THE WILD FRONTIER

THE WILD FRONTIER

ATROCITIES DURING
THE AMERICAN-INDIAN WAR
FROM JAMESTOWN COLONY
TO WOUNDED KNEE

William M. Osborn

RANDOM HOUSE

NEW YORK

Grateful acknowledgment is made to the following for permission to reprint
previously published material:

FACTS ON FILE, INC.: excerpt from *Atlas of the North American Indian* by Carl Waldman.
Copyright © 1985 by Carl Waldman. Reprinted by permission of Facts on File, Inc.

HARPERCOLLINS PUBLISHERS, INC.: excerpt from *The Indian in America*
(New American Nation Series) by Wilcomb E. Washburn. Copyright © 1975 by
Wilcomb E. Washburn. Reprinted by permission of HarperCollins Publishers, Inc.

HARVARD UNIVERSITY PRESS: excerpt from *The American Indians* by Edward H. Spicer.
Copyright © 1980, 1982 by the President and Fellows of Harvard College. Reprinted by
permission of the publisher, The Belknap Press of Harvard University Press (Cambridge, MA).

SIMON & SCHUSTER: excerpt from *God Gave Us This Country* by Bil Gilbert.
Copyright © 1989 by Bil Gilbert; excerpt from *The Long Death* by Ralph K. Andrist.
Copyright © 1964 by Ralph K. Andrist, renewed 1992 by Ralph K. Andrist; excerpt from
The Indian Wars by S. L. A. Marshall. Copyright © 1972 by S. L. A. Marshall.
Reprinted with permission of Scribner, a division of Simon & Schuster.

PAGE AND ELOISE RICHARD SMITH TRUST: excerpts from *A New Age Now Begins: A People's
History of the American Revolution* by Page Smith. Copyright © 1976 by Page Smith.
Reprinted with permission of Page and Eloise Richard Smith Trust (smithtrust.com).

UNIVERSITY OF CHICAGO PRESS: excerpt from *Indians of North America*
by Harold E. Driver. Copyright © 1961, 1969 by Harold E. Driver.
Reprinted by permission of the University of Chicago Press.

UNIVERSITY OF OKLAHOMA PRESS: excerpt from *Indian Removal: The Emigration of the Five
Civilized Tribes of Indians* by Grant Foreman. Copyright © 1932 by the University of
Oklahoma Press. Reprinted by permission of the University of Oklahoma Press.

Library of Congress Cataloging-in-Publication Data
Osborn, William M.
The wild frontier: atrocities during the American-Indian War from Jamestown Colony
to Wounded Knee / William M. Osborn.
p.   cm.
Includes bibliographical references.
ISBN 0-375-50374-9
1. Indians of North America—Wars—United States.   2. Indians of North America—
Government relations.   3. Atrocities—United States—History.
4. Frontier and pioneer life—United States.   I. Title.
E81 .O72   2000
973'.00497—dc21   00-27171

Random House website address: www.atrandom.com
Printed in the United States of America on acid-free paper
2 4 6 8 9 7 5 3
First Edition

Book design by Victoria Wong

This book is dedicated to the memory of the victims of the atrocities on the wild frontier. Settlers, soldiers, and Indians often fought dishonorably there in our longest and cruelest war.

Acknowledgments

My debts to some of the many people who contributed to this book must be acknowledged.

First, to the Indians, explorers, settlers, soldiers, officials, and others who reported events relating to the American-Indian War. These were the raw materials from which this book was made.

Second, to the scholars and authors who took these reports, which often conflicted, and wrote about them in a coherent way. This is especially true of William Brandon, George Catlin, J. Hector St. John de Crèvecoeur, Angie Debo, Harold E. Driver, Alvin M. Josephy, Jr., Fanny Kelly, Duane Schultz, and Carl Waldman.

Third, to Robert D. Loomis, my editor at Random House, who was always willing to contribute his advice, his wisdom, and his brilliance to the book.

Finally, to my wife, Pat, who saw too little of me while the manuscript was in preparation, and to our daughter, Amy, who provided inspiration in many ways, including presenting me with a beautiful pen for book signings even before the first draft was completed.

Contents

Introduction

The wild frontier commenced in 1607 with the arrival of the first permanent settlers and was declared ended by the Bureau of the Census in 1890. The war between the settlers and the Indians began in 1622 in Virginia and also ended in 1890 in South Dakota. The outcome of this war determined who would control the North American continent. It was played on a stage that was new to European peoples, and many of its dramatic events had not been seen before in history and would never be seen again. This was a first-time clash between 2 cultures.[1] Robert Hughes, in *Culture of Complaint,* said, "Surprises crackle, like electric arcs, between the interfaces of culture."[2] Surprises also crackle with atrocities. The war lasted 268 years, the longest in the history of our nation. The United States itself will not be 268 years old until the year 2044.

IN *The West: An Illustrated History,* edited by Henry Steele Commager, an article by M. A. Jones pointed out that "the realities of frontier life have regularly given way to the requirements of myth."[3] Myths cloud history and impair its classic function—to help us solve present-day problems. This accurate analogy has been drawn by Arthur M. Schlesinger, Jr., in *The Disuniting of America:*

> For history is to the nation rather as memory is to the individual. As an individual deprived of memory becomes disoriented and lost, not knowing where he has been or where he is going, so a nation denied a conception of its past will be disabled in dealing with its present and its future.[4]

The Indians agreed. There is an old Sioux saying—"A people without history is like wind upon the buffalo grass."[5]

Military historian S. L. A. Marshall in *Crimsoned Prairie* said in some despair, "Taken as a whole, books about the Plains wars have one salient characteristic, that of discrepancy."[6] As Carl Waldman noted in his preface to *Who Was Who in Native American History:*

> A book covering such a wide range of material can be no more accurate than its sources. Much of the material comes from writers who were explorers, missionaries, traders, or army officers first, in addition to amateur historians or anthropologists. Hearsay and legend play a part in what has been passed down. Contradictions abound.[7]

Edwin T. Denig, who lived with the Indians from about 1800 to 1850 and married 2 Indian women, noted another disagreement. "We find two sets of writers, both equally wrong, one setting forth the Indians as a noble, generous, and chivalrous race above the standards of Europeans, the other representing them below the level of brute creation."[8]

Generally speaking, most of the earlier writers were settler advocates, while many who came later were Indian advocates. Fergus M. Bordewich, who spent much of his childhood living on Indian reservations, put it this way in his book *Killing the White Man's Indian:*

> Until not long ago, Americans were generally taught to view the nation's westward movement as a saga of heroic pioneering and just wars that carried European immigrants from the shores of the Atlantic to those of the Pacific. At the center of that essentially mythic vision stood the Indian, simultaneously noble and barbaric, man of nature and bloodthirsty savage, and destined for tragic extinction. The epic of the Indian wars added color and grandeur to the saga of national expansion: in their apparent savagery, Indians dramatically underscored Euro-Americans' notions of civilization, while their repeated military

defeats seemed unchallengeable proof of the white man's technological and moral superiority.

More recently, revisionist scholars and educators have tended to portray that same history as one of deep, unredeemed tragedy, of which the destruction of the Indian is a central, equally mythical example, apparent proof of the barbarism of Euro-American civilization.[9]

The word *settler* is meant to include colonists, soldiers, militia, government people, farmers, hunters, trappers, merchants, miners, and other Americans who came in contact with the Indians between 1607 and 1890, as well as the English colonists before the American Revolution.

This war was a "complex and intense struggle,"[10] fought over a time span of more than 26 decades. Hundreds of Indian tribes were involved. The tribes were not only fighting one another, but the Dutch, the Spanish, the English, the French, and the settlers, often at the same time. European wars were frequently fought in part in North America. Participation in those wars by the Indians depended upon the wishes of each tribe. During the American Revolution, most tribes sided with Great Britain. One author, Carl Waldman, in *Atlas of the North American Indian,* concluded that if the British had given the tribes better support, they "probably would have won the war."[11]

No one knows for certain where the Indians originally came from. Some experts today believe that they came from some unknown part of Asia centuries ago over the Bering Land Bridge when Asia and America were connected. A growing number of other experts say the glacier there prevented use of the Bering route to our eastern seaboard until 11,500 years ago.[12] These experts believe Asians and perhaps even Europeans hugged the ice sheets in animal skin kayaks and reached America long before the Bering people.[13] There are also fairly recent archeological finds that hint that the Bering people may not have been in the first group to migrate to America. Anthropologist Walter Neves flatly stated, "We can no longer say that the first colonizers of the American continent came from the north of Asia."[14] The Indians encountered in Virginia, Massachusetts, and elsewhere may or may not have been in the first group and, if not, would not have been the First Americans.

The Indians had no word for themselves similar to the word *Indian.*[15] According to Alvin Josephy,

Many groups of native Americans were given their historic names by white men who either contrived descriptive terms of their own for them (Creeks) or adopted expressions by which they were known to other tribes.[16]

When they gave themselves a tribal name, however, as Clark Wissler in *Indians of the United States* noted, often it was something like "we, the people."[17]

SOME HAVE referred to the skirmishes and battles considered here as the Indian wars. Others have preferred to call them simply one war, the Four Hundred Year War (1492 to 1890) or the Four Century War. The latter is the approach taken here because the separate "wars" have been characterized by Alan Axelrod in *Chronicle of the Indian Wars* as "barely differentiated."[18]

Cheyenne chief Black Kettle said, according to Dee Brown in *Bury My Heart at Wounded Knee,* "There are bad white men and bad Indians. The bad men on both sides brought about this trouble."[19] The war in the main was "ugly and dark," according to Axelrod.[20] For Marshall, "The war was waged with excessive brutality on both sides."[21] Furthermore, as John Tebbel and Keith Jennison pointed out in *The American Indian Wars,* "There was little to choose in placing the blame for the atrocities."[22]

A partial chronology up to the end of the war may be helpful to the reader.

1607—First English settlers arrived in the Jamestown area
1622—War between Jamestown settlers and Powhatan Indians began
1675—King Philip's War began
1754—French and Indian War began
1763—Pontiac's Rebellion began
1775—Revolutionary War began
1812—War of 1812 began
1824—Bureau of Indian Affairs established
1830—Indian Removal Act became effective
1831—Trails of Tears began
1832—Black Hawk War began
1848—California atrocities began
1861—Civil War began

1862—Santee Sioux Uprising in Minnesota
1864—Sand Creek Massacre
1866—Fetterman's Massacre
1876—Battle of the Little Bighorn (Custer's Last Stand)
1890—Wounded Knee Massacre
1890—Census Bureau declared the frontier ended

THE WILD FRONTIER

CHAPTER 1

Settler and Other American Attitudes About the Indians

There was a "long-standing American ambivalence over Indians," according to John M. Coward in *The Newspaper Indian*.[1] Changes in settlers' attitudes resulted in part from the changes in writers' attitudes. The *New York Times* editorials from 1860 to 1890 often reflected these changes. Although the *Times* was not as influential then as it is today, nevertheless it was a strong voice and, perhaps even more important, a spokesman for the East on Indian issues. The *Times* generally supported the Indian causes and concluded that most instances of open conflict between Indians and settlers were caused by settler injustice.[2] Paradoxically, the *Times* treated many of the chiefs harshly. Sitting Bull, Geronimo, and Satanta especially were the subject of editorial wrath.[3]

Brian W. Dippie, in *The Vanishing American*, summarized the important east-west division of opinion about the Indians:

So vivid was the contrast between eastern and western attitudes that few writers on the Indian question failed to mention it. One experienced observer pictured the states "divided into two great parties, one crying for blood, and demanding the destruction of the Indians, the other begging that he may be left in his aboriginal condition, and that the progress of civilization may be stayed." Their views, another writer noted, were conditioned "by contact, cupidity and prejudice, on the one hand; and enthusiasm, benevolence and remoteness, on the other." The pertinent point was that easterners had solved their problem by moving the Indians out of the way, and had "long since forgotten the savage war whoop"; while in the West, "the Indian question is a live question," men live "in constant danger," and their "only appellation" for the Indians is "red devils."[4]

The *Times* pointed out that "contemporary treatment of Indians in the West simply paralleled what had begun on the East Coast a century ago."[5]

FROM THE beginning of the European invasion of the New World, those attempting to exploit the Indians claimed that they "were not normal people but rather members of a subhuman or animal species, lacking souls."[6]

The first settlers were English for the most part, and a flood of reports from the New World presented a grim picture of what they might encounter. Gary B. Nash gave one example in *Red, White, and Black:*

> Crafty, brutal, loathsome half-men whose cannibalistic instincts were revealed, as one pamphleteer wrote in 1578, by the fact that "there is no flesh or fishe, which they finde dead, (smell it never so filthily) but they will eate it, as they finde it, without any other dressing [cooking]."[7]

Other more dread aspects of Indian conduct circulated among settlers before they left their ships, according to Michael Kraus in *The United States to 1865:*

> The "noble savage" had, however, a terrifying aspect also; stories were told of how he attacked in the dead of night with blood-curdling yells, how he set houses afire with flaming arrows, and how he scalped the fleeing inhabitants. There were horrifying narratives, too, of cannibalism told with all the grisly details. The earliest settlers, leaving the comparative safety of their ships, were understandably fearful about the reception that awaited them.[8]

But as Page Smith pointed out in *A New Age Now Begins,* there was another view vying for settlers' consideration, that of Voltaire and Rousseau, whose philosophy was so important to the framers of the

Constitution of the United States, but who had never been to the New World. These philosophers romanticized the Indians, whom they saw as being natural men:

> The European mind was captivated by the idea of the noble savage as it had been by few ideas in its history. Both Voltaire and Rousseau, philosophers who nurtured the Enlightenment, saw society as corrupt and decadent, far removed from the wholesomeness and simplicity of the natural man. They romanticized the savage man, whom they saw as being close to nature, his intelligence unclouded by priestly superstition, by social conventions, fashion, greed, and ambition.[9]

The settlers were thus faced with strongly conflicting attitudes toward Indians. They chose to emigrate in great numbers. Why would they continue if these terrible stories were true?

INDEED, THEY lived in relative peace with the Indians for almost 15 years from their arrival at Jamestown, Virginia, in 1607 and Plymouth, Massachusetts, in 1620, although there were skirmishes. Then attitudes changed dramatically with the Powhatan Wars, which also were the beginning of the American-Indian War. In 1621, before war had even commenced, a Virginia poet wrote that Indians were irrevocably "Rooted in Evill, and opposed in Good; errors of nature, of inhumane Birth, The very dregs, garbage and spanne of Earth."[10] Opechancanough became the dominant leader of the powerful Powhatan Confederacy in 1618. He attacked Jamestown and other settlements on the James River in 1622 without warning, killing hundreds.[11] After that, according to Roy Harvey Pearce in *The Savages of America,* the settlers "ceased trying to understand the Indian; for such understanding would avail them little."[12] And in retaliation for the massacres noted, Bernard W. Sheehan in *Seeds of Extinction* said, "the Virginians followed a policy of extermination."[13] The Indian attitude toward the settlers hardened as well.

When the administrators of the Virginia Company protested that the colonists had gone too far in dealing with the Indians following the 1622 attack, the Virginia Council of State replied that

> wee hold nothing inuiste [unjust] . . . that may tend to theire ruine. . . . Stratagems were ever allowed against all enemies, but with these neither fayre Warr nor good quarter is ever to be held, nor is there other hope of their subversione, who ever may inform you to the Contrarie.[14]

This was about as bad as settler attitudes could get.

The American-Indian War—rightly characterized by Bil Gilbert in *God Gave Us This Country*—was one of

> unique ferocity. . . . Generally the antagonists believed that this was a winner-take-all competition, that compromise and accommodation were neither possible nor desirable. . . . The savages—red and white—did things to each other which sensitive outsiders found unbelievable.[15]

That ferocity surely arose out of the 2 parties' conflicting cultures and characters involved, a principal theme of this book.

TO THE north, the attitude of the Massachusetts colonists toward Indians was much the same. William Bradford was governor of the Plymouth colony from 1621 until 1656 except for the years Edward Winslow served. He maintained peaceful relations with the Wampanoags, but made war on the Pequot.[16] Bradford wrote in his history of the colony that the English had come expecting the "continual danger of the savage people, who are cruel, barbarous, and most treacherous," which made "the very bowels of men to grate within them and make the weak to quake and tremble."[17]

The Reverend Cotton Mather, who was influential in Massachusetts Bay Colony government, believed it was futile to attempt to Christianize and civilize Indians. He contended they were sent to North America by Satan and should therefore be exterminated.[18] Mather preached after the Indians were defeated in a battle of the Pequot War that "in a little more than one hour, five or six hundred of these barbarians were dismissed from a world that was burdened with them."[19]

BEFORE THE Revolutionary War started (1775–83), Prime Minister North in Parliament tried to defend use of Indians as British allies. Opposition leader Lord Chatham called Indians scalpers, cannibal savages, roasting and eating, torturing, murderous barbarians, and savage hell-hounds,[20] statements not likely to improve settler attitudes. The war itself only aggravated settler feelings against the Indians. The Declaration of Independence, written by Thomas Jefferson, declared that one of the charges against King George III was that he "had endeavored to bring on the inhabitants of our frontiers, the merciless Indian Savages whose known rule of warfare is an undistinguished destruction of all ages, sexes and conditions."

English governor William Tryon urged the British ministry to "loose the savages against the miserable Rebels in order to impose a reign of terror on the frontiers."[21] It was done. There were depredations by Indians against settlers that had far-ranging effects. Scars were left by the Revolution which led to atrocious conduct by the settlers.

ONLY 4 DAYS after the Revolution ended, George Washington wrote to James Duane outlining a policy of purchasing land occupied by Indians instead of seizing it:

> I am clear in my opinion, that policy and oeconomy [*sic*] point very strongly to the expediency of being on good terms with the Indians, and the propriety of purchasing their Lands in preference to attempting to drive them by force of arms out of the Country; which as we have already experienced is like driving the Wild Beasts of the Forest which will return as soon as the pursuit is at an end and fall perhaps on those that are left there; when the gradual extension of our Settlements will as certainly cause the Savage as the Wolf to retire; both being beasts of prey tho' they differ in shape. In a word there is nothing to be obtained by an Indian War but the Soil they live on and this can be had by purchase at less expense, and without that bloodshed, and those distresses which helpless Women and Children are made partakers of in all kinds of disputes with them.[22]

Secretary of War Henry Knox also opposed taking by force the lands acquired from England that were occupied by Indians.[23] He also believed that the view of many contending it impracticable to civilize the Indians was "probably more convenient than just."[24] Even at this early date and so soon after the conclusion of the Revolutionary War, a high government official was concerned about justice for the Indians. However, that same year, Knox took Washington's idea of buying land occupied by Indians several steps further. He foresaw that if the settlers would approach the Indian land and drive the game away, making the land less valuable to the Indians, they would be willing to sell cheaply, and they would be reduced to a very small number.[25]

Washington's attitude toward the Indians changed dramatically, however, after the embarrassing victory of the Miamis and their allies in 1790 over General Josiah Harmar's army, which Washington had sent to the Northwest Territory to pacify the Indians. Washington no longer talked about peacefully occupying the West. He now decided that the Indians must be punished severely in order to defend the frontier and national honor. He sent General Arthur St. Clair to fight the Miami allies, but St. Clair was even more roundly beaten by the Indians in 1791.[26]

After the Miami allies were finally defeated by General Anthony Wayne in 1794, however, the government "adopted a relatively conciliatory policy in its dealings with the natives. Government officials could afford to be benign" because control over the Northwest Territory had been established and settlers' hunger for land in that area had been satisfied temporarily.[27] Washington then followed the policy formulated by Secretary of War Henry Knox, which recognized the Indians' claim to the land they occupied and denied that the government was entitled to that land by the right of conquest. He shared Knox's view that the government's authority over land occupied by the Indians consisted only of the exclusive right to negotiate with Indians for its purchase. Washington also started the practice of meeting with delegations of tribal leaders.[28]

BEFORE HE became president, Thomas Jefferson supported military actions against Indians. As president, he was the first to advocate removal of the tribes to the West as a solution to the conflict between Indians and settlers. He proposed locating settlers as near to tribal areas as possible, hoping to impede the Indians' hunting-based culture. Jefferson also believed that if Indians could be protected from white civilization for a period of at least 50 years, that might be enough time for assimilation. He regarded the Indians as noble savages.[29] But after he had left office, Jefferson changed his views about the Indians. He came to believe that "ferocious barbarities justified extermination."[30] The transformation was startling. It came about, of course, because of the atrocities.

President James Madison reported in his first annual message to Congress in 1809 that "our Indian neighbors" had remained at peace.[31] War with Britain was approaching again, however, and in 1811 Madison's attention was drawn to the Indian murders and depredations on the northwest frontier.[32] On June 18, 1812, Congress declared war on Britain. Several tribes fought with the British, so Madison announced that "the hand of friendship, extended in vain, was now withdrawn."[33] In 1815, after the war was over, Madison was "happy" to report that tranquility had been restored in the northwest and that "our Indian neighbors" were back in the government's good graces.[34]

But the War of 1812 "had permanently altered Indian-white relations in North America." Furthermore, according to Dippie, "by siding with the British, the ungrateful Indians had forfeited any claim to sympathy. The country owed them nothing; its sense of fair play was now their sole protection."[35] Novelist Washington Irving wrote in 1814 that there was a hardening of "popular feeling" toward the Indian. He urged restraint, a view not held by many settlers at that time.[36]

President James Monroe declared in his first inaugural address in 1817 that "with the Indian tribes it is our duty to cultivate friendly relations and to act with kindness and liberality in all our transactions. Equally proper is it to persevere in our efforts to extend to them the advantages of civilization." The concept of "cultivating friendly relations" with Indians seems to have disappeared by 1818, however, when President Monroe wanted to take "complete and undisputed control" over them. But 3 years later, he was talking about "real benefactors" and "Great Father" ideas.

SOME SETTLERS viewed Indians as wild animals. After the settler murderers of 9 Indians in Indiana were apprehended in 1824, their defense was that it was "no worse to kill an Indian than to kill a wild animal."[37] Similarly, Helen Hunt Jackson in *A Century of Dishonor* told how around 1878 in Dakota County, Winnebago Henry Harris, who was employed to cut wood, was shot through the heart. Harris had had several disputes with a white man named D. Balinska, and Balinska had threatened Harris's life a few months before. Investigators found footprints in the snow leading from Balinska's home to the place from where the shot was fired. The rifle ball which killed Harris was the same weight as one found in Balinska's shot pouch. The grand jury was unwilling to indict for the apparent reason "that it was only an Indian that was killed."[38]

Missionaries of course believed the Indians could be saved. They held that view "in relative isolation," however, until about 1850, when others began to feel that way too.[39] There was interest growing in the government in helping the Indian as well. Secretary of War John C. Calhoun reported to House Speaker Henry Clay in 1818 that "helplessness has succeeded independence" among the western Indians, and "the time seems to have arrived when our policy towards them should undergo an important change. . . . Our views of their interest, and not their own, ought to govern them."[40] This analysis favorable to the Indians was widely accepted. Calhoun created the Bureau of Indian Affairs within the War Department in 1824. He sent military expeditions west for several purposes, 2 of which were to contain Indians within treaty lands and to prevent settlers taking such lands. (Later he saw the Indians as an obstacle to settler westward expansion.)[41]

DURING THE 1820s the idea became common that the Indians were dying out and when they did, there would no longer be an Indian problem. In 1820 Massachusetts orator Edward Everett predicted that if the red man could change from savagery to civilization on his own, that was good, but if he could not, he should be left to the operation of his character and habits, and when he was gone a civilized man would take his place.[42] Secretary of State Henry Clay in an 1825 cabinet meeting said that Indians were by nature incapable of civilization, were essentially inferior to the Anglo-Saxon, and were destined to extinction probably within 50 years.[43]

President Monroe in his 1818 annual address argued that to civilize the Indians

> and even to prevent their extinction [it] was indispensible that their independence as communities should cease, and that the control of the United States over them should be complete and undisputed.[44]

Monroe later added that to use force to do this would be "revolting to humanity and entirely unjustifiable."[45]

THE RESERVATION system required Indians to remove to west of the Mississippi. But Wilcomb E. Washburn sounded a dark note about settler attitudes toward Indians in his book *The Indian in America:*

> Whatever else the reservation system may represent it does mark an acceptance of the Indians' right to live and to retain land and resources for their support. While such a concession may not seem exceptional, on balance it ran against a persistent current of thought—not solely in America—that cared little whether aborigines disappeared from the face of the earth.[46]

Andrew Jackson wrote to William Henry Harrison in 1811 accusing Indians of being deceitful, unrelenting barbarians and adding that "the blood of our murdered countrymen must be revenged. The banditti ought to be swept from the face of the earth."[47] Jackson also likened Indians to wolves.[48]

However, in his first inaugural address in 1829, President Jackson promised,

> It will be my sincere and constant desire to observe toward the Indian tribes within our limits a just and liberal policy, and to give them that humane and considerate attention to their rights and their wants which is consistent with the habits of our Government and the feelings of our people.

This is a breathtaking apparent change in attitude from wanting to sweep the Indians from the face of the earth in 1811 to desiring to treat them justly and liberally only two decades later.

But by this time, most settlers no longer thought that the Indian could improve. A religious writer noted in 1830 that although missionaries never doubted the Indians' capacity for improvement, "the great mass of the community" did not share that view.

By the 1840s, it was obvious there was an impending crisis in Indian affairs because continued settler expansion impaired Indian isolation in the West. There were many different views concerning how to solve this worsening situation,[49] but at least there was some thinking about the Indians and their problems.

ROBERT G. Hays in *A Race at Bay* noted the change in attitudes toward Indians brought about by the Civil War. "Inevitably, attention to the Indian problem diminished as the nation moved closer to civil war."[50] The earlier general interest in improving the lot of the Indians waned. Horace Greeley went to the West Coast by train in 1859 and sent back dispatches as he proceeded:

> I have learned to appreciate better . . . than hitherto . . . the dislike, aversion, contempt, wherewith Indians are usually regarded by their white neighbors, and have been since the days of the Puritans. [One] needs but little familiarity with the actual, palpable aborigine to convince any one that the poetic Indian—the Indian of Cooper and Longfellow—is only visible to the poet's eye.[51]

In 1860 a California paper reported, "The Indians are in a starving condition; they kill stock to live. The whites cannot afford horses and cattle for their sustenance, and will not. Ergo, unless Government provides for the Indians, the settlers must exterminate them."[52]

The Santee Sioux Uprising in Minnesota in 1862 caused settler goodwill, according to Marshall, to "run out."

> One tribe of the Dakota [the Santee Sioux] had proved to be not only treacherous but barbarous in the extreme. It would not be forgotten by the whites of the frontier. The Indians were no less served warning that when crossed, Government and its security forces would retaliate beyond reasonable limits, exiling or exterminating a great body of people, if that were deemed the expedient course.[53]

Following the Sand Creek Massacre by the Colorado militia in 1864, however, some newspapers condemned the attack against the Indians. The *Louisville Journal* expressed the opinion that the Indians were "poor children of nature" and they deserved "pity from the philanthropic world." The attack "should excite for those poor creatures the generous pity of the nation, and we are gratified that it is to be subjected to Congressional investigation."[54] On the other hand, the superintendent of the Denver mint worried that "every band of Indians of any size on the plains is united for the purpose of exterminating and driving all the white men from these mountains and plains."[55]

IN 1865 there were several comments in the *Times* about the post–Civil War period. It "openly called on the government to treat the Indians . . . more fairly."[56] Matters did not improve, so the *Times* suggested that it would be a happy thing for both Indians and settlers if the Indians would move to Mexico, where the bulk of their race was concentrated.[57] The *Times* also reported that "many of the Western settlers are very anxious for a war of extermination against the Indians, and assert that outrages and atrocities will never cease until this is adopted and ended."[58]

In the 1860s, the *Times* again changed its attitude concerning Indians. Its principal interest became the protection of settlers on the frontier, and it was outspoken in condemning policies it believed were too lenient on warlike tribes.[59] In later decades, although it could not condone Indian atrocities, it tended to blame the government for them, leaving the implication, at least, that the atrocities were justified.[60]

John M. Coward concluded that "many post–Civil War newspapers and their readers were advocating a more complex view of Indians: They might still be 'savage,' but they could also be seen as innocent victims of their 'degraded' state."[61]

AFTER FETTERMAN'S Massacre in 1867, General Sherman urged that the army should act with vindictive earnestness against the Sioux, even to the extermination of men, women, and children. Congress didn't agree and created a peace commission instead.[62]

A committee of investigation was appointed which included four generals: Alfred Sully, Ely S. Parker, John Buford, and John B. Sanborn. The committee's report in 1867 was sobering. Frontiersmen and army contractors had made false reports of alleged massacres by Indians, then called on the government to send troops to protect them.[63] The *Times* supported the view that the settlers constantly provoked the Indians:

> It has justly been said in Congress by those who have investigated the matter, that the Western settlers are a constant source of irritation to the Indians, committing petty depredations upon them, driving them from their lands, and in a thousand little ways stirring up their ill-blood.[64]

In 1868, after President Grant had been elected but before he took office, some members of the Sac and Fox tribes met with President Andrew Johnson to protest that a thieving Indian agent had them put in prison. Johnson remarked that "the agent of the Government should have been put in jail instead of the chiefs."[65]

By the following year, the *Times* observed that the "extermination remedy" was gradually dropping from the range of possibilities in deciding what to do with the Indian. Wryly it noted that a London newspaper nevertheless thought it was a proper thing to do.[66] The *Times* further hoped that the Indian might receive fair play "now that the army officers have so strenuously taken his part." The Indians' worst foes were the settlers, the sutlers, the peddlers, the traders, and the frontiersmen who had defrauded them.[67]

Finally, near the end of the year, the *Times* concluded that "the new view is not to exterminate, but to civilize the Indian."[68] To the extent that this was the majority attitude, progress was being made in settler attitudes.

Ulysses S. Grant announced a new federal Indian policy when he assumed office in 1869. Quakers played such a dominant role in Grant's Peace Policy that it was called the Quaker Policy by some. Grant is reported to have said that if his policy could make Quakers out of the Indians, it would help take the fight out of them.[69]

Yet, during Grant's second administration, there was a growing public reaction against numerous Indian aggressions, and the Peace Policy collapsed. Robert F. Berkhofer, Jr., summarized the situation in *The White Man's Indian*. Many vocal westerners opposed the Peace Policy as just another example of "sickly sentimentalism" toward savage Indians, while eastern humanitarians looked to new ways of converting the Indian to Christian civilization after the 1870s.[70] For instance, about 1870, the *Montana Post* was fed up:

> It is high time the sickly sentimentalism about humane treatment and conciliatory measures should be consigned to novel writers, and if the Indians continue their barbarities, wipe them out.[71]

But by 1871 the *Times* had become optimistic about the future of the Indian:

> If the Indian is to survive on this continent at all, it must be by elevating himself to the social, industrial, and political level of the white man. With time and opportunity, it is pretty obvious that he can do this.[72]

When a group of chiefs came to New York in 1872, the *Times* observed that easterners might smile at such names as Red Cloud, Red Dog, Blue Horn, and Slow Bull, "but in the North-west their names recall a long series of bloody massacres, and they are mentioned with hatred and dread."[73]

THE POOR condition of the Indians in 1875 was the subject of another *Times* editorial decrying that the Indians were "practically friendless and helpless. On the frontier, between the settlers and the adventurers, closing in on them alike from the West and the East, and with the treatment they are sure to receive from the Government, the Indians might as well be between the upper and nether mill-stones."[74]

After several Indian uprisings earlier in 1875, the *Times* apparently came to feel that readers were becoming bored with Indian stories and cared little for either their present or future condition. All that changed with the Battle of the Little Bighorn in 1876. That battle (Custer's Last Stand) was an unprecedented shock to the settlers and spoiled the country's centennial celebration.

Edward Lazarus in *Black Hills/White Justice* wrote that "not since Lincoln's assassination, and some said not even then, had there been such an outpouring of public grief. . . . Grief soon gave way to rage and rage to calls for revenge. . . . Nebraska Senator Algernon Paddock introduced a bill calling for the extermination of the Indians."[75] If ever the proposition of Indian extermination could succeed, it was in 1876. But the Paddock bill did not pass even though the *Times* openly asserted on July 7 that Custer's command had been butchered by the Indians.[76]

After the Battle of the Little Bighorn, the *Bismarck Tribune* expressed what many in the West were feeling:

> Let that christian philanthropy which weeps over the death of a lazy, lousy, lying and stealing red skin, whose hands are still reeking with the blood of defenceless women and children, slain on the frontier, and who are ever ready to apologize for these murderers, take a back seat. Invite the soldier to the front and sustain him while he causes the Indians to realize the power, and those that still live to respect the white man. Wipe out all treaties, rub out all agencies and reservations, and treat the Indians as they are, criminals and paupers.[77]

IN THE 1870s Selden N. Clark of the Bureau of Indian Affairs published a pamphlet that concluded that the theory that the Indian was destined to decline and finally disappear "should probably be abandoned." This created a "minor sensation."[78] Many were beginning to take this view. On the other hand, Indians were sometimes receiving respectful treatment in the courts. Two Poncas and some Sioux were visiting the Yankton Reservation in 1875. The Sioux attacked the Poncas outside the reservation's agency, killing one and seriously wounding the other. Charges were brought, but the case was dismissed on the grounds that the court had no jurisdiction over crimes committed by one Indian against another in Indian country.[79]

Four years later, a group of Poncas were taking the son of Chief Standing Bear to his boyhood home for burial. Due to government bungling, they were detained by the military. Indians had been generally excluded from the judicial system until federal judge Elmer Dundy held that the Poncas were "persons" under the Constitution and could apply for a writ of habeas corpus. He released them from detention. The realization that Indians were now afforded some protection by the judicial system "jolted" the country.[80] After that decision, Robert G. Hays concluded, the Poncas (and the settlers) understood that "the Indian is just as good as a white man, as long as he behaves himself," at least in a court of law.[81]

Still, Indians were seen as a menace by some. The *New York Herald* called for their extermination in 1879. "The continent is getting too crowded." But William Brandon in *Indians* correctly observed that "no one really took that seriously anymore."[82]

In spite of this progress, in 1881, the *Times* reported that the Colorado legislature considered a bill "for the destruction of Indians and skunks." A committee recommended that it pass. "To class Indians and skunks together is the habit of the free and boundless West. Only the sickly sentimentalists of the East demur at such a classification."[83] The bill did not pass. That same year, "several hundred thousand people addressed a memorial to Congress asking that body to keep faith with the Indians." A significant number of people thus supported the Indian cause.[84]

The perceived success of the Carlisle and Hampton Indian schools, where young Indians were sent to be "civilized," convinced the country that Indians were capable of receiving a Christian education. President Grover Cleveland told Congress in 1888 that the "capacity of the Indian no longer needs demonstration."[85]

THE *Times* editorialized after the Battle of Wounded Knee that it was "proof of a high degree either of desperation or of fanaticism that the captives should have preferred to trust the chance of resisting an irresistibly superior force of whites. They must have known when they emptied the rifles they were required to surrender into the ranks of armed soldiers that surrounded them that they were sealing their own doom."[86]

James Wilson in *The Earth Shall Weep* asserted that Justice Oliver Wendell Holmes (who died in 1894) described Indians as "this sketch in red crayons of a rudimental manhood[,] to keep the continent from being a blank until the true lord of creation should come to claim it."[87]

Near the end of the century, the *Times* decided that culture even among the civilized tribes was seldom deemed noteworthy and that the Indian "was not a particularly creditable specimen of humanity."[88]

THEODORE ROOSEVELT was the last president to undergo a change in attitude toward Indians. Shortly before he became president in 1901, he said, "I don't go so far as to think that the only good Indians are dead Indians, but I believe nine out of every ten are, and I shouldn't like to inquire too closely in the case of the tenth. The most vicious cowboy has more moral principle than the average Indian."[89] His position was that the Indian was a savage, the Anglo-Saxon a civilized man, and civilization always had priority over savagery.[90] However, Roosevelt's views soon altered. After he took office, his policy was to prepare Indians for freedom from the reservation system while protecting them from their inexperience in the hard world.[91] He later said that each Indian should be given a piece of land and "thrown loose to shift for himself, as a citizen amongst other citizens, as soon as he can be prepared for the ordeal."[92] In his diary, moreover, he wrote that he "regretted he didn't have a strain of Indian blood" in his veins.[93]

IN THE decades from the 1920s to the 1940s, Indians began agitating in a way that did not sit very well with most whites and perhaps with most Indians. Cayuga chief Deskaheh went to the League of Nations in 1922 unsuccessfully seeking recognition of his tribe's sovereignty. The Senecas issued a declaration of independence to the state of New York in 1939. In World War II, although many Indians fought and died heroically for the United States, the Iroquois League independently declared war on Germany; others, including Iroquois, Ute, Papagos, Hopi, and Seminole, ignored Selective Service and were put in jail.[94]

Many whites found renewed Indian activism in the 1960s unacceptable. Those activities seem to have divided Indians as well and even retarded Indian progress. Peter Matthiessen's *In the Spirit of Crazy Horse* reported that they were directed by the radical American Indian Movement, or AIM. Its predecessor was founded in 1962 by 2 Ojibway inmates of Minnesota's Stillwater State Prison, Clyde Bellecourt and Eddie Benton Banai. In 1968 Bellecourt, Banai, George Mitchell, and Chippewa Dennis Banks formed AIM.[95]

AIM people were connected with a number of events ostensibly meant to further the Indian cause. They occupied the former federal prison on Alcatraz Island in 1969. They occupied federal buildings in Littleton, Colorado; Fort Lawton, Washington; Mount Rushmore; Stanley Island; Ellis Island; Plymouth Rock; a replica of the *Mayflower;* and a Coast Guard station in Michigan. According to Wilson, in 1971 AIM established the International Treaty Council, which tried to win recognition of Indian sovereignty from the United Nations and other countries.[96]

There was a march on Washington called the Trail of Broken Treaties Caravan in 1972 and a subsequent 6-day demonstration during which AIM occupied the Bureau of Indian Affairs offices and destroyed public files.[97] The National Tribal Chairmen's Association, headed by Webster Two Hawk, chairman of the Rosebud Sioux, denounced the occupiers. AIM carted off dozens of documents and looted and defaced the building.[98]

In 1973 AIM and its supporters occupied the Sioux Pine Ridge Reservation, where the Wounded Knee Massacre had occurred. AIM wanted to throw allegedly corrupt tribal leaders out of office. They held out for 71 days, and during that time 2 Indians were killed and a United States marshal wounded. Two years later, there was another shoot-out at Pine Ridge, and 2 FBI agents were murdered.[99]

William T. Hagan, author of *American Indians,* reported that these and other AIM activities caused whites to "become alarmed at the violence and property destruction associated with" the occupation of the Bureau of Indian Affairs and the Pine Ridge Reservation. There was a "shift in public opinion—a white backlash" suggesting that "such confrontations had become counter-productive, particularly for a people increasingly dependent upon the good will of Congress."[100] Edward Lazarus, who had a chapter in his book about AIM and related movements, concluded that some of these events further deepened divisions among Indians.[101] Middle-of-the-road tribal people were sometimes affronted by the fundamentalist fervor of "born-again Indians." One Sioux said, "I don't need some urban activist to come and tell me how to be an Indian. I've always been an Indian. I don't have to put on feathers to prove it."[102] And Washburn observed this about AIM:

> AIM does not represent a majority viewpoint among Indians. . . . The dominant white majority, upon whose goodwill any major change in Indian policy is ultimately dependent, does not stand behind the radical outlook presented by AIM. . . . AIM leaders at Wounded Knee proved unable to relate their demands to the context of American political realities, thereby letting slip an opportunity to promote Indian advancement. In their assault on elected tribal leaders like Richard Wilson of the Oglala Sioux, and by their demands that such leaders be summarily removed and the elective system abolished, AIM leaders

threatened one of the major props of Indian autonomy and self-government. . . . Even AIM's cavalier asssumption that its members could not be hurt by the white man, no matter how violently they acted in destroying the symbols of his authority, smacks of the belief of the Ghost Dancer followers . . . that their Ghost Shirts were invulnerable to the white man's bullets.[103]

In the last few decades, the view of the western migration and of Indian history has changed dramatically for some, from the belief that the migration was heroic to the belief that it was a deep tragedy. This radical transformation came about in part because of the 1970 Dee Brown book, *Bury My Heart at Wounded Knee,* which "stunned the nation"[104] and exerted a great influence on white attitudes about Indians. Wilson said that book, "perhaps more than anything else, helped to promote the more sympathetic view of Indians."[105]

The revised view also came about because of the political correctness movement. Almost everyone remembers the turbulent sixties and seventies and the Vietnam War protestors, many of whom are now college professors and leaders in the political correctness movement, which admittedly has contempt for American history. Indians hold a special place in politically correct hearts. Columnist John Leo described the movement as an attempt "to portray American Indian cultures as unremittingly noble, mystical, gender-fair, peace-loving, and living in great harmony with nature."[106]

One's attitudes toward Indians today will as likely as not be governed by one's political views. Liberals argue that the present dismal state of the Indian results from the failure of government to remedy mistreatment. Conservatives argue that their state results from Indian failure to adapt to American society. Something can be said in support of both positions.

CHAPTER 2

Some Indian Cultural Characteristics

Some view Indians as angels, while others view them as devils. (The former view is advanced by numerous recent motion pictures and television programs.)[1] The truth of course lies somewhere between heaven and hell.

The hundreds of Indian tribes that existed in 1622 were diverse in many ways, yet they also had many common characteristics. Edward H. Spicer said in *The American Indians* that

> in the early 1600s at least 75,000 American Indians lived along the coast from Maine to North Carolina. Divided into approximately 40 groups, they differed from one another in language, customs, and sense of collective identity. However, all of their languages belonged to one linguistic family—Algonkian—and they shared many basic cultural traits, such as the small-scale cultivation of corn, beans, and squash; a religious belief centered on the acquisition of supernatural power through shamans; and a strong tradition of absolutist and hereditary political authority with tribute payments to a principal headman.[2]

Angie Debo noted that these characteristics have influenced their history and persist to the present day in many of their descendants.[3]

Clark Wissler came to the conclusion more than 50 years ago that "the white man defeated the Indian, traded with him, sometimes married his women, usually held his opinions and ways in contempt, *but never understood him*" (emphasis added).[4]

George Catlin, the famous Indian portrait painter, gave up his law practice, painted portraits in Philadelphia and Washington, D.C., and then spent from 1831 to 1839 visiting Indians from 48 tribes. He was armed with letters of recommendation from President Jackson and his secretary of war. By the time he returned, he had additional recommendations—he had been made a medicine man in 3 tribes because of his magnificent Indian portraits. He wrote a book about his experiences called *Letters and Notes*. Catlin called himself a "professed philanthropist"[5] and an Indian advocate. He respected and admired them: "The North American Indian in his native state, is an honest, hospitable, faithful, brave, warlike, cruel, revengeful, relentless—yet honourable, contemplative and religious being."[6] If the reader could only read one book about the character of Indians during this period, Catlin's book is the one to read.

A PRINCIPAL common characteristic of Indians, love of warfare, understandably related directly to atrocities. Several writers and historians, however, have reached the stunning conclusion that the Indian tribes were peaceful. Tebbel and Jennison said as much in *The American Indian Wars:*

> Before the white man came, the vast, magnificent, and comparatively empty region that is now the United States was inhabited by one million Indians, organized into six hundred distinct societies and scattered from the desolate wastes of the Far North to the hot swamps of the South; from the great forests of the East to the plains, deserts, and mountains of the West. These Indian societies existed in balance with themselves. . . . The tribes of eastern North America were relatively free of warfare.[7]

S. L. A. Marshall observed with sarcasm that "quite familiar is the saying that the American Indian was a peace-loving, peace pipe–smoking being until the white man came."[8] James Adair, for instance, claimed, "The Indians did not wage war on each other unless prompted to it by the white traders."[9] Larry Lee Carey similarly argued that "although some tribes (notably the Mohawks) had a predilection for warfare, most Indians did not become hostile except when seeking redress for blatant injustices."[10] John Collier in his *Indians of the Americas* asserted that Indian warfare "was limited, not unlimited or excessive."[11] James Wilson claimed that Indian warfare "was seldom undertaken either to exterminate or to dispossess an enemy,"[12] and that "after inflicting limited damage, the victors usually withdrew."[13] The fighting "was (in some ways) closer to a sporting contest than to total war."[14]

But the 500 or so tribes were emphatically not "in balance with themselves," nor were they "relatively free of warfare," and they were certainly not "peace-loving . . . until the white man came." Widespread fighting started long before then. Indian war was not limited or even close to a sporting contest. The fact is, according to Page Smith, the Indian loved warfare. "Cruelty, violence, and constant warfare were the facts of [Indian] daily life."[15]

In a tract published around 1504–06, Amerigo Vespucci observed that "the nations wage war upon one another without art or order. The elders by means of certain harangues of theirs bend the youths to their will and inflame them to wars in which they cruelly kill one another."[16]

The Iroquois Confederacy illustrates the Indian love of warfare. No Indians were more addicted. The first explorers of the American coast, and settlers as well, found many Algonquins fighting one another and the Iroquois.[17] The situation became so bad that the Iroquois Confederacy, or League of Five Nations, was formed among 5 tribes in an attempt to end the constant feuding.[18] The confederation consisted of the Mohawk, Oneida, Onondaga, Cayuga, and Seneca tribes. Even after that, however, said Gary Nash, there was "an impressive amount of fighting . . . between the Five Nations and surrounding Algonkian people."[19]

From 1638 until 1684, 46 years later, the Iroquois* fought the so-called Iroquoian Beaver Wars against 13 other tribes—the Hurons, Tobaccos, Neutrals, Eries, Ottawas, Mahicans, Illinois, Miami, Susquehannocks, Nipissings, Potawatomis, Delaware, and Sokokis.[21] The Iroquois, according to Alvin Josephy, "were almost constantly engaged in wars with Algonquians or with other Iroquoian peoples."[22] They killed more than 10,000 Hurons. "They hated the Huron intensely, like brother against brother."[23]

---

*The Iroquois boys trained with knives, war clubs, and bows and arrows. They became warriors when in their teens. The confederation expanded in all directions in order, among other reasons, to get new sources of fur.[20]

The fall of the Iroquois has been attributed to fighting among those tribes. Wissler put it as bluntly as possible:

> It was not the white man who destroyed the Iroquois Family, but a case of brother against brother. Probably this is a case of what was going on in America before the white man came and would have continued indefinitely had he stayed away.[24]

Similarly, Sheehan noted that

> one of the more gruesome episodes in the history of Indian warfare had been the Iroquois conquest of the Hurons. From it the Five Nations acquired their reputation for military superiority. Whatever the real reasons for the conflict and for the decisive victory of the Iroquois, it constituted a startling sample of the violent propensities supposedly inherent in the primitive state. And it occurred, in the Jeffersonian view, without the influence of the whites. Indian set upon Indian. Surely the inherent viciousness of the natives had caused the conflict.[25]

About 1670 the Iroquois, who were based in New York, invaded the western country (what is now Indiana and Illinois) and caused a panic among the tribes there. They had succeeded in getting firearms from the Dutch about 1630. During the next 40 years they waged incessant and victorious war on all their neighbors—the Delawares on the south, the Eries on the west, and the Hurons on the north and northwest.[26]

The war between the Iroquois and the Hurons finally ended in 1684. Francis Parkman had little sympathy for what happened:

> It was a strange and miserable spectacle to behold the savages of this continent at the time when the knell of their common ruin had already sounded. Civilization had gained a foothold on their borders. The long and gloomy reign of barbarism was drawing near its close and their united efforts could scarcely have availed to sustain it. Yet in this crisis of their destiny these doomed tribes were tearing each other's throats in a wolfish fury, joined to an intelligence that served little purpose but mutual destruction.[27]

About 1776 there was an Iroquois civil war. Mohawks attacked Oneidas, and Oneidas attacked Mohawks. Iroquois fought Iroquois at the Revolutionary War battles of Bennington and Saratoga, both of which were won by the Continental army.[28]

Speaking of the Iroquois, Albert Gallatin,* secretary of the treasury to Jefferson and Madison, tellingly noted that Iroquois "conquered only to destroy; and, it would seem, . . . solely for the purpose of gratifying their thirst for blood. . . . They made a perfect desert of the whole country within 500 miles of their seats."[30]

In the 1830s, Catlin discovered that the Crow and the Blackfeet "are always at war, and have been, time out of mind."[31] The Mandans were engaged in "almost continued warfare."[32] He generalized that "many different and distinct nations, [were] always at war with each other."[33]

Catlin learned that little parties of 6 or 8 Delawares† from 2,000 miles away had visited tribes in the Upper Missouri. In several instances, the visitors, after being feasted and having solemnized articles of everlasting peace, received many presents, "and [having] taken affectionate leave, have brought away 6 or 8 scalps with them."[35]

In 1846 an Indian agent in the Upper Missouri Agency remonstrated with a Sioux chief about the perpetual wars Indians had with one another. The chief answered, "If their great-grandfather desired them to cease war with their enemies, why did he not send each of them a petticoat, and make squaws of them at once?"[36]

In 1855 a group of 250 Comanche warriors out on a buffalo hunt encountered by chance a group of their old enemies, the Apache. There was a battle in which both sides lost about 17 men. Nelson Lee, who had been captured by the Comanche, observed that

> at that time a deadly strife existed between the tribes, and it would have been a scandalous violation of an Indian's idea of manhood to have separated without a bloody tilt at arms. . . . When a warrior dies on the field of battle, their joy knows no bounds.[37]

Dozens of writers have commented on the warlike nature of the Indians. The warlike nature and bold provocations of some tribes or groups of warriors led to violence and injustices that might not otherwise have taken place.[38] An important conclusion was that "combat among differ-

---

*Albert Gallatin lived with the Abnaki Indians for a while. He was a congressman and held several diplomatic posts. Interested in Indian culture, he supported a federal policy of educating Indians in order to assimilate them into mainstream society.[29]

†The Delaware lived at first in New York, New Jersey, Pennsylvania, and Delaware. Settlers pushed them into the Ohio River area, then to the Great Lakes area, Missouri, Kansas, Texas, and Oklahoma. They sold Manhattan to the Dutch for 24 dollars even though the Manhattan Indians held the island.[34]

ent tribes or among different bands within a tribe was, if anything, far more frequent than war between Indians and whites."[39] Harold E. Driver even concluded in *Indians of North America* that "probably as many Indians were killed fighting each other after White contact as were killed in wars with the Whites."[40] The *World Book Encyclopedia* states forthrightly that

> the European settlers did not bring the first warfare to North America. Indian tribes had fought among themselves for thousands of years. They struggled constantly for the best hunting grounds and village sites, for revenge after the killing of a tribesman, and for personal glory. . . . But not all tribes were equally warlike. Some, including the Iroquois and the Apache, fought almost all the time.[41]

Edward H. Spicer in *The American Indians* agreed:

> A . . . characteristic of the . . . peoples of the northern plains was that they became especially concerned with and adept in warfare. The competition for hunting grounds was intense as more and more Indians moved into the region. Thus for survival they developed fighting techniques, and warfare became a major orientation of their cultures.[42]

Warfare performed several valuable functions for the tribes. Bil Gilbert reported a Cherokee chief in the 1700s saying to an English agent that the idea of making peace with another tribe was not attractive because the Cherokee must then immediately look for another tribe with whom they could engage in "our beloved occupation."[43]

Carl Waldman listed a variety of functions served by war in tribal culture:

> as ritual, a rite of passage to manhood or a means of achieving godlike qualities, such as among the Plains warrior societies; as economy, for a source of sustenance through raiding, as practiced by the Apaches of the Southwest; as limited political purpose, a way to establish tribal confederacies, as in the case of the Iroquois League of the Northeast; and as official state policy, as demonstrated by the Aztecs of Mesoamerica, who maintained their social structure through military expansion.[44]

The Cheyenne fought for the joy of combat and to gain the approval of others. War was a great hunt, and the young braves went to war with pleasure. To enjoy life fully, to feel satisfied, they needed someone to fight, and in their wanderings across the Plains, it was seldom difficult to find strangers to attack. To the Cheyenne, anyone who was not of their own tribe was an enemy.[45]

THE SIOUX started west around 1750 because their enemies, the Chippewa, had obtained guns from the French. The Sioux forced western tribes to move.[46] Sioux author Vine Deloria candidly admitted that the Sioux

> have a great tradition of conflict. . . . And when we find no one else to quarrel with, we often fight each other. . . . During one twenty-four-year period in the last century the Sioux fought . . . against the Crow, Arapaho, Cheyenne, Mandan, Arikara, Hidatsa, Ponca, Iowa, Pawnee, Otoe, Omaha, Winnebago, Chippewa, Cree, Gros Ventre.[47]

Francis Parkman expressed the same view about the Sioux attitude toward warfare:

> War is the breath of their nostrils. Against most of the neighboring tribes they cherish a rancorous hatred, transmitted from father to son, and inflamed by constant aggression and retaliation.[48]

Harold E. Driver found even more significance in the Indian obsession with war:

> No young man ever thought of getting married or of being accepted as an adult citizen until he had slain an enemy and brought back a scalp to prove it. So important was this achievement to the individual that when war parties failed to contact the enemy and to obtain the necessary scalps, they sometimes killed members of their own tribe, whom they accidentally encountered on their way home, rather than return empty-handed and in disgrace.[49]

In the 1780s, Jefferson came to a similar realization. "Their [Indian] souls are wholly bent upon war. This is what procures them glory among the men, and makes them the admiration of the women. To this they are educated from their earliest youth."[50]

Intertribal warfare finally reached the point where, Brian Dippie claimed, "[m]any treaties negotiated by the government . . . attempted to establish boundaries between the tribes in the hope of ending internecine warfare."[51] Clark Wissler, who lived with 10 Indian tribes in

1905,[52] noted another indication that Indians were natural enemies. "Many Indians were ambitious to collect scalps but usually preferred Indian scalps."[53]

Carl Waldman, however, concluded that land was the central issue in a majority of Indian wars.[54] He stated that the fighting among the Indians was for the same purpose that had occurred before and that would occur again when the settlers came, namely, "a stronger people pushing aside a weaker one while expanding territorially."[55] Robert M. Utley and Wilcomb E. Washburn also found in *Indian Wars* that the Sioux (this applies to almost every tribe) "fought for possession of hunting grounds, in defense against the forays of equally aggressive enemies, and in reprisal when an enemy scored a success."[56]

The depth of feeling one tribe could have against another was illustrated when General George Crook was trying to get Crow scouts in the Great Sioux Wars. He called a general council with his officers and tribal chiefs. Old Crow, the paramount chief, made this statement:

> These are our lands by inheritance. The Great Spirit gave them to our fathers, but the Sioux stole them from us. They hunt upon our mountains. They fish in our streams. They have stolen our horses. They have murdered our squaws, our children. . . . Our war is with the Sioux and only them. We want back our lands. We want their women for our slaves, to work for us as our women have had to work for them. We want their horses for our young men, and their mules for our squaws. The Sioux have trampled upon our hearts. We shall spit upon their scalps.[57]

Crow-Sioux enmity erupted again in 1877 when 5 Sioux chiefs approached the camp of General Nelson A. Miles under a flag of truce. They were a peace faction which was gathering strength. Miles had anticipated their arrival, so he had instructed his Indian scouts to honor anyone approaching under a white flag. As the Sioux approached the camp of the Crow scouts, the Crows ambushed and massacred the Sioux, their ancient enemies.[58]

A trapper and hunter named Wootton—but called Uncle Dick—noted that before the settlers came, the Indians not only robbed and plundered and stole from one another, but killed, scalped, mutilated, tortured, and enslaved. When the settlers came, they did these same things to them.[59]

THE SIGNIFICANT wars among Indians are described in Appendix A, which lists more than 500 known intertribal wars[60] between 1622 and

1890. Wars that are not important to the subject of this book are merely listed in skeletal fashion, giving only the date and the belligerents. Probably there was not a time between 1622 and 1890 when Indians were not fighting other Indians.

Many of these intertribal wars occurred before the settlers arrived in any significant numbers, and more than 450 occurred after the Powhatan Wars began in 1622—that is, after the Indians became aware that battles with the settlers might occur. Earlier, King Powhatan had expressed fear that the settlers were going to invade and possess land occupied by Indians.[61]

ONE OF the most telling illustrations of Indian love of warfare is that Indians very frequently served as mercenaries and scouts for pay for the English, French, and American armies against other Indians, even other Indians from the same tribe. Such events are included in Appendix A. Marshall saw this as "another sad chapter in the story of Indian betrayal of Indians."[62] Cyrus Townsend Brady in his *Indian Fights and Fighters* believed that this situation was instrumental in the success of American arms against the Indians:

> It is a singular thing to note the looseness of the tie with which the members of the various tribes were bound. Frequently we find bands of the same tribe fighting for and against the United States on the same field. One of the most fruitful causes of the success of our arms has been this willingness on the part of the Indians to fight against their own people, of which the government has been willing to avail itself.[63]

The conflicting views about Indians in general also applies to the effectiveness of their warfare. On the one hand, Waldman believed that the Indians were "among history's most effective warriors, and their guerrilla tactics—emphasizing concealment and individual initiative"— were adopted by many modern armies.[64] William Brandon praised the Indians' "remarkable courage."[65] Roy Harvey Pearce observed that the Indian "will defend himself against a host of enemies, always choosing to be killed rather than to surrender."[66] Harold E. Driver similarly noted that

> few indigenous peoples in the world at the same level of culture have fought so valiantly against European intruders as did the Indians east of the Rocky Mountains in the United States. Man for man, bow for

bow, and gun for gun, they were a match for the best troops sent against them and were overwhelmed only because of the greater numbers and superior armament of the English and French colonizers.[67]

On the other hand, Page Smith made a detailed critique of the Indian as a warrior. He said that the Indian had a basic weakness in warfare in that he was not prepared for protracted campaigning. The Indian preferred stealthy raids, was unwilling to sustain heavy casualties, and did not have the will to persist in the face of heavy odds. He fought for glory and spoils but not for victory, was capable of effective attack but not defense, and could not be restrained or controlled once aroused. The Indians would stand fast in the face of attack by a superior force only when confronted with death or surrender, in which event death was almost always chosen.[68]

Lack of Indian staying power in battle has also been noted by others.[69] Indians had a tendency to run away from a battle. Old West writer Bret Harte put it like this:

> The red men had different ideas of bravery than those to which whites had been schooled. Most Indians saw no glory in dying nobly for a doomed cause when it was possible to get away and resume the battle elsewhere under better conditions.[70]

General Philip Henry Sheridan discovered that "Indians seldom [make a] stand when the force is able to defeat them. . . . They will scatter."[71]

"Indians rarely fought," according to Axelrod, "unless they enjoyed substantially superior numbers."[72] Cyrus Townsend Brady put it another way: "The well-known disinclination of Indians to fight pitched battles is a factor which enters largely into every campaign."[73] And he noted another drawback:

> One of the curious Indian superstitions, which has often served the white man against whom he had fought to good purpose, is that when a man is killed in the dark he must pass all eternity in darkness. Consequently, he rarely ever attacks at night.[74]

And there was another inhibiting factor noted by Ralph K. Andrist—cold. "Indian war parties very seldom operated in winter."[75] Very few combatants have the advantage of knowing that the enemy will probably not attack at night or in the winter. Andrist further said the Indians often did not have "the ability to improvise tactics."[76]

Charles Robinson called attention to one more liability of the Indian as a fighter:

The average Indian thought almost entirely as an individual, and not as part of a larger organization. Strategy, communications, even numbers of people in a particular location—essential to any white history—were seldom noted because they did not affect most Indians as individuals.[77]

NOT SURPRISINGLY, ruthlessness in warfare was another Indian characteristic. When the Sioux were fighting the Ute, Sioux chief Red Cloud* saw that a Ute warrior trying to cross a stream was about to drown because of a wounded horse. Red Cloud went into the stream, saved the warrior from drowning, then scalped him. Later Red Cloud killed an Indian child who was tending a horse herd before running the horses away.[79]

CRUELTY IS an indispensable element of an atrocity—and was another characteristic shared by the Indians and the settlers. James Adair, an Irish trader who married many Indian women and fathered many Indian children, recalled that "once the contest began, the Indians had no sense of where to end it. Their thirst for blood of their reputed enemies is not to be quenched with a few drops—the more they drink, the more it inflames their thirst."[80] Catlin reported that "cruelty is one of the leading traits of the Indian's character. . . . In the treatment of their prisoners also, in many tribes, they are in the habit of inflicting the most appalling tortures."[81]

Missionary John Heckewelder, who was a friend of the Indians, acknowledged in 1818 "that the Indians are in general revengeful and cruel to their enemies. That even after the battle is over, they wreak their deliberate revenge on their defenseless prisoners."[82] Catlin also found that "the Indians are hard and cruel masters."[83]

Captive Mary Jemison married a Delaware, then later married a Seneca warrior named Hiokatoo, who was second in command to

---

*Red Cloud counted 80 coups (acts of courage). His warriors and other tribes fought the army in several battles, seeking to close the Bozeman Trail, which ran through Sioux territory. Finally, the government gave in to his demands and by treaty agreed to close its forts in return for the Indians stopping their raids.[78]

Joseph Brant, a Mohawk leader, at the Cherry Valley Massacre.[84] Her account of her life looked on the Indians with sympathy, but she candidly described Hiokatoo's early training:

> In early life, Hiokatoo showed signs of thirst for blood by attending only to the art of war, in the use of the tomahawk and scalping knife; and in practicing cruelties upon every thing that chanced to fall into his hands, which was susceptible of pain. In that way he learned to use his implements of war effectually, and at the same time blunted all those fine feelings and tender sympathies that are naturally excited, by hearing or seeing, a fellow being in distress. He could effect the most excruciating tortures upon his enemies, and prided himself upon his fortitude, in having performed the most barbarous ceremonies and tortures, without the least degree of pity or remorse. Thus qualified, when very young he was initiated into scenes of carnage, by being engaged in the wars that prevailed amongst the Indian tribes.[85]

Fanny Kelly, who wrote *My Captivity Among the Sioux Indians,* observed the same thing:

> Cruelty is inherent in them, and is early manifested in the young, torturing birds, turtles, or any little animals that may fall in their hands. They seem to delight in it, while the pleasure of the adult in torturing his prisoners is most unquestionable.[86]

Fanny Kelly, only 19 years old but a wife and mother, was headed across the Plains for Idaho when she was captured by a group of more than 1,000 Indians in 1864. She had remarkable experiences, and a Sioux related to Kelly "many instances of outrageous cruelties of his band in their murderous attacks on travelling parties and frontier settlers."[87]

Sometimes Indian cruelty was too much even for other Indians. The Iroquois were so cruel that their neighbors feared and hated them.[88]

USE OF torture was another Indian characteristic. It is closely related to cruelty, but of course there may be cruelty without torture. Frederick Drimmer compiled a book of narratives called *Captured by the Indians.* He said that "Indians often made a cult of torture, and young and old, male and female, took part in it. The squaws had a special reputation for ferocity."[89]

Some general observations about torture can be made. Alan Axelrod, in his *Chronicle of the Indian Wars,* wrote:

It is a fact that Indians were often cruel to their captives. The weak, the old, the infants, and the wounded—prisoners who would impede flight from the scene of a raid—were often summarily dispatched. Children were killed before the eyes of their parents. Elderly parents were killed in front of their children. . . . Cutting, flaying alive, dismemberment, piercing, beating, and burning were common. One usual torture was to cut off an ear, a strip of flesh, or a finger and force the victim to eat it. . . . [Running the gauntlet was a] . . . combination of torture, ritual, and sport [which] placed the captive at the head of parallel rows of club-wielding warriors (and often women and children as well); the captive had to run from one end of the "gauntlet" to the other as blows rained down on him. If he stumbled and fell, he was placed at the starting point again—or he was beaten to death.[90]

Harold E. Driver noted the same thing:

The most distinctive feature of the warfare pattern [among Indians] in the East as compared with other areas north of Mexico was the emphasis on the torture of prisoners. Most instances of torture on the Plains and Prairies seem to have been derived from the East in the historic period. Generally the prisoner was tied to a stake, frame, or platform, and tortured with fire, blows, mutilation, stabbing, shooting with arrows, or dismemberment while still alive. Such orgies lasted from a few hours to a few days, and the remains of the victim were often eaten in a cannibalistic feast.[91]

Howard Mumford Jones listed some of the crimes committed by the Indians during King Philip's War:

The contest was illustrated . . . by the raping and scalping of women, the cutting off of fingers and feet of men, the skinning of white captives, the ripping open of the bellies of pregnant women, the cutting off of the penises of males, and the wearing of the fingers of white men as bracelets or necklaces.[92]

William Brandon outlined tortures inflicted by the Iroquois, which included

prisoners being hamstrung, cords drawn through slits gashed at the tendons of their heels, and thus roped together being forced to march . . . to the town of their captors, there to be burned alive.

As among the people of the Southeast, a captive was supposed to continue singing his defiant death song while the jubilant, screaming women and children burned him with torches, gouged out bits of his flesh with jagged pieces of seashell, or while a warrior tore off his scalp and poured red-hot coals over his bleeding skull, all this cunningly managed so as to delay as long as possible the moment when the last glint of life, like a melting snowflake, died from the body.

Maybe Iroquois torture was a trifle too notorious, considering that most of their neighbors indulged in similar delights.[93]

Torture by Canadian Indians was apparently along the same lines. Charles Dennis Rusoe D'Eres was captured when 14 years old and spent 11 years with them. Gary L. Ebersole described what happened after a battle with an enemy:

Several of them were most inhumanely slaughtered by the tomahawk and knife, cutting open their bodies, and with their hands scooping up the warm blood out of their bodies, while alive, and drinking it greedily, whooping and dancing merrily, as if partaking of the most agreeable repast.

The prisoners who survived, were kept confined without any sustenance, and every day were whipt and tortured, by burning their fingers; forcing them into their pipes, when smoking, and there confining them until burnt to the bone, whooping and dancing round them—this was their practice day by day.[94]

Colonel Richard Dodge, an aide to General Sherman during the Civil War, related his extensive experience on the frontier upon leaving the service. He recorded that a favorite method of Indian torture was the stake-out. The victim

was stripped of his clothing, laid on his back on the ground and his arms and legs, stretched to the utmost, were fastened by thongs to pins driven into the ground. In this state he was not only helpless, but almost motionless. All this time the Indians pleasantly talked to him. It was all kind of a joke. Then a small fire was built near one of his feet. When that was so cooked as to have little sensation, another fire was built near the other foot; then the legs and arms and body until the whole person was crisped. Finally, a small fire was built on the naked breast and kept up until life was extinct.[95]

Indians sometimes tortured members of sister tribes under odd circumstances. The Fox and Sac (who were allies from 1734 to the present) were going to fight the Sioux, but the Fox were 20 horses short. They let the Sac know. The Sac came to the Fox village where the 20 young men who were "beggars for horses" were seated on the ground in a circle. Twenty Sac, on horses they had agreed to give away, rode into the village circling the men on the ground, each carrying a heavy whip. When a Sac rider had picked the man he wanted to have his horse, he gave him "the most tremendous cut with his lash" on his naked shoulders again and again as he rode around the men on the ground. Finally, the horse owner dismounted and presented his horse to the man he had whipped. Catlin said one man got a horse and the other "the satisfaction of putting his mark on the other man."[96]

Perhaps the ultimate sacrifice was torturing to death a member of the killer's own tribe. The practice is described by Harold E. Driver:

> Along the Gulf from Louisiana to Florida and then up the Atlantic Coast to Virginia, chiefs had absolute authority over their subjects, including the power of life and death. . . . Human sacrifice of members of the in-group . . . has also been reported for this region. Wives and slaves were also killed at the death of a chief so that they might accompany him to the afterworld. Such sacrifice was also thought to appease the wrath of powerful spirits. Men sacrificed their own children at public spectacles to gain the favor of the chief and be raised to the rank of nobility. . . . The Pawnee Indians of Nebraska were the only other people north of Mexico to practice human sacrifice. . . . They used to sacrifice a maiden of their own tribe by tying her to a rectangular frame and shooting her with arrows.[97]

There was an incredible Mandan religious ceremony to select young men who were best able to lead a war party against other tribes. Catlin witnessed 45 or 50 volunteer youths who 6 or 8 at a time went through the ordeal in the medicine lodge. They were without food, drink, or sleep for nearly 4 days. Finally, a candidate came forward. A cut more than an inch deep was made in each shoulder or breast, and skewers were placed in the wound. The lodge had a hole in its roof from which a number of rawhide cords were dropped. These were attached to the skewers, and he was instantly pulled up off the ground. Then he was cut again and skewers inserted on each arm below the shoulder, below the elbows, on the thighs, and below the knees. Weights, often buffalo skulls with horns, were attached to his arms and legs. (Catlin made sketches and was so close that he could hear the knife rip through the flesh, causing him to cry "uncontrollable tears.")

At this point, a warrior came forward with a pole and started turning the candidate's body around, gently at first, then faster and faster, until the candidate fainted. The important men in the tribe then checked him to be sure that he was "entirely dead." He was then lowered to the ground. When consciousness returned, he crawled, with the weights still attached, to another warrior with a hatchet and a dried buffalo skull before him. The candidate held up the little finger of his left hand, laid it on the buffalo skull, and the warrior chopped it off near the hand with the hatchet. Catlin saw some of the candidates who had already lost their little fingers put their left forefingers on the skull, and they, too, were chopped off. (Catlin did not witness it, but several chiefs and dignitaries of the tribe without little fingers on the right hand told him they had taken a third step at the ceremony.)

After all 6 or 8 candidates had undergone this ordeal, they were then taken, with their weights still attached and skewers in place on the legs and arms, into the presence of the whole village. Two warriors put leather straps on the wrists of each candidate, and they were pulled, faster and faster, around the Big Canoe (a large hogshead 8 or 10 feet high containing choice medicines). This part of the ceremony was called the last race. The object was to run longer than the others without "dying." When they faltered, the warriors dragged them by the wrists until the skewers were pulled out by the weights. Most fainted, then they were dropped, and appeared "like nothing but a mangled and loathsome corpse" to Catlin. When each regained consciousness and could rise, he went to his wigwam.[98]

The Sun Dance practiced by the Sioux was better known but similar to the Mandan dance. Two of the most famous Sun Dances involved Sitting Bull* and Rain-in-the-Face.† In 1875, Sioux war chief and medicine man Sitting Bull held a 3-day Sun Dance along the Rosebud River in Montana. About 10,000 to 15,000 warriors were in attendance. Edward Lazarus described the ceremony involving Sitting Bull:

> Sitting Bull offered his flesh to the Great Spirit, gouging fifty small strips from each of his arms. His blood streaming, the chief danced for eighteen hours without rest or food, staring at the sun and moon by

---

*Sitting Bull, a Hunkpapa Sioux, killed his first buffalo at age 10 and counted his first coup at 14 in a battle against the Crow Indians. He led many raids on nearby tribes. After the Santee Sioux Uprising he fought soldiers pursuing them. He and his warriors participated in the Battle of the Rosebud and the Battle of the Little Bighorn.[99]

†Rain-in-the-Face was also a Hunkpapa Sioux war chief. He fought the Cheyenne and the Gros Ventres. Rain-in-the-Face fought in the Fetterman Massacre and the War for the Black Hills. It was his claim that he killed Custer. He had 7 wives over the course of his life.[100]

turns. He fell into a trance and saw a vision: white soldiers falling into his camp, while a voice boomed in his head that these white men were a gift from the Great Spirit, Wakan Tanka.[101]

The Sun Dance of Chief Rain-in-the-Face was even more dramatic. He told an Indian named W. Kent Thomas that he "would rather fight than eat." Rain-in-the-Face described his Sun Dance, which took place in the presence of Sitting Bull, as follows:

> The Sun Dance is that ceremonial performance in which the young Sioux aspirant gives that final proof of endurance and courage which entitles him to the *toga virilis* of a full-fledged warrior. One feature of it is the suspension in air of the candidate by a rawhide rope passed through slits cut in the breast, or elsewhere, until the flesh tears and he falls to the ground. If he faints, falters, or fails, or even gives way momentarily to his anguish during the period of suspension, he is damned forever after, and is called and treated as a squaw for the rest of his miserable life.
>
> Rain-in-the-Face was lucky when he was so tied up. The tendons gave way easily, and he was released after so short a suspension that it was felt he had not fairly won his spurs. Sitting Bull, the chief medicine man, decided that the test was unsatisfactory. Rain-in-the-Face thereupon defied Sitting Bull to do his worst, declaring there was no test which could wring a murmur of pain from his lips.
>
> Sitting Bull was equal to the occasion. He cut deep slits in the back over the kidneys—the hollows remaining were big enough almost to take in a closed fist years after—and passed a rawhide rope through them. For two days the young Indian hung suspended, taunting his torturers, jeering at them, defying them to do their worst, while singing his war songs and boasting of his deeds. The tough flesh muscles and tendons would not tear loose, although he kicked and struggled violently to get free. Finally, Sitting Bull, satisfied that Rain-in-the-Face's courage and endurance were above proof [*sic*], ordered buffalo skulls to be tied to his legs, and the added weight with some more vigorous kicking enabled the Indian stoic to break free.[102]

The federal government prohibited the Sun Dance in 1910 because it constituted self-torture.[103] The purpose of this dance was quite similar to that of the Mandan ceremony—namely, to demonstrate the ability to withstand pain and therefore fight bravely in war.

John Rodgers Jewitt, who had been taken captive by the Nootka Indians, attended the annual celebration in honor of their god between 1803 and 1805. He saw 3 men, each of whom had 2 bayonets run through his sides between his ribs, walking back and forth in the room singing war songs and exulting in their behavior.[104]

There were other kinds of self-torture. Female relatives of slain Comanche warriors were expected to show their grief by self-torture for weeks, months, or years. They would withdraw from camp, wail until exhausted, and meanwhile slash their arms, faces, and breasts.[105] The Sioux, with captive Fanny Kelly, were fleeing General Alfred Sully and his troops in 1864. Several warriors were killed. Kelly reported a scene of terrible mourning that took place among the women:

> Sometimes the practice of cutting the flesh is carried to a horrible extent. They inflict gashes an inch in length on their bodies and limbs. Some cut off their hair, blacken their faces, and march through the village in procession, wailing and torturing their bodies to add vigor to their lamentations.[106]

The Hurons had a Dance of Fire, which called for the dancers to carry coals or heated stones in their mouths. They also plunged their arms into boiling water. It was thought this invoked a spirit to cure the sick.[107]

Several explanations for Indian torture have been advanced. William Brandon in *Indians* and Bernard W. Sheehan in *Seeds of Extinction* gave the most plausible one. Sheehan said that after "sating the urge for blood" in a battle, the Indian "took the few survivors prisoner to endure a more horrid fate on the return to the victor's country. These [were] atrocities saved by the Indians for the entertainment of the home village."[108] Brandon agreed and said that the practice had no underlying significance. "It is hard to escape an impression that simply the entertainment involved had become the main force behind the ritual torture of captives of war."[109]

Indian advocates sometimes imply or even assert that particular kinds of torture, such as scalping, were done first by the settlers and later copied by the Indians. That was not so. Explorers such as Jacques Cartier in 1535, Hernando de Soto in 1540, Tristan de Luna in 1559, and others reported Indian scalping before the settlers arrived.[110] No evidence of scalping in Europe has been found.[111] The findings of Bil Gilbert, Fergus M. Bordewich, and Alvin Josephy confirm that settlers did not scalp before Indians. Gilbert, for example, said that "a few captives were now and then put to slow, horrible deaths, a practice which, like prisoner taking itself, had originated before the coming of Europeans."[112] Bordewich noted that Indian words "for scalping and more imaginative forms of dismemberment existed in many Indian languages from the earliest times."[113] To the same effect, Josephy noted tortures and other conduct repulsive to the settlers were encountered when they went into Indian territory:

> Their [the settlers'] own intrusions into Indian homelands inevitably exposed them to practices such as horse thefts, raids for personal prestige, torture, and even cannibalism and human sacrifice and trophy-taking that repelled and angered them.[114]

Hatred was a strong Indian and settler characteristic. Hatred is a state of mind that may lead to revenge or even violence. It would seem that the Indians hated the settlers as soon as they realized the settlers intended to take land occupied by them. In 1607, years before the Powhatan Wars began in 1622, King Powhatan (predecessor and relative of Opechancanough) told John Smith, "Captain Smith, (saith the king) some doubt I have of your comming hither . . . for many do informe me, your comming is not for trade, but to invade my people and possesse my Country."[115] It would also seem the settlers began to hate the Indians as soon as they realized the Indians were committing atrocities. Henry Knox, the first secretary of war, reported to Congress in 1787 that

> the deep rooted prejudices, and malignity of heart, and conduct reciprocally entertained and practiced on all occasions by the Whites and Savages will ever prevent their being good neighbours. The one side anxiously defend their lands which the other avariciously claim. With minds previously inflamed the slightest offence occasions death, revenge follows which knows no bounds. The flames of a merciless war are thus lighted up which involve the innocent and helpless with the guilty.[116]

One of the strongest statements of hatred toward the settlers was given by the great orator Shawnee chief Tecumseh, speaking to the Creeks in Alabama:

> Accursed be the race that has seized our country and made women of our warriors! Our fathers, from their tombs, reproach us as slaves and cowards; I hear them now in the wailing winds. They seize your land; they corrupt your women; they trample on the ashes of your dead.[117]

Sitting Bull added a new concept, a similar settler hatred of the Indians: "No Indian that ever lived loved the white man, and . . . no white man that ever lived loved the Indian."[118] The frontier settlers from the viewpoint of the Indians

> were the men who squatted on Indian lands, cheated them in trading, and provoked their hatred. That hatred, in turn, led to wholesale, indiscriminate atrocities which the whites repaid by a deliberate policy of annihilation rather than simple defeat.[119]

Page Smith determined that "the most disastrous legacy of the Revolution could be found in the permanently embittered relations between the Western settlers and the Indians who confronted them."[120] The British promoted Indian raids, which were increasingly punitive, to punish the settlers for their presumption in revolting against the mother country. "With the involvement of the Indians, the frontier was devastated by a ruthless and barbarous total war."[121] Smith added that the settler who had built buildings and acquired animals and

> then saw the buildings put to the torch and the animals slaughtered, nursed an understandable hatred of the British and their Indian auxiliaries. If, in addition, he saw the livid crimson skull of a friend or relative who had been scalped by the Indians, the lust of vengeance burned in him as long as he lived. . . .
> Of all the policies pursued by the British in the Revolutionary era, their employment of Indians to kill Americans is the least excusable. . . . The British policy was as cruel and exploitive to the Indians as it was bloody and ruthless to the Americans. When the British departed, they left behind them a legacy of bitterness that could never be alleviated. From the Revolution on, those Americans who lived in the frontier settlements, which moved constantly westward, viewed the Indian as the enemy, cruel, deceitful, merciless; and they judged it a simple rule of self-preservation to match him in cunning and savagery, terror for terror, life for life, scalp for scalp, settler and savage caught in a terrible ritual of violence.[122]

Indian raids on frontier settlers during the Revolution were a matter of great significance:

> It was primarily an Indian war; without Indian allies the activity of the British in the West would have been confined to a few minor expeditions by British regulars and Tories. . . . With the involvement of the Indians, the frontier was devastated by a ruthless and barbarous total war. Indeed, the frontier settlers suffered, in the course of the raids and

counterraids of the border war, more casualties than Washington's Continental Army suffered in all its major engagements.[123]

The Indians' hatred was not directed only toward the settlers. That hatred was aimed at other tribes as well, presumably all those with whom the Indians made war. New York governor George Clinton, who was vice president from 1805 to 1812, under Jefferson and Madison, put it as graphically as anybody in an 1814 paper:

> With savages in general, this ferocious propensity was impelled by a blind fury, and was but little regulated by the dictates of skill and judgment. The Indian tribes . . . engaged in interminable conflict that stunted their cultural progress and kept their numbers small. They utterly destroyed their enemies by eating their bodies, not because they had an appetite for such fare but in order to excite themselves to greater fury. Those unfortunate enough to be captured would be killed with "the most severe and protracted suffering."[124]

James Mooney wrote from personal experience: "Only those who have known the deadly hatred that once animated Ute, Cheyenne, and Pawnee, one toward the other, . . . could appreciate the effect of the Ghost Dance religion on those tribes."[125] As late as 1982 hatred still existed between the Hopi and the Navajo.[126]

REVENGE WAS often inextricably a part of hatred. "For the Indians," wrote Utley, "this revenge was not merely casual retribution for specific injustices. It represented a strong and moral principle in Indian life. To fail to repay an injustice was not charity or mercy, but itself injustice."[127] Frederick Drimmer also emphasized that "nothing is more sacred to a savage than revenge."[128] He went on:

> The Indian had his grievances against the whites. To him, one American or Englishman was like another, and all were held responsible for the misdeed of one. Given the provocation and the opportunity, he often exacted the last full measure of revenge."[129]

Bernard W. Sheehan went so far as to say that some observers thought the Indians fought mainly for revenge:

> Revenge had the sound of an indiscriminate savage reaction; it made war arise from causes intrinsic to the Indian character. Jonathan

Carver wrote that "the passion of revenge, which is the distinguishing characteristic of these people, is the most general motive [for war]. Injustices are felt by them with exquisite sensibility, and vengeance pursued with unremitted ardor." John Heckewelder, a usually sympathetic observer of Indian life, admitted that "the worst that can be said of them is that the passion of revenge is so strong in their minds that it carried them beyond all bounds."[130]

THERE HAVE been frequent observations that the Indian was childlike. The Indian allies of the British in the Revolution frequently killed cattle just to get their bells.[131] Horace Greeley later found them to be "little more than children."[132] According to James Wilson, "Since the time of Columbus, Europeans had seen Native Americans as children—pastoral innocents or feckless, thoughtlessly cruel delinquents."[133]

Thomas L. McKenney was the chief administrator of Indian policy under 3 presidents. After he left office, he wrote a 3-volume history of Indians in North America, which noted, among many things, their childlike quality:

> Our Indians stand pretty much in the relation to the Government as do our children to us. . . . Indians are children and require to be nursed, and counseled, and directed as such. . . . Indians, I have found out, are only children, and can be properly managed, only, by being treated as such.[134]

Professor Logan Esarey noted something further:

> Their senses were keen but their reason rudimentary. They believed in sorcery and witchcraft. Spirits, friendly and unfriendly, animated everything around them. . . . Their reverent, childlike minds were lost in the confusion.[135]

This childlike behavior of the Indians was demonstrated in their attitude toward gifts. Columbus noted that they were "delighted" with small gifts. Often they could not resist the attractive trinkets offered by the speculators for vast areas of land. Sheehan observed that

> the artifacts of European civilization, although obviously increasing the efficiency of the Indian, set him adrift from his old manner of life, made him dependent on the white man, and gave him an insecure base on which to erect a new society.[136]

Fanny Kelly remembered this about the Sioux:

> They were much like children . . . easily offended, but very difficult to please. . . . I was constantly annoyed, worried, and terrified by their strange conduct—their transition from laughing and fun to anger, and even rage. I knew not how to get along with them. One moment, they would seem friendly and kind; the next, if any act of mine displeased them, their faces were instantly changed, and they displayed their hatred or anger in unmeasured words or conduct—children one hour, the next, fiends.[137]

In getting ready for their great expedition in 1803, Lewis and Clark recognized the need for vast quantities of beads, scissors, thimbles, thread, silk, paint, 288 knives, rifles, balls, powder, combs, arm bands, ear trinkets, brass buttons, tomahawks, axes, moccasin awls, mirrors, tobacco, and whiskey to give to the Indians.[138]

The Sioux continued to exhibit these qualities as late as 1916. Cattle prices were inflated then. The Sioux sold almost all their cattle and bought white status symbols, especially automobiles. When they had no more cash, they sold their horses until they were all gone.[139]

Perhaps this childlike characteristic was put into perspective by ecologist John Stewart Collis, who called attention to a unique fact: when Columbus came to America, "the whole of the North American continent was six thousand years behind European civilization."[140]

HUNTING WAS the favorite vocation of the Indians, next to war. The buffalo was the most important animal hunted on the Great Plains. Stephen E. Ambrose reported in *Undaunted Courage* that Meriwether Lewis and his hunting party killed 20 buffalo in a 2-day period in December 1804, but ate only the tongues.[141] In the 1870s, the buffalo were almost exterminated for commercial purposes and finally for sport when they were shot from passenger trains. Indians were properly critical of the senseless killing. But it would appear senseless killing was not the province of the settlers alone. Ralph K. Andrist found that

> the Indians did their part [in decreasing the number of buffalo]; they were not the great conservationists they are made out to have been, and did a great deal of wasteful killing. Many early travelers tell of Indians killing buffalo for nothing but the tongue, and the maneuver of stampeding a buffalo herd over a cliff, when one was handy, killing far more animals than could possibly be used, was standard practice. A

band of western Cree in Canada so thoroughly wiped out the buffalo in their area by driving them over cliffs that they were forced to move to new hunting grounds.[142]

A few days before Catlin went with the Sioux in 1832, an immense buffalo herd appeared. Five or six hundred Sioux horsemen went to the buffalo and came back in about 6 hours with 1,400 buffalo tongues, which were sold for a few gallons of whiskey. George Catlin sadly remarked on "this profligate waste of the lives of these noble and useful animals, when, from all that I could learn, not a skin or pound of the meat (except the tongues), was brought in."[143] Wilcomb E. Washburn determined that "buffalo might be driven into a buffalo pound, driven off cliffs, encircled with fire, or surrounded by mounted hunters using bows and arrows."[144] The great number of animal remains at excavated hunting sites raises the possibility that hunters may have lowered certain animal populations below the levels required for sustenance.[145] Beaver and otter were nearly exterminated in Iroquois country around 1640.[146] Great quantities of animals were killed just for the hides, leaving the meat to rot.[147]

Captive James Smith reported that the country around his tribe had been "hunted poor, so that few of even the best of hunters were able to kill game often."[148] Fanny Kelly saw the same wasteful activity:

> Sometimes these animals [buffalo] number tens of thousands, in droves. The Indians often, for the mere sport, make an onslaught, killing great numbers of them, and having a plentiful feast of "tatonka," as they call buffalo meat. They use no economy in food. It is always a feast or a famine; and they seem equally able to gorge or fast. Each man selects the part of the animal he has killed that best suits his own taste, and leaves the rest to decay or be eaten by wolves, thus wasting their own game, and often suffering privation in consequence.[149]

Even in thinly settled areas, tribes often carelessly exhausted the resources in the area and were obliged to move on.[150]

THERE ARE a number of other Indian characteristics relating to their collective behavior. Almost every tribe broke into 2 major factions, one favoring accommodation with the settlers and adoption of white ways, and the other holding firm to the old ways and resisting the blandishments of the whites.[151]

It is clear that most tribal governments were weak. Most tribes had several chiefs. There were war chiefs and peace chiefs.[152] The Sioux, for example, had 12 chiefs in 1878 and an unwieldy 63 chiefs in 1880.[153] When the Iroquois Confederacy was organized, it had a council of 49 chiefs.[154] This meant that Indians were handicapped in war because coordinated military action was usually impossible.[155] "The Indians overall," wrote Carl Waldman, "failed to present a unified and organized front because of long-standing feuds."[156]

Tribal decisions were characteristically reached by highly democratic means—often through innumerable meetings or councils, which frequently came to no unanimous conclusion at all. Moreover, individuals, if they disagreed with a so-called tribal decision, were usually not bound by it. In short, tribes could rarely enforce treaties on their own people. Nash even said that "no party in disagreement with a majority decision was compelled to act against its wishes."[157]

Grant's commissioner of Indian affairs was a Seneca Indian chief, Ely S. Parker.* His policies were fair and enlightened. In 1869 he made this assessment:

> The Indian tribes of the United States are not sovereign nations, capable of making treaties, as none of them have an organized government of such inherent strength as would secure a faithful obedience of its people in the observance of compacts of this character.[159]

Alvin M. Josephy, Jr., concluded that Plains Indian tribes in general

> had little formal government. Most bands were autonomous under their own leaders or chiefs. . . . But they gave advice rather than orders; councils of leading men made decisions based on unanimous agreement.[160]

Some tribes had no government at all. This was true of the Kiowa Apaches, the Lipans, the Jicarillas, the Mescaleros, the Western Apaches, and the Chiricahuas. With little or no government, it hardly need be said that "custom and tradition rather than law and coercion regulated social life."[161]

Indians frequently acted without authority—as did the settlers—

---

*Ely S. Parker studied engineering, then worked at several government jobs, including one where he met Ulysses S. Grant. Grant later commissioned him captain of engineers, and he served with Grant's army in two campaigns.[158]

which was a natural consequence of little or no government. Carl Waldman concluded that

> Indian proponents of peace, who believed that the long-term hope for their people lay in accommodation with whites, had their efforts undone by a constituency they could not control . . . often by young, volatile individualistic warriors in quest of personal honor.[162]

Washburn was not the only one who found that "Indian leaders could not easily control the warlike actions of youthful tribal members."[163] Stephen E. Ambrose explained that

> hostilities could break out at any time, for no apparent cause other than the restlessness of the young warriors, spurred by their desire for honor and glory, which could only be won on raids, which always brought on revenge raids, in a regular cycle.[164]

When the Virginians were fighting the Susquehannock* in 1676, Gary B. Nash reported that "the Susquehannock sachems could not control their own warriors, who were launching attacks even as their chiefs negotiated with the governor."[166] There was no peace until the Indians were crushed.[167]

Captive Charles Johnston observed that "young men of all the savage tribes frequently go out on raids without consulting their chief or nation."[168]

In 1864, the Cheyenne chief Black Kettle tried to call off his warriors who had been in a fight with troops in which Lean Bear and another chief were killed. Angie Debo described how the troops retreated to Fort Larned, "chased by some vengeful Indians that Black Kettle could not restrain. Then these warriors raided the trail between Fort Larned and Fort Riley on the Kansas."[169] Black Kettle and other Cheyenne chiefs "freely admitted they could not always restrain their young braves."[170]

MANY HISTORIANS have commented that Indians lacked unity, which made it more difficult for them to defeat the settlers. Debo put it

---

*Susquehannocks were bitter enemies of the Iroquois, and both tribes made frequent raids on the other. They were defeated by the Iroquois in 1675, and most left their original homeland. The tribe finally ceased to exist, with survivors living here and there among other Indians.[165]

directly: "Unrelated tribes never united in a general war."[171] Alan Axelrod concurred when he said, "The exultation of individual virtue meant that so-called tribes did not often act with unity, and one tribe rarely formed a strategically effective alliance with another."[172] There is no question, Carl Waldman concluded, "that the Indians were defeated by their own lack of unity."[173] Robert M. Utley and Wilcomb E. Washburn argued in *Indian Wars* that perhaps

> the tribes could have slowed the process, or compelled a more just conclusion, had they been able to unite against the common threat. But they failed to see the white advance as truly apocalyptic until too late, and they never overcame the cultural forces that made them see other tribes as greater enemies than the white people.[174]

Ironically, many Indians wanted Europeans to settle their lands. This matter is gone into in some detail by Alvin M. Josephy. Sometimes they were "encouraging white settlement in order to gain European support and auxiliaries."[175] Once in a while Indians begged or even demanded that forts be built in their territory in order to intimidate their enemies.[176]

ANOTHER IMPORTANT characteristic of the Indians from the time the war began was the refusal of many Indians to be assimilated into American life. To be assimilated in this context means to be absorbed or incorporated. But to the Indian it had bad connotations. This is because many Indians feared and still fear that assimilation would completely destroy the Indian culture and way of life.

The United States, speaking through its presidents, its Supreme Court, and its policy, has consistently urged assimilation. President Jefferson spoke to a group of Delawares, Mohicans, and Munries in 1808. He told them, "You will mix with us by marriage, your blood will run in our veins, and will spread with us over this great land."[177]

The Supreme Court said in 1823 in the case of *Johnson and Graham's Lessee vs. William McIntosh* that when a people is conquered,

> most usually, they are incorporated with the victorious nation, and become subjects or citizens of the government with which they are connected. The new and old members of the society mingle with each other; the distinction between them is gradually lost, and they make one people. Where this incorporation is practicable, humanity de-

mands, and a wise policy requires, that the rights of the conquered to property should remain unimpaired; that the new subjects should be governed as equitably as the old. . . . But the tribes of Indians inhabiting this country were fierce savages, whose occupation was war.[178]

Not all Indians, of course, resisted assimilation. As early as 1847 the Sioux chief Red Cloud sensed the futility of the struggle. He advised the tribes to note the settlers' example and follow it. But he put it rather sarcastically:

You must begin anew and put away the wisdom of your fathers. You must lay up food and forget the hungry. When your house is built, your storeroom filled, then look around for a neighbor whom you can take advantage of and seize all he has.[179]

Another influential Indian, Ely S. Parker, favored assimilation. Parker thought the Indians had more to lose by resisting assimilation, particularly the western tribes. "Unless they fall in with the current of destiny as it surges around them, they must succumb and be annihilated by its overwhelming force."[180]

The prevailing Indian view on assimilation, however, was held by Big Eagle, a Sioux leader, and it was uncompromising:

The whites were always trying to make the Indians give up their life and live like white men—go to farming, work hard and do as they did—and the Indians did not know how to do that, and did not want to anyway. . . . If the Indians had tried to make the whites live like them, the whites would have resisted, and it was the same way with many Indians.[181]

Jefferson urged Indians to become farmers. In 1863 and again toward the end of the Civil War, President Lincoln spoke at length to a group of Indian chiefs in Washington. He deferentially suggested that assimilation was best for them:

You have asked for my advice. I really am not capable of advising you whether, in the providence of the Great Spirit, who is the great Father of us all, it is best for you to maintain the habits and customs of your race, or adopt a new mode of life. I can only say that I can see no way in which your race is to become as numerous and prosperous as the white race except by living as they do, by the cultivation of the earth.[182]

(That the Indians have not taken Jefferson's and Lincoln's advice is shown by the 1990 census, which indicated that only 7,000 out of 1,960,000 Indians and Aleutians are farmers.)

At the Medicine Lodge Creek peace conference in 1865, a United States senator from Missouri and peace commissioner named Henderson addressed 5,000 Indians in a blunt if not threatening manner concerning assimilation. He reminded them that the buffalo would not last forever. "When that day comes, the Indian must change the road his father trod, or he must suffer, and probably die. We tell you that to change will make you better. We wish you to live, and we will now offer you the way."[183]

The first Peace Commission report of 1868 elaborated on assimilation:

> The white and Indian must mingle together and jointly occupy the country or one of them must abandon it. If they could have lived together, the Indian by this contact would soon have become civilized and war would have been impossible.[184]

Ten years later, General Sherman observed,

> I have seen some Indians willing and able to take farms, build houses, and join in the white man's ways; and I honestly believe the Army could induce hundreds, if not thousands, of others to do the same, but if left wandering about, hoping to restore the old order of things, an Indian will be a curiosity here in twenty years.[185]

Senator Henry L. Dawes, however, predicted after Wounded Knee in 1890 that "without doubt these Indians are somehow to be absorbed into and become part of the 50,000,000 of our people. There does not seem to be any other way to deal with them."[186]

Some tribes, like the Cherokee, did assimilate to a considerable extent. Helen Hunt Jackson believed that "there is no instance in all history of a race of people passing in so short a space of time from the barbarous stage to the agricultural and civilized [as the Cherokee]."[187] Assimilation had widely begun as early as the start of the nineteenth century. By then, Fergus M. Bordewich observed, almost all tribes east of the Mississippi were abandoning wigwams for cabins, buckskin for cotton clothes, and hunting for agriculture.[188] The commissioner of Indian affairs reported in 1860 that

> the Winnebagos continue steadily on the march of improvement. . . . The progress of the Winnebagos in agriculture growths by individuals

is particularly marked with success. There have been raised by individuals as high as sixty acres of wheat on a single farm. . . . Wigwams are becoming as scarce as houses were two years ago.[189]

The next year, the commissioner

was much surprised to find so many of the Sioux Indians wearing the garb of civilization, many of them living in frame or brick houses, some of them with stables or out-houses, and their fields indicating considerable knowledge of agriculture.[190]

Around 1875, Helen Hunt Jackson noted that the Winnebagos were nearly civilized, with all engaged in civil pursuits and the men working with their own hands.[191]

By the twentieth century, the process had gone much further, as Russell Thornton explained in *American Indian Holocaust and Survival*:

A point will be reached—perhaps not too far in the future—when it will no longer make sense to define American Indians in genetic terms, only as tribal members or as people of Indian ancestry or ethnicity.[192]

These conclusions follow in part at least from Indian intermarriage.

Yet the National Indian Youth Council reported in 1964, according to James Wilson, that "we do not want to be pushed into the mainstream of American life."[193]

Indians have things to gain and something to lose by assimilation. What they do is of course their decision. Some tribes have demonstrated that assimilation does not necessarily mean destruction of Indian culture.

INDIANS HAD completely different ideas about property than the settlers, and this created many difficulties. It is clear that the Indians maintained that personal property such as weapons and clothing could be owned by one individual Indian. Although their slaveholding was widespread,[194] there is no indication that slaves were held in common by the entire tribe.

Their attitude concerning land was communal. Alan Axelrod stated the most commonly expressed Indian view:

No one "owned" a particular parcel of land. A given tribe might claim the right to hunt or live on it and might defend that right by force of arms; however, most tribes were willing to make agreements allowing other tribes or individuals to hunt on "their" land. Such an agreement did not convey ownership of the land to the other party.[195]

Relying on the view that the Indians only possessed or occupied the land, Indians and Indian advocates charged in the past—and some of them charge today—that even though they signed treaties ceding the land to the federal government, the settlers "stole" the land from them. An 1864 speech of Sioux chief Tall Soldier is typical:

Let the wretches die, who have stolen our lands, and we will be free to roam over the soil that was our fathers'. We will come home bravely from battle. Our songs shall rise among the hills, and every tipi shall be hung with the scalp-locks of our foes. . . . The inferior race, who have encroached on our rights and territories, justly deserve hatred and destruction. . . . The Indian cries for vengeance.[196]

The treaties themselves do not bear out the Tall Soldier claim. A standard cessation clause is found in the first removal treaty, the 1830 treaty with the Choctaw. It reads in part, "The Choctaw nation of Indians consent and hereby cede to the United States, the entire country they own and possess east of the Mississippi River."[197] Both the ownership rights and the possessory or occupancy rights of the Indians are transferred by this language. They retained nothing for themselves.[198]

SEVERAL TRIBES were imperialistic. During the 1600s, the Iroquois "expanded their territories in every direction." In the mid-1600s, they decimated the Hurons, Tobaccos, Neutrals, and Eries. They attacked the Susquehannocks, Algonquins, Ottawas, Illinois, Miamis, Potawatomis, Delawares, Mahicans, and Wappingers. Their extended territory went from the Hudson River to the Illinois River and from the Ottawa River to the Tennessee River.[199] In the late 1600s, Crees and Chippewas drove the Sioux westward, taking their land. The Sioux later developed faith in their own superiority, according to Bordewich, and "seized land with virtual impunity from the Ioways, Omahas, Arikaras, and Mandans."[200] By 1776, the Sioux had reached the Black Hills on the western edge of the Dakotas, where, in the early nineteenth century, they expelled the Kiowas and the Cheyennes.[201]

ALTHOUGH WOMEN often had unique roles in the tribes, more often than not their position was weak. The Shawnee war chief Tecumseh made a mistress leave him for the sole reason that she had improperly boned a turkey, causing him disgrace.[202] Comanche chief Big Wolf had 4 wives. He tied a deerskin cord to the corner of the mattress of each so that with a small pull the wife he wished would come to him.[203] Roy Harvey Pearce observed that one tribe even had "the wondrous custom of offering maidens of the village to distinguished visitors."[204] Sioux chief Black Buffalo offered Lewis and Clark young women as bed partners. Clark later wrote that "a curious custom with the Sioux is to give handsome squars [*sic*] to those whome they wish to Show some acknowledgements to."[205] The Arikara offered women to all the men in the Lewis and Clark party; many accepted, and left with venereal disease.[206] Clark wrote that the Chinooks "will even prostitute their wives and daughters for a fishinghook or a stran [*sic*] of beads."[207]

Jefferson charged that Indian women "are submitted to unjust drudgery."[208] Catlin went further. He said that Indian wives not only "stand rather in the light of menials and slaves," but "are kept at hard labour during most of the year."[209] He noted, "I have never seen an Indian woman eating with her husband. Men form the first group at the banquet, and women and children and dogs all come together at the next."[210]

In many other tribes, however, women occupied much stronger positions. In Iroquois political life, women held important posts. The mother and all her children constituted a "fireside," which was the foundation of society. All authority came from the groups and the women who headed them. The group named the sachems or peace chiefs who made up the ruling council of the Iroquois and the Five Nations as well.[211] Half of the 6 priests were women.[212] Shawnee women were organized like the men. Their chiefs directed matters such as farming, certain ceremonies, and women's affairs. Although they didn't go into battle, female chiefs helped with logistics. They held something like a veto power over the deliberations of the men.[213] The Navajo women were very influential in family life.[214]

Indian women sometimes did take part in the fighting. In a battle in Powder River country in 1864 against the Arapaho, one of General Connor's officers observed, "I was in the village in the midst of a hand-to-hand fight with warriors and their squaws, for many of the female portion of this band did as brave fighting as their savage lords."[215] When the army was fighting the Modocs in the lava beds in 1872, the soldiers moved close to the Modoc stronghold and were met with fire from both male and female warriors.[216] According to Cyrus Townsend Brady, Sioux leader American Horse was trapped by soldiers in 1876 with four warriors and several women and children in a cave. "Even the women had used guns, and had displayed all the bravery and courage of the Sioux."[217] Chief Joseph of the Nez Perce reported after the 5-day Battle of Bear Paw Mountain in 1877 that on the first day his tribe had lost "eighteen men and three women."[218]

As we have seen, Indian women could be as cruel as Indian men. A U.S. Army captain described how after a battle Cheyenne squaws helped "scalp and torture the wounded, shooting arrows into their bodies and cutting off fingers and toes, even when they were alive."[219]

MANY AUTHORS have commented on how much the Indians loved their children. "He is affectionate to his children, careful of them, and indulgent in the extreme," wrote Roy Harvey Pearce. "His sensibility is keen, even the warriors weeping most bitterly on the loss of their children."[220] "The Indians were usually affectionate toward their children," observed Harold E. Driver, "rarely punishing them, and an Indian mother would treat an adopted white child as her own."[221] Indian Commissioner George W. Manypenny also praised them in this regard: "His love for his offspring is intense."[222]

Infanticide was practiced, however, in many tribes. If the mother died at childbirth and no wet nurse could be found, the infant usually was buried with its mother. If the father died, the mother might kill the baby to free herself for other children. Where illegitimacy was strongly disapproved, the mother might put such a baby to death. Deformed infants were often killed. Infants would sometimes be killed in times of famine.

There were some instances where mothers killed their children because of the exigencies of warfare. Sometimes they would be killed so that the mother could fight without encumbrance. Some Seminole women and children were captured in 1836. One of the women gave her 3 children a drink from a coffeepot. She escaped, but her children remained in captivity. The children were then found dead from poison administered by their mother.[223] The same year, the Seminoles were defeated in battle; before they retreated, "they strangled their children by stuffing their mouths and nostrils with mud moss."[224] Some of the Creek women trying to escape from their group, which was being removed to Oklahoma in 1836, killed their young children, perhaps because they might make noise betraying their parents when secrecy and silence were vital.[225]

The elderly sometimes fared no better. Captain William Clark, when he was among the Mandans, heard what happened when an elderly Indian asked for something to ease the pain in his back. His young grandson said it was not worthwhile, "that it was time for the old man to die."[226] Later, George Catlin told about being directed by the Indian agent, Major Sanford, to a member of the Puncah tribe, "one of the most miserable and helpless looking objects that I had ever seen in my life, a very aged and emaciated man." He had once been a chief and was now too old to travel with the tribe, which was going to move to where there was more food. He told Catlin he was "to be exposed," that is, left to die when the others departed. He sat by a small fire with a few sticks of wood within reach, a buffalo's skin over his head, a few half-picked bones, a dish of water, and nothing else—nothing even to defend himself with against the wolves.

Before they left, his children gathered around him and he said,

> My children, our nation is poor, and it is necessary that you should all go to the country where you can get meat,—my eyes are dimmed and my strength is no more; my days are nearly numbered, and I am a burthen to my children—I cannot go, and I wish to die. Keep your hearts stout, and think not of me; I am no longer good for anything.[227]

Catlin went to the old chief after this farewell, they talked, they shook hands, the chief smiled, they shook hands again, then Catlin left to catch his steamboat on the Missouri. He returned a few months later and found everything as it had been except that the chief's skull and some of his bones had been picked clean by the wolves. Catlin concluded that "this cruel custom of exposing their aged people, belongs, I think, to all the tribes who roam about the prairies."[228]

FREQUENT ADOPTION existed among the tribes before and after the settlers came.[229] Some tribes gave a widow or a mother who had lost a child the option of adopting a captive to replace the lost relative. The person might be inducted into the tribe as an equal or as a semislave. Many settler captives eventually found Indian life so attractive that they resisted being rescued. Frederick Drimmer outlined what often happened:

It is interesting to observe that a captive was usually adopted in the place of someone who had died or been killed in war. He was given not only the name, but also the privileges and responsibilities of the person whose place he took—was expected to be a husband to the dead man's wife and a father to his children. Sometimes a party of warriors would set out with the express aim of taking a white captive to replace a deceased member of their family or clan.[230]

There was even a "significant number of whites who resisted or declined 'rescue.'" Benjamin Franklin put the problem this way in 1753:

When an Indian Child has been brought up among us, taught our language and habituated to our Customs, yet if he goes to see his relations and makes one Indian Ramble with them, there is no perswading [sic] him ever to return. When white persons of either sex have been taken prisoners young by the Indians, and lived a while among them, tho' ransomed by their Friends, and treated with all imaginable tenderness to prevail with them to stay among the English, yet in a short Time they become disgusted with our manner of life, and the care and pains that are necessary to support it, and take the first good opportunity of escaping again into the Woods, from whence there is no reclaiming them.[231]

Eunice Williams was captured by the Iroquois in the 1704 Deerfield raid. Her father found her in Montreal in 1714 and tried to persuade her to leave her Indian husband and return. He said, "She is yet obstinately resolved to live and dye [sic] here, and will not so much as give me one pleasant look."[232] Frances Slocum was captured in the Wyoming Valley of Pennsylvania in 1778. She married a Delaware Indian, who left her, and later married a Miami chief. After searching for many years, her brothers found her in 1837 and urged her to return, at least for a visit, but she said, "I can not. I can not. I am an old tree. I can not move about. I was a sapling when they took me away. It is all gone past. I am afraid I should die and never come back. I am happy here."[233]

Another captive who refused to return to settler civilization was Cynthia Ann Parker, mother of Comanche chief Quanah Parker. She was captured in Texas in 1836 by Caddos Indians when only 9 years old. The Caddos sold her to the Comanches, and she became the wife of a Comanche chief, by whom she had 3 children. She preferred Indian life to settler life. She was recaptured, but died 4 years later.[234] Angie Debo observed that "no other tragedy of frontier life brought such anguish [as

Cynthia's kidnapping], no other phase of Indian warfare aroused such hatred as this capture of children."[235]

Children below the age of 12 taken captive by Indians were easily assimilated or Indianized, but older children often retained the desire to return to their families.[236] Those who had been captive for many years eventually took on Indian dress, talk, thought, and values. Frequently they took on an Indian identity. Such captives often faced prejudice if they returned to white society. Many never found themselves completely accepted or assimilated there.[237]

Why did some captive settlers not want to return? Several reasons suggest themselves. Gary L. Ebersole observed that

> captivity was not a negative experience for everyone. For some individuals, captivity opened up hitherto unimagined opportunities and lifestyle choices. Some individuals enjoyed a newfound freedom, unknown in the white world. This was obviously the case with many black slaves, but others, too—indentured servants, battered wives, overworked young boys, and young women—also realized an independence or a new social identity among the Indians that literally opened new worlds to them.[238]

Indian child-rearing practices may also have been a factor. The maxim "Spare the rod and spoil the child" was followed by most settler parents. In many families, children were viewed primarily as a source of labor and were exploited as such. One 12-year-old who had been forced by his father to watch sheep alone for long periods of time joined an Indian band after Indians had glowingly described to him a life of hunting, fishing, and riding and even promised him a pony if he would come with them. He did.[239]

Another reason white captive males might not want to return was that, as Alexander Kellet put it in 1778, "Indian maidens positively desire white men because they are better lovers and know what women want."[240] From what he had seen, Indian men treated their wives coldly; therefore, Indian women "are consequently very prone to European attachments, where they are agreeably surprised by a fondling and dalliance which is quite novel to them, and not the less captivating."[241]

J. Norman Heard, in his book *White into Red*, concluded, "The number of captives living out their lives with Indians was probably considerably smaller than the number restored to their white families."[242]

THE INDIAN certainly had a sense of humor. William Brandon quoted a writer in the 1800s who said about one tribe, "Wit, merriment and practical jokes enliven all their gatherings."[243] The Indian humor has come down to us as a black humor sometimes, perhaps because of the circumstances out of which it arose.

One day in 1808, Tecumseh called William Henry Harrison* a liar. Harrison drew his sword, the soldiers aimed their guns at the Indians, and the Indians raised their tomahawks at the soldiers. Harrison declared the meeting ended, and no one was hurt. The next morning, Tecumseh apologized. Harrison then visited the Indian camp, where the two sat on a log. Tecumseh kept scooting over toward Harrison; Harrison kept moving away, but finally reached the end of the log and objected to Tecumseh. Tecumseh laughed, saying that was what the white man was doing to the Indians.[245]

Indian removals to Oklahoma began in the 1830s. Eventually more than 25 tribes went there, and many others were shifted to new locations. Sioux chief Spotted Tail asked, "Why does not the Great Father put his red children on wheels, so he can move them as he will?"[246]

Around 1850, an Indian agent told Kiowa chief Little Mountain that the government was going to teach the Indians how to farm. The chief's reply was that he hoped that since the government was so generous it would also send the Indians some land that would grow corn, since they had no such land on the reservation.[247]

A Paiute Indian told this story about his grandfather, who was a big eater. A white man who watched him eating at a barbecue said he wished he had the Indian's appetite. The Indian replied, "You white people took our buffalo, and our women, and our land. You took everything we had. You want our appetite too?"[248]

The Sioux orator Red Dog, who was overweight, spoke at Cooper Institute in New York in 1870. His comments about his size had a bite to them:

> When the Great Father first sent out men to our people, I was poor and thin; now I am large and stout and fat. It is because so many liars have been sent out there, and I have been stuffed full with their lies.[249]

---

*William Henry Harrison fought with General Wayne at the Battle of Fallen Timbers. After he resigned from the army, he became the Northwest Territory delegate to Congress, then gover-

Many have commented on the eloquence of the Indians. In discourse, wrote Clark Wissler, "they proceeded in a fine manner, often rising to high levels of oratory."[250] And Peter Matthiessen lauded Indians as "a people who prize eloquence as the great gift of the oral tradition."[251]

John Logan, also known as James Logan and Tahgahjute (His Eye-lashes Stick Out), was a Mingo, an Iroquois living in Ohio or Pennsylvania. In 1744, a mob of settlers murdered several Mingo Indians, including members of Logan's family, near present-day Steubenville, Ohio. British governor John Dunmore and Logan met to negotiate. Logan opened the meeting with these words:

> I appeal to any white man to say, if ever he entered Logan's cabin hungry, and he gave him not meat; if ever he came cold and naked, and he clothed him not. During the course of the last long and bloody war, Logan remained idle in this cabin, an advocate for peace. Such was my love for the whites that my countrymen pointed as they passed, and said, "Logan is the friend of the white man." I had even thought to have lived with you, but for the injuries of one man, Colonel Cresap, who last spring, in cold blood and unprovoked, murdered all the relations of Logan, not even sparing my women and children. There runs not a drop of my blood in the veins of any living creature. This called on me for revenge. I have sought it; I have killed many; I have fully glutted my vengeance. For my countrymen I rejoice at the beams of peace. But do not harbor a thought that mine is the joy of fear. Logan never felt fear! He will not turn on his heel to save his life. Who is there to mourn for Logan? Not one.[252]

Ten years later Jefferson commented that in all the orations of Demosthenes and Cicero, there was not a single passage superior to Chief Logan's speech.[253]

In 1834, a Tennessee weekly reported a story about a grieving Indian woman who spoke over the graves of her husband and child. She lamented that

> the father of Life and Light has taken from me the apple of my eye, and the core of my heart, and hid him in these two graves. I will moisten the one with my tears, and the other with the milk of my breast, till I meet them in that country where the sun never sets.[254]

---

nor of the Indiana Territory. Harrison fought the Shawnees at the Battle of Tippecanoe in 1811. Harrison defeated Shawnee chief Tecumseh in 1813. He became president in 1841.[244]

One of the most memorable moments of Indian eloquence is undoubtedly the October 5, 1877, speech of Nez Perce* chief Joseph. General Oliver Howard ordered the tribe to move from Oregon to Idaho. Joseph and his younger brother, Ollikut, agreed to the moving, but before the tribe left, some young members of the tribe who had been drinking killed 18 or 19 settlers, and it was decided they would head instead for Canada. In the last battle at Bear Paw, Joseph's young daughter became frightened and fled from the others. Joseph decided to surrender. The interpreter wept as he translated Joseph's words, which were recorded by the general's aide:

> Tell General Howard I know his heart. What he told me before, in Idaho, I have it in my heart. I am tired of fighting. . . . My people ask me for food, and I have none to give. It is cold, and we have no blankets, no wood. My people are starving to death. Where is my little daughter? I do not know. Perhaps, even now, she is freezing to death. Hear me, my chiefs. I have fought; but from where the sun now stands, Joseph will fight no more forever.[256]

The cause was lost. Brother Ollikut was dead, but his daughter was found and brought back to him.

General Howard had promised Chief Joseph that he could return to the Wallowa Valley in Oregon where he had lived, but the government refused to honor Howard's promise. When Joseph died, one of the general's aides commented, "I think that in his long career, Joseph cannot accuse the Government of the United States of one single act of justice."[257] Not all the eloquence was Indian eloquence.

THEFT WAS a characteristic of the Indians that repelled and angered the settlers. The intrusion of the settlers into Indian territory "exposed them to practices such as horse thefts . . . [which] outraged the intruders' sense of morality and were opposed and ended by force and violence." Alexander Whitaker, a minister from Henrico, Virginia, wrote in 1613 that Indians "esteem it a virtue to lie, deceive and steale as their master the divell teacheth to them."[258] Indians did not consider theft a crime, according to George Catlin, but instead called it "capturing . . . considering it a kind of retaliation or summary justice."[259]

---

*The Nez Perce did not farm, but wandered searching for food, fish, and game. After Joseph and his people surrendered, they were sent to Kansas, then to the Indian Territory, and finally to Washington State.[255]

The Sioux loved horses, and although wild herds were available to them, they "preferred to steal horses already broken to riding." The western Indians stole horses from the Spanish, the French, and the English. They stole horses from other tribes. Clark Wissler wrote that "all of the Plains Indians taught their youth that one of the most laudable acts was to steal the horse of a stranger. An Indian brought up under such a regime would be troubled by a guilty conscience if he passed a chance to steal a horse." This was the principal cause of friction between them and the settlers.[260] Most Comanche raids were for horses. If scalps were taken, the raid was all the more successful, "but the taking of human life was ordinarily a secondary matter." In *The Comanche Barrier to South Plains Settlement,* Rupert Norval Richardson related how Chief Is-sa-keep stated that his 4 sons were a great comfort to him because "they could steal more horses than any other young men in the tribe."[261]

In 1804, Lewis and Clark Expedition sergeant John Ordway wrote in his journal around the campfire that the Sioux would sing and "confess how many horses they had Stole."[262] Indian thefts from the expedition were frequent. In December of that year, the Sioux stole 2 horse-drawn sleighs and a horse.[263] But in December 1805, the situation was reversed. When the expedition was getting ready to leave the Pacific to return to the East, Lewis desperately needed a canoe. The Clatsop Indians would not sell him one for what he considered a reasonable price, so the expedition took matters into their own hands. Ordway reported how 4 men went "over to the prarie [*sic*] near the coast" and took a canoe "as we were in want of it."[264] Six days later, just as the party was starting back east, an Indian guide claimed the canoe was his, so Lewis bought it from him for an elk skin.[265]

As they entered Chinook country in April 1806, a series of new thefts began. First, the Indians tried to steal a piece of lead and a tomahawk, and did steal Lewis's dog, Seaman, an ax, an iron socket, a saddle, and a robe. Lewis ordered 3 soldiers to follow the Indians who had stolen the dog and recover it, which they did. Lewis was fed up. He later wrote that the Chinook were "the greatest thieves and scoundrels we have met with." He told a group of Indians who were hanging about the camp that "if they made any further attempts to steal our property or insult our men we should put them to instant death."[266]

In July 1806, 7 of the party's 17 horses were stolen, so Lewis sent the renowned woodsman George Drouillard, whose father was a French Canadian and whose mother was a Shawnee, to try to find them. He tracked them to where they crossed the Dearborn River, but gave up because the thieves had a 2-day head start.[267] Lewis, Drouillard, and 2 others then took a side expedition along the Marias River. They came upon about 8 Blackfoot Indians, whom they approached. After some tense moments, Lewis asked them to camp with him that night, and they agreed. The next morning at dawn, one Indian stole a soldier's rifle, and another stole Lewis's as well. The Indians were chased, and a soldier, Reubin Fields, stabbed to death an Indian who would not give the rifles up.

In the meantime, the main party of Blackfeet was trying to steal the party's horses. Lewis gave chase. An Indian with a British musket turned toward Lewis; Lewis (who was an expert marksman) fired, hitting the Indian in the stomach. The Indian raised himself to his knee and shot, coming so close that Lewis could hear "the wind of his bullet." Only 4 of the party's stolen horses were recovered, so Lewis stole 4 Indian horses to replace them.[268]

S. L. A. Marshall saw this stealing by the Plains Indians as part of their culture:

> It was no more possible for Indians to keep their hands off of a carelessly guarded horse corral or a vulnerable herd of cattle than it was for the white man to abandon the rule that private property was sacred. The Indian knew no law against raiding. Horse stealing or the running off of someone else's beeves was to his mind an achievement, a stroke to his credit, a coup.[269]

Harold E. Driver estimated that "a hundred times as many horses were stolen on the Plains as were obtained in legitimate trade."[270] Helen Hunt Jackson guessed that in 1860 the Sioux had stolen more than half the horses the Poncas owned. The Poncas moved down the Niobrara River to try to get away from the Sioux.[271]

In 1855, Nelson Lee* was captured by the Comanche together with 20 other men while driving some mules and cattle to California. Only 4 of them lived. Lee was held as a slave and a medicine man for 3 years. The first thing the Indians did after the attack, he said, "was to collect the plunder. Not only did they gather up all our buffalo skins, blankets, rifles and revolvers, culinary utensils, and the like, but the dead were stripped to the last shred, and everything was tied on the backs of their mules. Nothing was left behind."[273]

---

*Nelson Lee worked as a boatman and was a Texas Ranger, a horse breaker, and a trader.[272]

The paths of George Crook,* who fought Indians most of his professional life, and Apache leader Geronimo crossed more than once. Dee Brown reported that Geronimo led a raid into Mexico to steal cattle in May 1883. General Crook caught up with the Indians. They surrendered, but Crook allowed them to keep their weapons "because I am not afraid of you." Geronimo told Crook he would need several months to round up all his people before returning to Arizona. Crook agreed. Eight months later, Geronimo returned from Mexico, according to his cousin, Jason Betzinez, who was on the trip, "driving along with him a large herd of cattle which he had stolen from the Mexicans." Crook took the cattle away from Geronimo, had them sold, and sent the proceeds of $1,762.50 to the Mexican government with the request it divide the money among the owners.[275]

IT SEEMS generally agreed that it was and is characteristic of the Indians that many have difficulty avoiding intoxication. There is disagreement about whether Indians had intoxicants before the settlers came, but most commentators believe that some form of liquor was made and used by the Indians early on. The Indians in Mexico had 40 distinct alcoholic beverages. There are several early references to American Indians drinking tiswin beer, which was made from corn.[276] Southwest Indians made wine from cacti. Southeast Indians made a persimmon wine. Papagos and Pima Indians believed the ingestion of liquor would cause it to rain.[277]

Seneca mystic Handsome Lake, who was once an alcoholic, reported on the return of a 1789 Indian trading expedition:

> Now that the party is home the men revel in strong drink and are very quarrelsome. Because of this the families become frightened and move away for safety. So from many places in the bushlands camp fires send up their smoke.
>
> Now the drunken men run yelling through the village and there is no one there except the drunken men. Now they are beastlike and run about without clothing and all have weapons to injure those whom they meet.
>
> Now there are no doors in the houses for they have all been kicked

---

*George Crook was a West Point graduate. He fought in the Yakima and Rogue River wars against the Indians. In the Civil War he was in the Battles of Antietam and Chickamauga, and the Shenandoah campaign. Then he campaigned against the Paiute, the Apaches, the Yavapais, the Sioux, and the Cheyenne.[274]

off. So, also, there are no fires in the village and have not been for many days.[278]

In 1796 a government Iroquois agent wrote in understated fashion that "they have recd their payments and immediately expended it for liquor & in the course of a frollick have killed one or two."[279]

Fur trader Alexander Henry stayed with the Indians from 1800 to 1807 at a small trading post. His journal notes that during that time there were 77 gatherings of Indians for drinking purposes, during which there were 65 injuries ranging from death to minor wounds. "Love of liquor is the ruling passion, and when intoxicated they will commit any crime to obtain more drink."[280]

John Gannt built a trading post on the Arkansas River in Colorado in 1832, when he introduced the Plains Indians to hard liquor. According to Duane Schultz, "The Indians clamored for more, trading nearly all their possessions for the drink—valuable furs and skins, armloads of blankets, horses and weapons, even their clothing, and then their wives and children."[281]

The devastating effects of liquor on Indians have been described many times. Wilcomb E. Washburn reported that

no evidence is more voluminous than that detailing Indian drunkenness. Whatever the area, whatever the time, report after report expressed the surprise of whites at the ardent desire of Indians to acquire "strong waters," and, having obtained them, their proclivity to total inebriation, often followed by injury or death to themselves or to their fellow tribesmen.[282]

Whole villages, including women and children, fell into chronic alcoholism. Health deteriorated, and social cohesion inevitably dissolved.[283] Superintendent of the Indian Trade Thomas L. McKenney left a graphic description of the Indian addiction:

No one who has not witnessed it, can conceive the sacrifices an Indian will make for whiskey; how far he will travel, laden with the returns of his winter's hunts; how little he foresees, or regards the consequences to himself, or any body else, of his indulgence in this final poison. The awakening from his delirious dream, and finding his furs and peltries gone, and in their places a few worthless articles, unsuited in quality or quantity to screen himself and his family from the winter's cold, may distress him, and kindle his revenge for the time being, but it is forgotten whenever a new occasion happens in which he can indulge the same excess![284]

The detrimental consequences of alcohol on the Indians were even worse than might at first be expected. Alan Axelrod pointed out the remarkable speed with which the Indians degenerated in the early 1800s. He said, "The Miamis, for example, a numerous and proud people in the eighteenth century, had become a diseased, drunken group of 1,000 by 1810."[285] Lazarus was writing about the Sioux when he observed the following, but he could have been speaking about most tribes:

The Indians craved the traders' brew—usually well-watered, loaded with molasses, pepper, tobacco juice, even gunpowder—but they had no tolerance for it. Many a drunken Indian lost the fruits of his winter hunt when a sober frontiersman tricked him out of his goods. Nor was poverty the only result. Alcohol made the Indians violent, so violent that many traders added sedatives to their drinks. These drugs were not always available and drunken homicide became commonplace in the Indian camps. Other Sioux simply passed out on the way home and froze to death on the prairie tundra.[286]

The Comanche captive Nelson Lee reported the following after watching the chief during a night of the "usual":

An Indian's dignity, whether chief or subject, never rises to that elevated degree which prevents his getting drunk every opportunity that offers. The sedate old chief became beastly intoxicated—forgot his customary decorum—vainly attempted to be funny—danced out of place—and whooped when there was no occasion for it—in fact, was as boisterous and silly as about half a gallon of bad Mexican whiskey could make him.[287]

Ralph K. Andrist completed the scene:

During the debauch that followed [Indian excessive drinking], drunken rows flared into stabbings, women wailed, adulteries were committed without discretion, and initial euphoria sagged into soddenness so deep the victims lay in their own vomit.[288]

And George Catlin was forced to observe that

after his [the Indian's] first means, in his wild state, are exhausted, he becomes a beggar for whiskey, and begs until he disgusts, when the honest pioneer becomes his neighbour; and then, and not before, gets the name of the "poor, degraded, naked, and drunken Indian," to whom the epithets are well and truly applied.[289]

Even today, the Indians suffer from extensive alcoholism. In 1964 the drink-associated crime rate of Indians was 12 times higher than the national rate.[290] The Indian Health Service reported that in the late 1980s, the Indian mortality rate from alcoholism in the United States was 667 percent greater than that of the general population.[291]

Brian W. Dippie expressed the modern view about this problem:

> For the Indians, alcohol brought with it a whole train of destructive consequences—quarrels disruptive of family and social life, the breakdown of traditional moral sanctions, impaired health due to exposure during bouts of drinking, maiming, prostitution, venereal disease, murder, and a lowered birth rate. . . . Tribal leaders over the centuries have struggled with the effects of intoxicating liquors on their people.[292]

Fergus M. Bordewich included a whole chapter on the subject of Indian alcoholism in *Killing the White Man's Indian*. He reported that some studies imply that the alcoholism of Indians and other ethnic groups may be genetic in nature because of structural differences in certain enzymes.[293]

Dippie concurs in this idea and adds some other possible causes. In the 1970s, scientists at the Oklahoma Center for Alcohol-Related Research entered a thorny area of controversy by suggesting that Indians might have a genetic intolerance to distilled spirits. Two Canadians have pointed to the possibility that hypoglycemia, exacerbated by severe stress and nutritional deficiencies, accounts for the Indians' susceptibility to strong drink.[294]

FINALLY, THE Indians were markedly religious, but in a uniquely Indian way. Religion was not a new thing for them. The subject of Indian religion, however, is a complicated one. Harold E. Driver perhaps encapsulated it best:

> Every thought and act [of the Indian] was hedged or bolstered by religion or magic, which ranged all the way from an amorphous feeling of reverence to the performance of elaborate rituals where every word and gesture was prescribed in advance. The distinction between the

natural and supernatural was never sharply drawn by Indians, who tended to blend the two into one harmonious whole. . . .

Gods, ghosts, and other spirits are supposed to have intelligence, emotions, and free will comparable to those of man. They may intervene in the affairs of the world of man in a manner consistent with a system of ethics or according to their whims of the moment. Because of their humanlike emotions, they may experience love, hate, joy, anger, jealousy, fear, courage, and may act according to their emotional state at the time. They may be benevolent, malevolent, or merely unconcerned, but they are generally susceptible to human pleading, and bend an ear to prayers, sacrifices, and other forms of emotional appeal to their egos. . . .

Some men are able to maneuver impersonal supernatural power as well as to compel spiritual personalities to do their bidding. Their technique is called "magic." If the proper spell is recited, if the proper manipulation of physical materials and objects [is] carried out, or if a symbolic pantomime is reenacted, a certain result is destined to follow. A mere human being therefore is able to compel supernatural forces or personalities to fulfill his desires. . . .

The term "sorcery" or "witchcraft" is applied to magic used for antisocial purposes. The harming or even the killing of a person by magical technique, when he is regarded by his society as a criminal, is not an antisocial act, because the people may agree that he should be killed. But when evil (black) magic is directed against an innocent person, only then does it become sorcery or witchcraft. It is then a form of unapproved aggression against a fellow member of a society. Magic, good and bad, was likewise universal in Indian America.[295]

Two additional aspects of Indian belief were vision quests and dreams. Young boys and girls could acquire a spirit helper by going on a vision quest. He or she would go to an isolated spot with a reputation as an abode of spirits and would remain several days, naked, fasting, mutilating the body, and praying. Frequently there would be a hallucination or vision, sometimes in the form of an animal, which would speak, teach a song, or show designs to paint on the body for protection against enemies.[296] George Catlin and others described this practice.[297]

Dreams were important because they were regarded as wishes of the soul, which should be satisfied for the health of the dreamer. A man who dreamed he was captured and being tortured by the enemy would ask his friends to tie him up and burn him. If he dreamed he was ordered to cohabit with a married woman or 2 for several days, village authorities would allow it for fear the dream spirit would bring disaster if he disobeyed. One Cayuga dreamed he had killed and eaten a girl. The chiefs selected an innocent victim, but when the dreamer was about to kill her, he decided his dream had been satisfied, and she was not killed.[298]

Dreams of torture by the enemy were common among warriors. One warrior described by Harold E. Driver told the council about such a dream, and the council seized him and tortured him with fire. After he was tortured in this manner, he seized a dog and offered it as a sacrifice. The dog was roasted and eaten in a public feast "just as they would eat a human captive."[299]

J. Hector St. John de Crèvecoeur concluded that the religious aspect of Indians made them in many ways superior to settlers:

> Without temples, without priests, without kings, and without laws, they are in many instances superior to us; and the proofs of what I advance are that they live without care, sleep without inquietude, take life as it comes, bearing all its asperities with unparalled patience, and die without any kind of apprehension for what they have done or for what they expect to meet hereafter. What system of philosophy can give us so many necessary qualifications for happiness?[300]

The government, however, did not believe that the medicine men who dispensed the sorcery or witchcraft were of benefit to the Indians at all. Secretary of the Interior Henry M. Teller criticized them in his 1883 annual report:

> Another great hindrance to the civilization of the Indians is the influence of the medicine men, who are always found with the anti-progressive party. The medicine men resort to various artifices and devices to keep the people under their influence, and are especially active in preventing the attendance of the children at the public schools, using their conjurers' arts to prevent the people from abandoning their heathenish rites and customs. While they profess to cure diseases by the administering of a few simple remedies, still they rely mainly on their art of conjuring. Their services are not required even for the administration of the few simple remedies they are competent to recommend, for the Government supplies the several agencies with skillful physicians, who practice among the Indians without charge to them. Steps should be taken to compel these impostors to abandon this deception and discontinue their practices, which are not only without benefit to the Indians but positively injurious to them.[301]

There were many instances where Teller's conclusions proved all too true. Medicine men frequently assured the warriors that they would not be hurt in battle, and especially that the settlers' bullets would not harm them.

The Comanche prophet Isatai was said to have great magic. He claimed he could vomit wagonloads of ammunition from his belly, stop white men's bullets in midair, bring the dead back to life, and cure all diseases. He used magic paint to effect some of these things.[302]

A group of Kwahadi Comanche, Cheyenne, and Arapaho rode to attack some white buffalo hunters at Adobe Walls. On the way, Isatai reassured them. He said the hunters could not shoot them, he would stop all their bullets with his medicine, and that the Indians would wipe them all out when they charged. Isatai bullet-proofed all the warriors, and made incantations so that all the buffalo hunters would be asleep and all the doors would be open. He rode into battle wearing a cap of sagebrush stems and nothing else. The warriors finally lost confidence in him when he completely covered his horse with bullet-proof paint only to have it shot out from under him while he was observing the battle.[303]

The warriors were defeated. "They turned their rage and frustration against Isatai," Carl Waldman reported, "who had promised them protection from the white men's bullets and a great victory. An angry Cheyenne lashed Isatai with his quirt, and several other braves came up to join in."[304]

Ottawa chief Pontiac also had a medicine man known as the Delaware Prophet. He claimed that he talked with the Master of Life.[305]

Tecumseh's medicine man and brother, Tenskwatawa, or the Prophet, had a variety of magic that would protect the warriors from the settlers' bullets. He communicated, he said, directly with the Great Spirit. In 1805 he experienced a deep trance and announced that he had visited the spirit world, where he had received a message from the Master of Life.[306] At the Battle of Tippecanoe in 1811, he predicted that the soldiers would be defeated because of his magic, but they were not, and he subsequently moved to Canada.[307]

In 1871, an owl hooted in Texas. Medicine man Mamanti told his people 2 parties of Texans would pass by. The hooting of the owl meant that the first (which would be small) should be allowed to pass by without being attacked, but the second one could be attacked successfully. The first party consisted of 18 people and was not attacked. The second, consisting of 10 wagons with 12 people, was attacked, and several in the second party were killed. (The atrocity aspect of this episode is discussed below.) The owl had not indicated that the first party contained

4-star general William Tecumseh Sherman, one of the most effective Indian fighters ever, who was on an inspection trip. The 2 chiefs who led the attack on the wagon train, Satanta and Big Tree, were apprehended, tried, found guilty, and sentenced to be hanged. The governor commuted their sentences to life imprisonment. The governor then freed the 2 in response to eastern pressure. Public opinion had allowed Satanta and Big Tree to escape the gallows. General Sherman was not happy. His letter to the governor in its entirety said this:

> I believe in making a tour of your frontier, with a small escort, I ran the risk of my life, and I said to the military commander what I now say to you, that I will not again voluntarily assume that risk in the interest of your frontier, that I believe Satanta and Big Tree will have their revenge, if they have not already had it, and that if they are to have scalps, that yours is the first that should be taken.[308]

Modoc medicine man Curly Headed Doctor told Chief Captain Jack, or Kintpuash, in 1873 that if he killed the army leaders at a peace conference, he would render the troops helpless. Captain Jack did kill the army commander, General Edward Canby, and another warrior, Boston Charley, killed one of President Grant's 2 peace commissioners, the Reverend Eleasar Thomas. The troops were not rendered helpless, however. They captured Captain Jack, Boston Charley, and the others who were with them.[309] They were hanged after a 10-day trial.[310]

Not all medicine men were unsuccessful. George Catlin noted about the medicine men of one tribe that "when the Mandans undertake to make it rain, *they never fail to succeed,* for their ceremonies never stop until the rain begins to fall."[311]

Fanny Kelly met Sioux chief Red Cloud in Washington after her release from captivity. She invited him to church, telling him about the great organ and the fine music he would hear. "Red Cloud replied with dignity that he did not have to go to the big house to talk to the Great Spirit; he could sit in his tipi or room, and the Great Spirit would listen. The Great Spirit was not where the big music was."[312]

The Paiute Wovoka was the most influential medicine man of all. He played a pivotal part in the Battle of Wounded Knee, perhaps the most well-known battle of this war. Dee Brown in *Bury My Heart at Wounded Knee* devoted considerable space to Wovoka. (His story is told by Kicking Bear.) The Messiah returned to earth again. A voice told Kicking Bear to meet the ghosts of Indians who were to return after the flood. He and 9 other Sioux went far west to a Paiute camp in Nevada.

The Paiutes told them Christ had come again. They went to Walker Lake, where Wovoka was born and where hundreds of Indians were waiting to see the Messiah. On the third day, he appeared. Kicking Bear had always thought Christ was a white man. He was surprised he looked like an Indian. He spoke to them. He taught them the Ghost Dance. They danced until late at night.

The next day, Christ told them white men had treated him badly, leaving scars on his body, so he had gone back to heaven. He gave them a message. Wovoka told them that the very next spring he was going to wipe out the white man for being so wicked to him at his first coming to earth.[313] A few days later they got on their horses to return home. The Messiah flew above them in the air, teaching them new songs. They found a group of dead Indian friends and visited with them for some time. They also found a herd of buffalo, ate one, left it lying as Wovoka instructed, and it reassembled into a new buffalo.[314]

THIS CHAPTER'S listing of Indian characteristics, good or bad, is not complete by any means. Helen Hunt Jackson, a great Indian advocate, wrote in *A Century of Dishonor* that one or more tribes had these characteristics: there was no difference between educated white and educated Indian; they were religious; kind and honorable; had sound judgment; lively imaginations; ready conception; wonderful memories; they prosecuted ends by sure means; evinced coolness and composure; never indulged in passion; had a sense of honor and greatness of soul; were high-minded and proud; courageous; valorous; intrepid; heroic; had equanimity; were affable; generous; hospitable; the intellectual equivalent of Europeans; eloquent; had less criminality than among the French; no beggars; were temperate in their mode of living; not affected by suffering. But she also added that Indians were suspicious, vindictive, and cruel.[315]

Those who believe the Indians were or are innocent, noble, and non-savage victims are, in all probability, romanticizing a people with many good qualities, some of which are outlined in this chapter. For example, the painter George Catlin correctly referred to Indian men as "red knights of the prairie" and "red sons of the forest."[316] From the time of James Fenimore Cooper to the present, many people have tended to view the Indian emotionally instead of intellectually, just as some others have tended to romanticize Wild West train and bank robbers such as Butch Cassidy and the Sundance Kid.

John M. Coward discussed the concept of romanticizing the Indian at some length:

> On a more psychological level, the Noble Savage was also an object of desire, a strange, exotic, and satisfyingly romantic figure. Romantic Indians, after all, were romantic precisely because they appeared to possess qualities highly desired by pioneering Americans: strength, dignity, boldness, and freedom. From colonial times onward, these ideals became exaggerated in the American psyche, a fact that reveals a deep-seated envy of Indians and Indian ways. Some eighteenth- and nineteenth-century Americans came to love the Indian.[317]

What causes this perhaps misdirected admiration? Possibly it is because Indians are usually handsome and dignified people who at first glance can be admired without questioning their past. Columbus wrote that Indians were "well built and of handsome stature."[318] Robert F. Berkhofer described the concept of "the good Indian" to include handsomeness of physique and dignity in bearing.[319] Their eloquence may play a part—few can fail to be moved by the speeches of Mingo John Logan and Nez Perce chief Joseph. It may be that it is the political anti-government feeling that makes itself known in certain quarters from time to time, an attempt to show that the government was wrong in displacing the Indians and in its dealings with them thereafter. Whatever the cause, to romanticize the Indians does them no good, because it masks their present-day problems and ignores some parts of their past that have contributed to those problems.

CHAPTER 3

Some Settler Cultural Characteristics

J. Hector St. John de Crèvecoeur* was perhaps more intimately ac-
quainted with the English and French colonies, the frontier, and the
wilderness than any other man.[1] His letters are said by some to be a
mixture of fact and fancy, but, nevertheless, they are full of wise observations and conclusions about Americans. He was the first to ask,
"What, then, is the American, this new man?" His much-quoted answer
was this:

> The American is a new man, who acts upon new principles; he must
> therefore entertain new ideas and form new opinions. From involun-
> tary idleness, servile dependence, penury, and useless labour, he has
> passed to toils of a very different nature, rewarded by ample subsis-
> tence. This is an American.[2]

"No sooner [he said] does an European arrive, no matter what his condition, than his eyes are opened upon the fair prospect."[3] Settlers arriving from Europe ceased to be Europeans after a time and became
different from them.

---

*Frenchman J. Hector St. John de Crèvecoeur (1735–1813) fought in two battles in the French
and Indian War. He learned about America while a traveling salesman and a surveyor.

Crèvecoeur described the American melting pot and predicted that the country would be influential. "Here individuals of all nations are melted into a new race of men, whose labours and posterity will one day cause great changes in the world."[4] (If the reader could read only one book about the settler character, it should be Crèvecoeur's *Letters from an American Farmer.*)

The settlers came to the New World to escape desperately hard conditions. Many fled Europe for spiritual betterment. A good many even came to escape hanging. European people arrived in the New World beginning around 1609, when the Jamestown colony was founded. There were emigrants from Scotland, Ireland, the Netherlands, and Russia as well, but the colonists were predominately English.[5]

There was a depression in England—and thousands of gin shops.[6] "The hard liquor consumed in one year (1733) in London alone amounted to 11,200,000 gallons, or some 56 gallons per adult male."[7] Page Smith sketched this picture of conditions in eighteenth-century England:

> It has been estimated that London in the eighteenth century had 6,000 adult and 9,300 child beggars. In the entire country of some 10,000,000 persons, there were estimated to be 50,000 beggars, 20,000 vagrants, 10,000 idlers, 100,000 prostitutes, 10,000 rogues and vagabonds, 80,000 criminals, 1,041,000 persons on parish relief. Indeed, over half the population was below what we would call "the poverty line," and many, of course, were profoundly below it—below it to the point of starvation.[8]

This was the involuntary idleness, servile dependence, penury, and useless labor about which Crèvecoeur spoke. "In such circumstances there was ample incentive to emigrate almost anywhere."[9] There was great opportunity in the colonies. "Anyone willing to work could be put to worthwhile labor, and might (and often did) in a few years establish himself as an independent farmer or artisan."[10] There was a growing need for labor there. Agents would pay for the passage of those willing to work off the cost of the transportation.[11] In addition, land was cheap and often free.

English law in the 1600s made almost 300 offenses punishable by hanging. It became an increasing practice of English judges to pardon those sentenced to hang on condition that the defendant would leave England. From 1650 to 1700 thousands received such pardons, and most immigrated to the American colonies and to the West Indies. From

1619 to 1640 all pardoned felons were sent to Virginia. From 1661 to 1700, more than 4,500 convicts were sent to the colonies. From 1745 to 1775, 8,846 convicts were sent to Maryland.[12] Criminals were not the best of settlers, and, Page Smith noted, "in one contingent, twenty-six had been convicted for stealing, one for violent robbery, and five for murder."[13] To a considerable extent, the frontier got the worst of the worst. In view of that fact, it is no surprise that the settlers as well as the Indians committed atrocities.

AFTER A time, the colonists began heading into the frontier in great numbers. The consequences, according to Bernard W. Sheehan, were that

> the worst representatives of the white men's society went into the wilderness first, fought with the natives, learned to hate them, and gave the impression of utter incompatibility between the white man's world and the Indian's world.[14]

William Franklin understandably concluded that "some of the worst People in every Colony reside on the Frontiers."[15] By 1800, 50,000 families had settled along the Ohio River, 100,000 in Tennessee, and 200,000 in Kentucky. T. Walter Wallbank and Alistair M. Taylor in *Civilization—Past and Present* said, "Here land was to be had for the asking."[16] Out west between 1841 and 1859, more than 300,000 people and at least 1.5 million oxen, cattle, horses, and sheep had moved along the Sante Fe Trail alone.[17] Author Howard H. Peckham reiterated that the frontier attracted the most undesirable settlers, "the congenitally dissatisfied, the fugitives from justice, the army deserters, the debtors, the swindlers, all were churned out of seaboard society and thrown to the frontier."[18] An anonymous English author wrote in 1812 that at the beginning of the war "the lower order of the white people in the United States of this new world, are, if possible, more savage than the copper-coloured Indians."[19] On the frontier, the *Niles' Weekly Register* noted, "white traders encouraged the 'worst passions' and 'most abominable vices' among the Indians."[20] Crèvecoeur observed that

> men appear to be no better than carnivorous animals of a superior rank, living on the flesh of wild animals when they can catch them. . . . There, remote from the power of example and check of shame, many families exhibit the most hideous parts of our society. . . . Thus are our

first steps trodden, thus are our first trees felled, in general, by the most vicious of our people.[21]

Perhaps the principal characteristic of the settlers was their love of land. The Indians loved warfare, and the settlers loved land—the land occupied by the Indians—thereby making conflict between the 2 inevitable. Page Smith more generally stated that the disparity of 2 cultures was the problem:

> Whether the aborigines of North America were "squalid savages" or nature's noblemen; whether the English settlers were ruthless exploiters or pious Christians anxious to save heathen souls, it is hard to imagine how the two cultures could have coexisted on the same continent without the bitter conflicts that marked their historic encounter.[22]

The conflict over land started almost at once. Not long after Jamestown was founded, the settlers simply began taking over Indian fields rather than clearing new fields themselves.[23]

Once the colonies had been established, there was a flood of land-hungry Englishmen, depicted by Carl Waldman:

> They came to North America primarily as families and farmers, and they came to stake a claim and stay. The overflow from the British Isles was furious. . . . Boatload after boatload of hopeful settlers arrived in the busy harbors. . . . It was the English drive toward privately held land that pushed most Indians . . . further and further back from the Atlantic seaboard, across the Appalachian Mountains and, eventually, after American Independence, across the Mississippi Valley as well.[24]

Denis William Brogan in *The American Character* described the allure of the land:

> Land was abundant in America, scarce in Europe; owning land was socially and financially the aim of all climbing Europeans in the seventeenth century—and it was a climbing century. . . . The poor who came to America—the majority of the settlers—had fewer illusions to shed than the gentry. . . . The move to America was important and final. They did not expect to go back; if they were religious or political refugees they did not want to.[25]

Crèvecoeur asked, "Does he [the settler] want uncultivated land? Thousands of acres present themselves, which he may purchase cheap."[26] As early as 1616 free land was available in Virginia. Gary B. Nash pointed out how easy it was to get it:

> Again the company raised the inducements for going to the Chesapeake. This time 100 acres of land were offered outright to anyone in England who would journey to the colony. Instead of pledging limited servitude for the chance to become sole possessor of land, an Englishman trapped at the lower rungs of society at home could now become an independent landowner in no more time than it took to reach the Chesapeake.[27]

In the Carolinas, settlers were offered 150 acres of free land.[28]

By 1770 more than 400,000 Scotch-Irish and other immigrants had spread through Pennsylvania, the valleys of the Appalachians, and the Carolinas. "As good eastern land became scarce," noted Alan Axelrod, "they moved into the forests further west. Armed only with an ax and a flintlock, they knew great hardship and almost constant strife with the Indians."[29]

Secretary of War Henry Knox reported to Congress in 1787 that the settlers and the Indians were ever prevented from being good neighbors because "the one side [Indians] anxiously defend their lands which the other side [settlers] . . . claim."[30] The same year a congressional committee reported that "an avaricious disposition in some of our people to acquire large tracts of land and often by unfair means, appears to be the principal source of difficulties with the Indians."[31]

Elliott West put it somewhat differently: "Whites did not set out, directly at least, to destroy the Indians' life. They were simply following a script that had no Indians in it, except as exotic relics."[32]

President Jefferson's government wished ultimately to distribute the vast Indian-occupied acres among the members of civilized society, and consequently intended to take most of the land away from the Indians.[33]

The Jefferson position demonstrates one of the defects of a democracy. It was difficult for any president to resist the settlers' demands that their need for land be satisfied by the government, or at least that the government stand aside while they satisfied that demand themselves. Sheehan found the expansion inevitable:

> By the time Jefferson became president, all the efforts made by the government to protect the tribes from intruders seemed doomed to failure. The frontier could not be controlled. Threats to use the courts or to send in troops, instructions to agents to clear the native lands, all came to nothing. Even granting the Indian the right to kill the settlers' cattle

or drive the animals out of the tribal territory did not stop the avalanche of intruders. Tribal leaders petitioned the government, appealed to state authorities and to the intruders themselves, and attempted to curb the belligerence of their own younger tribesmen. Nothing helped; the white man kept coming.[34]

And just after the Civil War, the federal Peace Commission with some sarcasm concluded that

> members of Congress understand the Negro question and talk learnedly of finance, and other problems of political economy, but when the progress of settlement reaches the Indian's home, the only question considered is "how best to get his lands."[35]

Settlers were aggressive in displacing Indians on the frontier; more bluntly, they often stole lands occupied by Indians. The *New York Times* spoke of it frequently. In 1867 an editorial stated that "it has justly been said in Congress by those who have investigated the matter, that the Western settlers are a constant source of irritation to the Indians, committing petty depredations upon them, driving them from their lands, and in a thousand little ways stirring up their ill-blood."[36] Two years later, the *Times* said, "It looks as though the Indian might receive fair play, now that the army officers have so strenuously taken his part. Though, to say the truth, it is not the soldiery, but the settlers, and the sutlers, that have been the Indians' worst foe."[37]

ONCE THE Declaration of Independence was adopted, an element of anxiety invaded the settler character. The Declaration was revolution against the British Empire. It was also treason and every delegate who voted for it knew it. The English punishment for treason was very specific, as J. W. Erlich pointed out in *Erlich's Blackstone:*

1. That the offender be drawn to the gallows, and not be carried or walk; though usually . . . a sledge or hurdle is allowed, to preserve the offender from the extreme torment of being dragged on the ground or pavement.
2. That he be hanged by the neck, and then cut down alive.
3. That his entrails be taken out, and burned, while he is yet alive.
4. That his head be cut off.
5. That his body be divided into four parts.
6. That his head and quarters be at the king's disposal.[38]

In addition, the settlers on the frontier lived with the anxiety of what the Indians might do to them. (The Indians were equally desperate, of course. They were aware early on that the settlers wanted the land they lived on. They realized that if the settlers got it, their way of life would be completely changed. "They lived in constant fear of dispossession," according to Angie Debo.)[39]

HATRED OF Indians was a pervading characteristic of the settlers, as demonstrated by this assessment from *The West: An Illustrated History:*

> Continually exposed to the dangers of Indian hostility, white frontiersmen came to hate the red men with an intensity which Americans elsewhere could not understand. To the settlers there seemed only two possible solutions. Either the army must conquer the savages, then put them under close guard on reservations, where they could never again make trouble; or the cause of civilization demanded that they be exterminated.[40]

The Virginia legislature in 1711 appropriated 20,000 pounds "for exterpating all Indians without distinction of Friends or Enemys."[41] Killing your friends as well as your enemies shows a savagery not shared by many Indians, if any at all. Crèvecoeur observed that between settlers and Indians "there is a sort of physical antipathy, which is equally powerful from one end of the continent to the other."[42]

Hatred, of course, led to calls for revenge. Just as Indians had sought revenge, Andrew Jackson wrote William Henry Harrison in 1811 stating, "The blood of our murdered countrymen must be revenged. The banditti ought to be swept from the face of the earth."[43]

HATRED AND revenge were not the only attitudes held by the settlers. They felt they had actually conferred a great favor on the Indians by invading the land they occupied. This view was stated by Chief Justice John Marshall in the *Johnson's and Graham's Lessee vs. William McIntosh* opinion:

> On the discovery of this immense continent, the great nations of Europe were eager to appropriate to themselves so much of it as they could respectively acquire. Its vast extent offered an ample field to the ambition and enterprise of all; and the character and religion of its inhabitants afforded an apology for considering them as a people over

whom the superior genius of Europe might claim an ascendancy. The potentates of the old world found no difficulty in convincing themselves, that they made ample compensation to the inhabitants of the new, by bestowing on them civilization and Christianity, in exchange for unlimited independence.[44]

James Fenimore Cooper was the first major author to depict sympathetically the plight of the Indian in the onslaught of the settlers. The prevalent view at the time was to consider Indians savages without redeeming qualities, but Cooper wrote about them as noble savages. William T. Hagan understood why this was:

> As usual, moral indignation over the plight of the red man varied with the distance from him. Those whites avid for Indian land or fearful for their scalps were ever inclined to classify him as subhuman and devoid of rights. Those far removed from the frontier detected great potential in the Indian.[45]

Angie Debo pointed out much the same thing: "Too many white well-wishers had uncritically assumed that everything Indian was wrong."[46] She added that they were determined to dissolve plural marriages and educate Indian children to change them into white people. Wrong was done to the Indians by these well-meaning people.[47] Bernard W. Sheehan wrote an entire book in support of this proposition. His conclusion was this:

> The Jeffersonian brand of philanthropy could be justly accused of treating the native more like a precious abstraction than a living human being. For the Indian, it wanted only the best, but that meant ultimately the elimination of the tribal order, for which the Jeffersonian age must bear its share of responsibility. Its crime was a willful failure of the intellect but not of the will.[48]

SETTLERS, LIKE Indians, often acted without authority. The settlers had weak government and sometimes no government on the frontier. A law might be passed in the colonial, state, or federal capitol, but often there was no one to enforce it. When a sufficient part of the country did not want to abide by a law, it was easy for the democratic leaders to ignore any violations of it. Then, too, many of the settlers on the frontier were themselves by nature inclined to be lawless.

Wilcomb E. Washburn concluded that "although discipline and control were perhaps more commonly accepted facets of European organization, white leaders were often unable to control the actions of their ordinary citizens."[49]

Alvin M. Josephy, Jr., also wrote about how difficult it was to control events on the wild frontier:

Jefferson, John Marshall, and many other leaders tried to inject morality, justice, and strict legal procedures in the headlong dispossession of the Indians. Almost without exception, however, their decrees, pronouncements, and pleadings were nullified by events on the frontier and by champions of the anti-Indian elements.[50]

There are many specific instances of settlers acting without authority. When the Powhatan Nemattanow (or Nemattanew) came out of the woods wearing Trader Morgan's hat, Morgan's servants killed him without trial. John Smith reported that Nemattanow "so moved their patience, they shot him."[51] But creating impatience was not a capital crime. It seems very probable that Morgan's people had no authority to kill Nemattanow. The Powhatan Wars resulted.

In 1646, Jamestown concluded a peace treaty with Opechancanough's successor, Necotowance. Boundaries were set. The treaty provided that neither the Indians nor the settlers were permitted to enter the other's land without permission of the governor.[52] According to Alan Axelrod, "The peace was an uneasy one. As would be the case well into the early 1800s, frontier settlers obstinately refused to recognize any limit to settlement. The government could not regulate westward expansion, though [Governor] Berkeley and Parliament tried."[53]

The Virginia Assembly in 1656 authorized an expedition to remove foreign Indians (Indians not subject to English authority), but "explicitly ordered restraint in the removal." The commander, Edward Hill, called 5 chiefs out to parley with him, and when they came, they were killed by some soldiers.[54]

Twenty years later, in 1676, the situation was about the same. Settlers in Virginia would go to Indian lands, turn loose their cattle and hogs, then if any were lost, would "beate and abuse them (notwithstanding the Governor's endeavour to the contrary)."[55]

The Seven Years' War between Great Britain and France (called the French and Indian War in America) resulted in France losing its interests in North America. The British then wished to separate the colonists and the Indians. The Proclamation of 1763 provided in part that the Indians should not be molested or disturbed in the Possession of such Parts of our Dominions and Territories as, not having been ceded to or purchased by Us, are reserved to them, or any of them, as their Hunting Grounds.[56]

Note that the proclamation referred to these lands as "our Dominions and Territories." They were not considered lands owned by the Indians.

In order to carry out this purpose, it was provided that no further surveys or land grants were to be made west of the Appalachian watershed. All such land was specifically reserved for Indian nations, and all settlers already west of the Appalachians were to withdraw back east.[57]

As British subjects, the settlers were of course obliged to obey the proclamation. It was not obeyed. In fact it was "immediately violated."[58] Gary B. Nash candidly noted that

the Proclamation Line of 1763 existed only on paper, and neither colonists nor Indians took it seriously. . . . Few colonists on the frontier held back their land hunger when they saw that the Indians were bereft of a European ally [France] and an alternate supply of trade goods. Nor could anybody in England discover a means of compelling the Americans in the West to obey Crown commands at a time when even along the Atlantic seaboard the King's authority was being challenged.[59]

The British government was unable to hold the Proclamation Line. When colonial governors were instructed to enforce the policy, Pennsylvania defiantly responded by declaring a scalp bounty, attracting a horde of bounty hunters who raided the Indian borderlands and pushed back Indian settlement.[60]

AFTER THE Revolutionary War ended, the 13 new states needed an Indian policy. General Washington wrote to James Duane in 1783, a letter that became the basis of the Indian policy of the Continental Congress. Washington said that the government should "establish a boundary line between them [the Indians] and us beyond which we will *endeavor* to restrain our People from Hunting or Settling, and within which they shall not come [Washington's emphasis]."[61]

Washington was prescient. The Congress under the Articles of Confederation could not restrain the frontier. Settlers disregarded boundaries, advanced, and seized lands occupied by Indians.[62] Watauga

settlers seized Cherokee land. The Continental Congress issued a proclamation warning the invaders, but was too weak to enforce it. Squatters
made what Angie Debo called "tomahawk claims" along the Ohio
River, defying Congress and the Indians.[63]

In 1783 Congress warned against purchasing or squatting on land occupied by Indians. In 1785 it ordered frontiersmen to stay south of the
Ohio River. They disobeyed. Congress sent troops to evict the squatters
and burn their cabins. The fighting between the squatters and the Indians simply increased.[64]

The Continental Congress in 1785 authorized a 700-man militia
under Josiah Harmar and charged it, as Alan Axelrod said, "with the
hopeless task of keeping white squatters off public lands."[65] In 1790,
after Washington had taken office, the Congress of the United States created a regular federal army of 1,216, augmented by 1,500 militia. This
army was to police federal lands and keep order among settlers and Indians as well.[66] Washington ordered that a line be drawn between the
United States and the Cherokee. He said, however,

> The Indians urge this; The Law requires it; and it ought to be done; but
> I believe scarcely anything short of a Chinese Wall, or a line of Troops
> will restrain Land Jobbers, and the Incroachment of Settlers, upon the
> Indian Territory.[67]

The Cherokee sued Georgia for passing oppressive legislation. The
Supreme Court of the United States, speaking through Chief Justice
Marshall, held in 1832 in *Worcester vs. Georgia* that "the Cherokee nation . . . is a distinct community . . . in which the laws of Georgia can
have no force." Jackson, however, "ignored the court ruling and advised
the Georgia officials to continue their persecutions of the Cherokees."[68]
This is the only known instance of a high federal government official refusing to obey the law in an Indian area. It was politically popular, however—an important factor in a democracy.

A Joint Special Committee of Congress (the Doolittle Committee) reported in 1867 that

> even after territorial governments are established over them in form by
> Congress, the population [of settlers] is so sparse and the administra-
> tion of the civil law so feeble that the people are practically without
> any law but their own will. In their eager search for gold or fertile
> tracts of land, the boundaries of the Indian reservations are wholly dis-
> regarded; conflicts ensue; exterminating wars follow, in which the In-
> dian is, of course, at the last, overwhelmed if not destroyed.[69]

———

RELIGION HAD a great effect on most of the settlers' lives, even though many were not particularly religious. In fact, said Crèvecoeur, "religious indifference is imperceptibly disseminated from one end of the continent to the other, which is at present one of the strongest characteristics of the Americans."[70] The settlers who came to America for spiritual betterment came in large part because the Protestant king James I of England refused to recognize the Puritans, who opposed him in Parliament. He said that if they did not recognize the authority of his bishops, "I will harry them out of the land." Many of them left. Page Smith has assessed the influence Puritans had on their new country:

> If he [King James] did not thereby lay the foundations for English America (Virginia, after all, was founded without any direct reference to James's hostility to the Puritans), he for a certainty provided the colonies with a company of settlers who, by transplanting that Puritanism that so enraged the king to the New World, determined the character, temper, consciousness—call it what you will—of that New World more conclusively than any other body of people who came to the English colonies.[71]

Converting the heathen Indian to Christianity was important to the settlers.[72] The missionary effort did not succeed to any great extent. Washburn discussed that failure in detail and pointed out that "very rarely was the pious ideal of conversion realized."[73] One of the problems was European hypocrisy, preaching Christian love but killing Indians. Another was that when he was converted, "the Indian often felt deracinated."[74] Yet another problem was that the Indian was confused and disillusioned by competing missionaries bearing conflicting theologies.[75] In 1870, for example, Nez Perce chief Joseph advised an Indian commissioner that his people did not want schools because they would teach the Indians to have churches, and churches would teach them to quarrel about God "as the Catholics and Protestants do. . . . We may quarrel with men sometimes about things on this earth, but we never quarrel about God. We do not want to learn that."[76] Crèvecoeur asked, "Shall we yet vainly flatter ourselves with the hope of converting the Indians?" and answered, "We should rather begin with converting our back-settlers."[77]

Seneca chief Red Jacket complained eloquently about the missionaries among his people:

The black coats [priests] tell us to work and raise corn; they do nothing themselves and would starve to death if someone did not feed them. All they do is pray to the Great Spirit; but that will not make corn and potatoes grow; if it will why do they beg from us and from the white people?[78]

A final problem, wrote professor Page Smith, was candidly stated by soldier John Smith:

Captain John Smith, who had his hands full contending with the deceitful Powhatan, was constantly exhorted by the officers of the Virginia Company to make more progress in converting the Indians to Christianity. To one such admonition, the captain replied testily that he needed some soldiers to force the Indians to pay attention to the preachers.[79]

John Smith added, "It was difficult to convert an Indian who was shooting arrows at you or was plainly intent on trying to scalp you."[80]

Massachusetts Bay Colony governor John Winthrop considered that the Puritans had a divine right to the land occupied by the Indians. He thought that the Indians themselves were "evidence of a Satanic opposition to the very principle of divinity."[81]

The whole earth is the Lord's garden, and he hath given it to the sons of Adam to be tilled and improved by them. Why then should we stand starving here for the places of habitation . . . and in the mean time suffer whole countries, as profitable for the use of man, to lie waste without any improvement.[82]

As a result, Roy Harvey Pearce wrote, "for those who lived in the frontier settlements . . . it came to be, simply enough, destroy or be destroyed; this was yet another skirmish in man's Holy War against Satan."[83] Claims were made that there was even biblical authority for the invasion. Genesis 1:26 says, let man "have dominion . . . over all the earth." The fact that the Indians had already obtained dominion over the earth of America could be overlooked because they weren't Christians.

The *Times* complained in 1870 that "thus far the churches [have] done almost nothing, being so much occupied with the foreign heathen that they have almost utterly neglected these wards of the nation."[84]

Religious leaders supported the Allotment Act of 1887, described below, which was detrimental to the interests of the Indians. Angie

Debo charged that as late as 1944, "the first attempt to turn public sentiment away from the [Indian] reform policy came from the churches."[85]

THE PHILOSOPHY of colonial leaders and other colonists was Lockean. John Locke believed that people had the rights to life, ownership of property, and liberty (political equality), and the state had the duty to protect these rights. The philosophy concerning land was stated in the credo of newspaper editor John L. O'Sullivan in the *New York Morning News* in 1845. He said,

> Our manifest destiny is to overspread and possess the whole of the continent which Providence has given us for the development of the great experiment of liberty and federated self-government entrusted to us.[86]

Americans and their then president, James K. Polk, fervently believed in the philosophy of Manifest Destiny.[87]

THE SETTLERS had a great advantage in their numbers. This superiority, compared to the Indians, was the principal reason they won the war. "In the end, the Indians lost the Four-Hundred-Year War," Carl Waldman concluded. "They were defeated . . . by overwhelming numbers—the spillover from an overpopulated Europe."[88] That superiority also kept Indian atrocities against the settlers down to a level permitting the frontier to advance. The *Times* made two predictions, said Robert G. Hays, one right and one wrong: "Civilization must ultimately overrun and surround them [the Indians], and gradually extinguish their existence as completely as it has that of the Mohawks and Senecas."[89] Although they were overrun and surrounded, they were not extinguished.

In 1862, before the Santee Sioux Uprising began, when some in his tribe wanted to attack the settlers, Sioux chief Little Crow said,

> See!—the white men are like the locusts when they fly so thick that the whole sky is a snowstorm. You may kill one—two—ten; yes, as many as the leaves in the forest yonder, and their brothers will not miss them. Kill one—two—ten, and ten times ten will come to kill you. Count your fingers all day long and white men with guns . . . will come faster than you can count.[90]

There are several problems in comparing settler populations with Indian populations. The United States Census did not begin until 1790 and did not include Indians until 1860. Any figures before 1790 for settlers and before 1860 for Indians are mere guesses and they vary wildly. The unreliability of such estimates is demonstrated by the following speculations as to the Indian population in the area of the United States in 1492: 200,000—Smith (p. 28); 750,000—Waldman (*Atlas*, p. 29), who said that this was "the number most often heard"; 800,000 to 900,000—Leupp (p. 350); 850,000—Josephy (*Indian Heritage*, p. 52); over 900,000—Drimmer (p. 15); 1,000,000—Collier (p. 172); as many as 3,000,000—Nash (p. 17); over 7,000,000 north of the Rio Grande River—Thornton (p. 36); between 10,000,000 and 12,000,000 for the continental United States and Canada—Waldman (*Atlas*, p. 29); and 1,000,000 to 18,000,000 in 1513 (not 1492, of course)—Steele (p. 3). The variations in population estimates for the entirety of North America are enormous as well. Kroker's estimate was 4,200,000, but Dobyn's was about 60,000,000.[91]

Here is a rough estimate concerning how many Indians were available in the east to fight how many settlers:

Year	Est. Indian Population	Est. Settler Population	Indian to Settler Ratio
1630	295,500	4,600	64:1
1650	284,000	50,400	6:1
1670	272,500	111,900	2:1
1690	261,000	210,000	1:1
1700	255,500	250,000	1:1
1720	244,000	466,200	1:2
1750	227,000	1,170,800	1:5
1770	215,500	2,148,083	1:10
1780	210,000	2,780,300	1:13

These figures make it apparent which side was likely to win the war. Robert M. Utley and Wilcomb E. Washburn put it succinctly: "The regular army supposed that it had conquered the Indians. But the real conquerors were the pioneers who tramped westward by the thousands and then the millions."[92]

———

TREACHERY WAS a characteristic of the settlers and soldiers as well as the Indians. Several such acts of treachery (in addition to those outlined above) are mentioned briefly here.

In 1777 the Shawnee chief Cornstalk was talking neutrality with the Americans in the Revolutionary War. He went to the American Fort Randolph under a flag of truce. Fort commandant Matthew Arbuckle imprisoned Cornstalk, his son Elinipsico, and others. A party of settler hunters heard the prisoners were under light guard and shot, killed, and mutilated Cornstalk, his son, and a warrior named Red Hawk.[93]

The Sac leader Black Hawk decided he would try to make peace with the soldiers in 1832. When a cavalry detachment led by Major Isaiah Stillman approached, Black Hawk sent out a party of 3 under a flag of truce. He sent a second party of 5 to observe. The troops attacked both groups, and 3 were killed.[94] Three months later, Black Hawk tried again. He sent out a large party under a flag of truce to try to negotiate. Soldiers ignored the flag, fired on the Indians, and in the battle that followed, 23 warriors were killed.[95]

Washington State territorial governor Isaac Stevens in 1855 encouraged the Nez Perce, Cayuse, Umatilla, Walla Walla, and Yakima Indians to give up most of the land they occupied in exchange for reservation land, homes, schools, horses, cattle, and annuities. He promised that they would be able to stay on their old land for 2 to 3 years after the treaty was ratified. The Indians agreed. Twelve days later, Stevens declared the Indian land open to homesteading. The Yakima War started soon after because of the broken promise.[96]

The Apache chief Mangas Coloradas agreed in 1863 to meet with General Joseph West. He was immediately seized and delivered the next day to the general. West let it be known to the guards that night that he did not want the chief to awake to another day, because he had left a trail of blood for 500 miles. A witness, a miner named Connor, stated that the guards heated their bayonets in the fire, applied them to the chief's feet and legs, and when he jumped up to protest, fired 4 shots into his head, killing him. General West conducted an investigation, which concluded that Mangas Coloradas had made 3 efforts to escape and was shot on the third attempt.[97]

A Sioux war party under Sitting Bull saw some soldiers camped along the Powder River in 1865. Some of the young warriors rode to them under a flag of truce to see if they could get some tobacco and sugar. The soldiers waited until the Indians were in easy rifle range, then fired, killing and wounding some of the Indians. The survivors were able to steal some of the soldiers' horses before retreating.[98]

After the Battle of the Washita in 1867, the Indians fled. Two Kiowa chiefs, Satanta and Lone Wolf, approached General Philip Henry Sheridan to try to make peace. He put them under arrest and sent word to the Kiowa by Satanta's son that the 2 would hang unless the tribe came into the fort. The tribe came in.[99]

The next year, Custer, under Sheridan's command, went out on a supposed peace mission to the Cheyenne. He invited their chiefs to his camp. When they came, he seized 3 of them. He then prepared a tree and ropes to hang them unless the tribe would carry out his demands, which were to surrender 2 settler women captives and to bring the tribe into the post. The women captives were released, and Custer accepted the tribe's promise to come to the post when the grass was green enough for traveling. They either did or didn't keep their promise, depending on whom you believe. Everyone agrees, however, that Custer kept his captives. Two of them were later killed by their guards.[100]

IT IS not surprising that none of the presidents of the United States before 1890, the date of the Wounded Knee Massacre, was an Indian advocate. Many of them fought against the Indians. It is unlikely that this experience was helpful to the Indians during their administrations. Certainly Washington and Jackson said some harsh things about them, and Jackson did some harsh things to them. George Washington fought against them and for the British in the French and Indian War and was at the battle in 1755 where General Braddock and 1,500 British were killed by Indians allied with the French.[101] He fought against them again in the American Revolution and ordered the Iroquois country destroyed because of their depredations against settlers in their area. William Henry Harrison fought against the Indians as early as his 1794 victory on the Miami River. He fought the Shawnee and other tribes in the 1811 Battle of Tippecanoe. Two years later he fought the British and their Indian allies at the Battle of the Thames. Andrew Jackson fought against the Creeks in 1813 and against the Seminoles and other tribes in 1818. Zachary Taylor fought the Shawnee in the War of 1812, the Sauk and Fox tribes in the Black Hawk War starting in 1832, and the Seminoles in 1837. Even Abraham Lincoln served briefly in the Illinois militia in 1832 during the Black Hawk War, but he did not see combat. The

Santee Sioux Uprising in 1862 and the Sand Creek Massacre in 1864 both occurred during his administration.

CAESAR SAID, "In war, actions of great importance are [often] the result of trivial causes."[102] We have seen and shall see trivial happenings escalate into serious conflicts resulting in loss of life because neither side would stop the escalation. A similar statement of the rule is "It is always easy to begin a war, but very difficult to stop one."[103]

Two classic examples of escalation happened in the 1850s. The first was in 1856, when 2 Cheyenne warriors hailed a mail coach near Fort Kearny in Nebraska. Their party, led by Little Spotted Crow and Little Gray Hair, had sent them to ask the driver for tobacco. The rattled driver saw them gesturing, lashed his mules, pulled his pistol, and started firing. The Cheyenne responded with a volley of arrows. One hit the driver in the arm. When the Cheyenne leaders heard about the incident, they whipped the 2 warriors, then the party returned to camp. The next day, soldiers from the fort attacked the camp in retaliation, killed 10, wounded 10, and destroyed all lodges and supplies. The outraged Cheyenne struck back, killing at least 12 settlers, and then returned to their winter camp. Secretary of War Jefferson Davis ordered a chastising expedition against the Cheyenne. Eight companies were sent. More than 300 warriors met them. Two soldiers were killed and 9 wounded. Apparently, 9 Indians were killed. The soldiers then found a large Cheyenne village 15 miles away. They burned its 200 tipis and most of its supplies. At least 33 people were killed over a misunderstanding about some tobacco.[104]

The second example of escalation occurred in 1859 when 2 Kiowa, subchiefs Satank and Pawnee, both slightly drunk, entered George Peacock's store at Walnut Creek Station on the Arkansas River. They demanded goods, but the clerk told them to leave. Satank grabbed a sheep, slit its throat, and filled his mouth with blood. He went back into the store and spit the blood into the clerk's face. There was a brief fight. Satank withdrew, but then climbed up and began tearing and throwing the sod roof. When he left, he promised to destroy the store. Soldiers called to investigate killed Pawnee the next day. Within 48 hours the Kiowas had attacked a mail stage and killed 4 prospectors.[105] Six more settlers were killed by Comanches and Kiowas after the incident at Peacock's store.[106] Almost exactly a year later, Satank killed Peacock.[107] Eleven people were killed because Satank refused to leave the store.

——

ARMY DISCIPLINE, which was very strict, played a part in this story. In 1795, a private deserted from Fort Defiance. The officers offered 2 Shawnee a reward of 10 dollars to bring him back alive and 20 dollars for his scalp. The next day, they brought the scalp to the fort.[108] The Lewis and Clark Expedition, described by Jefferson as one to extend external commerce, was staffed for the most part by soldiers. Early in the expedition, Private John Collins was guarding the liquor just after midnight, tapped a barrel, became drunk, then offered Private Hugh Hall enough liquor to get him drunk as well. At the court-martial, Collins was given 100 lashes and Hall 50.[109] Two weeks later, Private Alexander Willard fell asleep at his post. He was sentenced to 100 lashes for each of 4 days, but he could have received the death sentence.[110] In the fall of 1804, Private John Newman, encouraged by another private, made statements that led to his court-martial on grounds that he had "uttered repeated expressions of a highly criminal and mutinous nature." He was found guilty and sentenced to 75 lashes and "discarded" from the party.[111] The last court-martial in the Lewis and Clark Expedition was that of private Thomas Howard in December 1804. The party was at stockaded Fort Mandan. Howard got to the fort late and scaled the wall. An Indian saw this and scaled the wall as well. Lewis tried to convince the Indian he had done wrong, gave him some tobacco, and dismissed him. Howard was sentenced to 50 lashes, which were forgiven.[112]

S. L. A. Marshall said that by 1860 army enlisted men were "too often criminals, toughs, drunkards, and fugitives." The post–Civil War enlisted men knew nothing about Indian warfare.[113] The Colorado militia that participated in the Sand Creek Massacre in 1864 has been described by author Duane Schultz in his *Month of the Freezing Moon: The Sand Creek Massacre, November, 1864* as

> chicken and watermelon stealing, casual AWOLs, late sleeping, trout fishing, bitching, drunken officers, saloon fights, and tumbles in the hay with country maidens much impressed by new blue cavalry uniforms. No one wanted to drill, guard duty was ignored, and none of the volunteers, apparently, obeyed any order unless the mood was on him and the tone of command suitably civil.[114]

But there was no lack of courage in general on the part of the soldiers. Although given more freely in this war than in later wars, a total of 428

Congressional Medals of Honor were awarded during the Indian wars, a number exceeded only by those earned in the Civil War and World War II. Here is a summary of the citations of 5 of the medal recipients:

- Glynn, Michael. Private, Company F, 5th U.S. Cavalry. Place and date: Whetstone Mountains, Ariz., 13 July 1872. Citation: Drove off, single-handed, 8 hostile Indians, killing and wounding 5.
- Harrington, John. Private, Company H, 6th U.S. Cavalry. Place and date: Wichita River, Tex., 12 September 1874. Citation: While carrying dispatches, he was attacked by 125 hostile Indians whom he and his comrades fought throughout the day. He was severely wounded in the hip and unable to move. He continued to fight, defending an exposed dying man.
- Herron, Leander. Corporal, Company A, 3rd U.S. Cavalry. Place and date: Near Fort Dodge, Kans., 2 September 1868. Citation: While detailed as mail courier from the fort, voluntarily went to the assistance of a party of 4 enlisted men, who were attacked by about 50 Indians at some distance from the fort, and remained with them until the party was relieved.
- Irwin, Bernard J., Dr. Assistant surgeon, U.S. Army. Place and date: Apache Pass, Ariz., 13–14 February 1861. Citation: Voluntarily took command of troops and attacked and defeated hostile Indians he met on the way. Surgeon Irwin volunteered to go to the rescue of Second Lieutenant George N. Bascom, 7th Infantry, who with 60 men was trapped by Chiricahua Apaches under Cochise. Irwin and 14 men, not having horses, began the 100-mile march riding mules. After fighting and capturing Indians, recovering stolen horses and cattle, he reached Bascom's column and helped break his siege.
- Jordan, George. Sergeant, Company K, 9th U.S. Cavalry. Place and date: Fort Tularosa, N. Mex., 14 May 1880. Citation: While commanding a detachment of 25 men at Fort Tularosa, repulsed a force of more than 100 Indians. At Carrizo Canyon, N. Mex., while commanding the right flank of a detachment of 19 men, on 12 August 1881, he stubbornly held his ground in an extremely exposed position and gallantly forced back a much superior number of the enemy, preventing them from surrounding the command.

The settlers, as opposed to the militia or soldiers, usually had no military training. They knew how to use guns, however, in shooting deer, bear, fowl, or other animals to feed their families. That skill and their courage and great numbers were formidable factors. The army didn't give them much help until late in the war. Meanwhile, said Denis William Brogan, "the early settlers long needed to acquire a craft equaling the craft of the savages and a savagery not much inferior."[115] As a group, they survived the Indian attacks, although many individuals did not.

OVER THE years, there have been 2 different schools of thought on whether the settlers and soldiers had an overwhelming advantage in weaponry. In 1622 the Indians had bows and arrows and stone tomahawks. The settlers had muskets, one-shot muzzle-loading weapons that, although cumbersome, were arguably better than a bow and arrow. The musket was used for 50 years after the settlers arrived. But the guns were so heavy that they had to be supported in a forked rest. It took 2 minutes to load, and it misfired about 30 percent of the time.[116] The first guns were so deficient that "their superiority over the bow and arrow was debatable."[117] According to Harold E. Driver, "As late as our own Revolutionary War, George Washington and other military leaders had considerable discussion on whether the bow and arrow should be a part of the armament of the thirteen colonies."[118]

In the 1600s, the Dutch, French, and English began selling guns to the eastern Indians. Some of them attacked their neighbors who did not have guns and drove them west. For example, in Minnesota the Ojibway and Cree drove the Sioux out of the area.[119] Of course, the guns were used against the settlers as well. In 1675 Benjamin Church of Rhode Island found that his forces were confronted by a salute of 50 or 60 guns from the Indians.[120]

The settlers next got breech-loading rifles, then repeating rifles. But traders sold the latest repeating rifles to the Indians.[121] There was a time after the Civil War when the army was using old single-shot Springfield rifles while the Indians were using repeating rifles furnished them under treaties for the ostensible purpose of hunting buffalo. The rifles, of course, worked just as well against soldiers or settlers.[122]

The army rifles were very good—the seven-shot Spencer, with a range of about 1,750 yards; the single-shot Springfield, which was much more accurate and had a 3,500-yard range (almost 2 miles); and the Sharps.[123] In 1874, the Comanche besieged the fort at Adobe Walls, now in Texas. Sharpshooter Billy Dixon saw a Comanche sitting on his horse some distance away. He carefully fired his Sharps, and the Indian fell from the horse. The shot afterward was measured. It was found to have been 1,538 yards, or 0.88 miles.[124]

The army also had Gatling guns and 12-pound howitzers. The Gatling gun was a 10-barrel crank-revolved weapon theoretically capable of firing 400 shots a minute. Its barrels frequently fouled, however. Although the 12-pounder was bulky, it could lob 2 shells a minute that killed anything they hit and raised a lot of dirt.[125]

When the character of the Indians is contrasted with that of the settlers, it is not difficult to understand how confrontations and atrocities occurred.

CHAPTER 4

Pre-Colonial Atrocities

The word *atrocity* when used here indicates an act of intentional extreme cruelty against another person during this war. The killing of an opponent in battle is not an atrocity because this was war, and such killings were acceptable.

Although there were many atrocities during the American-Indian War, they began long before then. The atrocities in the New World were not unique. They were committed by both Europeans and Indians long before Jamestown and Plymouth were settled.

Reminiscent of Governor Wyatt calling the Indians to a peace conference at the colony and then trying to poison them, legend has it that before the birth of Christ, Roman cofounder Romulus invited the Sabine people surrounding Rome to a festival. The Romans then carried off the Sabine women by force and raped them. The Sabines, of course, then went to war with the Romans (as did the Indians with the Virginians).[1] Roman law made use of torture. Emperors often ordered condemned persons burned at the stake, a practice followed by Indians but interestingly enough apparently never adopted by the settlers, even though they committed other kinds of atrocities.[2]

Charlemagne of the Franks has been called "the civilizer." He wanted to subjugate as many peoples as possible and force them to become

Christians. He finally conquered the heathen Saxon tribes, but only after executing 4,500 of them at Verden in 782. Twelve years later, Pope Leo III crowned him emperor of the Holy Roman Empire.[3]

The Spanish Inquisition began in 1231. Roman Catholics accused of heresy were tried in the Court of the Inquisition, which was established by Pope Gregory IX in that year.[4] If the heretics confessed, they were reconciled with the Church after performing penance. If they did not confess, they could be tortured. The most common form of torture was the rack, which wrenched the limbs of the victim. If torture failed to make the victim confess, then he or she was turned over to civil authorities.[5] In the Spanish region of Castile alone, thousands of people were burned to death.[6] The total number of people tortured and killed is not known.[7]

Heresy is the unacceptable deviation from Church doctrine. Witchcraft, on the other hand, is the claimed performance of a supernatural act. Saint Joan of Arc was tried for both and burned at the stake in 1431. She was found innocent 25 years later by Pope Calixtus III.[8]

The sophisticated Aztec Indians of Mexico used military aggression to maintain their trading empire and to take "captives for human sacrifice, which served as a function of the state for keeping order."[9] Religion dominated the conduct of the Aztecs. Their war god, Huitzilopochti, demanded great tribute. Thousands of prisoners were slain at the top of his temple pyramids, their hearts subsequently torn out by the priests. Sometimes the hearts were still beating because they had been cut from the chests of living victims.

Legend says that at the coronation of Montezuma II in 1502, more than 5,000 people were sacrificed.[10] Sometimes the devout Aztec offered his or her own blood drawn from cuts in the tongue through which sticks and strings were sawed back and forth. Often the body of a sacrificed victim was eaten at a religious feast.[11]

The capital of the Aztec empire was Tenochtitlán. There the heads of the victims were impaled on a towering skull rack in the main square. Captured warriors were given mock weapons, tied to a stone, then killed in mock combat by warriors with real weapons. Priests danced wrapped in the skins of their victims, which were dripping with blood. Captives were lashed up as targets and shot with arrows and darts so their blood would fertilize the earth. Children were sacrificed to Tlaloc, the rain god. Victims were burned alive to celebrate the harvest.[12]

The paradox of the Aztecs was that they had "a complex, sophisticated culture with high intellectual pursuits and a refined sense of esthetics; yet here also was a ferocious culture that fed on the ritualistic death of others."[13]

In addition to the heresy atrocities, witchcraft atrocities were committed in both Europe and America. About 300,000 women were put to death for witchcraft by Christian churches between 1484 and 1782. All were innocent in the sense that they could not perform supernatural acts (although they may have claimed they could, often after torture).[14] Tens of thousands were killed in Europe.[15] The Reverend Cotton Mather in Salem, Massachusetts, aroused the citizenry against the witchcraft danger, and in 1692 20 were killed (19 burned at the stake and the other pressed to death) and 150 more sent to prison.[16]

The Portuguese explorer Vasco da Gama was the first to sail around Africa to India in 1497. Arab traders resented his presence and turned the Hindus against him. In 1502 and 1503 he made a second voyage there to avenge Indian violence against Portuguese sailors.[17] He burned an Arab ship containing hundreds of men, women, and children, ignoring the pleas of mothers who held up their babies to beg for mercy. "At one settlement da Gama captured about eight hundred sailors from small craft, hanged them at the yardarms, cut off their hands and heads, loaded them in a vessel, and let it drift ashore."[18]

By the time his reign had ended in 1509, King Henry VIII of England had banished, beheaded, or disemboweled those who had offended him, even loyal friends. An errant cook was boiled in oil.[19]

When the Spanish came to the New World, their cruelty continued. The first priest ordained in the New World, Bartolomé de las Casas, reported the conduct of the Spanish soldiers in the Caribbean islands. They would rip open the bellies of pregnant women, take out the fetus, and hew it to pieces. They would wager on who could with the greater dexterity cut a man in half. They would wager who could cut off his head with one blow. They would take children by the feet and dash their heads against the rocks. They would throw children into the water and call on them to swim. They would sometimes run a pregnant woman and her baby through at one thrust of the sword. They would erect a gallows for 13 people so low that the feet of the persons being hanged would touch the ground. As the 13 were being hanged, the soldiers would say they did it in honor of Jesus and the 12 Apostles. Then they would burn the 13 alive.[20]

The first 2 Spanish ships to drop anchor in the 1520s off the Carolinas found a "gentle, kindly, hospitable" people whom they named the Chicoreans. The Spaniards invited scores of them aboard, offered them a view of the lower decks, then locked them in and sold them as mine slaves in Santo Domingo. This was repeated by other slavers, so that by the end of the 1600s, the tribe was extinct. The same was true of inhabitants of many of the West Indian islands.[21]

Pánfilo de Narváez, a Spanish roughneck soldier, pillaged in Mexico, then came to the area around Tampa Bay in 1529. An Indian chief and his family were lured into his camp, where he cut off the chief's nose, then ordered the chief's mother torn apart by dogs. His army of 400 was eventually destroyed by Indians, exhaustion, exposure, and disease. Only 4 soldiers survived, according to one author;[22] another says 242 survived.[23]

Perhaps one of the most depressing things about the Spanish in the New World was that under their *encomienda* system, a land grant included not only the land, but also the people on the land.[24] The land and the slaves were packaged together.

About 1541, near Albuquerque, Spanish explorer Francisco Vásquez de Coronado burned 100 or more men at the stake and took the bulk of the women and children as slaves.[25]

An engraving from a 1594 edition of a book by Theodor De Bry entitled *America* appears in literature relating to Indian atrocities with some frequency.[26] The foreground shows 2 Indians holding a bound Spanish soldier on the ground while a third pours molten gold down his throat. The background shows a human arm and leg being cooked on a fire while 2 Indians are bringing an additional arm and leg for roasting. In the right center, a nude Spaniard lies on the ground; one Indian is severing his right arm and another his left leg.

In 1598, in what is now New Mexico, the Spanish commander, Juan de Oñate, ordered his second in command and his nephew, Vincente de Zaldivar, to wage war without quarter on the Pueblo Indian town of Acoma because the Indians there had killed 13 Spanish soldiers.[27] After 2 days of fighting, the town was destroyed, 500 men and 300 women and children were killed in cold blood, and about 500 women and children and 80 men were taken alive. All people over 12 years of age were condemned to 20 years of slavery. Men over 21 had one foot cut off as an additional penalty, girls under 12 were turned over to the friars to be distributed wherever they chose, and the boys were given to Zaldivar.[28] Two Hopi were captured. Their right hands were cut off, and then they were set free to let others know about what happened to those who revolted.[29]

English captain Thomas Hunt in 1614 called on several ports in New

England pretending to seek trade. Instead he seized about 30 Indians and sold them as slaves in Spain.[30] (Alvin M. Josephy, Jr., in Chapter 3 of *500 Nations* described many more Spanish atrocities.)

Historians do not dispute these atrocities. Neither do they dispute the hard-to-believe atrocities committed by settlers and Indians after 1614. One commentator has said, "The degree of violence that was woven into the texture of early frontier life fairly boggles the mind of our, in some ways, far more delicate age."[31] Atrocities were a vice shared by settlers and Indians alike, although there sometimes is disagreement as to who started the dispute that led to an atrocity.

Indian and settler atrocities are presented together here, usually in chronological order. Deaths from Indian atrocities are summarized in Appendix B; deaths from settler atrocities in Appendix C. The figures for numbers of deaths are conservative because not all deaths are known and because such deaths are frequently not reported. For example, if it was said the soldiers shot "Indians," only 2 deaths are counted, and if the report was that the Indians scalped "many settlers," only 3 deaths are counted, even though the context indicated that there possibly were many more.

A good deal of information about Indian atrocities is available from written reports from persons who were captured by the Indians. Some background about these captives and their narratives is useful in evaluating the atrocities described. J. Norman Heard noted that

> the tradition of captive-taking goes back to prehistoric times among North American Indians. Centuries before white men came to these shores, captives were taken from neighboring tribes to replenish losses suffered in warfare or to obtain victims to torture in the spirit of revenge.[32]

During the French and Indian War alone, perhaps as many as 2,000 American captives were taken to Canada as prisoners by the Indians. (Canada was controlled at the time by the French, who were the Indians' allies.) "The Indian captivity was a massive historical reality."[33] Captivity was so common at times that abductions came to be accepted as part of life on the frontier.[34] While the Puritan captives saw the Indians as fiends from hell, the later Quaker captives saw them as savage men in need of enlightenment.[35] Quaker captive Jonathan Dickinson referred to the "cruelly devouring jawes of the inhumane cannibals."[36]

Mary Rowlandson's narrative is an example of how these captive narratives reveal Indian characteristics. Others are found in Frederick Drimmer's book *Captured by the Indians,* which deals with the captivities of James Smith, Thomas Brown, Alexander Henry, Moses Van Campen, John Knight, John Slover, John Tanner, Charles Johnston, John Rodgers Jewitt, Elias Darnell, John W. B. Thompson, Nelson Lee, Lavina Eastlick, and Fanny Kelly. The Smith, Knight, Jewitt, Darnell, and Kelly narratives are firsthand. It is not known whether or not the Henry, Van Campen, Johnston, Lee, or Eastlick narratives are firsthand, and the Slover narrative was told to a Pittsburgh lawyer named Hugh H. Brackenridge. Richard VanDerBeets, in *Held Captive by Indians: Selected Narratives, 1642–1836,* explained how avidly the public took to these stories:

> These narratives were tremendously popular, and "first editions are rare today because they were quite literally read to pieces, and most narratives went through a remarkable number of editions."[37]

Although there are claims that some captive narratives were exaggerated, romanticized, mere propaganda, and misrepresented facts, no such claim has been made against any of the narratives relied upon here, so far as can be determined. Gary L. Ebersole, in *Captured by Texts,* analyzed 41 captive narratives, 7 of which are relied upon here: Jewitt, Johnston, Kelly, Lee, Rowlandson, Tanner, and Van Campen. He flatly concluded in his last paragraph, "I have no problem accepting at face value the accounts of the white Indians mentioned above."[38]

Some captives were undoubtedly prone to exaggerate, but historian R. W. G. Vail emphasized that many narratives of captivity were "simple, vivid, direct and, generally, accurate pictures of the exciting and often harrowing adventures of their authors."[39] J. Norman Heard, author of *White into Red,* acknowledged that, "while individual narratives may contain inaccuracies and exaggerations, taken in the aggregate they provide a generally reliable source of information on assimilation."[40] James Gordon Meade asserted that captive narratives were "honest accounts of experiences charged with meaning to authors and readers alike."[41] Indeed, Richard VanDerBeets complimented them:

> Many captive narrators were excellent observers, and their accounts of Indian warfare, hunting, customs and manners, religion, and council procedures are in some cases our only glimpse of . . . past realities. For the historian, many of the narratives of Indian captivity are repositories of eyewitness information relating to the major Indian-white conflicts throughout the course of American history.[42]

Drimmer pointed out that the narratives he included "have been accepted as authentic since their earliest publication, and have frequently been used as sources by historians and anthropologists."[43] Larry Lee Carey characterized Johnston's narrative as genuine and believable and found that Kelly was a "dispassionate, objective commentator."[44]

Jules Zanger, who reprinted Fanny Kelly's account of her captivity, which was originally published in 1871, called attention to the fact that it

> came buttressed with affidavits from Army officers and Indian chiefs [Indian affidavits are Xd by Sioux chiefs Spotted Tail, Swift Bear, Red Cloud, and assorted majors, captains, lieutenants, and an assistant surgeon] attesting to its authenticity.[45]

Kelly's captivity was well known before her escape, perhaps because her brother-in-law was a Union general. President Lincoln ordered the army to try to buy her freedom. After her escape, she went to Washington, where President Grant asked to meet with her and expressed his sympathy (the Sioux had killed her daughter). Congress passed a bill appropriating $5,000 for her services during her captivity in saving a wagon train from Indian attack, and in warning Fort Sully about another Indian attack.[46]

The motivation given by the narrators for writing the captive narratives was quite varied. Mary Rowlandson put it this way:

> One principall ground of my setting forth these lines is to declare the Works of the Lord, and his wonderfull power in carrying us along, preserving us in the wilderness, while under the Enemies hand, and returning us to safety again.[47]

Anne Jamison wrote so that her children and others might be excited to acknowledge God, submit to him, and put their trust in him.[48] John Johonnot also wrote from religious motives.[49] The Reverend J. J. Meethvin offered the captivity of Andele for the "pleasure and profit" of young readers.[50] Nathaniel Segar said he wanted to get full compensation for his military service in the Revolution and his captivity in Maine.[51] Moses Van Campen was struck by the rare specimens of enterprise, bravery, and conduct that were exhibited.[52] The Reverend Reuben Weiser told about the captivity of Regina Hatman because "our children should know something about their [Indian] cruelties, and thus see why God has permitted them to be banished from their native land."[53] The Reverend John Williams wanted to report God's providential dealings with himself.[54] Peter Williamson hoped to move his readers to sympathize with his plight as a wounded veteran and former captive "and thus to open their purse strings."[55] He earned a living with his captivity narrative and other writings and by exhibiting himself in Indian costume at his coffeehouse.

Ebersole saw an appeal in these narratives of captivity quite beyond their sensationalism:

> The theme of captivity was widely employed in the seventeenth, eighteenth, and nineteenth centuries in diverse literary genres because it represented a striking instance of sudden reversal of fortune, whether this was understood to be divine affliction or not. The theme of sudden reversal of fortune of the good and apparently blameless was, of course, as old as the story of Job.[56]

He added that captivity tales also

> were offered as an invitation to readers to engage in an inquiry into the human condition and, with the comparative knowledge gained, to meditate on the blessings and the costs of civilization. Still other tales were presented as affording the reader "an opportunity of observing the mind of man in its progress from the original savage to civilized life; as well as in its retrograde movements from civilization to the savage state."[57]

He also found that a desire to entertain drove some of these authors:

> Few works were written exclusively to provide entertainment to the reader. At a minimum, there was a nod toward providing some form of rational entertainment or moral instruction, however trite.[58]

There was a heyday of atrocity accounts. Zanger commented on this and other aspects of captive narratives:

> The Indian captive narrative, though it has antecedents and parallels in other cultures, developed as a particularly American literary form. It appeared, flourished, and declined during ... [the] American experience on the Indian frontier ... during which the Indian presented an obstacle to the expanding civilization of the white man. With the disappearance of that frontier—and with it of the threat of the Indian—the captivity narrative ... disappeared, merging finally with the stream of Western sensational literature.[59]

The narrative was usually published at the urging of friends and relatives or at the suggestion of journalists or printers. Although narratives were generally brought out as soon as the captive had returned from the wilderness,[60] a puzzling aspect is that so many captives waited so long before telling their interesting stories. Cordova-Rios told his story when he was 75 years old; Alexander Henry was 70. Anne Jamison waited for 46 years after her captivity was over, Mrs. Johnson waited 40 years, Charles Johnston waited 37 years, and Leith at least 58 years. Mary Jemison was 80 when her account was published; James Smith waited almost 40 years to tell his story and Steele almost 40 years. No one has attempted to explain this strange fact except Frank Buckelew, who was captured in 1866 at age 13 by the Lipan Indians in Texas. His narrative was not published until 1932, 66 years later. The preface of his book states that he "long hesitated to present his story as an Indian captive lest it be condemned as fiction."[61] In short, he thought many settlers would refuse to believe the horrors recited in most captive narratives.

The captive narratives were understandably reflective of the times, and VanDerBeets thought they "draw and shape their materials from the very wellsprings of human experience."[62] It has been said that this body of literature "emphasizes the fact that it was the line of fluid frontiers receding into the West that changed the colonists into a new people."[63]

INDIAN CANNIBALISM occurred over a long period of time, indeed, longer than the war itself. It terrified the settlers and is discussed independently here (the other atrocities will be treated in chronological order for the most part).

The first report of cannibalism in the New World occurs in a 1493 letter from Christopher Columbus. He indicated that he had found no monsters, nor had he had a report of any "except in an island 'Carib,' . . . which is inhabited by a people who are regarded in all the islands as very fierce and who eat human flesh."[64] The word *cannibal* comes from the Carib Indians.

Some Indians in the Caribbean prized human flesh. The Caribs and Tupians "relished human flesh and ate it in preference to other food."[65] They were tribes who made war to get victims and ate the heart and other parts of the body in the belief they would get the courage or other qualities of the victim.[66] Others found it repellent.[67]

Cannibalism was not confined, however, to the Carib island. It was described in detail by Amerigo Vespucci, who made important voyages to the New World and whose writing was published around 1504. He related that the Indians of Brazil

> cruelly kill one another, and those whom they bring home captive from war they preserve, not to spare their lives, but that they may be slain for food; for they eat one another, the victors the vanquished, and among other kinds of meat human flesh is a common article of diet with them. Nay be the more assured of this fact because the father has already been seen to eat children and wife, and I knew a man whom I also spoke to who was reputed to have eaten more than three hundred human bodies. And I likewise remained twenty-seven days in a certain city where I saw salted human flesh suspended from beams between the houses, just as with us it is the custom to hang bacon and pork. I say further: they themselves wonder why we do not eat our enemies and do not use as food their flesh which they say is most savory.[68]

Indian cannibalism in English literature first appeared in a translation of a Dutch pamphlet published about 1511. In describing Indian life it reported Indians "ete also on[e] another[.] The man eteth his wyfe[,] his chylderene as we also have seen and they hange also the bodyes or persons fleeshe in the smoke as men do with swynes fleshe."[69]

Richard Slotkin, among others, stated that almost all the Indian tribes practiced ritual cannibalism.[70] Harold E. Driver said cannibalism (as well as torture and human sacrifice) occurred in all tribes from the Iroquois in the northeast to the Gulf tribes in the southeast:[71]

> The pattern of warfare in a particular region is partly determined by the contacts with peoples on the outside and by the ideas and values derived from these contacts. For example, the torture of prisoners, or their sacrifice to the supernatural, and cannibalism, occur in a continuous area from the Iroquoians in the Northeast to the Gulf tribes in the Southeast, thence south through Northeast Mexico to Meso-America and the Caribbean.[72]

Christy Turner II believes that the skeletal remains of at least 286 Hopi (radiocarbon-dated to about 1580) indicate that they had been cannibalized by other Hopi. He also believes that 12 percent of 870 Anasazi skeletons he examined indicate cannibalization, an additional 69 people. (Turner has admitted that he has no direct evidence to support these conclusions, and many anthropologists disagree with him, suggesting the physical evidence he found might result from bizarre mortuary practices or the execution of witches.)[73]

The Iroquois would force their male captives to run the gauntlet, accept some of those who made it into the tribe, perhaps give those who did not to the widows of warriors, and "still other captives might be cooked and eaten so that their strength could be absorbed by the Iroquois warriors."[74]

Pierre Esprit Radisson was captured by Mohawk while duck hunting in Quebec. He was adopted into the tribe. He went on a hunting trip with 3 Mohawk warriors and a Huron captive. The Huron captive proposed that they kill their captors and escape, which they did. But other Mohawks caught up with them 14 days later. "The Huron was killed and his heart eaten by the Mohawks."[75]

Alan Axelrod wrote that "cannibalism was widespread and was reported among Indians well into the nineteenth century."[76]

Cannibalism was not confined to Indians. In 1607, after widespread starvation, some settlers ate corpses and at least one ate his wife.[77] Other settlers considered it. In 1703, William Clap wrote a letter recounting how he had been taken prisoner by the French and forcibly marched to Canada. The party was in such dire straits that the 2 French guards considered killing and eating him. Clap prayed in their presence, and one of the Frenchmen, who seemed to have tears in his eyes, told him to get up and they would try one day longer.[78]

After Barbara Leininger was captured in 1755, she was put with a captive Englishwoman, who later tried to escape. The Indians scalped her, laid burning splinters on her body, and cut off her ears and fingers. A French officer "took compassion on her, and put her out of her misery." An English soldier named John had escaped from prison at Lancaster and joined the French. He cut a piece of flesh from the Englishwoman's body and ate it. She was then chopped in two and her body devoured by the dogs.[79]

Anne Jamison wrote that she and her children were in a large party fleeing Indian attacks by floating down the Mississippi on a raft. They ran out of food. The only surviving adult male in her party proposed consuming a child chosen by lot. Jamison dissuaded him.[80]

There were reports of Indian cannibalism in New England. Puritans said that Indians gnawed flesh from settler bones after tying their captives to trees.[81] Around 1625, the Mohegan sachem Wonkus ate part of the body of the Narraganset sachem Miantonomo, then commented, "It is the sweetest meat I ever ate."[82] In 1676 Nathaniel Saltonstall told about an incident in New England where the Indian executioner flung one end of a rope over a post and hoisted the victim up like a dog "and with his Knife made a Hole in his Breast to his Heart, and sucked out his

Heart-Blood."[83] The Algonquins as well as the Iroquois were cannibals.[84]

In 1724 the Creeks offered to mediate a war between the Seneca and the Cherokee. The Seneca replied that they could not afford to make peace because "we have no people to war against nor yet no meal to eat but the Cherokees."[85] A French half-breed, Charles Langlade, led Ojibway, Potawatomis,* and Ottawas against the Miami capital, Pickawillany (near Piqua, Ohio) in 1752. One trader and 13 Miami warriors were killed. Three other traders and Miami chief Memeskia were captured. "Chief Memeskia was killed and ritually devoured by his assailants."[87]

In 1754, the *Boston Evening Post* reported that

the Enemies had 2 kill'd and as many wounded in the Engagement, which being over, the Indians cut open Capt. Donahew's Breast, and suck'd his Blood and hacked and mangled his Body in a most inhuman and barbarous Manner, and then eat a great part of his Flesh. They also suck'd the Blood and mangled the Bodies of the other Slain.[88]

After Fort William Henry fell in 1757, Paul Roubaus, missionary to the Abnaki Indians, ordered them not to participate in ritual cannibalism as the Ottawas had done before.[89]

Governor Clinton reported before 1814 that the Indians "utterly destroyed their enemies by eating their bodies, not because they had an appetite for such fare but in order to excite themselves to greater fury."[90] French officer Louis Antoine de Bougainville, comte de Bougainville, wrote to his mother that "her child shudders at the horrors which we will be forced to witness" in combat employing these most "ferocious of all people, and cannibals by trade," his Indian allies. He wrote to his brother that the Indians had been "drawn from 500 leagues by the smell of fresh human flesh and the chance to teach their young men how one carves up a human being destined for the pot."[91]

While John Tanner was a captive of the Indians between 1789 and 1817, he encountered medicine man Aiskawbawis. Tanner admitted he never thought well of Aiskawbawis, who claimed to talk with the Great Spirit, beat his drum incessantly at night, driving all the game away, and

---

*The Potawatomi tribe fought against the English in Pontiac's Rebellion and for the English in the American Revolution. They fought against the United States in Little Turtle's War, Tecumseh's Rebellion, and the Black Hawk War. Soon afterward, their situation became hopeless, and they were relocated west of the Mississippi.[86]

had "once eaten his own wife because of hunger." The Indians wanted to kill him for this, but didn't.[92]

Some of the tribes on the northwestern coast were cannibals. They had secret societies. Alvin M. Josephy told about them:

> One of the best known was the Kwakiutl Cannibal Society, whose initiates were possessed by the Cannibal Spirit at the North End of the World. Working up to a frenzy, the dancers bit flesh from the arms of those watching them, and then ate of the body of a specially killed slave or of an animal masked to resemble a human.[93]

In the 1860s, 3 Indian tribes attacked the Tonkawa Indians, who were hated for their adherence to Texas and accused of practicing cannibalism.[94] The Comanche fought the Tonkawas in 1874 and lost. The Comanche hated them because they served the army as scouts against other Indians and because they were, or had been, cannibals.[95]

The Tonkawas practiced cannibalism for food, not ritual. A Tonkawa band, together with settlers in Texas, chased some Comanche horse thieves. Three Tonkawas killed a Comanche rear guard, then rode to a neighboring farm. Noah Smithwick was invited to their feast and remembered what happened:

> Having fleeced off the flesh of the dead Comanche, they borrowed a big wash kettle . . . into which they put the Comanche meat, together with a lot of corn and potatoes—the most revolting mess my eyes ever rested on. When the stew was sufficiently cooked and cooled to allow of its being ladled out with the hands, the whole tribe gathered round, dipping it up with their hands and eating it as greedily as hogs. Having gorged themselves on this delectable feast, they lay down and slept till night, when the entertainment was concluded with the scalp dance.[96]

The Lipans in Texas practiced cannibalism. Texas Ranger Robert Hall was invited to dinner after a Lipan skirmish with the Comanche. " 'They offered me a choice slice of Comanche,' he remarked, 'but I politely informed them that I had just eaten a rattlesnake and was too full to eat any more.' "[97]

The fact that some Indians were cannibals was a serious impediment to a satisfactory relationship between Indians and settlers. Bernard W. Sheehan put it like this:

> No fantasy-ridden portrayal of savage violence cut more deeply into the Indian's reserve of humanity than the charge of cannibalism. Some

commentators denied the accusation; others made palliating distinctions over the circumstances in which Indians would eat human flesh. James Adair protested that they consumed only the heart of the enemy in order to inspire them with his courage, and at the same time, he denied that Indians were cannibals. An occasional account took pleasure in a blood anecdote. John Long quoted the story of a Jesuit missionary who described an Indian woman feeding her children when her husband arrived with an English prisoner: "She immediately cut off his arm, and gave her children the streaming blood to drink," asserting at the priest's protestation that she wanted her children to be warriors "and therefore fed them with the food of men." A sergeant named Jordan wrote to his wife from the Northwest in 1812 and told of an incident that occurred immediately following his capture by "four damned yellow Indians." One of the natives agreed to spare his life because Jordan had once given him tobacco at Fort Wayne. But the savage went to the body of Captain Wells who lay nearby, "cut off his head and stuck it on a pole, while another took out his heart and divided it among the chiefs, and they ate it up raw." The fact could not be disputed, Indians had eaten human flesh and thus had offended against the moral basis of human existence. No amount of explanation could quite cover the crime, nor would any fanciful description replace the accusation.[98]

Paradoxically, James Wilson, author of *The Earth Shall Weep,* had some good things to say about cannibals, quoting Michel de Montaigne about some Brazilian cannibals he had met in Paris: "Those peoples . . . seem to me to be barbarous only in that they have been hardly fashioned by the mind of man, still remaining close neighbours to their original state of nature."[99]

The way Indians usually handled their prisoners (in Texas at least) terrified the settlers as much as their cannibalism:

The Indian customs of mutilation, torture, rape, and wanton murder were seen as total depravity. Marauding Indians generally killed their victims outright or tortured them to death soon after capture. They rarely kept prisoners because they did not have the means to confine them, and very often did not even have the means to feed them. Boys and girls beyond the age of infancy were spared because they were useful—the boys to be groomed as warriors and the girls as wives. Infants, however, often were killed as liabilities. Captive women and even young girls could expect to be gang-raped, although sometimes a warrior with prestige might claim a captive as exclusively his own. Girls placed under the supervision of Indian women might be subject to routine acts of sadism, such as burning with firebrands or hot irons, or laceration.[100]

As a general rule, when Indian captives were taken, they were held for ransom, adopted by the Indians, or "put to slow, horrible deaths, a practice which, like prisoner taking itself, had originated before the coming of Europeans."[101]

> Customs varied from nation to nation, but as a rule war criminals were ritually shaved and painted, then secured loosely, so as to allow some interesting freedom of movement, to a post around which slow-burning firewood had been piled. Before and after the flames were lighted, victims were stoned, slashed, and partially dismembered, care being taken so that these preliminary torments did not bring about their untimely end. Skillful torturers could keep a man, or at least the charred, mutilated hulk of one, alive for many hours. Somewhat like hangings and witch or heretic burnings among Europeans, these were great public occasions which engaged the entire community and were thought to be instructive particularly for youths.[102]

The plight of the Moore family illustrated the kind of treatment settlers captured by Indians might receive:

> There was, for example, the case of Martha Moore and her family. After their men were killed defending a farm in southwestern Virginia, they were captured by Shawnee raiders led by a minor chief, Black Wolf. Two of the children, a crying infant, Peggy, and a retarded son, John, were immediately killed. . . . Returning to his village in Ohio, Black Wolf found a band of Cherokee visiting there. They had also been raiding but without success and were consequently sore and disgruntled. To cheer them up, Black Wolf made a present of Martha Moore and her daughter Jane. (Another daughter, Mary, and a servant girl, Martha Evans, were kept by the Shawnees and treated well until they were ransomed several years later.) The Cherokee tied the women to a stake and commenced to roast them very slowly. Martha Moore cried out and begged to be released quickly, but her pleas were directed to her own God. They were heard by a Shawnee matron who, disgusted by the unheroic sport of the Cherokee, entered their fire ring and with two quick hatchet blows ended the ordeal of the Moore women.[103]

Bil Gilbert, who described this scene, added that "such horrible happenings became increasingly frequent and involved the Shawnee as well as Cherokee and other nations."[104]

The matter of Indians murdering prisoners was, of course, a serious one, and Frederick Drimmer said, "The Indian put to the tomahawk all but a small proportion of those who fell into his power."[105] Clark Wissler concluded that the purpose of an Algonquin raider in torturing the settler to death was

> to shock and enrage the white man's relatives. He took care to leave behind the most hideous evidences of brutality, even the revelation of his tribal identity. No wonder the settlers came to look upon the Indians as devils and to vent their rage against them in much the same way, even carrying off their women and children to be sold as slaves in the West Indies.[106]

There is no indication that the purpose of the other tribes was any different.

CHAPTER 5

Colonial Atrocities

The colonial era began with the arrival of the first white settlers in America from Great Britain. The Spanish conquistadores came to the New World to search for gold and glory for their sovereign. The corporate merchants of Great Britain, however, "went looking for money-making opportunities for themselves and their investors."[1] Three years after Queen Elizabeth I died, King James I granted settlement charters to the Virginia Company of London to develop the South and the Virginia Company of Plymouth to develop New England. These were capitalistic companies. Great Britain "deliberately set out to populate the New World." The Spanish had had few settlers.[2]

The Virginia Company of London settled at Jamestown, Virginia, in 1607. A swampy area had been selected to deter Spanish attacks, and it was a breeding ground for malaria, typhoid, yellow fever, and dysentery. The emigrants knew little about farming, and after a severe drought, there was widespread starvation. The company persisted and provided supplies to any colonist willing to make the voyage west. Captain John Smith* arrived and saved the colony by stopping the practice of having

---

*John Smith was an English soldier of fortune who fought for the French and the Austrians before he brought settlers to Virginia and founded Jamestown. After the events discussed here, he was injured in a gunpowder explosion and had to return to England in 1609. Smith came to

everyone draw from the common stores. Instead, he encouraged individuals to work harder "by giving each his share in direct proportion to his production."[4]

The *Mayflower,* headed for Virginia, was blown off course by a storm and landed on Cape Cod, Massachusetts. Although the ship remained through the winter to give shelter, by April half the colonists had died. The others had survived in part because the Abnaki Indian Samoset (who was visiting the Wampanoag) and the Wampanoag Squanto arranged a treaty with the local Wampanoags and introduced them to native crops such as corn.[5]

John Smith's adversary in the Powhatan Wars was Chief Opechancanough, brother of Powhatan. In 1607, Smith was hunting with some Indian guides. His party was ambushed by Opechancanough and his 300 Indians. Smith was the only settler who survived. He was captured, but later released.[6]

The next year, he was getting some corn from Opechancanough when he learned he was surrounded by several hundred well-armed Indians. Smith grabbed Opechancanough by the scalp lock and stuck his pistol in his ribs. He told the Indians that they had promised to load his ship with corn, and if they did not, he would load it with their dead carcasses. The corn was loaded.[7] This was only one of several times Opechancanough and John Smith would take turns capturing each other.

In 1622, Opechancanough began a war that became a series of conflicts. It started in Jamestown as the result of an event involving 2 men. Trader Morgan (whose first name is not known) had gone into the woods to do business with the Indians in March. His friends never saw him again. But, shortly afterward, Nemattanow, or Nemattanew, a prominent Powhatan (the English called him Jack of the Feathers because he would often dress himself with feathers "as though he meant to flye"[8]), came out of the woods wearing Morgan's hat.[9] One author stated that Nemattanow announced Morgan's death.[10] Morgan's servants shot and killed him.[11]

Opechancanough immediately threatened revenge, even though he had told the settlers only a few months before that "he held the peace so firme, the sky should fall [ere] he dissolved it."[12] He knew that the lucrative tobacco crop had brought too many settlers to Virginia. By

---

the New World again in 1614, when he explored around Cape Cod, and he made his last visit in 1615, during which he was captured by French pirates, then shipwrecked.[3]

1622, Indian hunting grounds and even the Indian way of life had been impaired by the settlers. The Morgan incident made up his mind. Only 2 weeks after Nemattanow's death, Opechancanough directed an attack against settlements and plantations along the James River; on the first day alone, 347 men, women, and children were killed out of a population of only 1,200.[13]

Governor Wyatt called a peace conference. Opechancanough and several hundred Indians attended, and Wyatt tried to poison all of them. Some 200 became violently ill, and "many, helpless, were slaughtered,"[14] but Opechancanough escaped.[15] (The poisoning led to the complaint of the Virginia Company noted earlier, to the effect that the colonists had gone too far.)

Opechancanough signed a peace treaty with the settlers in 1632, but 12 years later, in 1644, he attacked again, this time killing 500 out of the 8,000 settlers. At the time of this attack, he was about 100 years old, very feeble, blind, and had to be carried on a litter. He was captured for the last time. Governor Berkeley ordered that he be treated with courtesy, but a guard shot him in the back, killing him.[16]

As so often occurred in conflicts between settlers and Indians, both sides were losers. Opechancanough brought about not only the bankruptcy of Virginia, but also the end of the Powhatan Confederacy. Chief Powhatan's successor, Necotowance, granted the settlers the legal right to the lands they had occupied.[17]

Father Isaac Joques was a missionary to the Mohawk. He was captured in the 1630s, whereupon his thumb was amputated and presented to him. He publicly offered it to God as a sacrifice, but one of his comrades told him to stop because otherwise the Indians might force it into his mouth and compel him to eat it. He flung it away. Cutting off an ear, a strip of flesh, or a finger and making the victim eat it was a "usual torture."[18]

In 1632, the Delawares killed 32 Dutch settlers at Swaanendael on Delaware Bay.[19]

The settlers in the Massachusetts Bay Colony learned that the Indians, presumably Pequots, flayed some prisoners alive with "ye shells of fishes," cut off the members and joints of others piecemeal and broiled them on the coals, and ate clumps of the flesh of others in their sight while they lived.[20] A group of settlers in Massachusetts was killed in 1637. One was put to death by roasting.[21]

In retaliation, in May 1637 Captain John Mason led an expedition that took an Indian prisoner who answered the English interrogation with mockery. The soldiers tied one of his legs to a post, pulled on a rope tied to his other leg, and tore him apart. Captain Underhill shot the Indian as an act of mercy.[22]

Other atrocities were committed by the settlers (sometimes with the help of other Indians). In June 1637, an army composed of 240 English colonists, 1,000 Narragansets, and 70 Mohegans made a night attack on a Pequot town near the Mystic River in Connecticut, burned the town, and killed its 600 inhabitants. Many of the casualties were women and children who burned to death. The governor said it was a fearful sight to see them frying in the fire. Some Pequots were later trapped in a swamp and surrendered. The adult male captives were killed, the boys sold to the West Indies, and the women and girls parceled out to the settlers as slaves.[23]

Toward the end of the Pequot War in 1637, the English received the severed heads of Pequots from surrounding Indian tribes.[24]

In the first year of the Beaver Wars, a war party of 100 Iroquois met 300 Hurons* and Algonquins. Normally Indians did not attack unless they had substantially superior numbers, but Iroquois (Oneida) chief Ononkwaya persuaded the Iroquois to attack anyhow. Only 4 or 5 Iroquois survived, one of whom was Ononkwaya, and they were killed by torture. His execution was reported by a Jesuit missionary.

Ononkwaya was roasted, but did not flinch. When the Hurons believed him dead, one of them scalped him. He leaped up, grabbed some burning sticks, and drove the crowd back. He was pelted with sticks, stones, and live coals. He was thrown into the fire, but he leaped out with a blazing brand in each hand and ran toward the Huron town. The Hurons tripped him, cut off his hands and feet, and again tossed him into the fire. He crawled toward the crowd on his elbows and knees glaring at them ferociously. They rushed forward and cut off his head.[26]

In 1639, the Hurons captured 113 Iroquois. Some were from war parties. Others were casual travelers. All 113 were burned to death.

A Dutch Staten Island farmer was killed in 1641 by a group of Raritan Indians, a subtribe of the Delawares. The Dutch then offered bounties for Raritan scalps or heads.[27]

The Wappinger Indians asked Dutch governor Willem Kieft in 1643 for help against the Mohawk, who were trying to get tribute from them. Kieft instead turned the Mohawk loose on the Wappingers, who killed

---

*The Hurons burned their own villages and scattered when the Iroquois invaded their territory. Some went with the French and were granted land near Quebec City; others migrated westward into Michigan, Wisconsin, Illinois, and Ohio.[25]

70 and enslaved others. Kieft then sent Dutch soldiers to Pavonia, the present site of Jersey City, to murder the surviving Wappingers, mostly women and children, whom the Mohawk had not harmed. They returned bearing the severed heads of 80 Indians. The soldiers and settlers used them as footballs on the streets. Thirty prisoners were tortured to death "for the public amusement." The night became known as the Slaughter of the Innocents.[28]

The governor had a houseguest both before and after the slaughter. His name was David Pietersz de Vries, an artillery master. He could see the firing in Pavonia from the residence that night and hear the shrieks of the Indians. He learned that the soldiers had taken babies from their mothers' breasts, hacked them to pieces in the presence of their parents, and thrown the pieces in the fire and in the water. Some babies were thrown in near the shore, and when their parents jumped in to save them, the soldiers would not let them come back to land, and they drowned. The next day some survivors came in to beg for food and get warm. They were murdered and tossed in the water. When de Vries returned to his country home, survivors straggled by with hands or legs amputated. Some were "holding their entrails in their arms."[29]

Kieft mismanaged the Indians and pursued policies of exterminating them, thereby provoking a full-scale war. He was dismissed as governor and succeeded by Peter Stuyvesant. On his return voyage to Europe, he was lost at sea.[30]

A number of crimes against Indians, including murder, were committed by the Dutch in New Amsterdam. A pamphleteer charged that a Hackensack Indian was publicly tortured by Dutch soldiers, skinned in strips, fed his own flesh, flayed from his fingers to his knees, castrated, dragged through the streets alive, and put on a millstone, where his head was beaten off.[31] The authorities ignored these crimes. Finally, some Dutch went to Staten Island to kill all the Indians they could find. The Indians were quick to retaliate.

In 1644 the Susquehannocks, aided by settlers from New Sweden, fought Maryland militia. The Susquehannocks took 15 prisoners. They tortured 2 of them to death.[32]

There was a Jesuit mission in Huron country. The priest was Father Antoine Daniel. In 1648, just after he had concluded mass, it was learned that enemy Iroquois were coming. Apparently everyone wanted to be baptized, so Daniel remained to baptize all who wished it. He urged them to escape, promising to remain to continue with the baptisms. The Iroquois attacked, shot Daniel, hacked his body apart, and threw it in the flames of the burning town.[33]

In 1649, some Hurons who had escaped from another town under Iroquois attack warned the Indians in the New York town of St. Louis to flee. All who could did, leaving 80 to their fate. Two Jesuit missionaries, Fathers Jean de Brébeuf and Gabriel Lalemant, remained behind to baptize. After a fierce battle, the Iroquois captured the town, burned it, and tortured and beat the survivors, especially the 2 priests. The torture included a mock baptism in which scalding water was poured over their heads.[34]

In 1655, a Delaware Indian woman was caught pulling peaches from the tree of a settler, who then shot and killed her. He in turn was ambushed and killed by her family. Soon about 2,000 armed Indians walked into town, terrifying the city. The Indians destroyed houses, killed indiscriminately, and took 150 settlers captive before leaving town.[35]

In 1659, Stuyvesant called for a parley during a fight with the Esopus Indians. Their chiefs entered the town of Wiltwyck for the peace conference. The Dutch killed them as they slept that night. The Indians then took 8 Dutch soldiers captive and burned them alive.[36]

The sachem of the Wampanoag Indians* was Metacom. His father was Chief Massasoit, who was very helpful to the Pilgrims. The settlers called Metacom King Philip. He was incensed with the settlers' treatment of his people, however, and tried to organize a rebellion to oust the British from New England. When the British tried 3 Christian Indians of his tribe in 1675, then hanged them, King Philip went to war. This war, called King Philip's War, lasted from 1675 to 1678. The Nipmuc, Narraganset, and other tribes joined him. More than 1,000 settlers were killed. The settlers eventually won due to superior numbers and firepower. They were aided by Indian allies from 4 tribes: the Massachusetts, Mohegan, Niantics, and Wampanoag. The war went against Philip. His wife and 9-year-old boy were captured and later, together with hundreds of other Indians, sold into slavery in the West Indies and Spain for the going rate, 30 shillings a head. This happened even though the preacher John Eliot, who was known as the Apostle to the Indians, opposed it. Eliot's view was that "to sell souls for money seemeth to me a dangerous merchandise."[38]

Cotton Mather said, "It must have been as bitter as death to him [King Philip] to lose his wife and only son, for the Indians are marvelously fond and affectionate toward their children."[39] Philip's other

---

*The Wampanoags, through Squanto and Samoset, were friends of the New England colonists in the early 1600s, but during King Philip's War, they became enemies. Those who did not fight kept their lands, particularly on Martha's Vineyard and Nantucket.[37]

relatives were killed. A Wampanoag warrior named Alderman counseled surrender. Philip killed him with his own hands. In 1676 Alderman's brother deserted, led the militia to Philip's hiding place, then
killed King Philip. Captain Benjamin Church, who had headed the successful settler army, described how

> [King Philip] was taken and destroyed, and there was he (Like as Agag
> was hewed in pieces before the Lord) cut into four quarters, and is now
> hanged up as a monument of revenging justice, his head being cut off
> and carried away to Plymouth, his Hands were brought to Boston. *So
> let all thine enemies perish, O Lord!!*[40]

In this war, it has been said, "the Puritans distinguished themselves by
wholesale massacres of noncombatants that could scarcely be credited if
not for the fact that it is the Puritans themselves who record them, with
relish."[41] Three tribes, the Wampanoag, the Nipmuc, and the Narraganset, were nearly wiped out.[42]

King Philip was succeeded by Annawan. When confronted by soldiers, he surrendered, ending the war. He was tried in Plymouth and
sentenced to death. Captain Church had come to respect Annawan and
argued for his life, but while Church was away, a mob seized Annawan
and beheaded him. He was the last leader of the Wampanoag Confederacy.[43]

Atrocities in the war were committed by the Indians as well. Author
Howard Mumford Jones related that during King Philip's War, the Indian atrocities consisted of

> the raping and scalping of women, the cutting off of fingers and feet of
> men, the skinning of white captives, the ripping open the bellies of
> pregnant women, the cutting off of the penises of the males, and the
> wearing of the fingers of the white men as bracelets or necklaces.[44]

In 1675 a group of militia went to Philip's own village, which was deserted. They found the heads of 8 settlers staring down at them from
poles.[45]

A group of settlers went on a peace mission to the Nipmucs. The Nipmucs attacked them, killing several. The mission retreated to the town
of Brookfield, where there was a garrison. The Nipmucs were close behind, and not all the militia reached the safety of the garrison. One was
captured and decapitated. His head was kicked among the Indians, then
stuck on a pole in front of his own home.[46]

That same year, 2 Massachusetts towns, Middleborough and Dartmouth, were attacked by Indians who

> barbarously murdered both men and women in those places, stripping the slain whether men or women, and leaving them in the open field as naked as the day wherein they were born. Such is also their inhumanity as that they flay of[f] the skin from their faces and heads of those they get into their hands, and go away with the hairy Scalp of their enemy.[47]

The subject of scalping is perhaps the most notorious one related to the American-Indian War. Around 1721, a delegation of Cherokee presented the king of England with 4 scalps of Indian enemies. The king was reported to have said he was "graciously pleased to accept."[48] The Pueblos had a Scalp Chief.[49]

There is some disagreement concerning why scalps were taken. The earlier practice was to take the entire head as a trophy, but of course that was a little awkward, especially if there were several, so eventually just the scalp was taken.[50] The Timucua tribe of Florida took arms and legs as well as scalps.[51] Tribes in the St. Lawrence area stretched the skin of the dead man's face on hoops.[52] Another view about why scalps were taken is that Indian religion held that a scalped person could not enter the happy hunting ground. If your enemy is scalped, he or she won't be there to bother you.[53] A third view is that scalping was for the purpose of releasing the spirit of the victim.[54]

Here is a description of fairly typical scalpings that happened during the Second Seminole War:

> Through Gen. Thompson were shot fifteen bullets, and sixteen through Rogers. The Indians scalped all, taking off the scalp clear around the head as far as the hair extended, and then beating in their skulls. The heads of Rogers and Suggs were shockingly mangled.[55]

But the method of scalping differed among tribes. The whole skin of the upper head was taken by some. Only the crown was removed by others. Later, when the Indians had steel weapons, many used a faster method, holding on to the hair, making one cut in the front, and taking the scalp lock with a sharp pull.[56] The River Yumans tribe (which included the Mojaves and Maricopas) had scalping specialists who acquired powers in dreams that enabled them to take off the skin of the entire head, including the ears.[57]

Several Indian practices were connected with scalping. The captive

James Smith was present when a Mohawk scalped his comrade. As they approached the Mohawk village, the Indians gave the usual scalp halloo, which was a long yell for every scalp or prisoner taken, followed by shouts of joy or triumph.[58] The Pueblos had a women's society "created to care for the scalps."[59] The Sioux captive Fanny Kelly described a scalp dance, which was held only at night. First the warriors came out and boasted of their prowess in war. Then their young women came with the scalps. The warriors leaped around in a circle, whooping and yelling the war cry. They made motions of cutting one another to pieces. They became furious, excited, ground their teeth, and tried to imitate the sound of death in battle.[60]

Scalping did not always cause death. A man living in northern Mexico described in detail how he was scalped by a Comanche. Some Blackfeet reported that Indians who survived scalping wore caps to cover the area. It was not uncommon for Plains Indians to scalp an enemy, then send him back to his people as an insult.[61] The daughter of Hepzibah Wells survived a scalping in 1690, as did others.[62]

Scalp bounties—the payment of money for a scalp—were common. In the early 1600s, the Spanish and the Apache did not get along at all. The Spanish then offered another tribe a bounty for Apache scalps.[63] In 1675, both the Plymouth colony and Connecticut offered the Narragansets a bounty for Wampanoag scalps or captives during King Philip's War.[64] The French in 1703 paid the Choctaw and Chickasaw a bounty for the scalps of Alabama Indians.[65] The same year Massachusetts paid 12 pounds for each scalp, but by 1722 they had raised it to 100 pounds.[66] During the French and Indian War, between 1749 and 1763, New England and Pennsylvania offered scalp bounties.[67] Some Pennsylvania settlers got $1,500 in 1763 by scalping 3 old Indian men, 2 women, and a boy who were making baskets in a nearby town.[68] Pennsylvania offered a bounty of $1,000 for the scalps of all hostile Indians in 1780 during the Revolution.[69] In 1776 New Hampshire offered 70 pounds for the scalp of each hostile male Indian and more than 37 pounds for that of each female or child over 12 years old.[70] All 13 colonies eventually offered scalp bounties.[71]

The British offered the Indians bounties for white scalps. In 1778 alone, British colonel Henry Hamilton, headquartered in Detroit, reported that the Indians (mostly Miamis) had brought in 110 scalps.[72] Two Mexican states offered bounties for Apache scalps in 1847.[73]

At times, scalp bounties were offered for Indians who had allegedly committed crimes, but bounties were paid even though the scalp wasn't that of the alleged criminal. It was enough if it was the scalp of a person belonging to the designated group. Of course, except for the terror factor, scalp bounties weren't very productive. Indians and others soon learned that whites couldn't distinguish between an enemy scalp and that of a friendly tribe, so scalps were brought in from the heads of any tribe. Finally, the Indians learned that the whites couldn't distinguish between an Indian scalp and a white scalp. Indians then got bounties for white scalps.[74]

There are reports of scalp bounties in California well into the nineteenth century. In 1859, the Marysville newspaper announced that

> a new plan has been adopted . . . to chastise the Indians for their many depredations during the past winter. Some men are hired to hunt them, who are recompensed by receiving so much for each scalp, or some other satisfactory evidence that they have been killed.[75]

In 1861, the *Shasta Herald* reported that at a meeting "measures [were] taken to raise a fund to be disbursed in payment of Indian scalps for which a bounty was offered."[76] Communities and individuals in California even offered money for Indian heads. Shasta City, for example, awarded 5 dollars for each head. Residents of Honey Lake in 1863 paid 25 cents for each scalp.[77]

Soldiers and sometimes settlers scalped Indians from time to time, but such conduct was exceptional. The worst instance was by the soldiers at the Sand Creek Massacre in 1864. Major Scott Anthony testified at a congressional hearing that "he saw the soldiers committing many acts of mutilation but he noted that those were no worse than what Indians had done to whites."[78] According to Duane Schultz, his rationalization was this:

> The only way to fight Indians is to fight them as they fight us; if they scalp and mutilate the bodies we must do the same. It is the general impression of the people of that country [the Colorado Territory] that the only way to fight them is to fight as they fight; kill the women and children. At the same time, of course, we consider it a barbarous practice.[79]

Atrocities other than scalping continued. Captain Richard Beers was dispatched with 36 men in 1675 to relieve the garrison in Northfield, Massachusetts. He and about 20 of his men were killed by Indians in an ambush. The next day, Major Treat with 100 men approached Northfield in pursuit of Indians and were "much daunted to see the heads of

Captain Beers' Soldiers upon poles by the way side." They turned back as a result.[80]

Mary Rowlandson, the wife of a minister, wrote about the events leading to her captivity by the Narragansets that same year in Lancaster, Massachusetts. Twelve settlers were killed in a raid and 24 taken captive:

> Hearing the noise of some guns, we looked out; several houses were burning and the smoke ascended into heaven. There were five persons taken in one house; the father and the mother and suckling child they knocked on the head; the other two they took and carried away alive. . . . Another there was who was running along was shot and wounded and fell down; he begged of them for his life, promising them money (as they told me), but they would not hearken to him but knocked him in [the] head, stripped him naked, and split open his bowels.[81]

The Wampanoag then came to the Rowlandson house and set it on fire, which forced the occupants into the hands of the Indians.

> No sooner were we out of the house, but my brother-in-law (being before wounded, in defending the house, in or near the throat) fell down dead; whereat the Indians scornfully shouted, hallooed, and were presently upon him, stripping off his clothes. The bullets flying thick, one went through my side, and the same (as would seem) through the bowels and hand of my dear child in my arms. One of my elder sister's children, named William, had then his leg broken, which the Indians perceiving, they knocked him on the head. Thus were we butchered by those merciless heathens, standing amazed, with the blood running down to our heels.[82]

Rowlandson described the Indians as "a company of hell-hounds, roaring, singing, ranting and insulting."[83] Other settlers were very much interested in this event. Her book, published in 1682,[84] was America's first bestseller.[85] In the raid, her baby was shot dead in her arms, she was shot in the side, her sister was killed, her brother-in-law was killed, her house was burned, another child died after 9 days of forced marching, and she spent 11 weeks in captivity. She was sold by one Indian, Quinnapin, to another and became the servant of the latter, Wetamoo, sister-in-law of King Philip from an earlier marriage. She appeared before King Philip twice.[86] She was freed for a ransom of 20 pounds, 2 coats, half a bushel of corn, and some tobacco.[87] Cotton Mather commented on her captivity in a sermon, pronouncing that it was not individual courage and heroism, but faith in the power of God that had helped her.[88]

About the same time Rowlandson was captured, Maryland Nanticoke or Doeg Indians got in a dispute with a farmer named Thomas Mathew over an account. Before matters were over, 5 Indian chiefs, 27 Indians, and at least 49 settlers had been killed.[89]

A year later, Connecticut major John Talcott and his men pursued the Pocasset Indians. The Pocasset chief and sachem was the female Wetamoo. An Indian betrayed her and led Talcott's men to her camp, where they captured everyone but Wetamoo. She jumped onto some wood and tried to escape out to sea. Her naked body was found later by the colonists. They severed her head and displayed it on a pole in Taunton.[90]

In 1689, the Pennacook, Ossipee, and Pigwacket Indians assaulted settlements in Maine and then attacked Dover, New Hampshire, where they killed 20 or 30 English. One of them was the 75-year-old fur trader Major Richard Waldron, an old enemy from King Philip's War. They cut off his fingers one by one. Then they took turns slashing his chest, stating they were crossing out their accounts.[91]

In 1676, the Christian Indians of Loretto burned an Iroquois to death in the presence of the governor-general of New France, Louis de Buade, comte de Frontenac. Other Frenchmen viewed the burning as well.[92]

Louis de Buade was in the military service of Venice, France, and the Netherlands and was then appointed governor-general of New France, an area that included what is now Canada and the central Mississippi Valley.[93] Frontenac sent a party of 160 French-Canadians and 100 Indians from Montreal in 1690 to attack Albany. They found Albany too difficult because it was too far to go in freezing weather, so they chose to attack Schenectady instead. They attacked and found the gates open and guarded only by 2 snowmen. For 2 hours they hacked men, women, and children to death.[94] It is said they acted without provocation and were motivated only by brutal lust and wantonness. It was also reported that pregnant women were ripped open and their babies thrown into the flames or dashed against posts.[95] Sixty colonists were killed.[96]

The Abnaki Indians* and the French attacked Fort Loyal, now Fal-

---

*The Abnakis were a confederation of Passamaquoddys, Penobscots, Micmacs, Malecites, and Pennacooks. They launched many raids against British settlements in the French and Indian War. Their stronghold, Norridgewock, fell into British hands in 1724, and the Abnaki withdrew to Quebec. They have land in Canada, Maine, and Vermont.[97]

mouth, Maine, 2 years later. The fort surrendered on the condition that the soldiers would be granted safe conduct. As they marched out of the fort, however, they were massacred, and at least 100 of them died.[98]

The Abnakis had agreed by treaty to refrain from hostilities until May, but instead they with some Canadians attacked York, Maine, on February 5. They killed 48 and took 70 prisoners. In June they attacked Wells, Maine, and Deerfield, Massachusetts. Widow Hepzibah Wells and her 3 daughters were scalped. The Thomas Broughton family of 5 was killed.[99]

The Abnakis captured Mrs. Hannah Duston when they raided Haverhill, Massachusetts, in 1697. She had had her eighth child the week before and was resting inside. Her farmer husband told the other children to run to a fortified house while he tried without success to reach his wife. The Indians carried off Hannah, the baby, and a nurse, Mary Neff, who was caring for them. While they were going through the forest, the baby cried, and an Indian smashed its head against a tree, killing it. Hannah and the nurse were then turned over to a group of 2 warriors, 3 women, and 7 children. The group went north for more than a month, with the Catholic Indians pausing twice a day to say their rosaries.

On the last night of her captivity, Hannah Duston, the nurse, and 10-year-old Samuel Lennardson got up quietly from the campfire, took hatchets, and killed 4 adult Indians and most of the children. An old woman and a boy escaped. Hannah remembered that Massachusetts was offering a scalp bounty at the time, so she scalped the Indians and returned home, where she found all the other members of her family alive. She collected her 25-pound scalp bounty even though the time for collecting such bounties had expired. Of course, Cotton Mather incorporated her experience—like that of Mary Rowlandson—into his sermons, attributing the evil of the Indians to their conversion to Catholicism and citing her escape as an example of the Protestant ideal of divine deliverance from evil.[100]

Sieur d'Iberville explored the lower Mississippi region for France and discovered the Mississippi Delta.[101] There he and other French officials encountered the Natchez tribe* in 1700. They were present later at an "orgy of ritualistic human sacrifices" after the female chief, the Great Sun, died. Later, a French commandant ordered a Natchez town to be removed from the site where he planned to build a settlement. Because a

---

*The Natchez were governed by a king or queen known as the Great Sun, who had absolute power over his or her subjects. Warriors were tattooed from head to foot. There was a class system of royalty, nobles, and commoners.[102]

Natchez sacred temple with ancestral bones was there, the Natchez massacred the garrison. The French, with 700 Choctaw allies, counterattacked and almost annihilated the tribe. The 427 survivors were shipped to Haiti as slaves.[103] The tribe gradually lost its identity.[104]

In 1703, about the same time the massacres were going on in the Mississippi Delta, the Abnakis from Maine and the Mohawk from Quebec again attacked Deerfield, Connecticut, killing 49 settlers and capturing at least 100. The town minister, John Williams, wrote his account of this raid. He said he was awakened by the Indians trying to break open the doors and windows and saw them enter the house. Williams ran to his bedroom to get his pistol, put it to the breast of the first Indian to come up, but it misfired, and he was seized. Two of his children were murdered together with a black woman. He and his wife (and their baby, born only a few weeks before) were marched in the winter in separate groups toward Quebec, which was 300 miles away. Williams inquired about his wife from other prisoners he passed. He finally learned she had slipped and fallen down in a river she was crossing, and the Indian who took her shortly after that killed her with his hatchet at one stroke. His daughter, Eunice, was carried almost all the way to Quebec by an Indian. The French eventually ransomed most of the prisoners, but Eunice was adopted by the Mohawk and later married the Indian who had carried her. Years later she returned to Deerfield to visit, but then went back to the Mohawk.[105]

In 1711, a group of Swiss colonists organized by Baron Christoph von Graffenried went to a tract of land in North Carolina only to find it occupied by the Tuscarora Indians. The baron complained to the surveyor general, who assured the colonists they had clear title. He suggested they drive the Indians off without payment. The Indians attacked, killing almost 200 settlers, including 80 children. Raids and counterraids followed. The baron was captured. In consideration of his release, he agreed not to make war on the Indians. William Brice, one of his settlers, decided the promise was "contemptible softheartedness," captured one of the chiefs of a tribe allied with the Tuscarora, and roasted the chief alive. The fighting escalated, and eventually the Tuscarora were so badly beaten that they went north and joined the Iroquois Confederacy.[106]

North Carolina sought help from South Carolina. South Carolina sent an expedition of 30 militia and 500 Indians, many of whom were Yamasees. The Indians exposed some of their white prisoners and tortured others in view of the Carolina lines, forcing the militia to negotiate. Eventually they defeated the Tuscarora. British commander John

Barnwell, a slave trader, reported in his journal that he had "ordered immediately to be burned alive" several of the prisoners they had taken. Barnwell felt inadequately rewarded by North Carolina, so he invited the Tuscarora to a friendship parley. They came, and in violation of the truce he had just made with them, Barnwell trapped a large number of the Indians and sent them into slavery. The remaining Tuscarora went to war again.[107]

A second expedition went against the Tuscarora in 1713. This one was led by slave merchant Colonel James Moore and was composed of 33 colonists and almost 900 Cherokee, Yamasees, Creeks, and Catawbas. A Tuscarora fort was stormed and taken. Several hundred of the Indians were burned alive, and 166 male Indians were slaughtered as unsuitable for slavery. Sent into slavery this time were 392 Tuscarora, mostly women and children.[108]

Around 1715, North Carolina settlers made repeated raids on Indian villages to get slaves. As a result of this treatment, the Yamasees fled to Florida, the Catawbas "were overcome by disease, drink, and attacks by other Indians," and the Shawnee* moved north.[110]

Benjamin Franklin reported Shawnee torture in his *Pennsylvania Gazette* in 1729:

> They made the Prisoner Sing and Dance for some Time, while six Gun Barrels were heating red hot in the Fire; after which they began to burn the Soals of the poor Wretches Feet until the Bones appeared, and they continued burning him by slow Degrees up to his Privites, where they took much Pains. . . . This Barbarity they continued about six Hours, and then, notwithstanding his Feet were in such a Condition, they drove him to a Stake . . . and stuck Splinters of Pine all over his Body, and put fire to them. . . . In the next Place they scalp'd him and threw hot Embers on his Head. . . . At last they ran two Gun Barrels, one after the other, red hot up his Fundament, upon which [he] expired. . . . P.S. They cut off his Thumbs and offer'd them him to eat and pluck'd off all of his Nails.[111]

In the middle of the 1700s, the Apache took adult captives, but not to sell as slaves. They were taken so they could be killed by the female relatives of men killed in battle. Grenville Goodwin interviewed an Apache who described what happened to these Apache prisoners. The women did not kill the captives, so that they could prolong the suffering. They

---

*The Shawnee were widespread, living in 14 states. They migrated often. In the 1800s they were relocated by the whites to Indian Territory.[109]

would shoot at the captive with bows and arrows. Some of the arrows stuck in his or her body, but others just bounced back and fell on the ground. The women also shot at the prisoners with rifles. Once the men cut off the arms and legs of 2 captives who had been shot and then danced with the severed limbs. Sometimes they danced with the scalp after it was taken. After defeating the Pimas, the Apache killed all the older women, "saving the good, younger ones to take back with them." Sometimes a prisoner would be made to dance all night with the men, then they would kill him or her in the morning.[112]

Twelve-year-old Peter Williamson was alone at his farm in Pennsylvania in 1754. The French and Indian War had been going on for 5 years. Indians surrounded the house and told him he would be burned alive unless he surrendered. He surrendered and the Indians burned his house, barn, and livestock. He was tied to a tree all that night. The next morning, his face, head, hands, and feet were burned with flaming sticks and coals. He shed silent tears, and when they were discovered, coals were applied near his eyes with the statement that his face was wet and would be dried for him. Williamson then described how the group walked 6 miles to the Jacob Snider house. Both parents and the 5 children were immediately scalped. A servant was captured, but when the servant complained about the heavy load he was carrying, he was tomahawked and also scalped. They then went to the John Adams house. The wife and 4 children were scalped in the presence of Adams, who was an old man. After the wife was murdered, "they acted with her in such a brutal matter, as decency will not permit me [Williamson] to mention." Adams begged to be killed, but the Indians would not do it. He was stripped naked, painted all over with various colors, tied to a tree, whipped, and burned with red coals applied to his cheeks and legs.

Twenty-five other Indians then arrived with 20 scalps and 3 captives. They had also captured a trader and "not only scalped him, but immediately roasted him before he was dead; then, like cannibals, for want of other food, ate his whole body, and of his head made what they called an Indian pudding." The 3 new captives escaped but were shortly captured again. Two were tied to a tree, a great fire was made near them, and they were scorched and burned. Archibald Loudon* reported that one of the Indians then

---

*Loudon was a Pennsylvania newspaper publisher. He put an ad in his paper asking those who had knowledge about atrocities during the Revolutionary War to advise the paper about them. Loudon then compiled their responses and published them in Harrisburg, Pennsylvania.[113]

with his scalping knife opened their bellies, took out their entrails, and burned them before their very eyes, whilst the others were cutting, piercing, and tearing the flesh from their breasts, hands, arms and legs, with red hot irons, till they were dead. The third unhappy victim was preserved a few hours longer, to be, if possible, sacrificed in a more cruel manner: his arms were tied close to his body, and a hole being dug, deep enough for him to stand upright, he was put into it, the earth rammed and beat in all around his body, up to his neck, so that his head only appeared above ground; they then scalped him, and there let him remain for three or four hours, in the agonies; after which they made a small fire near his head, causing him to suffer the most excruciating torments . . . such agonizing torments did this unhappy creature suffer for near two hours before he was quite dead. They cut off his head, and buried it with the other bodies.

Williamson made his escape one night when his guards were asleep.

In 1755, Mohawk captive James Smith saw the warriors leave the Indian fort in the morning to fight General Braddock's army. He had high hopes that he would see them vanquished and that Braddock would take the fort and rescue him. That afternoon, a runner arrived and said that Braddock was losing. Later that day, he heard a number of scalp halloos, then saw the Mohawks and French returning with a great number of scalps and much British equipment. They said Braddock was defeated. A second group of about 100, mostly Indians, came in. Almost all of them were carrying scalps. Then a third group with wagon horses arrived with more scalps. About sundown a small party of warriors came in with around a dozen prisoners. They were naked, with their hands tied behind them and their faces and part of their bodies blackened with coal and water, which meant they were to be burned. The prisoners were all burned to death opposite the fort on the Allegheny River. The first man was tied to a stake and repeatedly touched with firebrands and red-hot irons. He screamed pitifully, and the Indians yelled like devils. Smith was too shocked by this scene to watch any further.[114]

Upon Braddock's defeat in 1755 in the French and Indian War, the Delaware Indians did a lot of scalping on the western borders of Pennsylvania, Maryland, and Virginia. Braddock had offered his troops 200 pounds for the scalp of Delaware leader Shinngass.[115] In the same year, the British offered 40 pounds for each scalp from an enemy tribe.[116]

In 1756, Indian chief Jacobs and his warriors burned and destroyed the little town of Coves, Pennsylvania. Settler Hugh M'Swine was away at the time, but when he returned, Jacobs took him prisoner and put him, with an Indian prisoner, under the care of a white named Jackson, who "had joined the Indians" and had been instructed to find more settlers. That night Jackson gave M'Swine an ax and told him to cut rails to make a fire. M'Swine immediately split the Indian with the ax, and after a fight shot and killed Jackson. M'Swine scalped them both.[117]

Blacksmith Robert Eastburn was fearful in 1756 that his town would be attacked by Indians. He therefore asked a British soldier if he could enlist. He was told he could. He walked with his unit half a mile out of town, heard a shot, climbed a large pine tree, and saw 2 Indians. He fired one shot, hoping he could kill them both, but he didn't know at the time what the result was. His unit retreated, he fell behind in the mud, and the Indians captured him. They took off all his clothes except his vest, put a rope around his neck, and began a 400-mile march to Montreal. One of the other prisoners with him revealed that his shot had killed one Indian and wounded another. He was fed porcupine, which he didn't like, and horse flesh, "which tasted very agreeably."

One night the Indian Eastburn had wounded took his blanket away and ordered him to dance around the campfire and sing. He refused because he thought it would be sinful. The Indian then tried to push him into the fire. When they reached Canada, the wounded Indian told a Frenchman about his refusal. The Frenchman tried to get him to dance and sing; he again refused, and the Frenchman took away Eastburn's vest, "which was my all." They were then joined by 8 more prisoners from his unit. All were made to lie down and were painted by the Indians. The rope was taken off his neck for the first time. They came to an Indian village where all the Indians came out and fell on the prisoners with their fists. Eastburn alone was taken to another town. As they entered the town, about 150 young Indians pelted him with dirt, gravel, and small stones. An Indian threw him into very cold water. He worked as a smith in Montreal for a time, then escaped, and was eventually reunited with his family.[118]

In 1756, Hugh Gibson was captured in an Indian raid in which his mother was killed. Whenever the Indians were to torture someone, all the captives were brought to watch. An Indian woman had fled to the settlers. During a skirmish, she got lost and fell back into Indian hands. She was stripped naked, tied to a post, and hot irons were applied to her skin until she died. Gibson saw the rule invoked that if one man kills another and the murderer cannot be found, the friends of the victim may kill the murderer's next of kin. The brother of an escaped murderer was killed under this rule.[119]

The house of Simon Girty's stepfather, John Turner, was raided by the

Delaware the same year in western Pennsylvania. The Girtys were taken west to the Delaware town of Kittanning. John Turner was tortured with red-hot gun barrels; blazing faggots were piled on his stomach and "a scalping knife slipped over his skull." After 3 hours, he was tomahawked to death. Turner's wife (who was Girty's mother), Simon Girty, who was 15, and Girty's brothers all were forced to watch. His mother was then killed. The family was split up among the Delaware, the Shawnee, and Simon Girty went to the Seneca. There he ran the gauntlet twice, then was adopted by the tribe.[120] The Seneca released him to the British, and he worked as a military scout and interpreter for them in the Ohio Valley from 1759 to 1776. In that year, he changed sides and joined the Virginia militia. He changed sides a second time, defecting to the British in 1778 and thereafter used Iroquoian methods of torture and execution against pro-Revolutionary captives.[121]

During the French and Indian War in 1756, the French under General Louis-Joseph de Montcalm captured Fort Oswego in New York. Montcalm promised the defeated commander of the fort safe conduct for his men. The Indian allies of the French, however, ambushed the men as they were leaving.

The next year, Montcalm took Fort William Henry and its 2,372 men. Again Montcalm promised safe conduct. Again the Indians ambushed the soldiers and plundered the fort. Montcalm had insisted that special protection should be given the sick and wounded, yet the Indians entered the hospital, scalped smallpox patients, and carried the disease home with them. Perhaps as many as 1,500 soldiers, women, and children were killed or taken prisoner at Fort William Henry. It is not known how many Indians died from smallpox because of the warriors' unauthorized conduct.[122]

In 1757, Indian allies of the French returned to Montreal with prisoners. The governor bought some of the prisoners from the Indians for 2 kegs of brandy each. The drunk Indians "killed one of the prisoners, put him into the kettle, and forced his wretched countrymen [the British] to eat of him." Another witness swore the Indians "compelled mothers to eat the flesh of their children."[123]

In the spring of 1757, General Montcalm and 2,000 Indian allies recruited from the upper Great Lakes region marched toward Lake George, destroying British soldiers along the way. The Indians scalped the dead and ate some of them as well.[124]

Massachusetts soldier Thomas Brown remarkably was captured 4 times by the Indians. He was serving as a scout for British major Robert Rogers's Rangers in 1757 when the group discovered about 50 French and Indian ice sleighs on Lake Champlain. Seven prisoners were taken (including one by Brown), then Rogers's men were attacked by about 400 French and 30 or 40 Indians. Brown was wounded in the first volley. "When I was able, I went to the rear, to the prisoner I had taken on the lake. I knocked him on the head and killed him—we did not want him to give information to the enemy." Brown and 2 other badly wounded soldiers made a small fire, discovered the British had retreated, and decided to surrender to the French. An Indian came toward them; Brown hid himself, and the Indian went to Captain Spikeman, who was so badly wounded he could not resist. The Indian stripped him and scalped him alive. The third soldier, Baker, pulled out his knife to stab himself, but the Indian carried him away. Spikeman saw Brown and asked him to give him a tomahawk so he could end his life, but Brown would not, telling him to pray because he could not live long.

Brown was captured (he had been captured not far from the same spot less than 3 years earlier) and led back to the place where Spikeman had been scalped. His head had been cut off and fixed on a pole. Brown was then told by an interpreter that all the British prisoners were to be hanged the next day because all 7 French prisoners had been killed. "Afterward he was so kind as to tell us this was done only to terrify us." The French decided to take all the prisoners to Montreal. They traveled about 9 miles on frozen Lake Champlain. Brown's hair was cut off, and his clothes were taken away.

Another prisoner resisted having his hair cut. The next night, the Indians made a fire, stripped that prisoner, and tied him to a stake. The Indian women then cut pieces of pine like skewers, stuck them in his flesh, and set them on fire. The Indians began to whoop and dance. They made Brown do the same. The Indians cut the prisoner's cords and made him run back and forth. Finally, in extreme pain, he pitched himself into the flames and died. The next day, they came to an Indian town near Montreal. The women stripped Brown naked, then told him to run to a wigwam. He was beaten with sticks and stones all the way. Brown was given to a French merchant who was returning to his home on the Mississippi. They got to the Ohio River.

At this place the Indians seized one of the prisoners, ripped open his belly with a knife and took one end of his guts and tied it to a tree. Then they whipped the miserable man round and round till he died. They obliged me to dance while they had their sport with the dying man.

Brown escaped, was caught, but finally the merchant released him. The next year he was captured by the Indians again. Finally, after 3 years and 8 months of captivity, "I was able to return in peace to my father's house."[125]

In 1758, British major Putnam was watching a French force less than 2 miles away. The Indians and French attacked, but Putnam refused to retreat. His gun "missed fire, while the muzzle was pressed against the breast of a large and well proportioned Savage." The warrior gave a war whoop, lifted his hatchet, and compelled Putnam to surrender. He tied Putnam to a tree, then returned to the battle. The area of the battle then changed, so that Putnam was in the line of fire from both sides. Many shots hit both the tree and his coat. Archibald Loudon continued the story:

> At one moment, while the battle swerved in favour of the enemy, a young Savage chose an odd way of discovering his humor. He found Putnam bound. He might have dispatched him at a blow. But he loved better to excite the terrors of the prisoner, by hurling a tomahawk at his head, or rather it should seem his object was to see how near he could throw it without touching him;—the weapon struck in the tree a number of times at a hair's breadth distance from the mark.[126]

A French officer then came to the tree and held his gun within a foot of Putnam's chest, but his gun misfired. Putnam boldly told the Frenchman he was a prisoner of war. The Frenchman's response was to hit Putnam on the jaw with his gun. The Indians then returned, untied Putnam, stripped him except for his pants, tied his hands, and led him into the woods. They decided to roast him alive. He was stripped completely, tied to another tree, dry brush and other fuel was piled around him, and it was set afire. A sudden downpour put out the fire. The Indians got it started again, and Putnam was painfully burned. This caused the Indians to yell and dance. A French officer named Molang was attracted by this, rushed to the tree, scattered the fire, untied Putnam, and delivered him to the well-proportioned savage who had originally captured him. The savage laid him on his back and tied him spread-eagled to four saplings. Poles and bushes were put over him, then Indians lay down on all sides to prevent his escape in the night. Putnam was turned over to the French and repatriated. He later became a general.[127]

In 1758, a miller named Richard, his family, and others were at home when 19 Delaware Indians attacked. Promised they would not be killed, the Bard family surrendered. Other captives were then taken. About 1,000 feet from the Bard home, a cousin, Thomas Potter, was killed by the Indians for no apparent reason. A few miles later, without warning, an Indian repeatedly tomahawked a small child in the breast, then scalped the child. The next day Samuel Hunter was tomahawked to death and also scalped.

The day after that, Bard was severely beaten because an Indian who had taken his hat was incensed when it blew off and the Indian had to go down to a stream to get it. Bard escaped that night. Mrs. Bard and 4 children were taken into an Indian town. Their hair was pulled, their faces scratched, and they were beaten. Captive Daniel M'Manimy was also beaten with sticks and tomahawks, tied to a post near a large fire, tortured with burning coals, scalped, and his scalp put on a pole before his face. A red-hot gun barrel was passed over his body, and finally he was pierced repeatedly with a red-hot bayonet. The Indians sang and shouted at him until he died.

Mrs. Bard traveled more than 500 miles. She met a white woman she had known earlier who was married to an Indian and had his child. She said she was told she would be burned unless she married him. She also said that as soon as captive women could speak the Indian language, they would either marry an Indian or be put to death. Although Mrs. Bard was in captivity for more than 2 years, she shrewdly never learned to speak the Indian language. Mr. Bard spent years looking for his wife, finally found her, and ransomed her.[128]

John M'Cullough kept a memorandum concerning the number of people killed and captured by the Indians in different settlements from November 1755 to July 1759. Many of the people are named. Ninety-five were killed, 171 either killed or captured, and 91 captured, a total of 357 deaths or captives.[129]

The British appointed General John Forbes to lead a new assault on Fort Duquesne (now Pittsburgh) in 1758. He sent 800 Scot Highlanders out to scout in September, but they lost one third of their strength to the Indians. In November the British advanced to within a few miles of the fort. They heard a loud explosion, and when they got to it the next day, they found it deserted except for a row of stakes on which were fastened the heads of the Highland troops who had been lost. Each had a Scottish kilt tied beneath it.[130]

The Shawnee captive Mary Jemison passed a Shawnee town on the Ohio River in 1758. She saw the charred heads, arms, and legs of white settlers who had just been burned.[131]

In 1758, Cherokee warriors who had abandoned the campaign of

General Forbes against Fort Duquesne got a few wild horses. Virginians who claimed the horses were theirs attacked the Cherokee, killing 12. The Virginians sold the horses and collected scalp bounties, falsely announcing that the scalps had been taken from hostile Indians. In return, the Cherokee killed 20 to 30 settlers. The southern frontier shortly thereafter was in a full-scale uprising.[132]

The year 1763 was an unusually bad year for Indian atrocities. In that year, a leader emerged to bring the Indian tribes together against the British. He was Pontiac,* an Ottawa chief, a commanding presence, and a great orator. Pontiac favored the French over the British not only because they gave presents to chiefs, but also because the English were settling on Ottawa land while the French were not. The French would also extend credit for supplies, unlike the British.[134] He then commenced Pontiac's Rebellion, which in the spring and summer cost the lives of an estimated 2,000 settlers and more than 400 soldiers.[135] He eventually enlisted many allied tribes: Ottawas, Chippewa, Delaware, Hurons, Illinois, Kickapoos, Miamis, Potawatomis, Seneca, and Shawnee.[136]

In order to retain his leadership, in May Pontiac took a tomahawk and "exhorted his followers to attack every white man outside the fort." His warriors immediately killed a woman and her 2 children a mile from the fort, a retired sergeant, his wife, one of their children, and 2 visiting soldiers. Also in May a war party of Ottawas and Hurons attacked and captured Fort Sandusky, killing 14 of its 15-man garrison as well as the merchants who operated the fort's storehouse.[137]

In June there was a lacrosse game outside Fort Michilimackinac (on the south shore of the Straits of Mackinac) between Chippewa† and Sauk.‡ British major George Etherington and his 35-man garrison were watching it from outside the fort for some reason. Indian women filtered into the fort. A ball went over the stockade, apparently by accident, and the players ran after it through the open gate. Once inside, they dropped their sticks and grabbed guns the women had concealed

---

*Pontiac believed that, united, the Indians could drive the British out of the Great Lakes area. During his rebellion, he unsuccessfully tried to take Fort Detroit, then put it to siege. With the aid of other tribes, he attacked many British forts and settlements. With the coming of winter and upon the advice of a French commander, the rebellion died out.[133]

†Chippewa, or Ojibway, were more widespread than most tribes. The French gave them firearms with which they drove the Sioux westward and the Sacs, Foxes, and Kickapoos southward out of what is now northern Wisconsin. They fought with the British in the Revolution, and when it was over, they ceded much of their land to the United States.[138]

‡The Sauk, or Sac, for much of their history were allied with the Fox tribe. After defeat in the Black Hawk War, the Sauk moved to Kansas, then to Oklahoma.[139]

under their blankets. The captain and a lieutenant were captured immediately. Another lieutenant was wounded and beheaded. The fort was overrun. A young British trader, Alexander Henry, was there and witnessed what happened after his own capture. The dead were scalped and mangled. The dying were shrieking under the knife and tomahawk. The bodies of some soldiers were ripped open, and the Indians "were drinking the blood, scooped up in the hollow of joined hands and quaffed amid shouts of rage and victory."[140]

Later that month Henry heard an unusual noise in the fort's prison. He looked in and saw the bodies of 7 white men being dragged across the floor. He was told that a Chippewa chief had put the 7 to death with his knife to show his approval of the attack. Shortly after that, the Indians took the fattest body, cut off the head, and divided the whole into 5 parts. These were put in 5 kettles over 5 fires. A message came for Henry's Chippewa friend, Wawatam, whom he had known before his captivity, to take part in the feast. Wawatam left the room with his dish and spoon. He returned half an hour later with his dish, which contained a human hand and a large piece of flesh. He told Henry it was the custom among all Indian nations when returning from war to make a war feast from among the slain. He said it inspired courage among the warriors in attack.[141]

While in a canoe with the Chippewa, Henry was offered bread, which was cut with the same blood-covered knives they had used to kill the soldiers. The bread was offered to him and the other prisoners with the comment that they should eat the blood of their countrymen.[142] Henry escaped after many harrowing experiences. He wrote a book about it all 46 years later.[143]

In June, the Iroquois took the garrison at Venango. The commander, Lieutenant Gordon, was forced to write down a dictated list of grievances addressed to the king of England. After he had finished the document, he was tortured for 3 days, culminating in the Seneca roasting him to death.[144]

The fort at Erie, Pennsylvania, agreed to surrender if the garrison was allowed to go to Fort Pitt. An agreement to that effect was signed by the Indians, who then divided the garrison among themselves as prisoners "for later amusement."[145]

The same month the Delaware, Mingos, and Shawnee turned to Fort Pitt. The fort was commanded by a Swiss soldier of fortune, Captain Simeon Ecuyer. He sent the Indian delegation, which had demanded his surrender, away with presents—blankets and handkerchiefs from the smallpox hospital. Soon there was a smallpox epidemic among the 3 tribes which lasted into the next year and which removed them from full-time participation in the war. British governor-general of North America Jeffrey Amherst had encouraged this tactic in a letter to Ecuyer.[146] Amherst also wrote to his subordinate Lieutenant Colonel Henry Boquet the same month, stating, "I need only Add, that I Wish to Hear of no prisoners, should any of the Villains be met with in Arms."[147]

On July 4 at the siege of Fort Detroit, Chippewa or Ojibway chief Wasson insisted that Pontiac turn over Captain Donald Campbell to him because Wasson's nephew had been killed by the British that day. Pontiac did. Wasson immediately scalped and killed Campbell, then threw his body in the water so that it would float past the defenders of the fort.[148]

On August 1, Captain James Dalyell led 247 men on a sortie. They were met by Pontiac with 400 Ottawa and Chippewa warriors. The French had told Pontiac about the sortie the night before. Nineteen British were killed, including Captain Dalyell. Pontiac's men recovered his body, took it back to their village, cut out his heart, wiped their prisoners' faces with it, hacked off his head, and mounted it on a pole.[149]

In December a group of 75 Presbyterians from Paxton, Pennsylvania, unhappy because of the failure of the colony's Quaker-dominated assembly to take more aggressive action against Indians, attacked some Christian Indians and murdered and scalped 3 men, 2 women, and a boy. The Paxton Boys, as they were called, claimed the attack was made because one of the Indians had melted down a stolen pewter spoon. Some Indians who had been away were given sanctuary by settlers in the Lancaster jail. Governor John Penn, the son of William Penn, issued a proclamation condemning the raid and prohibiting further violence.

Thirteen days after the first raid, the Paxton Boys broke into the jail and killed the remaining 14 Indians, including all the children. Benjamin Franklin wrote a pamphlet calling the Paxton Boys "Christian white savages." He added that the Indians "would have been safe in any part of the known world, except in [this] very neighborhood." Two months later, the Paxton Boys went to Philadelphia to kill the city's Indians. The peaceful Quakers defended the Indians. A group headed by Franklin met with the Paxton Boys and worked out a settlement. The Paxton Boys agreed to call off the attack in return for bounties for scalps of Indians from warring tribes.[150]

An anonymous narrator told this story of his close encounter with death sometime in 1763. Five of his neighbors were killed by Indians. He literally had to run for his life to escape them. Later he and 100 soldiers came upon 3 Indians who were about to fire on them, but surrendered instead. He asked another soldier what should be done with them. The soldier replied that they should be delivered to the commander. He reminded the other soldier about the deaths of the 5 neighbors and how he had had to run for his life. He told the soldier, "I have declared revenge on the first Indian that I saw, and the opportunity now offers." He got 5 soldiers to agree to his plan. The Indians were told to walk ahead of the soldiers, who then shot them from behind. Two were killed and the third wounded. The third was then scalped. He got up, however, and made his escape.[151]

Near the close of 1763, Chief Pontiac invited several prominent French settlers to a celebration feast. When it was over, he asked one of the guests how he liked the very good young beef. Pontiac said, " 'Come here, I will show you what you have eaten.' Whereupon he opened a sack lying on the ground behind him and displayed the bloody head of a British soldier, which he held up by the hair and added, with a grin, 'There is the young beef.' "[152]

Benjamin Franklin wrote that in 1764, a soldier named David Owens, who had deserted to the Indians in the Seven Years' War (the French and Indian War), returned, accompanied by a white boy who had been an Indian captive. They came upon a party of 9 Indians:

> In the Night Owens made the White Boy get up from among the Indians and go to the other side of the Fire; and then taking up the Indian's [sic] Guns, he [Owens] shot two of the men immediately, and with his hatchet dispatch'd another Man together with the Women and Children. Two Men only made their Escape. Owens scalp'd the 5 grown persons.[153]

Five years later, in 1769, Pontiac was visiting a trading post in Cahokia, Illinois, when he was struck on the head and murdered by an Illinois Indian, Black Dog, believed to be in the pay of the British.[154] The Ottawas, Chippewa, Potawatomis, Sac, Foxes, and Kickapoos united against the Illinois as a result of Pontiac's murder and defeated them, reducing the number of the tribe from 1,800 to 150. The few survivors took refuge at the French settlement of Kaskaskia. Later they sold their land and went to Kansas. Earlier, in the 1680s, the Illinois Indians had stopped the long westward expansion of the Iroquois when the Iroquois failed to take Fort St. Louis on the Illinois River.[155]

Atrocities During the Eras of the British Wars: The Revolutionary War and the War of 1812

The American colonists were as loyal to King George III* as were the British back home when the French were defeated in the French and Indian War. Britain was soon a global power, but America, "while civilizing rapidly, was still largely a wild and untamed place."[2] But the British in the motherland didn't understand the problems the colonists faced dealing with the Indians. George Grenville became prime minister in 1763. It was important to him that the colonists profit Britain, but they did not.[3]

Britain might have overlooked the commercial mediocrity of the colonies, but it could not overlook their "brazen and repeated flouting of British laws."[4] Parliament passed act after act that many of the colonists deemed oppressive, and many ignored them—the Molasses Act, the Navigation Acts, the Sugar Act, and the Stamp Act.[5]

Then there was violence. On the same day that the chancellor of the exchequer, Lord North, announced there would be no new taxes from London, a mob of radical colonists, unaware of North's announcement,

---

*King George assumed the throne in 1760 at age 22. The king, who was not bright, "could neither understand the American colonies nor grasp the need to try; he knew only that he wanted to keep them subject to Britain."[1]

attacked the Boston customs house. Snowballs were thrown at the British guards, who fired and killed 5 and wounded several more in what became known as the Boston Massacre.

North came up with a plan to tax tea. In protest, John Hancock and Sam Adams formed a group poorly disguised as Mohawk Indians to board the tea ships on December 16, 1773. They dumped 342 chests of tea owned by the East India Company in the harbor. The event was ever after known as the Boston Tea Party. North was furious, and Parliament passed the Boston Port Act, which closed the port until the colony paid Britain for the cost of the tea. (The bill was never paid.) Then Parliament passed the Massachusetts Government Act (closing the Massachusetts legislature), a new Quartering Act, the Administration of Justice Act, and acts favorable to Canada, including extending its boundaries into the Ohio Valley. The colonists called these the Intolerable Acts.[6]

Young plantation owner Thomas Jefferson published his *Summary View of the Rights of British America,* which denied Parliament's right to legislate for the colonies because "the God who gave us life, gave us liberty at the same time." On the other hand, Benjamin Franklin and John Dickinson, principal draftsman of the Articles of Confederation, urged caution.[7]

The British governor of Massachusetts, General Thomas Gage, was ordered to strike a blow at the rebels. He found out where they were and sent troops to seize them and then destroy their supply facility at Concord, Massachusetts. Boston silversmith Paul Revere set out on horseback to warn everyone the British were coming. The British arrived in Lexington, Massachusetts, on April 19, 1775, and were met by 70 armed men, some of them "Minutemen," local militia formed to fight on a minute's notice. Some unknown person fired a shot; 8 Minutemen were killed and 10 wounded. The British marched on to Concord and destroyed the few colonist supplies there. On their way back to Boston, however, local farmers in the Lexington area organized into a fighting unit and fired on the British from every house, barn, and tree. Casualties were 93 colonists and 273 British soldiers.[8] The colonists were colonists no more. They were revolutionaries and free men—if the Revolution could be won.

A prophetic statement was made by a British sympathizer, a Tory, as he watched a Minuteman go by his window on the way to Lexington. He said, "There goes a man who will fight you in blood up to his knees."[9] If the Minutemen were willing to fight part of the army of the world's greatest power, they and their descendants surely would fight the less powerful Indian tribes if necessary.

In 1777 British general John Burgoyne (who was also a playwright) drove down the Hudson Valley with his army of about 9,000 from Canada in an attempt to isolate New England from the rest of the colonies. Indians, probably one of the Algonquin family of tribes, were part of his command. Two of those Indians, one a Wyandot named Panther, were escorting an American named Jane McCrea, who was on her way to marry one of Burgoyne's officers, David Jones. Her long hair may have made her a target.[10] The Indians tomahawked her to death, stripped off her clothing, scalped her, and perhaps raped her. The Indians then took her scalp with that of an American officer back to camp, where they had a victory dance. Her body was found later. Word spread quickly through the British army.[11] The Americans were horrified. American general Horatio Gates damned Burgoyne for hiring "the savages of America to scalp Europeans and the descendants of Europeans, nay more, that he should pay a price for each scalp so barbarously taken."[12]

General Washington heard about the incident and wrote urging the Massachusetts and Connecticut militias to "repel an enemy from your borders, who, not content with hiring mercenaries to lay waste your country, have now brought savages, with the avowed and expressed intention of adding murder to desolation."[13] A record number of militia turned out and eventually defeated Burgoyne. Meanwhile, Burgoyne faced a dilemma. If he executed the Indians, his Indian allies might be turned into enemies. If he took no action, he would seem to condone the murder. He ordered Panther shot, but his superior argued that the Indians would desert unless Panther was turned loose. Burgoyne then pardoned the Indians and gave them a stern lecture. They resented this. A few days later, a large number of them deserted anyway.[14] American soldiers began silently killing British sentries, as well as killing or scalping Indians and pinning notes on the bodies reading "For Jane McCrea."[15]

The war was dragging on for the British, and they were frustrated. At the beginning they had employed Indians primarily for military ends. Gradually, they started using them to punish and frighten the Americans. Englishman William Tryon, who was the royal governor of North Carolina, then, later, governor of New York, urged the British ministry to "loose the savages against the miserable Rebels in order to impose a reign of terror on the frontiers."[16] (Governor Tryon favored terror in other directions as well. He masterminded an unsuccessful assassination attempt on the life of General Washington.)[17] Tryon's recommendation became British policy. When Prime Minister North tried to defend it in Parliament, Lord Chatham declared he was astonished to hear such principles confessed! . . . Principles equally un-constitutional, inhuman, and unchristian! . . . What! to attribute the sacred sanction of God and nature to the massacres of the Indian scalping knife? To the cannibal savage, torturing, murdering, roasting and eating; literally, my lords, *eating* the mangled victims of his bar-barous battles! Such horrible notions shock every precept of religion, divine or natural, and every generous feeling of humanity. . . . They shock me as a lover of honorable war, and a detester of murderous bar-barity. . . . We turn loose these savage hell-hounds against our brethren and countrymen in America, of the same language, laws, liberty and religion, endeared to us by every tie that should sanctify humanity.[18]

Unquestionably, the object of Indian raids was to devastate the white enemy, burn his house, kill his livestock, scatter his possessions, scalp his women, carry off his children, and if possible torture him to death.[19]

Henry Knox, the first secretary of war, reported to Congress in 1787 that "the deep rooted prejudices, and malignity of heart, and conduct reciprocally entertained and practiced on all occasions by the Whites and Savages will ever prevent their being good neighbors."[20] Smith noted that when the British departed after the Revolution, they left be-hind a legacy of bitterness that could never be alleviated. "Settler and savage [were] caught in a terrible ritual of violence."[21]

Not all the atrocities involved actual physical pain or death—a threat would do. In 1777, Fort Schuyler (old Fort Stanwix) in New York, de-fended by 750 Americans, was surrounded by 1,800 British soldiers and 600 Indians under the command of Colonel John Butler and Mohawk chief Joseph Brant. The British obtained a parley. Colonel Barry St. Leger threatened that if the fort did not surrender, the Indians could not be restrained and would destroy the American men, women, and chil-dren. The American commander, Lieutenant Colonel Marinus Willett, made this reply to Colonel John Butler, the British officer carrying the St. Leger message:

Do I understand you, Sir? I think you say, that you come from a British colonel . . . and by your uniform, you appear to be an officer in the British service. You have made a long speech on the occasion of your visit, which, stript of all its superfluities, amounts to this, that you come from a British colonel, to the commandant of this garrison, to tell him, that if he does not deliver up the garrison into the hands of your Colonel, he will send his Indians to murder our women and chil-dren. You will please to reflect, sir, that their blood will be on your head, not on ours. We are doing our duty; this garrison is committed to our charge, and we will take care of it. After you get out of it, you may turn around and look at its outside, but never expect to come in again, unless you come as a prisoner. I consider the message you have brought, a degrading one for a British officer to send, and by no means reputable for a British officer to carry. For my own part, I declare, before I would consent to deliver this garrison to such a murdering set as your army, by your account consists of, I would suffer my body to be filled with splinters, and set on fire, as you know has at times been practiced, by such hordes of women and children killers, as belong to your army.[22]

The British threat of mass murder proved counterproductive. Willett went through enemy lines for help. A plan was worked out "to make such an exaggerated report of General [Benedict] Arnold's force [which had relieved the fort] as to alarm them and put them to flight." The plan worked: 500 or 600 Indians fled, and the British then gave up the siege "in the greatest hurry and confusion."[23]

Pennsylvania and New York bore the brunt of Indian raids. The worst of these attacks occurred in 1778 at Wyoming Valley, Pennsylvania, which is near Wilkes-Barre. It was designed to wreak vengeance and furnish plunder. A force of 1,200 British and Indians went through western Pennsylvania murdering and looting. Crèvecoeur, who lived near these towns, reported, "Many families were locked up in their houses and consumed with the furniture. Dreadful scenes were transacted which I know not how to retrace."[24] Every house in Wilkes-Barre was destroyed.[25]

The Indians captured 2 white men and a black man at a mill near Wyoming Valley, took them back to the Indian camp, and murdered them. The fort at Wyoming Valley was then surrounded in 1778. Sir John Butler, the British commander, set fire to a nearby fort to give the impression he was retreating; the Americans were deceived and followed. They were ambushed and slaughtered. Battle casualties were mutilated, scalped, and burned. An American soldier, Captain Bedlock, was taken prisoner. He was stripped naked, his body was stuck full of splinters of pine knots, then more pine knots were piled around him. These were set on fire. His 2 companions, Captains Ranson and Durgee, were thrown alive into the flames and held down with pitchforks.[26] Captives were tortured and burned.[27] Butler claimed his men had taken 227 scalps.[28] The Indians sent into the fort the bloody scalps of 196 people.[29] In addition, many settlers who fled the attack perished from hunger and exhaustion in the Pocono Great Swamp.[30] The Iroquois killed 360 settlers in a single day.[31] The press reported these atrocities, and "the Wyoming Valley Massacre became a byword for Tory and Indian brutality."[32]

During Indian attacks, the courage of settler women was displayed time and time again. In 1778, several families were living in the Bozarth house for safety. One of the children ran in from play to report that there were Indians outside. A man went to the window and was shot by the Indians. An Indian broke into the house and started fighting with a second man, who had no weapon. He called to Mrs. Bozarth for a knife. She did not have one. She took an ax and killed the Indian with one blow to the head. A second Indian came in and shot the man with no weapon. Mrs. Bozarth hit this Indian with the ax several times until his intestines appeared. More Indians, who had been killing children outside, came toward the house. When one stuck his head in the door, Mrs. Bozarth cut it in two with the ax. The man with no weapon survived his wound. She and he barricaded the house (with the dead inside) for protection against the besieging Indians until help arrived.[33]

British lieutenant colonel Henry Hamilton was lieutenant governor of Detroit. During the Revolution, he supplied the Shawnee, Delaware, and Miamis with guns, ammunition, and supplies and offered a bounty on white scalps. He was known among the settlers as the Hair Buyer. He reported that during 1778 the Indians in his district had brought in 110 scalps.[34]

Colonel John Smith of Pennsylvania and his men were fighting the Indians. His men took 4 scalps. In the fight, Captain John Hinkston pursued an Indian out of sight. He later returned with a scalp, stating he had tomahawked the Indian.[35]

Trouble continued in New York. Mohawk chief Joseph Brant with Mohawk and Seneca Indians attacked Cherry Valley, New York, in 1778 with a force of about 700. Friendly Indians had warned the commander of the fort there, Colonel Ichabod Alden from Massachusetts, that the Indians were going to attack the fort. The settlers asked Alden's permission to move into the fort or at least store their most important possessions there. Alden refused on the ground that the soldiers would be tempted to steal the settlers' goods. The officers also stayed outside the fort, for reasons unknown.

After 4 or 5 hours when Brant was still unable to take the fort, the Indians started burning and pillaging nearby settlements. The occupants of 6 farmhouses (who were mostly women and children) were killed. In one house alone the Indians massacred the owner, his wife, his mother, brother, sister, 3 sons, a daughter, and the soldiers billeted there,[36] more than 30 people.[37] The Seneca and some of the Mohawk scalped, dismembered, and indulged in ritual cannibalism. British lieutenant Rolf Hare stabbed Sarah Dunlop and saw a halfbreed called William of Canajoharie eat her flesh.[38]

Moses Van Campen was an American sergeant who rose to the rank of major helping to defend the frontier in Pennsylvania for 6 years except for the 2 years he was held captive by the Indians. He was with General Sullivan on his expedition against the Iroquois. In 1778 he and his father were building a fort with his brother and 2 others when the Indians attacked. His father was struck through by a spear and was scalped. His brother was tomahawked, scalped, and thrown into the fire before the sergeant's eyes. His uncle had been killed by the same Indians that morning and his cousin taken prisoner. He was captured, but later the prisoners killed or drove off their captors. Van Campen then turned his attention to scalping the Indians. He strung their scalps on his belt for safekeeping with the scalps of his father, brother, and the others.

He got to Fort Jenkins and was told his mother was inside. He took off the belt of scalps and gave them to an officer to keep before going in to see his mother. The next day he went to Sunbury, Pennsylvania, where his scalps were exhibited, the cannons were fired, and he was given an ensign's commission. Two years later, he was a lieutenant. A report came that about 300 Sinnemahoning Indians were preparing to attack the frontier. His commanding officer sent Van Campen and 4 others to investigate. They found a camp of an unknown number of Indians at night and decided to attack. The militia got among the Indians undetected, then started firing and tomahawking. The Indians fled. "We were masters of the ground and all their plunder, and took several scalps." They learned there were 25 or 30 Indians in the camp who had killed and scalped 2 or 3 families. Several scalps were found in their camp.[39]

Mohawk Joseph Brant then attacked the town of Minisink, less than 50 miles from West Point, in the Mohawk Valley, in 1779. The fort, the mill, and 12 houses were burned, some with sleeping people in them. A few were killed.[40]

The commander of the local militia at Goshen, 12 miles away from Minisink, was Colonel Dr. Tustin. He asked his men to meet the next day at Minisink. At a council of war, and over the objections of Tustin, it was decided to pursue the dangerous Brant. Dr. Tustin set up a field hospital for the wounded; the Indians scalped him and 17 of his patients. About 170 militia had started the battle, but only 30 returned to their homes. (There was an amusing sidelight. During the battle, Major Wood inadvertently made a Masonic sign. Brant, who had been to England, was a Mason. Wood was captured, Brant interrogated him, learned he was not a Mason, and was furious because he thought he had been tricked. He nevertheless spared Wood's life. When he was exchanged, Wood immediately joined the lodge.)[41]

In 1779, 2 Mohawk captured 16-year-old twin sisters Maria and Christina Manheim from their home in Pennsylvania. Their band had taken 23 settlers, then burned their houses. The 2 who had captured the twins couldn't agree whose property they were, so the chiefs decided the girls should be destroyed. The Indians sharpened a supply of pine splinters about 5 inches long, then dipped the blunt ends in turpentine. The twins were stripped naked, tied to a sapling with their hands high above them, then had more than 600 splinters stuck in their bodies from their knees to their shoulders. Each of the splinters was set on fire. It was almost 3 hours before they died. By that time they had lost "almost every resemblance of the human form."[42]

The same year, Indians captured 2 girls in Buffalo Valley, Pennsylvania. The Indians saw some reapers from the top of a mountain and left the girls with one Indian guard while the reapers were attacked. The guard lay down to rest. It began raining. One of the girls covered the Indian with leaves on the pretense of protecting him from the rain. When he couldn't see, she killed him with an ax. The girls then ran toward the reapers, but the Indians saw them, and one of the girls was killed.[43]

Because of his fear of Indians, farmer David Morgan and his family fled to a nearby fort close to Westmoreland, Pennsylvania, in 1779. Morgan was over 60 and infirm. He saw 2 Indians approaching some of his younger children, who were at work on the farm. He yelled a warning to the children, which caused the Indians to come toward him. He ran, but the Indians were gaining, so he turned, fired his rifle, and killed one of them. The other threw his tomahawk just as Morgan swung his single-shot rifle at the Indian. The tomahawk cut off his little finger and almost cut off the one next to it. The rifle broke off in the swing.

The Indian got on top of Morgan and tried to reach his knife, but an apron he had tied to his body interfered. Morgan got one of the Indian's fingers in his mouth "and deprived him of the use of that hand, by holding it, and disconcerted him considerably by chewing it." The Indian finally got his knife into the hand Morgan had in his mouth, but Morgan twisted it so that it badly cut the Indian's hand. Morgan wrestled the Indian's knife away from him and stabbed him in the belly. People came from the fort and found the second Indian still alive, hiding in a fallen tree. Rather strangely, the Indian asked the people from the fort how they were. They skinned both Indians "and they have made drum heads from their skins."[44]

George Rogers Clark was a surveyor in Kentucky before he became a captain in the Virginia militia. With the support of Virginia governor Patrick Henry, he mounted a military expedition against pro-British Indians in Illinois and Indiana. In 1779, Lieutenant Colonel Clark, with 350 Virginia militiamen, was trying to get Lieutenant Colonel Henry Hamilton to surrender the fort at Vincennes, Indiana, along with its 175 soldiers and 60 Indian warriors. By some psychological maneuvering, Clark persuaded Hamilton that he faced a greater force than he actually did. Clark attacked the fort, Hamilton asked for a cease-fire, the 2 met, and Hamilton asked for time to talk with his officers. Clark gave him an hour. During that time, his men captured 4 Indians, who were taken to a place in view of the fort, where Clark's men tomahawked them to death. This had an unsettling effect on the Indians in the fort. Hamilton surrendered. Clark was made a brigadier general the next year.[45]

General Washington ordered General John Sullivan* to invade Iroquois territory after the effective British-Iroquois raids on the settlers. There is some disagreement concerning what Washington specifically told Sullivan to do. Carl Waldman reported that Sullivan's instructions were that Iroquois country should not "be merely overrun but destroyed."[47] This might imply that no prisoners were to be taken. Page Smith, who has written more extensively about the Revolution than Waldman, said Washington instructed Sullivan that there was to be "the total destruction and devastation" of the Iroquois settlements and "the capture of as many prisoners of every age and sex as possible."[48] There is no factual basis for asserting, as some Indian advocates have done, that Washington ever favored extermination of all Indians at any time or place.

In 1779, a force of about 2,500 men under Sullivan attacked the Iroquois in Pennsylvania and New York. Towns and crops were destroyed. Even though they suffered few casualties, the Indians' cultural base in New York was destroyed.[49] Two Indians who had been killed were skinned to make boot tops.[50] James Wilson, in *The Earth Shall Weep,* asserted that during the Sullivan campaign Colonel Daniel Brodhead and his troops massacred hundreds of Iroquois women and children in a

---

*General Sullivan had practiced law in New Hampshire and was a delegate to the First Continental Congress. As a major general, he took part in Washington's victories at Trenton and Princeton, New Jersey. After the war, he was a governor, congressman, and federal judge.[46]

"squaw campaign."[51] (No other reference to a massacre of 200 or more Iroquois women and children has been found to confirm this assertion, and the Wilson book has no source notes.)

As Sullivan invaded Iroquois country in 1779, his advance guard under Lieutenant Thomas Boyd was ambushed. Pro-American Oneida chief Hanyerry was killed, his body hewn to pieces, and his scalped head impaled on a branch. Boyd himself was wounded and captured by the Indians. He was whipped, his fingernails pulled out one at a time, his nose and tongue cut off, an eye gouged out, his genital organs cut off, and his body pierced with spears in several places. He was then skinned alive and his head cut off. Sullivan's men found the body. General Sullivan wrote that there had been other tortures "which decency will not permit me to mention."[52]

That same year American colonel Archibald Lochry and 100 men were on their way down the Ohio River to join George Rogers Clark. Mohawk chief Joseph Brant captured part of an advance party and learned about Lochry's movement, which allowed him to ambush them. Lochry and several others were captured and tortured to death.[53] (For some reason, Wilson contended that "Joseph Brant . . . scrupulously avoid[ed] unnecessary killing."[54] This cannot be reconciled with the Cherry Valley, the Minisink, the Goshen, or the Lochry atrocities.[55])

In 1779, General Sullivan ordered Major Henry Dearborn* and others to destroy Cayuga towns. Dearborn burned 6 towns and took a crippled Indian boy and 3 women prisoner. The officer in charge ordered that a house be left to shelter them. As the troops were moving out, some of the soldiers, unobserved, made the door secure, then set the house and its inhabitants on fire.[57]

Quaker Benjamin Gilbert and his family lived on a farm in Pennsylvania. In 1780, 11 Indians appeared who had abandoned their territory on the approach of Sullivan's army. Two were Mohawk, 3 Cayuga, 1 was Delaware, and 5 were Seneca. They took 12 captives at the farm, including the children, then went to an adjoining farm, where 3 more were captured. After all the buildings were burned, the group headed for Montreal. They came to a place where 4 Indians had been killed a few days earlier. They told the settlers that they too would be killed and scalped that night. One captive was so terrified he managed to escape. The others were treated harshly after the escape. The Mohawk leader

---

*Dearborn was a physician from New Hampshire. He fought in the Battle of Bunker Hill in 1775 and was later captured by the British. After his release, he was promoted to major, fought at Ticonderoga and Saratoga, and wintered with Washington at Valley Forge.[56]

threw the Gilbert boy down and tried to strike him with his tomahawk, but his mother put her head on her son's forehead, pleaded with the Indian, and prevented it. He was so enraged, however, that he tied both of them to a tree by their necks.

As was the custom, the captives were beaten with clubs and stones as they entered Indian towns. They reached the St. Lawrence and were put on a boat in a steady rain. A shelter was made for father Gilbert, who was 69 and ill, to make him more comfortable. Then he was moved inside, but he died. His widow feared the French who operated the boat would throw the body overboard, and she appealed to British officers, who were in a following boat. They arranged for the boat to stop at a garrison the next morning, where a son was permitted to go to the commandant, get a coffin, and bury Mr. Gilbert under an oak tree near the fort.[58]

Ten male settlers from the Virginia and Kentucky border areas were captured by the Wyandots in 1781. One was 18-year-old Henry Baker. They were all forced to run the gauntlet. They were then taken to the Wyandot council house and condemned to be burned at the stake, one each day. Baker was to be last. When it was Baker's turn, the Indians came to get him and took him to the charred stake. At the last moment, the renegade Simon Girty saved his life.[59]

Colonel Brodhead was leading an expedition toward the Delaware town of Coshocton in 1781 when his scouts discovered Indians. They fired at them, but 2 escaped to warn the others. The troops ran into a heavy rain and managed to take Coshocton without firing a shot. They herded the occupants together, killed 15 braves with spears and tomahawks, then scalped them.[60]

The next morning, the Delaware chief asked to talk to Brodhead from the other side of the river. Brodhead told him to speak. The chief said, "Peace." Brodhead wanted some chiefs to come over, but the chief said he feared one would be killed. Brodhead assured him that would not happen. One of the chiefs then crossed the river in a canoe and started talking with Brodhead. But just as the Delaware had feared, the chief was killed from behind by a tomahawk wielded by a civilian traveling with the troops. "That ended the peace parley." Brodhead began the march back to Fort Pitt. The militiamen found the prisoners they had taken to be a nuisance and began murdering them.[61]

In 1782, Indians murdered John Fink in Ohio, took Mrs. Robert Wallace and her 3 children captive, and scalped the mother and the infant child. They also captured John Carpenter (who claimed 2 of his captors were Moravians), wounded, scalped, and mutilated William

White within sight of the fort, and captured Timothy Dorman and his wife.[62]

Moses Van Campen was captured a second time in 1782 when his unit of 20 or 25 men was attacked by 85 Indians. The chief warrior came before the captives. The 5 Indians killed in the skirmish were laid nearby. The chief warrior consulted the Great Spirit about whether to kill the prisoners immediately or spare their lives. Van Campen remembered the Indians he had killed recently "and thought that if I was discovered to be the person responsible, my case would be a hard one." The chief warrior then announced that he "came to the conclusion that there had been blood enough shed; as to the men they had lost, it was the fate of war, and we must be taken and adopted into the families of those whom we had killed." This spirit of generosity was not found very often in this war.

Van Campen then had to run the gauntlet. Young Indians with whips came after him. Two young Indian women came up with whips. He knocked them down and saw they had beautiful yellow underdresses. He was then adopted by Colonel John Butler, the British commander of the Wyoming Valley Massacre, whose son, Captain John Butler, had been killed by the Americans. In that capacity, he was confined to a private room but not put under guard. He was offered a British commission equal to his own, but he refused. Later, he was taken to a military prison in Montreal, where he found 40 or 50 other officers. On the Fourth of July, they managed to get some brandy and "we had a high time." The British found this very offensive. Two months later, he was paroled to return home.[63]

In response to attacks on American settlers by Delaware and other tribes in 1782, a force of 300 Pennsylvania Continental militia under Colonel David Williamson attacked the peaceful Moravian mission at Gnadenhutten, Ohio. Williamson told the Indians that they would be put to death because of the conduct of the Delaware.[64] Almost all of the 90 Delaware Christian Indians at Gnadenhutten were killed, including women and children.[65] It is reported that one of the militia, Charles Builderback, killed 14 Indians with a cooper's mallet.[66]

Williamson got the wrong Indians. British captain Matthew Elliott, who was in charge of Detroit in 1781, had destroyed all the possessions of the Christian Indians, then ordered them to leave. Because of a harsh winter and famine, they obtained British permission to move temporarily back to their original towns. They arrived at Gnadenhutten just after the Mohawk and Delaware had conducted unusually brutal raids in the area. The Pennsylvania legislature condemned the massacre, but did not reprimand Williamson in any way.[67]

The massacre inevitably led to acts of vengeance by the Delaware. Colonel William Crawford, a friend of General Washington, was sent with some soldiers to try to destroy Moravian, Delaware, and Wyandot towns along the Upper Sandusky River.[68] Crawford requested Dr. John Knight, who related these events, to go along as surgeon. Knight was a Virginian who served in the Revolution and learned medicine while in the army.[69] There were 465 men when they started out, but some soon returned home when they lost their horses. After some skirmishes during which both sides took scalps, Colonel Crawford, Dr. Knight, and some others were captured by the Delaware. Delaware chief Pipe painted the faces of all the captives black. Five of them were seated together some distance from Dr. Knight. A number of adult females and boys fell on these 5 and tomahawked them.[70]

"There was a certain John M'Kinley amongst the captives, formerly an officer in the 13th Virginia regiment, whose head an old squaw cut off, and the Indians kicked it about upon the ground. . . . Almost every Indian we met struck us either with sticks or their fists."[71] Dr. Knight described in detail what happened next:

When we were come to the fire the colonel [Colonel Crawford] was stripped naked, ordered to sit down by the fire, and then they beat him with sticks and their fists. Presently after I was treated in the same manner. They then tied a rope to the foot of a post about fifteen feet high, bound the colonel's hands behind his back and fastened the rope to the ligature between his wrists. The rope was long enough either for him to sit down or walk around the post once or twice and return the same way. The colonel then called to [Simon] Girty and asked if they intended to burn him?—Girty answered, yes. The colonel said he would take it all patiently. Upon this Captain Pipe, a Delaware chief, made a speech to the Indians, viz: about thirty or forty men, sixty or seventy squaws and boys.

When the speech was finished they all yelled a hideous and hearty assent to what had been said. The Indian men then took up their guns and shot powder into the colonel's body, from his feet as far up as his neck. I think not less than seventy loads were discharged upon his naked body. Then they crowded about him, and to the best of my observation, cut off his ears; when the throng had dispersed a little I saw the blood running from both sides of his head in consequence thereof.

The fire was about six or seven yards from the post to which the colonel was tied; it was made of small hickory poles, burnt quite through in the middle, each end of the poles remaining about six feet in length. Three or four Indians by turns would take up, individually, one of these burning pieces of wood and apply it to his naked body, already burned black with powder. These tormentors presented themselves on every side of him, so that whichever way he ran round the post they met him with the burning faggots and poles. Some of the squaws took broad boards, upon which they would carry a quantity of burning coals and hot embers and throw on him, so that in a short time he had nothing but coals of fire and hot ashes to walk upon.

In the midst of these extreme tortures, he called to Simon Girty and begged of him to shoot him; but Girty making no answer he called to him again. Girty then, by way of derision, told the colonel that he had no gun, at the same time turning about to an Indian who was behind him, laughed heartily, and by all his gestures seemed delighted at the horrid scene. . . .

Colonel Crawford at this point of his sufferings, besought the Almighty to have mercy on his soul, spoke very low, and bore his torments with the most manly fortitude. He continued in all the extremities of pain for an hour and three quarters, or two hours longer, as near as I can judge, when at last, being almost exhausted, he lay down on his belly; they then scalped him and repeatedly threw the scalp in my face, telling me "that was my great captain."—An old squaw (whose appearance every way answered the ideas people entertain of the devil) got a board, took a parcel of coals and ashes and laid them on his back and head, after he had been scalped; he then raised himself upon his feet and began to walk round the post; they next put a burning stick to him as usual, but he seemed more insensible of pain than before.

The Indian fellow who had me in charge, now took me away to captain Pipe's house, about three-quarters of a mile from the place of the colonel's execution. I was bound all night, and thus prevented from seeing the last of the horrid spectacle. Next morning, being June 12th, the Indian untied me, painted me black, and we set off for Shawanese town. . . . We soon came to the spot where the colonel had been burnt, as it was partly on our way; I saw his bones laying amongst the remains of the fire, almost burnt to ashes; I suppose after he was dead they had his body on the fire.

The Indian told me that was my Big Captain, and gave me the scalp halloo.[72]

Dr. Knight escaped from his captor the next day, before he could be delivered to Shawanese town for his execution.[73] (Washington wrote that "I learned the melancholy tidings of Colonel Crawford's death. . . .

The manner of his death was shocking to me.")[74] After his escape, Dr. Knight was discharged from service, married Crawford's niece, and raised a large family.[75]

On a Sunday in 1782, Reverend John Corly and his family were walking to his church when they were attacked by Indians. His wife was carrying a baby being breastfed. The baby was killed and scalped. His wife was struck, but did not fall, so an Indian shot her through the body and scalped her. They sank the hatchet into the brains of his 6-year-old son and killed him. Another daughter besides the baby was killed and scalped. One daughter hid in a hollow tree and came out when she thought the Indians were gone. They were not. They knocked her down and scalped her, but she survived. A final daughter was also scalped, "on whose head they did not leave more than an inch round, either of flesh or skin, besides taking a piece out of her skull." She also survived. The Reverend Corly fainted. He was rescued by a friend.[76]

John Slover was captured by the Miami Indians before 1773 when he was 8, after his father and 2 little sisters had been killed. He was a captive of the Miamis for 6 years. Then Slover was sold to a Delaware and finally to a Shawnee, with whom he lived another 6 years.[77]

During this time, another prisoner was taken and stripped and blackened with coal and water, the Indian sign that he was marked for death. He was made to run the gauntlet, and while he was doing this he was beaten and cut with tomahawks, and guns fired loads of powder into his body. Blood gushed from a wound in his shoulder. He got to the council house, where he thought he was safe. When he realized he was not safe there, he tried to grab a tomahawk, but was too weak. For a long time after that he was beaten, then finally killed.[78]

That evening a third prisoner was cut into pieces and his limbs and head put on poles. Slover also saw 3 other bodies in the same condition. He was told they had been killed the same way. These 3 bodies were dragged out of town, given to the dogs, and their limbs and heads stuck on poles.[79]

Alexander McKee,* an agent of the British Indian Department who had led Indians in many attacks against Americans, was present at most of the council meetings known to Slover. The animosity of tribes toward the settlers was shown at these council meetings, which were attended

---

*McKee was the son of an Irish trader and a woman thought to have been white raised by the Shawnee. He married a Shawnee woman. When the Revolution began, because McKee was a Tory, he and Simon Girty fled to Detroit. He became a British captain, and his troops, among other campaigns, took Rundle's Station in Kentucky, killing about 200 men, women, and children.[80]

by several tribes—the Mingo, Ottawa, Chippewa, Wyandot, Delaware, Shawnee, Munsee, and some Cherokee—and which lasted 15 days. All warriors could attend, but only chiefs could speak. On the next to the last day of the council, a speech sent from the British commander at Detroit was read. The commander said in part, "When any of our people fall into the hands of the Rebels, they show no mercy—why then should you take any prisoners? My children, take no more prisoners of any sort—man, woman, or child." Two days later, Indians from every nation in the area determined to take no more captives of any kind. It was decided that if an American child only 3 inches long should be found, it would be shown no mercy. At the end of the council, all tribes present agreed that if any nation not present did take prisoners, the nations present would rise against them and put the prisoners to death.[81]

About the time of the meetings, 12 men were brought in from Kentucky. Three were burned that day. The remainder were distributed to other Indian towns. Slover was told they were also burned. At the final council meeting he was to attend, the Indian woman with whom he was living hid him, apparently because she didn't want him to know it would then be decided he too was to be burned.[82]

The next morning, about 40 warriors and Girty surrounded the house where he was living, put a rope around his neck, tied his arms behind his back, and "blackened me in the usual manner." He was tied to a post; the flame was kindled. It was a clear day, but just as the fire began to blaze, there was a hurricane, extinguishing the fire. He was told he would be burned the next morning. He was tied with buffalo hide, but he got loose and stole a horse. He rode it until it tired, abandoned the horse, and then ran. He was lashed by nettles and bitten by mosquitoes because he was naked except for a piece of rug he had stolen as he escaped. He eventually reached Wheeling and was saved.[83]

When the Revolution started, although the Indians believed they had been mistreated by the British, they thought their best hope of keeping their land was with them. In addition, the British had more resources than Americans to bribe tribal leaders. Both sides courted the Indians at the beginning of the war, and the Indians became divided. Carl Waldman summed up the eventual effects the Revolution had on the Indians:

As it was, for their efforts in the American Revolution, the Indians suffered many casualties, experienced the devastation of villages and crops, lost much of their land in cessations, ended the unity of one of the oldest surviving Indian confederacies—the Iroquois League—and alienated the white population around them.[84]

Winning wars is often a grim business, and losing them is even worse.

ON SEPTEMBER 3, 1783, the Treaty of Paris was signed, ending the Revolutionary War and affirming the independence of the 13 American colonies. Unfortunately, the treasury of the Continental Congress was empty. During the last full year of the war, it had assessed the states to keep the government running. Twelve of the 13 had paid nothing. New Jersey had paid only $5,500 of its $485,679 assessment. A delegate wrote that "our Army is extremely clamorous, we cannot pay them—we can hardly feed them." Washington recommended that Congress not break up the Continental army, but Congress ignored that recommendation as a practical matter.

In 1784, only a year after the Treaty of Paris, the United States Army consisted entirely of a West Point artillery company of 58 men and 29 others at Fort Pitt, a total of 87 soldiers.[85] Trouble on the frontier could be expected, and it occurred.

Mutiny was in the air as well. Some impatient officers, in a group of propositions called the Newburgh Addresses, advocated either refusing to disband when peace was declared or, if the war continued, to "retire to some unsettled country," leaving Congress with no army. Washington appeared unannounced at a meeting of these officers and gave a critical speech inquiring about the author of the Addresses:

> My God! what can this writer have in view, by recommending such measures? Can he be a friend to the Army? Can he be a friend to this Country?

When he left, the officers resolved to reject the Newburgh Addresses. There was no further serious talk of insubordination or desertion.[86]

THE SCOTT family lived on the frontier in Virginia in 1785. One night, several Indians stormed into the house. Mrs. Scott believed they were from the Delaware, Mingo, and 2 other tribes. Mr. Scott jumped out of bed and was shot and killed. An Indian stabbed and cut the throats of the 3 youngest children in their beds, then dashed their bodies on the floor near their mother. The eldest child, a girl of 8, was awakened, ran to her mother, asking her mother to save her. Mrs. Scott pleaded with the Indians to spare the child, but they tomahawked and stabbed the girl while she was in her mother's arms. Mrs. Scott was taken away by the Indians. On the eleventh day of her captivity, she escaped.[87]

In 1786, Captain McGary was with a group of soldiers attacking Shawnee villages. When they came to his village, an old chief named Moluntha stepped out with a peace pipe, a cocked hat, and an American flag. McGary asked the chief if he had participated in a battle earlier that year in Kentucky where 70 soldiers led by McGary had been killed. Moluntha had little English, was old, confused, and knew only that the American was asking him something. He nodded his head, saying, "Yes, yes." McGary took his hatchet, brained the chief, and took his scalp.[88]

That same year, while working his farm in Kentucky, the grandfather of President Abraham Lincoln—also named Abraham Lincoln—was murdered by an Indian. Tom Lincoln, father of the president, was there at the time. Tom's older brother, Mordecai Lincoln, saw the attack and shot the Indian, saving their lives. President Lincoln commented years later about his grandfather's death: "He was killed by Indians, not in battle but by stealth, when he was laboring to open a farm in the forest."[89]

In 1788, Tecumseh's brother, Cheesekau, lost his life trying to break into a settler's log cabin in the Cumberland River Basin after a settler had been killed there.[90] Tecumseh* took revenge by raiding a small settlement on Drake Creek. He and his group of Shawnee murdered and scalped 3 men and took several women and children prisoner.[92]

George Ironside, a Scotch trader, was in Miami and Shawnee country in 1789. One of their warriors showed him a heart he had personally taken from a white prisoner. He kept it fastened behind him with the scalp.[93]

Charles Builderback, "who had stood literally in Delaware blood and brains while bashing in the heads of the praying Indians at Gnadenhutten," was rounding up cattle on the Ohio River with his wife the same year. A party of Shawnee captured them, and when they recognized him, they emasculated and dismembered him over a long period of time. Then his skull was smashed with hatchets.[94]

Charles Johnston was captured by Indians in 1790 while going down

---

*Tecumseh fought in all the battles of Little Turtle's War. Thereafter, he traveled widely, unsuccessfully advancing the idea of one Indian nation from Canada to the Gulf of Mexico. Tecumseh joined the British in the War of 1812 and became a brigadier general.[91]

the Ohio River just above the Scioto. A white man and a woman were killed during the capture. The dead were scalped and their bodies thrown in the river.[95] Johnston was then forced to help the Indians decoy a canoe of 6 settlers. He and 2 other white settlers, Divine and Thomas, were put on the bank of a river. When the canoe was in sight, Divine called out for an ax to repair a boat. As the canoe came close to shore, the Indians opened fire, killing 4 immediately and wounding the other 2, who were dragged to shore and tomahawked. All 6 were scalped and their bodies thrown in the river. Johnston had been captured by a similar ruse performed by Divine and Thomas. Although both had claimed the Indians had forced them to do so, another captive told Johnston that Divine had planned both schemes when the Indians promised they would release him if he got settler prisoners for them. Johnston thought Divine was "perfectly happy" in executing the ax ruse.[96]

After Johnston had been ransomed, a Shawnee warrior told him his friend and fellow prisoner, William Flinn, had been burnt at the stake and eaten at one of the Miami towns. The Shawnee added that he had shared in the meal and that Flinn's flesh was even sweeter than bear's meat, a food in high repute with Indians.[97]

General Josiah Harmar had been a lieutenant colonel under Washington. It was he who in 1783 brought the ratified Treaty of Paris to France, thereby ending the war. On his return to the United States, he was named commander of the army and assigned to the Old Northwest Territory, where he was the government's Indian agent to the Ohio Valley tribes. Carl Waldman said of him, "He commanded U.S. forces in the region, clearing Indians from ceded lands and evicting white settlers who trespassed on remaining Indian Territory in violation of treaty agreements."[98] This analysis succinctly states federal government policy toward the Indians throughout almost all of the American-Indian War: Obtain cessation of Indian lands, clear Indians from those lands who have sold but refuse to leave, and evict settlers who trespass on Indian lands in violation of treaties. This was the policy, but frequently it was not followed.

Chief Little Turtle* (part Miami and part Mahican) and his allies had

---

*Little Turtle formed an alliance of Miamis, Shawnee, Delaware, and Hurons against the American soldiers led by Harmar, then against those of General Arthur St. Clair. He then counseled peace, but his warriors disagreed, and he turned command over to the Shawnee Blue Jacket, whose forces were defeated by General "Mad Anthony" Wayne at the Battle of Fallen Timbers in 1794.[99]

killed around 1,500 settlers in the Old Northwest between 1783 and 1790.[100] Washington ordered Harmar's army into the field.

At the close of the 1700s, it was said that the Miami Indians were savages who massacred women and children, drank the blood of their victims, and made merry as they burned their captives at the stake. It was reported that more settlers were tortured at Kekionga, their principal village at present Fort Wayne, Indiana, than any other place in the state.[101]

Harmar and his men advanced into Miami territory* in 1790. Secretary of War Henry Knox, concerned about what the British would think of Harmar's strike, told General St. Clair to tell the British commander at Detroit, Major Patrick Murray, that Knox merely intended to chastise the Indians, but to keep all this secret. Of course Murray told the Indians at once. On the basis of this information, the Indians asked for and got help from other Indian allies. There were bloody skirmishes, and Harmar lost 75 soldiers and 108 militia, while the Indians lost 100 warriors.

Three American prisoners were interrogated, then, after learning what more they could from them, the Indians killed them. Harmar had to retreat.[103] British general Simon Fraser warned one group of American prisoners, who were lightly guarded, that if they should attempt to escape "no quarter would be shown . . . and those who might elude the guard, the Indians would be sent in pursuit of, and scalp them."[104]

Near Cincinnati, Ohio, several tribes surrounded Dunlap's Station, a fortified community. To weaken the resolve of the defenders, they took a prisoner, Abner Hunt, a surveyor, into a clearing in front of the stockade, tied him to a log on the frozen ground, stretched him out, built a hot fire around him, made knife slits in his body, and put hot coals in the slits. He screamed and cried until nearly dawn.[105]

Shortly after the ice broke on the Ohio River in the spring of the next year, Indians captured 2 riverboats, killing 24 settlers. Some Shawnee and Mingos recognized 2 of the passengers, brothers Michael and Daniel Greathouse. Daniel was supposedly the leader of the settlers who had murdered part of the family of Mingo chief Logan in 1774. Daniel Greathouse and his wife were stripped. Cuts were made in their abdomens and their intestines tied to a tree. Then they were forced to walk around the tree, pulling out their intestines.[106]

Americans responded to the murder of the Greathouses in a variety of

---

*After their defeat at the Battle of Fallen Timbers, the Miamis by treaty ceded all of Ohio and much of Indiana to the government and went to live in Kansas and Oklahoma.[102]

ways. Houses and barns were booby-trapped. Scalp bounties were offered for any Indian scalp (not just Shawnee and Mingo scalps). Shortly after the Greathouse incident, a ranger party led by Simon Kenton killed 5 Shawnee on the Ohio. All were scalped. The head of a young boy was mounted on a pole along the river.[107]

Jackson Johonnet was assigned to General Harmar's army in 1791 with the rank of sergeant. He had come from his native England to Boston when 17. He was unable to find employment until he met an army officer. "After treating me with a bowl or two of punch, I enlisted." Before he saw any action, he and 10 other soldiers were captured by the Kickapoos* on the Wabash River. After 2 days, one of the soldiers, George Aikins, could go no farther because of hunger and fatigue. Archibald Loudon reported his fate:

> The captain of the guard approached the wretched victim, who lay bound upon the ground, and with his knife made a circular incision on the scull; two others immediately pulled off the scalp; after this, each of them struck him on the head with their tomahawks; they then stripped him naked, stabbed him with their knives in every sensitive part of the body, and left him, weltering in blood, though not quite dead, a wretched victim of Indian rage and hellish barbarity.[109]

The Kickapoos with captive Johonnet reached an Indian village on the upper Miami, where the captives were severely beaten. Soldiers James Durgee, Samuel Forsythe, Robert Deloy, and Uzza Benton all fainted. They were "immediately scalped and tomahawked in our presence [including that of Johonnet], and tortured to death, with every affliction of misery that Indian ingenuity could invent." Twenty-six days after the capture, Johonnet and a fellow soldier, Richard Sackville, escaped.

Not much later they came upon the newly murdered, stripped, and scalped bodies of an old man, a woman, and 2 children. Not long after that, they accidently discovered 4 Wabash Indians guarding 2 prisoners. They killed 3 of the Indians, but Sackville also died. Prisoner George Sexton told Johonnet that 3 others had been taken captive with him; however, 2 were wounded and were immediately scalped and killed. Sexton was so grateful for being released from captivity by Johonnet

---

*Kickapoos have lived in many different places. Originally from Wisconsin, they helped other tribes defeat the Illinois and divide their territory. They moved to Illinois and ceded their land there to the government in 1819. For a time, they lived in Mexico.[108]

that he insisted on staying on watch 23 out of the 24 hours in the day and carrying all their baggage.

Johonnet thereafter fought with distinction with General St. Clair, winning a battlefield commission. His narrative, said Loudon, ended with the statement that it was written for the purpose, among others, of exhorting American youth

> to defend the worthy inhabitants on the frontiers from the depredations of savages; whose horrid mode of war is a scene to be deprecated by civilized nature, whose tender mercies are cruelties and whose faith is by no means to be depended on, though pledged in the most solemn treaties.[110]

RALPH K. ANDRIST has said that "every Indian conflict seems to have some blunder or stupidity that makes it worse than it need be."[111] General St. Clair's* defeat in 1791 is an example. Logan Esarey characterized it as a "misguided, mismated, misordered, misdirected affair."[113] Its mission was to go north from Cincinnati and fight the Indians under Little Turtle. Bil Gilbert reported that Cincinnati real-estate man John Cleves Symmes saw the troops and said that they had been recruited "from the prisons, wheel barrows [impressed labor gangs] and brothels of the nation at two dollars a month [and] will never answer our purpose of fighting Indians."[114] The army consisted of 2,300 men, half of whom indeed were federal short-term conscripts. In addition, there were about 200 female "cooks," who had been gathered by the men. St. Clair and his officers were convinced the men would not march without the women, so they were officially ignored.[115] The soldiers were never paid. Food was in such short supply that regular army troops had to be detached to guard the supply trains from their own men.[116]

By the time St. Clair got to the area where he hoped to fight, 600 soldiers had deserted.[117] The Indians attacked. The soldiers fought for 3 hours, then the order to retreat was given. The retreat became a rout, and St. Clair lost 623 soldiers and 24 civilian teamsters. Only 580 of his men got home. Twenty-one Indians were killed. "In proportion to the number of men fielded that day," wrote Axelrod, "it stands as the worst loss the U.S. Army has ever suffered."[118] Robert M. Utley thought it certainly was "the worst disaster in the long history of the Indian wars."[119] St. Clair resigned his commission as a result of this defeat.

---

*St. Clair became territorial governor of Ohio. When he retired to private life, he lost most of his fortune in land speculation and lived in relative poverty until his death.[112]

St. Clair's second in command, Richard Butler, was a survivor of that rout for a time. Butler was mortally wounded in a fight around the artillery. He was found by his brothers, Captain Edward Butler and Major Thomas Butler, who were also badly injured. Richard told them he was fatally wounded and that they should leave him, which they did. Two Shawnee later found him. They killed and scalped him. Simon Girty and others identified the corpse. The Shawnee cut out his heart, which was still warm, and divided it into 14 pieces, one for each of the Indian nations fighting there.[120]

After St. Clair's defeat, captives were roasted at the stake. Soldiers' intestines were pulled out bit by bit. Some were flayed alive and their limbs hacked or slowly wrenched away. The brains of children were dashed out against the trunks of trees. Some of the women were stretched naked on the ground and run through with wooden stakes. Other women's breasts were hacked away, then the women were cut in 2.[121]

When Washington learned of the defeat, he exclaimed,

O God, O God, he's [St. Clair's] worse than a murderer! how can he answer it to his country;—the blood of the slain is upon him—the curses of widows and orphans—the curse of Heaven![122]

The year after Johonnet enlisted in the British army, Massy Herbeson and her family were in their home near Pittsburgh. Her husband was away, and many Indians came into their home. She recognized 2 Senecas and 2 Munsees. The Indians then began taking the family away from the house. Her 3-year-old son was unwilling to leave. The Indians took him by the heels, dashed him against the house, then stabbed and scalped him. The next night, a 5-year-old son began to mourn for his dead brother. An Indian tomahawked and scalped him, too. Massy escaped the next morning.[123]

After the Battle of Fallen Timbers in 1794, some soldiers found 8 warriors looking for food. One warrior was killed and scalped.[124]

THOSE SETTLERS who had "abandoned civilization" were called white savages. Simon Girty was not the only one. There was also Alexander Outlaw. In 1795 he entered the Indian town of Citico. He murdered a few women and children, according to Bernard W. Sheehan, "exposing their private parts in the most shameful manner, heaving a young child, with both its arms broke, alive, at the breast of its dead mother." It was reported that he had "done everything in his power to drive the Indians to desperation."[125] Another white savage was Benjamin Harrison, who in 1795 murdered 17 Creeks. He decapitated some of them with a broadax.[126]

In 1798 Jedidiah Morse, "who maintained a scholarly interest in the Indians and held deep sympathies for their welfare,"[127] gave this compendium of Indian torture:

> They begin at the extremity of his body, and, gradually, approach the more vital parts. One plucks out his nails by the roots, one by one; another takes a finger into his mouth, and tears off the flesh with his teeth; a third thrusts the finger, mangled as it is, into the bowl of a pipe made red-hot, which he smokes like tobacco; then they pound his toes and fingers to pieces between two stones; they cut circles about his joints, and gashes in the fleshy parts of his limbs, which they sear immediately with red-hot irons, cutting, burning, and pinching them alternately; they pull off his flesh, thus mangled and roasted, bit by bit, devouring it with greediness, and smearing their faces with the blood, in an enthusiasm of horror and fury. When they have thus torn off the flesh, they twist the bare nerves and tendons about an iron, tearing and snapping them, whilst others are employed in pulling and extending his limbs in every way that can increase the torment. This continues, often, five or six hours; and sometimes, such is the strength of the savages, days together. They frequently unbind him, to give a breathing to their fury, to think what new torments they shall inflict, and to refresh the strength of the sufferer, who, wearied out with such a variety of unheard-of torments, often falls into so profound a sleep, that they are obliged to apply the fire to awake him, and renew his sufferings. He is again fastened to the stake, and again they renew their cruelty; they stick him all over with small matches of wood that easily takes fire but burns slowly; they continually run sharp reeds into every part of his body; they drag out his teeth with pincers and thrust out his eyes; and, lastly, after having burned his flesh from the bones with slow fires; after having so mangled the body that it is all but one wound; after having mutilated his face in such a manner as to carry nothing human in it; after having peeled the skin from the head, and poured a heap of red-hot coals or boiling water, on the naked skull—they once more unbind the wretch; who, blind and staggering with pain and weakness, assaulted and pounded on every side with clubs and stones, now up, now down, falling into their fires at every step, runs hither and thither, until one of the chiefs, whether out of compassion, or weary of cruelty, puts an end to his life with a club or dagger. The body is then put into a kettle, and this barbarous employment is succeeded by a feast just as barbarous.[128]

Morse makes it clear that this is a summary of Indian torture of a hypothetical victim, not an actual victim. Most of the types of torture he described unfortunately actually occurred.

The ship *Manchester* from Philadelphia was captured by the Nootka Indians of Canada around 1803. The chief told captive John Rodgers Jewitt that 7 of the crew had tried to run away but were captured and put to death. Four Indians held each man on the ground, forced his mouth open, and choked him by ramming stones down his throat.[129] Jewitt, an English armorer, was one of only 2 survivors of the brig *Boston,* which was captured as well. After the capture, he was confronted with a line of 25 heads. The chief asked Jewitt whose each was, but Jewitt had to tell him some were mangled beyond recognition.[130]

Medicine man Tenskwatawa, younger brother of Tecumseh, made some rousing speeches to the Delaware Indians in 1806. He said that those who spoke or acted against him were probably possessed by evil spirits, were witches, and must be reeducated or eliminated. The Delaware invited him to come to their communities on White River in Indiana in 1806 to help them purify the people. He went there and punished 5 witches. An old woman named Coltos was roasted over a slow fire for 4 or 5 days, then confessed she could secretly fly long distances in the air. She was killed. Then Joshua, a Christian Mohican, was found to have a giant man-eating bird. He was clubbed and burned. Two Christian Delaware subchiefs, Teteboxti and Billy Patterson, were found to have trafficked with evil powers, so they too were clubbed and burned. Billy Patterson's wife was also accused and convicted. As she was being tied to the fire stake, her young brother freed her and led her out of the building. Then he came back and declaimed, "The devil has come among us, and we are killing each other."[131] The witch hunt was suspended.

In 1807 Mary Jordan, her husband, and their 6 children were at home when 40 or 50 Indians broke in and dragged them naked from the house. Twenty Indians were ordered to take them to the Indian village 200 miles away. The rest stayed behind to pillage and fire the house. The family was marched 40 miles through wilderness the first night. Anyone who slackened the pace was beaten and threatened with death. They made another 40 miles the second day. They then were joined by the pillaging party, which had found and consumed part of the husband's keg of spirits. The children were beaten, cut with knives, and scorched with brands of fire.

The Indians decided the children could not walk farther. They dug holes in the earth and placed dried branches around them. The husband broke the ropes with which he was bound and attempted to escape, but was brought back. He was placed in a hole as were the 6 children. All 7 were buried in earth nearly to their necks. The branches were then set on fire. All were burned to death in less than 15 minutes.[132]

THERE ARE a number of recorded atrocities during this period whose dates cannot be determined, but most of them probably happened between 1770 and 1810, and the last (Blackwell) a few years before 1865.

Mrs. Boggs, with a suckling child, was captured by the Indians. The child was not permitted to nurse. It was thrown in the road from time to time. Sometimes the Indians kicked it before them. After treating the baby in this fashion for 3 days, it was carried in the woods, where it was murdered and scalped.[133]

George Woods was forced to witness an Indian torture. The Indians cut holes in a man's cheeks, passed a small cord through the holes, then tied the cord to a small sapling. Two Indians with heated gun barrels seared his naked body. His scalp was torn from his head, then hot ashes and coals were applied to his skull. His abdomen was opened, one end of his bowels cut and tied to a tree, then red-hot irons again were applied to his body to make him move around the tree until his bowels were all drawn out. His genital organs were cut off. A hot gun barrel was thrust into his heart, finally killing him. Woods also recounted that sometimes the Indians opened the wrists and ankles and then, with a forked stick, twisted out the sinews.[134]

Bookseller and whiskey dealer James Potts was a sutler in the rear of a 2-division army during the Revolution. The 2 divisions were a few miles apart. Potts decided to move to the forward division in order to improve his sales. He was captured by Indians while on the way. The Indians killed and scalped him, hung him upside down by a sapling, and cut him open so that his intestines hung down over his head. The rear division found him in that condition as it marched by.[135]

Another victim in a torture was stripped naked and tied to a pole with a grapevine. Before being tied to the stake, he was beaten by women and children with dry canes or pitch pines in a most barbarous manner. When the death signal was given, the victim's arms were tied and a vine was fastened around his neck, with the other end at the top of the pole. Clay was put on his head to secure his scalp from the torches. Women came at him from all sides with burning torches. Fire burned his body. He was then doused with water so the burning could start again. When he fell unconscious, he was scalped, dismembered, and all the extremities of his body, including his genital organs, were carried off in triumph.[136]

The Shawano tribe captured a Muskohge (a group of tribes later known as the Creeks) warrior called Old Scrany and prepared for the usual fiery torture. Scrany showed no concern. He told them he was a noted warrior who had gained most of his martial prestige at their expense and was going to show them while dying that he was still their superior as he was in battle. He added he could punish himself more exquisitely than "all their despicable ignorant crowd" could possibly do. He finally said if they would untie him and hand him a red-hot barrel, he would show them. When given the barrel, he seized it, brandished it from side to side, made his way through the crowd, leaped from a very high bank into a stream, and made his escape. "He proved a sharp thorn in their side afterwards to the day of his death."[137]

The Shawano also captured the warrior Anantooeah. He appeared to be as unconcerned as Old Scrany. And like Scrany he stated that they did not know how to punish a noted enemy, but he was willing to teach them if they would give him a pipe and tobacco. He then lit the pipe and sat down naked with no apparent concern on the women's burning torches. A Shawano head warrior stood up, said it was plain Anantooeah was not afraid of dying, and he would not have died except that he was now spoiled by the fire. "And then by way of favour," commented Loudon, "he with his friendly tomahawk, instantly put an end to all his pains."[138]

The Seneca were at war with the Catawbas. Seven Seneca warriors surprised a Catawba warrior who was hunting. He ran to a hollow rock he knew 4 or 5 miles away. While he was running, however, he managed to kill the 7 with his rifle. But he was captured by others and taken to the Seneca village for the fire torture. The women and children beat him severely at each town through which he passed. As he was being taken to the stake, he broke away, dived into a nearby river, and swam underwater until he reached the other shore. He climbed the steep bank on the other side. Many Seneca were in the water after him, many on land in pursuit of him, bullets were flying all around him, yet, Loudon reported, "his heart did not allow him to leave them abruptly, without taking leave in a formal manner. . . . He first turned his backside toward them, and slapped it with his hand . . . and darted off." He ran for 2 days, pursued by several Seneca. He then discovered 5 of the pursuing Seneca and waited until they were asleep. He took one of their tomahawks and killed them all. "He chopped them to pieces, in as horrid a manner as savage fury could excite, both through national and personal resentment,—he stripped off their scalps . . . [and] set off afresh with a light heart." He went to the place where he had killed the first 7 Seneca, "digged them up, scalped them, burned their bodies to ashes, and went home in safety with singular triumph." The Seneca met in war council and decided to leave him alone.[139]

The Chickasaw had also been at war with the Muskohge. A Chickasaw warrior went into Muskohge territory alone to revenge the death of a relative. He concealed himself for almost 3 days under the top of a fallen pine tree. He could see the ford of a river where the Muskohge sometimes passed. A Muskohge young man, woman, and girl came by. The warrior shot the young man, tomahawked the other 2, then scalped all 3 in full view of a Muskohge town. He was pursued and ran back to his tribe, a distance of 300 miles, in less than 3 days.[140]

Elizabeth Blackwell was found by Indians with badly frozen legs in the mountains. They nursed her, and after her legs were amputated in the east, she returned to the tribe. Another woman who had been captured from a train was brought on horseback into the Indian camp. When an Indian attempted to lift her from the horse, she shot him. The Indians cut her body in gashes, filled them with powder, then set fire to her. Blackwell was so distressed by the woman's suffering that she asked them to kill the woman immediately, and they did.[141]

NOT LONG after the Revolution, Britain and France were at war again, this time in the War of 1812. In the years leading up to the Americans' involvement in the war, they furnished the French with a vast quantity of military supplies; as a consequence, Britain started seizing ships headed for France. Congress prohibited the importation of many goods from Britain. The Embargo Act of 1807 ended all trade with foreign countries. Merchants persuaded Jefferson to end the act as it applied to all countries except Britain and France.[142] Napoleon persuaded Madison to remove the embargo on France but retain it against Britain. There were skirmishes on the high seas between American and British ships. At the same time, expansion by settlers into the Northwest Territory, according to Douglas Brinkley, "sparked ominous Indian uprisings." Hawks demanded preparation for a new war, and on June 1, 1812, Madison asked Congress to declare war on Britain.[143]

The Creek Red Sticks prepared for war against the settlers in 1813, said James Wilson, by chanting, "War now. War forever. War upon the living. War upon the dead; dig up their corpses from the grave; our country must give no rest to a white man's bones."[144]

The British burned Washington in 1814, but later that year the American navy won a decisive victory over the British on Lake Champlain; this defeat so upset the British that they retreated to Canada. A peace treaty was entered into later the same year at Ghent in Belgium.[145]

The War of 1812 was uncommonly important because after the peace treaty was signed, General Andrew Jackson*—unaware of the treaty—fought and won the Battle of New Orleans. A makeup army composed of Tennessee and Kentucky riflemen, free blacks, and various other irregulars kept firing on advancing British troops. The British suffered 2,037 casualties, while Jackson had only 21. Jackson became a national hero and later became president. He had a great influence on American Indian policy. The war also proved that the Revolution had been no fluke—once again, Americans had managed to defeat Europe's best army.[147]

During the first year of the war, Fort Dearborn (now Chicago) surrendered. When the troops and civilians left the fort, the Potawatomi Indians struck. A total of 35 whites were killed, many by torture.[148]

That same year, British colonel Henry Proctor had besieged Fort Meigs on the Maumee River with Tecumseh and his men. The fort was relieved by men from nearby Fort Defiance, so Proctor pulled back into Canada, although Tecumseh wanted to stay and fight. On the way to Canada, Tecumseh's men scalped 20 prisoners Proctor had taken.[149] (Wilson claimed that Tecumseh also scrupulously avoided unnecessary killing.[150] How it can be said that the 1788 revenge atrocity on Drake Creek and this atrocity were necessary is difficult to explain.)

Many lives were lost when hundreds of settlers took shelter in Fort Mims because of earlier Indian depredations. The fort was really the fortified home of Samuel Mims, a Creek half-breed. In 1813, about 1,000 Red Stick Creeks under Red Eagle attacked the fort. The commander, Major Daniel Beasley, had ignored warnings given by black slaves that there were Indians nearby and had left the gates open. The fort was taken. About 400 settlers were massacred; only 36 escaped.[151]

Soldiers themselves were not above such behavior. A scout for Andrew Jackson in 1813 in the Creek War, the famous Davy Crockett, bragged in his autobiography that in one skirmish against the Indians,

*When the British invaded his area during the Revolution, Jackson joined the state militia and at age 13 took part in the Battle of Hanging Rock. The next year he was captured by the British and was taken to a military prison, where he contracted smallpox. After the Creek Indians attacked Fort Mims in 1813, Jackson as a major general in the Tennessee militia defeated the Creek Red Sticks after several battles. Jackson attacked Pensacola, Florida, even though he had dysentery, then fought the Battle of New Orleans.[146]

"we shot them like dogs; and then set the house on fire, and burned it up with the 46 warriors in it."[152]

In 1813, William Wells, the chief federal Indian agent in Fort Wayne, Indiana, intercepted a British message about a troop movement. He thought he could help, so he collected 30 Miami warriors and started out. His force was attacked by Potawatomi. His 30 Miami fled except for those who joined the Potawatomi. Wells killed at least 2 Indians, then was cut apart. The Potawatomi took out his heart and ate pieces of it while it was still warm. His head was cut off, put on a spear, and shown to American prisoners.[153]

Early on in the war, in 1813, British and Indians occupied the village of Frenchtown (now Monroe, Michigan) on the Raisin River. Kentucky militiaman Private Elias Darnell described the battle there. He kept a journal that was published shortly after his captivity was ended.[154] The militia formed the line of battle and advanced on the town, which they soon took. Twelve Indians were slain and scalped. The next day, a militia party went out to bring in the soldier dead. All but one had been scalped and stripped. The British were reinforced. American commanding general Winchester was captured and surrendered the entire American army. The new American commander, Major Madison, would not agree to capitulate until British colonel Proctor promised that prisoners would be protected from Indians and the wounded taken care of. An Indian who spoke English said his company had gone after retreating militiamen, who surrendered, gave up their guns, and pleaded for quarter, but most of them were killed because the Indians tomahawked them without distinction.[155]

Darnell was helping take care of the American wounded, who included his brother Allen, when Indians rushed in, took the blankets and best clothes, and ordered them out. The Indians then burned the houses where the wounded had been, even though it was January. Those who were unable to get out were burned to death. Those who did get out were shot, tomahawked, scalped, and mangled by the Indians. A number of prisoners were marched toward the town of Malden but were unable to keep up and were massacred by the Indians. The next day, the road was strewn for miles with bodies. Darnell marched with the Indians. Two wounded fell behind. The Indians shot and scalped one. The other ran up to them and begged that he not be shot, but he was shot and scalped. Darnell's brother Allen was also killed for lagging behind.[156]

The Indian who had charge of Darnell decided to befriend him. He gave him food, a knapsack, and a gun and offered him a female Indian and shelter. The third night, while the Indian was asleep, Darnell escaped and went to Fort Malden, which was east of the Detroit River. He found the house where American prisoners were held by the British and entered it, feeling that "Providence had smiled on my attempt to extricate myself from the Indians."[157] There had been 960 Kentucky militia at the Raisin River. No less than 850 of them were massacred. Only 33 escaped alive. This "served to arouse American anger and resolve." Bil Gilbert concluded that

> when news of it [the Raisin River Massacre] reached the United States, the slaughter of the unarmed prisoners understandably increased the Americans' fear of the Indians. However, in a cold, objective way, the atrocity had an invigorating effect on the national war effort. Thereafter the western settlers did not have to refer to old massacres which had occurred in the 1780s and 90s. They had one of their own which needed to be revenged and which morally justified more or less anything they might be able to do to the savages. "Remember the River Raisin" stirred Americans in 1813, as slogans having to do with the Alamo, the battleship *Maine,* and Pearl Harbor would their descendants.[158]

The Battle of Fort Meigs in 1813 in central Ohio followed the pattern of the Raisin River Massacre. Indians under Tecumseh captured several prisoners. Just as had happened at Raisin River 4 months earlier, the Indians began massacring the prisoners. Tecumseh learned of this, galloped to the stockade, and physically drove the Indians from the prisoners. Forty had been killed before he got there. Because of this incident, the settlers started thinking of Tecumseh as the Noblest Savage.[159]

Tecumseh was never seen alive after the 1813 Battle of the Thames. There was speculation that a corpse that was found was his, but 6 people who had known him could not make a positive identification at the time. Many rumors and stories arose later. One was that troopers took pieces of his skin for souvenirs, but it is not known if this is true.[160]

ATROCITIES CONTINUED after the war ended. A band of the Pawnee tribe* had a ritual. A war party would go into enemy country, where it would kill and scalp, but the purpose of the raid was to bring back an adolescent girl unharmed. She was treated like a queen, with her every

---

*Pawnees were peaceful with their white neighbors, but they fought against the Sioux, Cheyenne, Arapaho, Kiowa, and Comanche.[161]

wish fulfilled for a time. Then a scaffold was erected, she climbed upon it with hands and feet bound, a priest would rush upon her, cut out her heart, and offer it to the gods. (Another version says 3 priests would murder her using a torch, an arrow, and a knife, then every male would shoot arrows into her body, which was left where she was killed to fertilize the earth.)[162] One year, when a young Comanche girl was to be sacrificed, a future chief named Petalesharo grabbed her before she was led to the scaffold and rode away with her. After he got her back to her people, he returned to his tribe. It was decided to discontinue the ritual after that.[163]

NOT ALL atrocities occurred on the frontier. Some happened after statehood had been attained. Indiana became a state in 1816, but in 1824 on Fall Creek, near Indianapolis, 9 friendly Indians (Miami and Seneca) were murdered. The settler murderers were caught, and goods were given to the victims' families by the Indian agent by way of reparation. Indiana governor Thomas A. Hendricks argued for quick prosecution to try to convince the Indians that the government did not countenance the crime, and the secretary of war and the commissioner of Indian affairs both supported prosecution of the case. All the defendants were tried (the bloody shirts of the Indians were literally waved in the courtroom) and convicted. One later escaped from jail, one convinced the judge that his father was responsible for his attending the murders, and the rest were hanged.[164]

Around 1827, trappers found sport in shooting defenseless Gosiute and Paiute Indians who lived along their routes in the Great Basin. Although there is no indication anyone was killed, the practice does show the low regard in which the trappers held the Indians.[165] The trappers who hunted Indians for sport were not alone. John M. Coward noted that many Western correspondents "happily fired at Indians whenever they had a chance."[166]

CHAPTER 7

Atrocities from the
Trails of Tears to the Civil War

The idea of removing the Indians to someplace where they would not be in contact with the settlers causing friction had been around for a long time. As early as 1776, Jefferson recommended that the Cherokee and all other tribes that supported the British should be driven beyond the Mississippi. "This then is the season for driving them off," he said.[1] The purchase of the Louisiana Territory by Jefferson in 1803 made removal a feasible matter.[2] There was now plenty of American territory west of the Mississippi. Voluntary removal was tried. Edward H. Spicer pointed out, however, that "tribes reluctant to move west were subjected to heavy pressures to do so."[3]

The westward removal of Indians—which resulted in many deaths—came to be called the Trails of Tears.[4] The genesis of this migration between 1831 and 1842 was the Removal Act of 1830. That legislation authorized the president to grant federal land west of the Mississippi to any tribe of Indians "as may choose to exchange if the land claimed by the Indians was owned by the United States."[5] The act permitted removal only of Indians who agreed to go.

Five southern tribes then signed treaties of removal with the government. The first treaty (and the pattern for the rest) was the Choctaw Treaty of Dancing Rabbit Creek signed September 27, 1830, in Noxubee County, Mississippi.[6] Under the treaty, numerous things of value were to be given to the tribe. Each chief got 2,560 acres plus $250 each year for life. Lesser tribal officials got smaller sums ranging down to $50 per year. Each head of a family got 640 acres, each unmarried child over 10 living with him 320 acres, and each child under 10 160 acres. Forty Indian children were to be educated at government expense for 20 years.

The government agreed to remove the Indians at its expense in wagons and with steamboats as might be found necessary and with ample corn, beef, and pork until 12 months after removal. Finally, the treaty stated, "Each Choctaw head of a family being desirous to remain and become a citizen of the States, shall be permitted to do so."[7] Up to half of those who wanted to go had to go by the falls of 1831 and 1832, and the remainer by the fall of 1833. The treaty stated these staggered departures were so that "a better opportunity will be afforded the Government, to extend to them [the Choctaw] the facilities and comforts which it is desirable should be extended in conveying them to their new homes."[8]

The Choctaw did not leave within the time required by their treaty, and this caused problems. By November 1831, only 4,000 had gone. The main body of the tribe had moved by 1833, but some remained after that date. The Choctaw* removed to Oklahoma from 1831 to 1834, the Seminoles† from 1835 to 1842, the Creeks‡ beginning in 1836, the Chickasaw§ beginning in 1837, and the Cherokee¶ in 1838 and 1839.[14]

---

*The Choctaw settled in Mississippi, Alabama, Louisiana, Arkansas, Texas, and Oklahoma. They supported the Americans in the Revolution and the War of 1812.[9]

†The Seminoles lived in Florida. The name means "one who has camped out from the regular towns." The reason for this is that the Seminoles broke off from other tribes (primarily Creeks) and moved south in the 1700s.[10]

‡The Creeks were in Georgia, Alabama, Florida, Louisiana, Tennessee, Texas, and Oklahoma. Their villages were organized into Red towns and White towns. The warriors lived in the former and the peacemakers in the latter.[11]

§The Chickasaw were in Mississippi, Alabama, Arkansas, Tennessee, Georgia, Kentucky, South Carolina, and Oklahoma. They supported the British in the French and Indian War, halted all French traffic on the Mississippi for a time, and successfully resisted the attack of French armies 3 times. Some warriors fought on both sides in the Revolutionary War.[12]

¶The Cherokee lived in Tennessee, North Carolina, South Carolina, Georgia, Alabama, Virginia, Arkansas, Kansas, and Oklahoma. They poisoned water to catch fish and used blowguns to kill small game. Tribal organization included a White Chief who helped make decisions about farming, lawmaking, and disputes, a Red Chief who advised about warfare, and a War Woman who went on war parties but did not fight and decided which prisoners would live and which would die.[13]

Substantially all of those Indians who were removed went to Oklahoma, escorted by the United States Army. Chicago attorney Grant Foreman read the "vast accumulation"[15] of government papers and wrote the removal's history.[16] Foreman's book, *Indian Removal,* is the most detailed work on the subject and is relied upon very heavily here. He was indignant about what happened on the Trails of Tears, but his indignation did not extend to the army. Foreman wrote,

> A conspicuous saving grace of this sorrowful story is the fidelity and skill with which the regular army officers and soldiers in the field discharged their unwelcome duties in connection with the removal.[17]

This is consistent with General Winfield Scott telling the soldiers before the Cherokee were removed that "every possible kindness must be shown by the troops" toward the Indians, but some claim they raped, robbed, and murdered their charges.[18] Serious crimes were committed against the Cherokee by soldiers, according to Alan Axelrod.[19] Grant Foreman himself, however, reported no crimes at all by the military against the Indians.

Immediately after the Choctaw signed the treaty, they sent exploring parties to Oklahoma who reported favorably on their new home. They found "good land," "streams," "plenty of game," and that "the timber is very good."[20] "The exploring Indians were very much pleased with the country."[21] George Catlin, who was there in the 1830s (and in other removed land as well), confirmed that it was "a large and rich tract of country."[22]

A half-breed Choctaw chief named Greenwood Leflore induced many Indians to remove at once, independently from the government. Leflore sent many families west the month after the treaty was signed, but of the first 1,000 he sent, only 88 arrived, and they were nearly starved.[23] The removal was commenced, but it was a bad start. Foreman outlined the problem:

> The government was launched without compass or rudder into the uncharted sea of Indian removal; for the first time it was about to engage on a large scale in the removal of its aborigines from their homes in which it was bound to collect and feed them, transport them across the great Mississippi River, carry them part way by steamboats and then overland through swamps and across streams, build roads and bridges, cut banks down to the streams, and finally locate these expatriates, men and women, the aged and decrepit, little children, and babes in arms, in their new country.[24]

Disease became the major difficulty. Cholera infested all the steamboats coming down the Mississippi. Lieutenant Gabriel J. Rains estimated the disease killed "one-fifth of the whole number."[25] Major Francis W. Armstrong and other soldiers also contracted the disease. Armstrong said from Nashville that "he and his wife had just recovered from it [cholera], and that business in the entire state [of Tennessee] had been entirely suspended in consequence of it."[26] Smallpox, dysentery, and measles were also prevalent.

Water, either too little or too bad or too much, created serious problems. Steamboats could not move when there was low water. Because of contaminated water, many Indians suffered from dysentery.[27] (Earlier, almost all American Revolutionary War soldiers got dysentery. Captain Lewis, for instance, suffered from it on the Lewis and Clark Expedition in 1805.)[28] In June 1833, the greatest flood in the history of the Arkansas River swept away Indian houses and government corn cribs. "Nearly all the people who lived upon the river," said Foreman, "have been ruined."[29] Captain William Armstrong reported that a swamp impeded progress. Many died from cholera.[30]

Cold weather also plagued the Indians. The Choctaw had left home in comparatively warm weather, were thinly clad, and only a few wore moccasins. Captain Jacob Brown wrote that many were "quite naked, and without much shelter."[31] For a week the temperature averaged only 12 degrees, there was snow, and on the tenth day the temperature was 0. For a time the river was impassable because of ice.[32]

Government bureaucracy aggravated almost every problem. Congress had appropriated large sums of money for government agents to buy supplies, horses, oxen, and the like for the Choctaw, but "no money was given them for months after they were in need of it."[33] Disbursing agent Lieutenant Rains wrote that the government was trying to get the Choctaw to eat pork rejected by Fort Gibson in Oklahoma because it was spoiled and unfit for consumption by soldiers. Rains scraped and re-brined 178 barrels, issued some of it, and hoped to furnish more.[34]

Starvation too was widespread. Joseph Kerr lived 68 miles from Vicksburg along the road over which the Choctaw passed. He wrote the secretary of war "a bitter arraignment of the inadequate provisions for caring for the Indians."[35] He added that there should be a blanket for each Indian, not just one for each family, and that they should be given shoes or moccasins or something with which to make footwear. General Gibson replied to Kerr, "The fall and winter were unparalleledly severe; the Indians poorly provided."[36] An officer led starving Choctaw to Kerr's small field of pumpkins, and "these they ate raw with avidity."[37]

An almost starving party of Indians camped in Arkansas near the Posey farm. Mr. Posey gave them permission to help themselves to his turnip patch; they did, and left absolutely nothing.[38]

Government agents were frustrated in dealing with those who sold supplies for the Indians. Dealers frequently conspired to force government agents to pay inflated prices. Captain Jacob Brown denounced "the whole sordid and avaricious combination against the Government."[39]

Indians hostile to the Choctaw often harassed them. The Choctaw petitioned the secretary of war:

> It is our wish that you would have troops stationed on the frontier immediately, as our people are settling up the Red river some distance; and unless we have troops stationed on the frontier immediately, our people will be in great danger of these hostile Indians.[40]

Three months later, some Choctaw seen traveling fast said they had been "run in by a band of Pawnee Indians."[41]

Even witchcraft caused problems. Shawnee living on Choctaw land executed a Choctaw woman as a witch, then the Choctaw executed 2 Choctaw for the same reason. Francis Armstrong gathered the chiefs and threatened death for anyone executing a witch and the lash for someone who made a charge of witchcraft in the future.[42] As might be expected, Armstrong's words badly aggravated the situation.

Lieutenant William S. Colquhoun reported that "drunkenness prevails to an extent beyond anything ever before experienced."[43] Lieutenant Jefferson Van Horne, disbursing agent for the Choctaw removal, stated that Indians of both sexes were drunk, and that one night "most of the Indians were drunk."[44]

Remarkably, the Choctaw prospered once they reached Oklahoma, as did some of the other tribes. Edward H. Spicer said this about them:

> Establishing themselves as the Choctaw Nation on their 3 million acres, they proceeded to make a rapid new adaptation. The wealthiest Choctaws of Mississippi had brought their slaves with them, some families with as many as 500. They immediately began breaking and cultivating the new land and were soon raising cotton, corn, pecans, hogs, and cattle. They developed transportation systems both across country and along the navigable Arkansas River.[45]

The 1832 Treaty of Payne's Landing with the Seminoles in Florida required them to go west within 3 years in exchange for the usual western land, money, and commodities. By the required time for removal, 1835, no Seminoles had gone.[46]

Seminole emigrations finally began in the middle of April 1836, when Lieutenant Joseph W. Harris took friendly Indians from Tampa Bay to New Orleans, where they were put on a steamboat. They arrived at Little Rock, Arkansas, on May 5. On the way, 25 died. Harris wrote that the deaths

> resulted from the perversity of the Indians in adhering to their own peculiar treatment of the sick; which being confined to frequent deluging the patient with cold water, & to a constant kneading of the body, terminated—inasmuch as the diseases consisted of coughs, slight disentaries [*sic*], &c—almost invariably in death. And this could not be obviated, although after having exhausted advice, entreaty and expostulation, we resorted to watching, threats and force.[47]

Harris himself became ill and had to leave the party near Little Rock. A physician, sometimes 2, apparently accompanied most groups, although some had none at all. The doctor with the Harris group thought the Indians were too ill to travel. He further advised, however, that the measles would increase unless they got away from the river, where the Seminoles were constantly bathing those affected in cold water, "which was sending them rapidly to the grave."[48] There was a heavy rain most of the time during this journey.

"A Choctaw introduced a Gallon of Whiskey into Camp, which I took from him."[49] Indians were dying every day. By the time the party got to Oklahoma, there had been 87 deaths within a 60-day period.[50]

Other Indians continued to harass them. An officer saw the bleeding scalp of one of the Seminole chiefs in the hands of a Creek warrior.[51]

Captain Pitcairn Morrison left Tampa Bay with a group, picked up more on the way, and arrived in Oklahoma with 305 Seminoles and 30 Seminole blacks on June 28, 1837. Lieutenant John G. Reynolds left New Orleans on July 11 with 66 Seminoles and arrived in Oklahoma on August 5. Apparently there were no deaths during either journey, an interesting fact. Several other groups were removed with no fatalities mentioned by Grant Foreman.[52]

On February 25, 1839, Seminoles left Tampa Bay. Sometime between March 28 and April 2, a steamboat boiler exploded, killing many of them.[53] A party of 200 left Tampa Bay on May 7 and arrived without deaths in Oklahoma.[54]

The last Seminole emigration occurred in 1857. Superintendent of Indian affairs for the southern superintendency Elias Rector gathered 165 Seminoles and some other Indians for removal. They all survived the journey, but later many were killed by a fever epidemic.[55]

A REMOVAL treaty was signed by the Creeks on March 24, 1832. Its terms followed the pattern set by the Choctaw removal treaty. The poorer Creeks were starving even before removal commenced. Governor George R. Gilmer reported to the president in 1831 that the Indians were "absolutely starving or subsisting upon the bark of trees."[56]

The first 630 Creeks were removed under Captain John Page in December 1834. They were poor, with little clothing, and the winter was unusually severe. There was rain, snow, and freezing temperatures nearly every day. Children and the sick had to lie on wet or frozen tents in the wagons because there was no time to dry them.[57] They arrived at Fort Gibson in March 1835, 3 months after they started. There were only 469 survivors.[58]

The Creek removal was now about to begin in earnest. On July 2, 1836, 1,600 Creeks left for the West, and their party eventually grew to 6,398. Seventy-nine Creeks died of disease during this trip, even though a surgeon went along. When one of the steamboats towing a bargeload of Indians was passing Columbia, Mississippi, many Indians came on deck to look at the town. The decayed deck collapsed, injuring some and killing one.[59]

The remainder of this group, consisting of 210 Creeks under Captain F. S. Belton, went by steamboat from Montgomery to New Orleans. Settlers secretly sold liquor to the Indians, who became drunk.[60] As they proceeded, Belton reported that "the heat is excessive and the water of the worst description."[61] By the time the Creeks reached their destination, 19 had died, 9 were missing, and Captain Belton was too ill even to keep his journal. He lay down by the side of the road, and the Creeks proceeded under Belton's assistant, Doctor J. Jones.[62]

In August 1836, a group of 3,022 Creeks, which soon grew to 3,142, left under William McGillivrey and Lieutenant R. B. Screven. Hungry Creeks in this party dropped out, and stole hogs and food to keep from starving. Only about 2,000 reached Fort Gibson.[63]

Lieutenant Edward Deas took another group of 1,170 from Georgia to Oklahoma the same month. In Tennessee, their number increased to 2,000. Deas returned to Georgia for another 2,320. The *Memphis Enquirer* reported, "They are generally in good health."[64]

That same August, some 2,700 Creeks who had helped the settlers fight hostile Indians started west under Lieutenant M. W. Batman and Chief Opothleyaholo. Batman reported that the Indians got drunk on whiskey furnished by settlers "in every town or village through which they passed."[65] The Memphis newspaper opinion that the Creeks were generally in good health is consistent with Foreman's failure to report any deaths at all in the 3 Creek parties, totaling 10,042, leaving in the August Screven, Deas, and Batman groups.

On September 5, a group of 1,984 Creeks left Tallassee, Alabama, in the charge of Marine Corps lieutenant J. T. Sprague. In his diary, Sprague himself argued it best that they leave:

> The necessity of their leaving their country immediately was evident to every one; although wretchedly poor they were growing more so every day they remained. A large number of white men were prowling about, robbing them of their horses and cattle and carrying among them liquors which kept up an alarming state of intoxication.[66]

Lieutenant Sprague then added,

> If liquor could be found upon the road, or within four or six miles of it, men and women would congregate there, and indulge in the most brutal scenes of intoxication. If any white-man broke in upon these bacchanals he did it at the imminent hazard of his life.[67]

Colonel John J. Abert said, "Their love of drink . . . will keep them in its vicinity while they have a shilling to procure it."[68]

Like others, the Creeks had little clothing. Sprague described their plight:

> The sufferings of the Indians at this period were intense. With nothing more than a cotton garment thrown over them, their feet bare, they were compelled to encounter cold, sleeting storms and to travel over frozen ground.[69]

They finally arrived at Fort Gibson on December 10. Sprague's diary summed it up. "Twenty nine deaths [out of 1,984 who started] were all that occurred; fourteen of these were children and the others were the aged, feeble and intemperate."[70] A group of Creeks wrote a letter to Sprague expressing their keen appreciation for his kindness and "for his efforts to ameliorate their misery and afford such comfort as he could."[71]

General T. S. Jesup had been ordered by the secretary of war to remove the Creeks. Jesup wrote to the secretary in 1837, when the removal was near completion, that he

> had seen an account in the newspapers of the removal of the Creek families, but was not aware of the brutal treatment which those families had been compelled to submit to. . . . The Creek families were plundered of the greater part of their property, and it is no more than just that they be remunerated.[72]

In 1837, 3,500 Creeks were waiting at Mobile for transportation to Oklahoma. Within a 5-month period, 177 died. Every officer and agent was sick (probably from dysentery). At Pass Christian, whiskey peddlers approached the Indians, and the officers destroyed several barrels of liquor.[73]

In late October, as the Creeks were on their way to Oklahoma in several steamboats, another tragedy occurred:

> The steamboat *Monmouth* with 611 Indians on board, was proceeding up the Mississippi River, when through the negligent handling of the boat she was taken through Prophet Island Bend on a course forbidden to upbound vessels; in this place at night she collided with the ship *Trenton,* towed by the *Warren:* the *Monmouth* was cut in two, and sunk almost immediately with a loss of 311 Indians.[74]

The *Monmouth* was apparently overloaded as well. Steamboat owners believed that no more than 400 or 500 people should be transported at one time; the *Monmouth* had 611 Indians on board.[75]

There was only one bright side to the horrible situation. The Creeks had been removed to land about which George Catlin said, "There is scarcely a finer country on earth."[76]

The treaty for removal of the Chickasaw was signed on Pontotoc Creek on October 20, 1832, and provided that the tribe would cede all its lands outright to the government. The government would then sell the land and hold the proceeds for the Chickasaw.[77]

The president appointed Colonel A. M. M. Upshaw superintendent of the Chickasaw removal. The first group of 500 Chickasaw passed through Memphis on July 4. They were imposing. According to Upshaw's diary:

> They presented a handsome appearance, being nearly all mounted, and, with few exceptions, well dressed in their national costume. It has been remarked by many of our citizens, who have witnessed the pas-

sage of emigrating Indians, that on no previous occasion was there as good order or more dispatch. Not a drunken Indian we believe, was seen in the company.[78]

Upshaw delivered 3,538 Chickasaw to Fort Coffee in Oklahoma on January 2, 1837.[79] Their land, according to Captain G. P. Kingsbury, was "one of the finest ranges for horses and cattle I have ever seen at this season of the year."[80] Upshaw's diary refers to few deaths.[81]

The negligence of the contractors, however, soon made itself felt. Upshaw wrote to Daniel Harris on May 1, 1837, that

I am here starving with the Chickasaws by gross mismanagement on the part of the contractors, and when our situation will be bettered it is hard for me to tell, for it is one failure after another without end. . . . I begin to think we will have to starve to death or abandon the Country.[82]

The government had greater difficulty making a removal treaty with the Cherokee. Georgia passed a law providing that Georgia law extended to the Cherokee Nation, that all Cherokee laws were null and void, and that anyone who tried to persuade anyone else not to go west would be jailed.[83] Foreman reported that President Jackson

warned the [Cherokee] Indians that the government was powerless to prevent the State of Georgia from exercising sovereignty over them and that if they insisted on remaining in the state, they did so at their peril, and that they need expect no help from him.[84]

Under these bleak circumstances, a removal treaty was signed by another group of Cherokee (the eastern Cherokee) on December 28, 1835, called the Treaty of New Echota. The Choctaw pattern was once more followed. A date was fixed by which they were required to leave, May 23, 1838, but less than one eighth had gone by that time.[85] When the deadline was reached, the Cherokee still resisted, were rounded up, and forcibly taken to Oklahoma.[86] Their removal was not complete until 1839.[87]

Lieutenant Harris was assigned to lead a group of Cherokee west.[88] A boat across the river furnished liquor and, Harris reported, "immorality & misrule have continued to be the order of the day—dancing, drunkenness, gambling & fighting the pastime of the night."[89]

Harris also reported "an alarming change took place with the introduction of a malignant type of cholera."[90] The Indians, panic-stricken, dispersed into the timber.[91] Harris himself got cholera.[92]

Harris left the party at Dwight Mission. By that time, there had been 81 deaths, 50 from cholera. Forty-five children under 10 "died chiefly of the measles, dysenteries, worms, &c, the result of exposure, confinement, want of proper cleanliness, the river water and the neglect of parents."[93] Of those in the Harris party who reached Oklahoma, nearly half died before the end of the year.[94]

A group of about 600 Cherokee who wanted to go west by themselves left New Echota, the Cherokee capital, in January 1837. Another party consisting of 466 Indians left Ross's Landing on March 3, 1837, under Dr. John S. Young. Liquor was introduced at many stops, and there was drunkenness.[95] Physician C. Lillybridge also went along and was in a good position to assess fatalities on the voyage, but he reported none at all.

The tenor of the removal changed after most of the Cherokee failed to leave by the date required by their treaty. James Mooney said, "It may well exceed in weight of grief and pathos any other passage in American history."[96] Nearly 17,000 Cherokee were gathered into stockades and brought in groups of about 5,000 to the river to embark. There were 2 physicians for each group.[97]

The next party was also in the charge of Lieutenant Deas and left Ross's Landing under guard on June 6, 1838. Deas determined that there were 489 in the group. He issued tenting material to protect the Cherokee from the weather. Fort Coffee was reached on June 19. Grant Foreman noted, "There had been no death in the party since their departure from Ross's Landing."[98]

Exactly one week after the party under Deas left, a second party, of 875 Cherokee, left Chattanooga under Lieutenant R. H. K. Whitley, whose assistants included 2 physicians and a hospital attendant. The results were dramatically different even though the conditions of the 2 journeys would appear on the surface to be about the same. Only 602 reached their destination. There were 273 deaths.[99] Why the June 6 expedition should have no deaths and the June 13 party 273 is not known.

On October 11, 1838, a group of 650 to 700 left, led by Deas. These were treaty-faction Cherokee who refused to go with the Cherokee Nation group under Ross. They arrived in Oklahoma without incident on January 7, 1839.[100]

The Cherokee Nation asked General Scott to permit the Cherokee to remove themselves in the fall after "the sickly season" had ended. Scott agreed.[101] On July 19, 1838, the *Army and Navy Chronicle* reported that there were 9,250 Cherokee in the stockades, with another 1,500 on the way there.[102]

There were now about 13,000 Cherokee gathered for removal, including their slaves.[103] On October 1, 1,103 Indians started under John Benge and on October 4 an additional group of 748 started under Elijah Hicks. By the 16th, it was apparent that the Hicks party did not have enough clothing. They reached their new home on January 4, 1839.[104] There were 114 deaths.[105]

Nine more Cherokee Nation parties left through October and 4 in November.[106] A party conducted by John Hicks left on November 4.[107] Cherokee leaving on October 5 included a Cherokee minister, the Reverend Jesse Bushyhead. He wrote that his party had been detained a month by ice in the Mississippi, and they did not reach Oklahoma until February 23. There were 32 deaths while they were on the road.[108]

The leaders of some of the other journeys gave reports of additional deaths: the Reverend Evan Jones reported 38; another Cherokee minister, the Reverend Stephen Foreman, 71; Mose Daniel's party, 48; James Brown, 34 "deaths and other causes"; John Drew, 55. These additional deaths total at least 269.[109]

There was some consolation in the quality of their new land. George Catlin described it as

> a fine tract of country; and having advanced somewhat in the arts and agriculture before they started, [the Cherokees] are now found to be mostly living well, cultivating their fields of corn and other crops, which they raise with great success.[110]

Edward H. Spicer even reported that "by 1887, the Cherokees . . . were on the way to political and economic development comparable to that of other Americans."[111]

SEVERAL TROUBLING questions are raised by the Trails of Tears. What are some relevant numbers? How many deaths were there? Were these deaths atrocities?

A Presidential Commission on Indian Reservation Economies in 1984 made its Report and Recommendations to President Reagan. That report said that only about 100,000 Indians were resettled. It also said that a problem with the act was that the Indians could not be removed far enough or fast enough to stay out of the path of advancing settlers.[112] The 1860 Census (29 years after removal began) indicated there were 340,000 Indians then. Although about 30 percent were removed under the act, about 70 percent of the Indians in the country (all over the country, not just in the South) were *not* removed.[113]

Grant Foreman and others have made estimates of deaths by tribes. Those estimates vary widely. Edward H. Spicer reported 5,000 Choctaw deaths.[114] Carl Waldman stated that approximately 3,500 Creeks "died of disease and exposure during and shortly after the ensuing removal."[115] Spicer said 2,000 Chickasaw failed to arrive in Oklahoma and "after arrival 3,500 more died."[116] Spicer said the Trails of Tears deaths "recorded in their [Cherokee] history" is 4,000.[117] Even when John Ross got permission from the government for the Cherokee to manage their own removal, the deaths continued. Out of 3,916 in the first 4 detachments, 573, or 14.6 percent, died.[118] These estimates total 18,000 deaths.

Foreman would appear to have made the most diligent investigation concerning the number of deaths. He noted that there was no way to assess the number of Cherokee deaths. He said in language that could apply to all the removed tribes,

> On the march there were many deaths, a few desertions and accessions and occasional exchanges from one party to another where some by sickness were obliged to drop out of the way and join those coming after; so that an accurate statement of the number removed and of those who perished on the way became impossible.[119]

The figures Foreman used in *Indian Removal,* taken for the most part from journals of eyewitnesses, give a far different picture than other writers. The deaths he reported on the Trails of Tears (not all the deaths he mentioned are referred to above) include 25 Choctaw deaths, 166 Seminole, 297 Creek, 556 Chickasaw, and 802 Cherokee, for a total of 1,846. (The Choctaw estimate of 25 deaths must be contrasted with his statements about the Leflore expedition, where 1,000 left and only 88 nearly starved Choctaw arrived. It seems unlikely all of the remaining 912 survived.) These specific estimates by Foreman, of course, are minimal estimates, because when the journal of the military officer stated that "many," "several," or "a number" died, a quantity cannot be determined.[120] The difference in estimates between 18,000 and 1,846 is clearly too wide. We do not know exactly how many Indians died on the Trails of Tears, but of course it was far too many and constituted a national tragedy.

Were the deaths in the Trails of Tears atrocities? An atrocity occurs only if the injury is intentional, and such injuries were not committed here by army personnel. The conduct of President Jackson would not appear to amount to intentional injury either, but it can be argued he did intend it.

The evidence that could lead one to believe he did intend the deaths consists of the fact that after the Creek War, Jackson was determined to eliminate all potential enemies of his country from the southern frontier.[121] But there are also indications that Jackson did not intend the many deaths. He stated in his 1829 first inaugural address that he desired a just, humane, and considerate policy toward the Indians. Robert Remini asserted that "no one these days seriously indicts Jackson as a mad racist intent upon genocide."[122] Remini concluded that

> some men, like Jackson, meant removal as a humanitarian means of preserving Native American life and culture in a place where they would not constitute a threat to the safety of the Union and a bother to the greed, arrogance, and racism of whites.[123]

Grant Foreman concluded his book on the removals on a cautiously optimistic note:

> The rehabilitation of these five Indian nations, their readjustment to their new surroundings, the recovery of their national spirit and enterprise, the building of their farms and homes, their governments and schools upon the raw frontier, bringing into being a higher civilization of Indians, this was an achievement unique in our history, that compares favorably with the best traditions of white frontier civilization.[124]

No more will be said about the sorrowful Trails of Tears. Atrocities, of course, continued throughout the country.

IN 1832, army captain Benjamin Louis Eulalie de Bonneville and his men established a trading post on the Green River in Wyoming. Helen Hunt Jackson told how one of his trappers discovered that his traps had been stolen, and he vowed to kill the first Indian he saw. He saw 2 Root Digger Indians fishing, killed one, and threw his body in the stream. Shortly after that, a party of trappers was about to cross a stream, saw unarmed Root Diggers on the opposite bank, and killed 25 of them. The survivors were chased, lassoed, and dragged until they were dead. Later on, the same group of trappers found that some of their horses had been stolen by the Riccaree Indians. They told them that unless all the horses were returned, 2 innocent Indians who had wandered into the trappers' camp would be burned to death. Two horses were released, and the Indians who had them fled. The 2 prisoners were burned.[125]

After the 1832 defeat of 275 Illinois militiamen by 40 Sac and Fox* warriors in the skirmish known as Stillman's Run, Black Hawk terrorized the frontier in the Black Hawk War. With 40 braves, mostly Potawatomi, he attacked the Davis farm at Indian Creek in Illinois. Fifteen were murdered and mutilated. Two girls, Rachel and Sylvia Hall, saw the Indians dancing, brandishing their parents' scalps. The sisters were captured, but later ransomed for horses. The Illinois frontier was disrupted by Stillman's Run and the Indian Creek Massacre. Settlers fled their homes, farming stopped, mining stopped. The Galena, Illinois, newspaper was quoted by Alan Axelrod as calling for a "war of extermination" against the Indians.[127]

A party of 29 Illinois militia finally caught up with 11 marauding warriors and killed them all. Militia colonel William S. Hamilton came on the scene an hour later with friendly Sioux, Menominees, and Winnebagos and turned them on the dead bodies. The Indians hacked them to bits.[128]

Black Hawk then went to Canada. When he returned in 1830, he found settlers occupying land in violation of the Treaty of 1804. They had appropriated Indian cornfields and plowed new fields among Indian graves.[129]

Moreover, half his warriors were gone, and his back was to the Mississippi River. Before he could cross, the steamboat *Warrior,* with a detachment of soldiers and a six-pound cannon, arrived. Black Hawk raised the white flag, but soldiers fired on the warriors. His men sought cover and returned fire. *Warrior* went downstream to refuel. The next

---

*During the French and Indian War, the Fox tribe fought against the French. The French and Chippewa drove them to new homelands. They and the Sac and others defeated the Illinois in 1769. They formed a temporary alliance with the Sioux to attack the Chippewa, but were defeated.[126]

morning, 1,300 volunteers and regulars stormed toward the Indians. The Indians tried to surrender, but the troops, according to Robert M. Utley and Wilcomb E. Washburn, "inflamed by weeks of panic," clubbed, stabbed, and shot them for 8 hours. The steamboat returned with its cannon, adding to the slaughter. One witness said the Mississippi was "perceptibly tinged with the blood of the Indians." The soldiers took 39 prisoners. Although 239 Sac and Fox warriors got across to the west bank of the Mississippi, hostile Sioux scalped or took all of them prisoner.[130]

When Black Hawk surrendered, he delivered a farewell speech to his tribe saying that "Black Hawk tried to save you, and avenge your wrongs. He drank the blood of some of the whites."[131] After his death in 1838, grave robbers raided his tomb and displayed his head in a traveling carnival—a double atrocity.

About the same time, George Catlin visited the grave of Omaha chief Black Bird, which was on top of a bluff overlooking the Missouri River. Black Bird had requested that he be buried astride his favorite war horse, and he was. Catlin dug into the burial mound, found the skull of the horse, then the chief's skull, secreted it, and took it away and put it "with others which I have collected in my route."[132]

THE SEMINOLE Wars in Florida (1816–58) seemed never to end. In 1837, commanding general Thomas Sidney Jesup decided to import 33 bloodhounds from Cuba to track down the Indians. The American public raised an outcry because of what they had heard bloodhounds did to runaway slaves. No bloodhound atrocities happened, however. The hounds had been trained to follow the scent of blacks; Indians smelled different from them and they wouldn't trail them. However, when bloodhounds did enter the Florida swamps where the Indians were, the Indians trained them to attack the soldiers.[133]

General Jesup decided he needed to deal with the Indian leadership. That same year he invited a young Seminole chief named Osceola to attend a peace council. When Osceola arrived, he and his people were arrested. Osceola was struck on the head and imprisoned in Fort Moultrie, near Charleston, South Carolina, where he died in 1838. The post surgeon, Dr. Frederick E. Weedon, displayed his remains there in a medical museum until it was destroyed in a fire.[134]

There was a truce in Florida in 1839, but a Seminole band led by Chekika killed several of the soldiers of Colonel William Harney in a night attack. The next year, his band did the same thing in the upper

Keys, killing 7. Harney with 90 soldiers killed Chekika and hanged his men.[135]

The Seminoles remained a problem. Colonel William J. Worth was sent to Florida in 1841. He methodically destroyed the Seminole shelters and crops. In doing so, he also captured the leading chief and 5 other leaders of the resistance. He sent word to all hostile Seminoles that the captives would be hanged unless they surrendered. They surrendered.[136]

The Seminole women did as the Creek women had done before them in the war, killing their small children so they would be free to fight beside their men.[137]

TEXANS INVITED Comanche* chiefs to peace talks in 1840. They then tried to seize the chiefs as hostages. The chiefs resisted. All were killed.[139]

The same year, there was an encounter between the Texans and the Comanche that resulted in the death of 7 Texans and the capture of 13. There were 35 Indians killed and 29 captured. When the Indians learned about the deaths of their people, they put 11 of their 13 captives to death "with great torture," sparing only the 2 children, who had been adopted into the tribe.[140]

Texas was admitted into the Union in 1845. In 1848, the Treaty of Guadalupe Hidalgo became effective. That treaty between the United States and Mexico provided that the United States would prevent incursions into Mexico by Indians from the United States. The Comanche were notorious for their raids into Mexico to steal horses. They were indignant about this provision of the treaty. Robert Simpson Neighbors had been appointed by President Polk to try to persuade the tribes in Texas to stay away from the settlers. He complained that "if a horse is stolen by an Indian . . . the first party of Indians that is fallen in with, is attacked and massacred" by the Texas Rangers.[141] A Ranger company heard a rumor about the murder of a settler, came upon a band of Wichitas, who fled, and massacred 25 of them. The Wichitas killed 3 surveyors in return. Soon there was an all-out war. Another wagon train was

---

*Through much of their history, Comanche raided whites and other tribes to steal horses. They had a long history of fighting the Texas Rangers and the army. The Native American Church was chartered by the Comanche in 1918; one of its practices involves the sacramental use of peyote. By the 1930s, about half the Indians in the country were members.[138]

attacked later by Kiowa,* and perhaps some Comanche. Troops arriving after the attack found that the ruins of the burned wagons contained 16 bodies.[143]

The settlers who came into the Oregon country in the 1840s got along with the Indians reasonably well for a time. Marcus Whitman, a physician and missionary for the Presbyterian Church, and his wife set up a mission to the Cayuse Indians with Henry Spalding and his wife near Fort Walla Walla in Washington. (The 2 wives were the first white women to cross the Rocky Mountains.) But the Cayuse began to resent the number of settlers coming into their area. There was a measles epidemic in 1847. Dr. Whitman treated both settler and Indian children, but the settler children tended to recover, while the Cayuse children tended to die.[144] Cayuse chief Tiloukaikt and warrior Tomahas believed Whitman was poisoning the Indian children. On November 29, the Cayuse attacked the mission, killing the Whitmans and 12 others. The settlers formed a volunteer army, and there was war until 1850. To make peace, the Cayuse turned over 5 of the perpetrators of the Whitman Massacre. They were tried, found guilty, and hanged.[145]

A volunteer army under clergyman Cornelius Gilliam with 550 Oregon militia went on a punitive expedition in 1848. Not all the Cayuse had supported the Whitman raid, but Gilliam attacked the first Cayuse camp he found. More than 20 peaceful Indians were killed, as well as 5 militia. When Gilliam accidentally killed himself with his gun, his troops lost interest in the campaign.[146]

CALIFORNIA ATROCITIES were unique. The Indians, at least in the north where the gold was, were unorganized, poor, and lacking in warlike spirit.[147] The miners, on the other hand, "were the extreme in frontiersmen, without respect for any law other than what they made themselves."[148] They have been described as including a "high proportion of 'hard cases': thieves, jailbirds, cutthroats, and assorted gallows bait."[149]

The California gold rush began in 1848. It has been said, "The gold rush of 1849–50 brought into California a large number of Anglos who were single men and less responsible than colonists in other areas."[150]

---

*Kiowa migrated frequently. Their first known home was in western Montana. Lewis and Clark found them in Nebraska in 1805. The Kiowa raided other tribes such as the Caddos, Navajos, Utes, Apache, Arapaho, Cheyenne, and Osages.[142]

The *Daily Alta California* newspaper in 1851 referred to "oppressions from the lawless and reckless scum of our countrymen and others, which the gold fever and the new order of things generally has brought into the country."[151]

California had a governor who announced that "a war of extermination will continue to be raised until the Indian race becomes extinct."[152] Ralph K. Andrist concluded that in no other part of the United States were the Indians "so barbarously treated and so wantonly murdered."[153] General George Crook described what it was like when he was a lieutenant in the mining town of Yreka, California:

> It was of no unfrequent occurrence for an Indian to be shot down in cold blood, or a squaw to be raped by some brute. Such a thing as a white man being punished for outraging an Indian was unheard of.[154]

When California was annexed to the United States in 1848, there were about 100,000 Indians there. By 1859 there were only 30,000, and by 1900 only 15,000. The causes of this catastrophe are not completely clear, but what is clear is that atrocities by the settlers (which included prospectors, miners, and ranchers) and disease played a significant part.

Before 1827, diphtheria, measles, and pneumonia "ravaged Indians." In 1833, other diseases such as cholera, smallpox, and syphilis "spread like wildfire," and approximately 4,500 Indians from 4 tribes died from disease in that year. "Other diseases spread unabated." From 1830 to 1848, almost 11,500 Indians died of "white man's diseases."[155]

Edward H. Spicer calculated that from 1769, when the Spanish missions were founded, until 1846, when California declared its independence from Mexico, the Indian population declined rapidly, perhaps by half, as a result of disease and poor living conditions. He added that by the late 1840s, the Indian population may have fallen to about 70,000.[156] Alvin Josephy suggested that from 1849 to 1859, 70,000 California Indians died from one cause or another. "Disease and poverty were prevalent."[157] It was reported in 1851 that sickness was ravaging the Indians in the vicinity of the Sacramento River, there were unburied bodies on the road, and many were lying prostrate with disease.[158] Disease and malnutrition undoubtedly killed more of the Indians than did violence.[159]

The Clifford Trafzer and Joel Hyer book *Exterminate Them!* compiled 115 California newspaper accounts dealing with settler relations with Indians. Trafzer is a Wyandot Indian. Many of the atrocity reports here are taken from that book. The number of atrocities will never be known, but Trafzer and Hyer claimed "volunteer militia units murdered thousands" of Indians and enslaved thousands more.[160]

In 1860 the *San Francisco Bulletin* was appalled by what was happening:

> We have been informed through the papers, of the murderous outrages committed on the aboriginal inhabitants of California by men with white skins. We regret to say that there is no exaggeration in these accounts. On the contrary . . . we can bring to light no circumstance to palliate or extenuate them in the slightest degree. In the Atlantic and Western States, the Indians have suffered wrongs and cruelties at the hands of the stronger race. But history has no parallel to the recent atrocities perpetrated in California. Even the record of Spanish butcheries in Mexico and Peru has nothing so diabolical.[161]

There was a form of atrocity in California seldom found elsewhere. Trafzer and Hyer, who are Indian advocates, asserted that because settlers had polluted the streams, driven off or killed local game, and disrupted traditional societies, "the actions of whites compelled many of California's Indians to steal cattle and horses."[162] Be that as it may, numerous Indian thefts occurred, and sometimes the thief was killed.

In the late 1840s, after the miners had taken land occupied by Indians, some Indians started robbing the miners and pilfering their property. In retaliation the miners formed posses and killed both guilty and innocent Indians alike.[163] One prospector accused Indians of stealing his pick. A chief visited the mining camp to inquire about it. He was shot. The Indians then wounded a prospector named Aldrich with 3 arrows.[164]

A Cahuilla Indian named Juan Diego was considered "loco," or crazy. He rode his horse to find work and tied it at the corral of a Mr. Temple. He came home on a stolen horse. His wife asked whose it was, and Diego seemed confused. Then Temple came up, shot Diego dead, and went to a justice of the peace and claimed the Indian had tried to knife him.[165]

In 1850, storekeeper Jim Savage* was informed that his Miraposa store had been raided. He went there and found that his 3 men had been

---

*Savage was from Illinois. He quit school at 14, lived for several years among the Sac and Fox and other Indians, then went to California, where he lived mostly among Indians and was like a chief. He spoke 5 Indian languages, plus German, French, Spanish, and English.[166]

murdered, his goods carried off, and his camp burned. Savage gathered 43 men and after walking many miles found an Indian camp. They were celebrating and "Savage could learn from what they said that they expected an attack from the Americans." The Savage group charged the Indians, killed 27 of them, and burned the camp, leaving an old woman who had fought well to die in the fire.[167]

In 1853 Indians destroyed about $5,000 worth of stock owned by ranchers Thomas and Toombe, who then "had two men employed, at $8.00 per month, to hunt down and kill the Diggers, like other beasts of prey." One of these men, John Breckenridge, armed only with a bowie knife, met 4 Indians (there is no indication they knew anything about the theft), and attacked them. They told him to leave, and when he did not, they shot arrows at him. Breckenridge killed one and captured one. The captured Indian was taken to Moon's Ranch, where he was hanged by the citizens. The same year, the store of Bragg & Drew near the Mckeiumne River was robbed. Drew thought he knew who the robbers were and went to an Indian ranch, where some of the goods were found. A chief threatened to kill Drew. He retreated and gathered a party of 16, who returned to the ranch and demanded the goods. An Indian fired and missed, both sides then fired simultaneously, and 4 Indians were killed.[168] In 1853, there was trouble near Tehama over some thefts. The miners slaughtered 15 or 20 Indians in retaliation.[169] In Sonora the same year, Indians stole some horses and mules. A party of 17 men pursuing them was suddenly surrounded by 300 or 400 Indians, who attacked. Three Indians were killed.[170]

Near Sugar Loaf Mountain in 1853, several deaths occurred. Some cattle were stolen from Mr. Middleton; 2 white men attacked the Indians, and 8 Indians were killed. Later, an Indian was killed for stealing. Another was hanged for the same offense.[171] Three years later, a miner's sugar had been stolen by Indians 2 or 3 times. He then mixed his sugar with an ounce of strychnine; 8 or 10 died, and others were made severely ill.[172]

These thefts were, of course, crimes, but apparently no Indian was ever convicted of any such theft because he never got to trial. An atrocity was committed against each murdered Indian by his killers. Other atrocities for other reasons follow.

There were, of course, thefts where the alleged thief was not killed. Indians stole the stock of John Sutter, whose discovery of gold started the gold rush, stole hundreds of Mexican cattle and horses after the Mexican War started in 1846, and stole livestock elsewhere. One rancher in 1850 had all his stock stolen 14 times in 3 years.[173] It has been claimed that the thefts were acts of Indian resistance, but the resistance was broader in scope:

> Besides stealing from Anglos and Chinese, Indians defended their homelands by attacking American settlements, burning ranches, and killing whites. They ambushed mail carriers, merchants, miners, and anyone else who trespassed on their lands. . . . Some fought American militia units.[174]

The Indians were driven from the land they occupied by the settlers. When the Indians resisted by attacking the gold miners, all the Indians in the area were hunted down, women were gang-raped, men were captured and forced to do field labor, and children were treated like slaves.[175] Edward H. Spicer put it as clearly as anyone:

> The coming of the Anglo-Americans in 1848–1849 after the U.S. war with Mexico extended the [California] Indians' condition of absolute subordination to the whole state. . . . The idea of Indian rights to land or to anything else was wholly foreign. Indians were murdered, plundered, pushed from what land they held, and then ignored in the constitutional government ultimately established (except for specific denial of the right to testify in court). The result was not only death and loss of property, but 75 years of social limbo, which no other Indians in the United States experienced. Despite efforts by a few reformers on behalf of white-Indian relations during the early 1850s, neither the federal government nor the state recognized the Indians' existence. They were not citizens, but neither were they wards of the state. The state appointed a superintendent of Indian affairs whose office did nothing, and the federal Bureau of Indian Affairs took no responsibility. The result was steady separation of Indians from nearly all their land, and frequent starvation. Some whites hunted Indians for sport and rounded up children and sold them.[176]

In 1849, prospectors from Oregon attacked a Maidu Indian village in California, raped many women, and shot some Indians who attempted to intervene. Soon after that, Maidu warriors in turn attacked Oregon miners, killing 5 of them. Oregon men stormed an Indian village and killed at least 12. The miners then murdered 8 Indian hostages.[177] The same year, an old Indian came to a mining camp. A miner claimed that one of the Indian's horses was his. The Indian said he had bought it from a white man. The miner took it, the Indian rode off, said something offensive to the miner, and the miner shot him.[178] Finally, in 1849 James M. Vail was missing and feared captured or killed by the Indians.

A search party found the smoking ruins of a house with tracks leading from it. The tracks were followed to an Indian, and he was killed.[179]

While California was still a territory, Captain Henry Naglee and his men, according to Clifford Trafzer and Joel Hyer, "indiscriminately murdered two chiefs."[180] Miner William M. Daylor took a group of his Indian employees to his mine in 1849. Six days later, a group of armed white men went there and killed an Indian while he was working on his knees. Another tried to escape and was shot through the arm, then the thigh, and finally his brains were beaten out with rocks and stones. The white men then followed the trail of the Indians who had escaped and slaughtered 14 more. The men camped near Daylor's house, where a family member was about to be buried. Four Indians left the grave and passed by the camp. They were fired upon, and one was killed and one wounded. The white men told Daylor they had killed 27 Indians before getting to the house. Forty-nine Indians were missing at the time this atrocity was reported.[181] Also in 1849, 2 white men, Andrew Kelsey and Charles Stone, had Pomo Indians working on their ranch. They exploited and even murdered some of them. The Indians killed the 2 ranchers. Soldiers came to the area to retaliate. They surrounded 300 Indians on an island and shot all in sight, killing dozens, including women and children. The commander, Captain Nathaniel Lyon, described it as "a perfect slaughter house."[182]

Dr. Able Lincoln from Tennessee built a ferryboat crossing the Colorado River in California at the mouth of the Gila in 1850. John Glanton from Texas, who had killed several men (the Mexican state of Chihuahua offered a reward of $8,000 for him), came along and became Dr. Lincoln's partner. They charged extortionate fees. A General Anderson and his men came to the ferry, objected to the fee, and built their own ferryboat. When the soldiers were across, Anderson gave the boat to some Indians, who set up a competing business. Glanton and a group of men marched to the Indian ferry, destroyed the boat, tied the hands and heels of an Irishman named Callahan, whom the Indians had hired to help, and threw him into the Colorado. The "old chief" argued with Glanton about the matter to no avail, so the Indians decided to kill Glanton, Lincoln, and all their men. After Glanton returned from a trip to San Diego, and while the ferry operators were taking a nap, they were attacked and 11 were killed. "Their mangled remains were thrown into a pile of combustibles and burned."[183]

The year 1851 was not a good one for California settlers either. Indians surprised and murdered 72 settlers near Rattlesnake Creek, according to the *Daily Alta California.*[184] Seven ferrymen were killed by

Indians at the Colorado River.[185] A settler was murdered between the Mariposa and Merced rivers.[186] Finally, at Four Creeks, 13 settlers were massacred and their entrails torn out.[187]

Cahuilla chief Juan Antonio and his men raided the J. J. Warner* ranch, killed a servant and burned him on the woodpile, destroyed his property, and drove off his stock. Later that day they killed 4 white invalids in Aguas Caliente. Antonio was caught, tried, and hanged.[188] Colorado Indians killed 4 sheepherders near Gila in 1851.[189] Not long after, Savage led another expedition against the Indians. With 28 men, he surprised an Indian camp and killed 10.[190] In 1851, an Indian was called from his home by a settler. When he was outside, the settler put a knife in his heart, causing instant death.[191] Seven whites were killed at the Red Banks on the Merced River in 1851.[192]

By this time, matters had degenerated to the extent that a settler wrote to the *Daily Alta California* in 1851 to say, "It cannot be disguised that there is an Indian war against Americans [settlers], solely. Almost the whole California population is disaffected with our institutions."[193]

Finally, in 1851 the president appointed a commission to negotiate treaties of peace with the various tribes. The commission tried to assess what had happened:

> In some of the difficulties which have recently occurred the Indians have been the aggressors—that the whites have had much provocation to justify the severity of their measures in retaliation, will not be denied. . . . [Since the gold rush] we are informed, the Indian has been by many considered and treated as an intruder, as a common enemy of the whites, and in many instances shot down with as little compunction as a deer or an antelope.[194]

The next year, Congress authorized the appointment of a superintendent of Indian affairs in California.[195]

In 1852 it was reported that miners met at the Orleans Bar and "after a meeting to discuss the Indian problem, voted to kill on sight all Indians having guns."[196] The same year some legislators wrote to Governor

---

*This is the same J. J. Warner, an Indian agent, who in 1856 told the Santa Isabel Indians that he intended to take all unbranded animals in their possession away from them, asserting that those animals were his property! The lieutenant commanding the local army post, William A. Winder, told the chief of the Santa Isabels that if any attempt should be made by Warner to take the animals, they should bring them to the lieutenant for safekeeping. Winder reported to his commander, Major W. W. Mackall, that "this is one of the many cases of injustice practiced upon these Indians, and by the very men whose duty it is to protect them."[188]

John Bigler, stating that in their 4 counties within a very few months, Indians had murdered at least 130 whites.[197]

Hupa Indian Jack Norton published through the Indian Historian Press a collection of oral histories taken from Indians about what happened in northern California in the 1850s. Norton charged that more than 600 Indians were murdered in separate encounters. One of them occurred in 1852 near Weaverville, where, Norton claimed, 153 Wintun Indians were killed in retaliation for some of them killing 5 cows.

The year 1853 saw many atrocities. Norton reported that at Yontoket several hundred Tolowa Indians were murdered during their harvest dance.[198] Allen Penrod from Illinois was murdered by Indians while working his claim.[199] The same year, an Indian chief tried to rectify a theft. A Cow Creek Indian stole some property from a rancher. When his chief, Numtarimon, learned about it, he pursued the Indian and started to take him back to the ranch. The Indian tried to escape, and the chief ordered him killed with arrows, which was done.[200] Again that same year, a mule train was attacked in California by Indians and a man named Dick Owen killed. Thirteen mules, one horse, and all the cargo were lost.[201]

At the Carter ranch $3,000 worth of stock was stolen. A posse was formed, which captured the half-breed Battedou. He agreed to take them to a cave "where the Indians were concealed." Rocks were thrown into the cave by the posse, and 13 Indians, including 3 women, were killed as they came out. The *Sacramento News* sanctimoniously said, "It is but doing justice to say, that the women who were killed were placed in front as a sort of breast-work and killed either by accident or mistake."[202]

At Frenchtown, a mining settlement, an Indian chief threatened vengeance on the whites for the wrongs done the Indians. A party of 8 whites was immediately formed. They arrested the chief, and after "a short deliberation" it was unanimously decided he should be hanged at once. He was.[203]

Major E. D. Townsend at Fort Miller learned that a white woman was supposed to have been kidnapped by Indians. A party of 25 soldiers was sent to the Indian camp. They demanded the woman and were shown an old Indian woman. The soldiers went to the opposite side of the creek and spent the night. The next morning, 8 or 10 Indians visited them and were told they would be killed unless the woman was delivered. When they tried to escape, 6 were killed.[204]

Inevitably, intoxication became a problem. The *Los Angeles Star* complained that "each Sunday morning . . . our streets are filled with drunken Indians, male and female. It is within bounds to set down the number of filthy drooling beasts, in human shape, at one hundred." The *Star* added that so far as it knew, no effort was being made to discover the people who were furnishing the liquor contrary to law.[205]

Captain H. W. Wessels reported to his superior that an inoffensive Indian had been barbarously murdered by a white man within a few hundred yards of the post. A warrant had been issued for the murderer's arrest.[206]

The situation of the California Indians had worsened by 1854. During the Rouge River War that year, a newspaper article stated, "Abducting Indian children has become quite a common practice. Nearly all of the children belonging to some of the Indian tribes in the northern part of the state have been stolen. They are taken to the southern part of the state and there sold."[207]

Some Indians of the Nason tribe in Oregon were killed in 1854. At a ferry house the Indians rode the horses of the whites without permission and constantly stole things. Their chief was fed at the ferry house, but upon leaving one day fired his gun at 4 settlers standing near the door. The chief was ordered in for a talk, and he declared he meant to kill all white men he could and burn their houses. The next day, about 20 settlers rode to the Indian ranches, killed 16 of them, and burned all their houses with one exception.[208]

This situation with variations was repeated all along the West Coast. The *Sacramento Union* in 1855 ran a report that tried to put the killings in perspective:

> The intrusion of the white man upon the Indian's hunting grounds has driven off the game and destroyed their fisheries. The consequence is, the Indians suffer every winter for sustenance. Hunger and starvation follows them wherever they go. Is it, then, a matter of wonder that they become desperate and resort to stealing and killing? They are driven to steal or starve, and the Indian mode is to kill and then plunder. . . . On the Klamath [River] the Indians have killed six white men, and I understand some stock. From the Salmon [River] down the whites are in arms, with determination I believe if possible, to destroy all the grownup males, notwithstanding this meets with the opposition of some few who have favorite Indians amongst them. I doubt whether this discrimination should be made, as some who have been considered good have proved the most treacherous.[209]

In 1857, in the vicinity of Round Valley, within a period of 3 weeks, it was reported that 300 to 400 Indians were massacred by settlers. The reason given was depredations by Indians on the settlers' stock and resistance to moving onto reservations. If true, this was the third-largest reported settler massacre of Indians anywhere—and the greatest west of the Alleghenies—but some caution must be exercised. The story was printed in the *California Farmer* for March 27, 1861, and was based on an article in *The Petaluma Journal* dated April 15, 1857, almost 4 years earlier.[210] Why the paper would wait such a long time before printing such a big story needs explaining.

In 1858, the Fresno Indians killed 6 or 8 of their medicine men because they could not cure the sick, and it was believed there would be no rain or green grass until they were exterminated. One of the medicine men, pursued by about 16 Indians, sought sanctuary at the Ridgway home. Sanctuary was given, but a few days later, the man went out and was killed.[211]

The *San Francisco Bulletin* reported that a young Indian boy (age 10 to 15) set fire to Colonel Stevenson's house in 1859. The sheriff left him in a room adjoining the courtroom, from which he was taken by a mob and hanged. The *Bulletin* commented, "Why not let him be hung in a legal manner?"[212]

Citizens of Humboldt and Trinity counties complained that too many settlers had been killed and property taken by Indians and that their lives were in danger. In response, Governor John B. Weller sent a company of 80 men to chastise the Indians, ordering that "the women and children must be spared." A newspaper said the order had been "strictly obeyed whenever possible" but that "75 to 100 [Indians] were killed."[213]

Another punitive expedition, a party of about 12 under John Breckenridge, encountered a group of 5 Indians and their white leader and killed them all. Breckenridge took the scalp of the white leader. The next day, the party found an Indian camp and killed 10 more.[214]

A letter to the *Sacramento Union* praised an army expedition that had killed 80 Indians and captured 400 more, adding that it "is worthy not only of repetition, but of much commendation."[215] According to Clifford Trafzer and Joel Hyer, a Captain Jarboe bragged that he and his men had killed 283 Indians.[216]

In 1860, Major G. J. Raines went to Indian Island between Eureka and Uniontown, where he reported that so-called volunteers had murdered all the women and children for no apparent reason. He found babies with brains oozing out of their skulls, babies cut and hacked with axes, and women with frightful wounds.[217] This would appear to be the third Norton atrocity—the result of the murderous activity of 3 to 7 white men who rowed a mile to an island where Wiyot Indians were dancing. Sixty to 70 were killed.

The *San Francisco Bulletin* described how, during another atrocity, an aged and feeble chief collected the women around him, assuring them that white men did not kill women and that they would be safe, but they all perished together. The number of Indians slaughtered in one night was about 240.[218] The *Bulletin* further reported that the Indians were particularly troublesome in Mendocino County. Stock had been stolen (Mr. Woodman lost 109 horses), and the settlers had formed a standing army. They attacked the Indians, killing another 32.[219]

The Eel River Rangers, under the command of Captain Jarboe, campaigned against the Indians in 1860. They battled with 90 Indians on the South Eel River, and about 30 were slain. The *Bulletin* called them "as thieving, marauding Indians as ever roamed the forests of California." Later Jarboe's men had a furious fight near Round Valley and killed 30.[220] The fourth and last claimed Norton California atrocity was a massacre of 200 or more Indians killed on a spit at the mouth of the Eel River.[221]

In 1860, settlers in Humboldt County attacked Indian villages in retaliation for cattle and other property stolen in raids. The *San Francisco Bulletin* reported that "bands of white men, armed with hatchets . . . fell on the women and children, and deliberately slaughtered them, one and all." A witness counted 26 such bodies in one camp.[222]

Not many months later, at the beginning of winter, the *Bulletin* ran a story about some settlers who had moved down from the mountains to protect their stock from the snow. When some returned to their houses to inspect them, they found "that the Indians had destroyed all that they had left." They tracked down the band that committed the damage and killed 39 Digger Indians.[223] The same week, the settlers in Upper Mattole also attacked the Diggers, slaying 7.[224] When Indians robbed the Larabee house and killed the cook, Ann Quinn, settlers killed 2 of the Indians.[225] And in 1862, Yahi Indians captured 3 white children and murdered 2 of them. One was found with 17 arrows in him, his throat slit, and scalped.[226]

Settlers in California were very unhappy about the inability of the army to stop claimed Indian misconduct. An editorial in the *Yreka Semi-Weekly Union* in 1864 took up the issue:

There is "A rottenness in Denmark" somewhere, in the management of our Indian affairs, and the citizens are now forming INDEPENDENT companies to follow the Indians into their mountain fastnesses and annihilate them.[227]

Near the Cottonwood River in 1865, 2 white men went to an Indian camp to abduct a 10-year-old girl. The mother and a crippled boy resisted. One of the men cut the throat of the boy, then stabbed him repeatedly until he died. The girl and her mother escaped. A few days later, the frustrated men returned and burned the camp.[228]

Some Indians concocted an extortion scheme called the Chinese Tax Collectors. Eight Indians visited Fairfield Bar on the Feather River in 1865 and requested that the Chinese owners produce their poll tax receipts. When they did, they were told the receipts were no good, and the Indians demanded cash. The Chinese had none, so the Indians beat them and stole all the valuables.[229]

Apparently in an attempt to make amends to some extent, both the California and federal governments belatedly enacted a claims statute in 1928 permitting Indians to sue the federal government for damages as a result of loss of land and resources. Thirty years later, the federal government gave land titles to all California Indians who asked for them, a program that remained in effect until the 1970s.[230]

There were many Indians killed by atrocities in California. In the 12-year period from 1849 to 1861, there were 2,017 California Indian deaths due to settler atrocities (see Appendix C); surely there were more never reported in that lawless time and place.

The great number of atrocities in California would seem to have resulted from a conflict between the characters of the criminal elements among the prospectors and miners and the poor and unwarlike Indians. These atrocities by whites represent the extreme point of atrocities throughout the war.

AROUND 1850, settlers chained the father of Modoc Scarface Charley to the back of a wagon and dragged him until he died.[231] In 1851, the Oatman family along the Gila River was attacked by some Indians, perhaps Yavapais, perhaps Apache. Everyone in the family was killed except 12-year-old Olive and her younger sister Mary, who were sold into slavery to the Mohaves. Olive was rescued 5 years later by a Yuma Indian. The Mohaves had tattooed her and Mary (who later starved to death) about the chin to discourage them from trying to escape. Olive was a sensation and went on a lecture tour across the country.[232]

These were not the only Indians who practiced tattooing their prisoners. Fanny Kelly said she "narrowly escaped tatooing [at the hands of the Sioux] by pretending to faint away every time the implements for the marring operation were applied."[233] A female captive in the Mississippi Valley refused to return to the settler community when ransomed by her father because her face had been disfigured by Indian tattooing and because she thought she was pregnant by a man who had taken her for his wife and who treated her well.[234]

An ox owned by a Mormon was shot with an arrow and killed in 1854 by High Forehead, a Sioux boy. He and 2 other boys ate it. They claimed the animal had been abandoned and was lame. The Mormon complained to the soldiers at Fort Laramie about what had happened. The matter was reported to Lieutenant J. L. Grattan. Grattan, who had perhaps been drinking (some say it was his French-Canadian interpreter, Lucien Auguste, who had been drinking and who mistranslated),[235] went to the Sioux camp with 30 men and 2 cannon and demanded either 25 dollars for the ox or the 3 Sioux boys. Grattan had no authority to make any such demand. There was an argument. Grattan barked an order, and the cannon fired on the Indians, killing Chief Bear That Scatters and several Sioux. The Indians beat and hacked the soldiers to death. Only one of the 30 escaped, but he died upon his return to Fort Laramie.[236]

This was the first time in the history of the army that a military unit had been completely wiped out. The event came to be known as Grattan's Massacre, or the Mormon Cow War. The country demanded action.[237] The next summer, Colonel William Harney and 1,300 soldiers marched out of Fort Leavenworth "to even the score." They came to the camp of the Sioux band of Chief Little Thunder, which had nothing to do with the cow incident, opened fire with cannon, killed 86 Indians, and took 70 women and children prisoner. Meanwhile, 5 of the warriors of Bear That Scatters sought to avenge his death by killing 3 settlers. They gave themselves up and were taken to Fort Leavenworth singing their death chants, but President Franklin Pierce pardoned them.[238]

Atrocities by the Sioux began to occur with greater frequency. In the Black Hills of the Dakotas, Sioux caught a trapper of mixed blood, Hercules Levasseuer, in 1855. They cut off his hands, then cut out his tongue. Three years earlier, 30 prospectors had gone there. Eight turned back after seeing Indians; the rest disappeared. A gold miner, Ezra Kind, scratched a last message on a rock indicating that all the others of his party of 7 had been killed by Indians. They got all the gold they could carry, and, Lazarus reported, "I have lost my gun and nothing to eat and Indians hunting me."[239]

In Washington Territory the same year, the Yakima chief Kamiakin properly did not trust Governor Isaac Stevens and therefore would not sign a treaty proposed by Stevens. Instead, he made alliances preparing for war. "Even thus allied, he thought it best to bide his time, organize, and plan before confronting superior white forces. As often happened when Indians contemplated war, hot-headed young warriors acted independently and rashly." Qualchin, who was Kamiakin's nephew, led 5 warriors who attacked and killed 6 prospectors. A. J. Bolen, the Indian agent, was sent to investigate, and he was also killed. The army sent a force, and Kamiakin's 500 warriors ambushed it, killing 5. Indians raided a settlement near Seattle, killing 9 more.[240]

Also that year, Colonel James Kelley led a unit of militia in Washington Territory, where Walla Walla chief Peo-Peo-Mox-Mox had just burned a fort. The colonel and the chief held a parley, and the chief sent a messenger back to the village purportedly to communicate the terms of Kelley's offer to the Indians. Kelley held Peo-Peo-Mox-Mox and 6 other chiefs as voluntary hostages. The chief's message no doubt was to attack the army, because Kelley's force was soon under attack by many Indians. Kelley ordered the chiefs tied up. Peo-Peo-Mox-Mox resisted, there was a struggle, the chief drew a dagger, and he was hit on the head by a gun barrel. After a 4-day battle, the Indians withdrew, and the Oregon volunteers showed the settlers the chief's ears and scalp. Kamiakin's other allies, the Umatillas and Cayuses, were enraged. They raided settlements, killing 31.[241]

The Rouge River War occurred in Oregon in 1855 at about the same time as the Yakima War in Washington. Captain Andrew Jackson Smith, the commander of Fort Lane, had tried to keep peace between the settlers and the Indians. At times he would even interpose his troops between them. In October, because of the threat posed by the settlers, he moved the Indian men to the fort. The women and children were to follow. Before they could, volunteers murdered 23 Indian old men, women, and children.

The next day, the Indians killed 27 settlers. General John E. Wool, the head of the Department of the Pacific, and commander of both Washington and Oregon, observed, "It has become a contest of extermination by both whites and Indians." Wool, like many other army officers, was not anti-Indian. "Wool openly sympathized with the Indians. He directed his field officers not to fight Indians unless forced to do so, and at all other times to persuade the tribes to become peaceful."[242]

That same year Nelson Lee* and 20 others were attacked by Comanches as they were taking mules and horses to California to sell. Four,
including Lee, survived, but were captured by the Indians. The next
morning, Lee's feet were unbound and he was conducted through the Indian camp so he could see what had happened to those who had not
made it. They had been cut and hacked. Some had their arms and hands
chopped off. Others had their tongues drawn out and sharp sticks thrust
through them. All had been scalped. When the Comanche village was
reached, the survivors were tied naked to posts with their hands and feet
stretched between them. A long line of perhaps 200 warriors approached them in single file carrying knives, tomahawks, and arrows.

As the procession passed a pair of these captives, 2 warriors broke
from the line, seized them by the hair, scalped them, then resumed their
places in line, and went on. The piece of scalp taken was about the size
of a silver dollar and did not necessarily kill them, but blood ran freely
over their faces and into their beards. The second time the line came
past, the warriors cut the same 2 prisoners with their arrows. The Indians returned an uncounted number of times, until the 2 were hacked
and covered with blood. After a couple of hours, the warriors started
singing their war song, approached the 2 slowly, then drew hatchets and
crashed them into the skulls of the prisoners. The bodies were thrown
on the ground. Dogs came and lapped the blood from the wounds.

After a time, Lee tried to escape, but was caught and taken to the tent
of Chief Spotted Leopard, where he was tied to stakes on his back. For
2 weeks he was kept tied down. The chief drew his knife across the ten-
don just below his knee. The chief frequently bent his leg back and
forth, breaking the wound open. The purpose of this procedure was to
cripple Lee so that he could not escape when he was finally allowed to
move about. Later, while on the way back to the Comanche camp, he
heard war whoops and shrieks of agony that grew fainter and fainter,
then stopped. When he got into camp he saw parts of an army uniform.
Lee never forgot what happened next:

> Moving on beyond the camp into a grove, a spectacle presented itself
> that froze my blood. A white man had been subjected to the torture. A
> sharp stick had been thrust through his heel cords, by which he was
> suspended from a limb, with his head downward, as a butcher sus-
> pends a carcass. He, also, had been sacrificed with the accursed flints,
> his ears cut off and tongue drawn out. A slight convulsive shrug of the

*Nelson Lee was born in New York City, fought in the Black Hawk War and the Mexican War,
was in the U.S. Navy, the Texas Navy, and was a Texas Ranger.[243]

shoulders indicated that life was not wholly extinct. I gazed upon him in silence and terror and was relieved when they led me away.[244]

Three Englishwomen were brought into the camp where Lee was held. They told him the men in their wagon train had been massacred, the children carried away, "and crying babies killed by cutting a hole under their chins and hanging them 'on the point of a broken limb.'" They said they had been repeatedly raped.[245]

Lee was sold twice during his captivity. Big Wolf sold him to Chief Spotted Leopard, who in turn sold him to Chief Rolling Thunder. Rolling Thunder liked him and asked if he would like to marry. Lee said yes, believing it would help his chances of escape. He was then given 6 daughters of the tribe from which to chose. He chose Sleek Otter, who proved to be a faithful and affectionate wife. His marriage did indeed improve his status in the tribe. "I was no longer made the center post at their war dances."[246]

One day, Rolling Thunder informed him that the 2 of them would go on a 3-day journey, alone. At the end of the first day, they entered the village of a small tribe. The chief got drunk. The next morning Lee was very thirsty, but there was no water. Finally they found a little muddy water, and Lee was given the horn to scoop it up, but he could only get 3 parts mud to one part water. Rolling Thunder saw the problem, got off his horse, threw his rifle on the ground, and lay down to drink the muddy water. His hatchet was on his saddle. Lee grabbed the hatchet, leaped toward the chief, and buried the hatchet a full hand's breadth in his brain. For 56 days he wandered lost in the wilderness, undergoing many hardships until a trader found him.[247]

Only 3 years after the Mormon Cow War, Mormons were again involved in atrocities. Utah had asked to be admitted to the Union as a state several times. Congress refused each time because some Mormons practiced polygamy. President James Buchanan appointed a new territorial governor in the place of Mormon governor Brigham Young. Buchanan sent federal troops to enforce the appointment. In 1857, a group of Indians and Utah citizens gathered to confront these troops. They attacked a party of 140 and murdered most of them.[248]

CHAPTER 8

Atrocities in the Civil War and Post–Civil War Eras

In the 1850s, soldiers in the West included some derelicts, drunks, and criminals hiding out from the law. This ragtag army was outnumbered by the Indians.[1] When the Civil War began in 1861, a substantial part of the army in the West was occupied trying to prevent clashes between the settlers and the Indians. That war would be the most destructive in world history up to that time.[2] The Union suffered horrendous casualties. More soldiers were needed, and they were taken from the West. Duane Schultz outlined what that meant:

> With the outbreak of the war . . . western lands found themselves virtually defenseless. Troops were ordered back east to fight the Confederates. Only thirty-nine soldiers of the Second Infantry remained on duty at Fort Larned on the Arkansas River. Fort Wise had 33 men, Fort Kearny 125, and 90 were quartered at Fort Laramie. In all the vast plains covering some 200,000 square miles, fewer than three hundred troops patrolled.[3]

After the Civil War, the army was reduced to about 30,000 men, and it remained at that strength (or perhaps even smaller) until the Spanish-American War began in 1898.[4] The peacekeeping forces were again spread very thin. Trouble and atrocities continued to occur—they could not be controlled.

In 1861, Apache chief Cochise vowed to exterminate all whites in Arizona.[5] Second Lieutenant George N. Bascom was stationed at Fort Buchanan. He was ordered to find Cochise and demand the return of a boy and some stock seized in an Apache raid near the fort. Bascom and Cochise met in Bascom's tent. Cochise, even though he had vowed to kill all whites, denied that his people had any part in the raid or its plunder. He truthfully blamed the White Mountain subtribe of Apache and offered to help get the boy and the stock back. Bascom told Cochise he and his party would be held hostage until the boy and stock were returned. Cochise drew his knife, slashed the tent, and escaped. The rest of his party—his brother, 2 nephews, and a woman with 2 children— were taken prisoner. Cochise already held 3 white prisoners before the meeting, but that night he seized a wagon train and got 2 more. The Apache also had 8 Mexican teamster prisoners, who were bound to wagon wheels and the wagons set on fire.

The next day, Cochise appeared under a flag of truce. Three Butterfield stagecoach employees who knew him went out to talk. The white flag was thrown down, the Indians seized one employee, James F. Wallace, both sides opened fire, the other 2 employees were hit, and one died. Bascom's troops later found the burned wagon train with the charred corpses of the Mexican teamsters still attached to the wheels. They also found the remains of Cochise's 6 white hostages, who were perforated by many lance holes and cut up to such an extent that Wallace could be identified only by his dental fillings.

Leaving behind the Indian woman hostage and her 2 children, Bascom took the rest of his prisoners (including Cochise's brother) to the scene where the bodies of Cochise's hostages had been found and hanged all of them. Their bodies stayed there for months as a warning.[6] This was the beginning of the Apache Wars. Cochise inflicted "frightful tortures" on his captives during that time.[7] During the next 2 months, it is believed his people killed 150 whites and Mexicans.[8]

In nearby New Mexico in 1861, settlers repeatedly raided the Navajo Indians and took captives who were later sold as slaves.[9] The same year at Fort Lyon in New Mexico, a series of horse races was run between the soldiers and the Navajo Indians. The feature race was between an army lieutenant on a quarter horse and Navajo chief Manuelito on a Navajo pony. Many bets were made. Manuelito lost control of his pony early on, and it ran off the track. The Indians charged that its reins and bridle had been cut with a knife. The soldier judges declared the lieutenant the winner. When the soldiers returned to the fort, angry Indians followed, and the gates were shut on them. One Indian tried to force his way in and was shot and killed.

Commander Lieutenant Colonel Manuel Chaves turned his troops on the 500 or so Indians gathered outside the fort. Captain Nicholas Hodt described what happened then. Indian women and children ran in all directions, but were shot and bayoneted. A soldier murdered 2 children and a woman. Hodt demanded that he stop, but he did not. The commander directed the howitzers to fire on the Indians. The sergeant in charge of the mountain howitzers pretended not to understand the command to fire, for he considered it to be unlawful, but being cursed by the officer of the day, and threatened, he felt he had to execute the order or else get himself in trouble. Thirty to 40 Navajo were killed. The rest fled and turned to raiding.[10]

Sometime before 1864, a Denver man reported what he had found after an Indian raid:

> About 100 yards from the desolated ranch [we] discovered the body of the murdered woman and her two dead children, one of which was a little girl of four years and the other an infant. The woman had been stabbed in several places and scalped, and the body bore evidences of having been violated. The two children had their throats cut, their heads being nearly severed from their bodies.[11]

Colonel Kit Carson* arranged for 5 Apache chiefs to go visit with Colonel James H. Carlton in Sante Fe around 1862. On the way, 2 of the chiefs met some soldiers commanded by Captain James Graydon, a former saloon keeper. Graydon offered them beef and flour, then the 2 groups parted, only to meet a second time. Graydon went into the chiefs' camp, had a drink with them, then shot them dead. The other 3 met with Carlton and told him they no longer wanted to fight.[13]

Herman Lehmann, who was captured as a boy and raised as a warrior, participated in a joint Apache-Comanche raid near the headwaters of the Llano River in Texas. He later admitted that they had "burned a house and killed a man, his wife and four or five children. We tortured them before we killed them."[14]

As usual, it wasn't just the Indians who were killing. In 1862, Con-

---

*Christopher Houston "Kit" Carson was a trader and trapper who lived with and married Indians. He fought Navajo, Comanche, and Kiowa during the Civil War, and he was made a brigadier general shortly after it ended.[12]

federate lieutenant colonel John Robert Baylor ordered one of his commanders to do away with all hostile Indians:

> The Congress of the Confederate States has passed a law declaring extermination of all hostile Indians. You will therefore use all means to persuade the Apaches or any tribes to come in for the purpose of making peace, and when you get them together, kill all the grown Indians and take the children prisoners and sell them to defray the expense of killing the Indians.[15]

THERE WERE two causes of the Santee Sioux Uprising in Minnesota, one chronic and one acute. The chronic cause was the failure of the government to pay the annuity due the Sioux so that they could buy food and other supplies from the government warehouses. The completely unrelated acute cause was the bravado of 4 young Sioux who had come home empty-handed from a hunting expedition.

By its 1851 treaty, the government agreed to make payments to the Sioux once a year. The payment due in mid-June was a large part of their income. In 1862 crops had failed. Their custom was to start their buffalo hunt in July, just after the payment was made, but July passed with no payment. The reason for this was that the government couldn't decide whether to pay in gold or Civil War greenbacks, and therefore made no payment at all. But the food and materials that could be purchased with the payment were already present in warehouses on the reservation.[16]

About 3,000 hungry Sioux confronted Indian agent Thomas J. Galbraith, demanding the food and other things due them. He told them that the provisions could only be distributed when he got the money. Galbraith asked that they go hunting and come back in a month. They did. When they returned on July 14, he told them that the money still wasn't there and that he would give them no food. On August 4, mounted warriors broke into a warehouse and started carrying away flour. Lieutenant Timothy J. Sheehan threatened them with a howitzer, and they left. Sheehan persuaded Galbraith to release some provisions. Sheehan also requested a meeting with the Sioux and local traders.[17]

Santee Sioux chief Little Crow* represented the Sioux at the council

---

*Little Crow was a hereditary chief of the Santee Sioux. He lived at the site of present South St. Paul, Minnesota. Little Crow had 6 wives and 22 children. He had good relations with settlers for a long time, and he fought the renegade band of Wahpekute Sioux who had attacked settlers at Spirit Lake in 1858.[18]

meeting. He protested they had no food and the warehouses were full, and asked that the Indian agent arrange for them to have food, "or else we may take our own way to keep ourselves from starving. When men are hungry, they help themselves."[19] Agent Galbraith put the matter to the traders, who could distribute provisions on credit if they chose. They deferred to Andrew J. Myrick, the most prominent trader, who, offended by Little Crow's statement, said, "So far as I am concerned, if they are hungry, let them eat grass!"[20] But Captain John S. Marsh, the commander at Fort Ridgely, ordered Galbraith to start distributing food at once. Then Galbraith visited the Lower Agency (there were two agencies) on August 15, observed that the harvest there seemed abundant, and told Little Crow he had changed his mind, and there would be no distribution until the money arrived.[21] The tinder was waiting for the spark.

The spark came about 2 days later, when 4 young Sioux, Brown Wing, Killing Ghost, Breaking Up, and Runs Against Something Crawling, were returning from an unsuccessful hunting trip. At the settlement of Acton, Minnesota, one of them stole a nest of eggs belonging to a settler. He was warned it would cause trouble, and the other 3 accused him of being a coward. He replied he wasn't afraid to kill a settler. The 4 then went to the farmer's house and started arguing with Robinson Jones, the owner of the hen, who was with his 15-year-old daughter and an infant son. Jones announced he was going to join his wife, who was visiting a neighbor, Howard Baker, and took his daughter with him, but left the infant at home. Later, the Indians followed Jones to the Baker house. In addition to Mrs. Jones and the Bakers, an immigrant couple, Mr. and Mrs. Viranus Webster, were there. The Indians proposed target shooting. The settlers agreed and shot first. They then stood back without reloading to see how the Indians did. The Indians shot and killed the 3 men, Mrs. Jones, and the daughter. They stole horses and fled, leaving Mrs. Baker and Mrs. Webster alive.

The Indian boys told their leaders what they had done, and there was a meeting at the home of Chief Little Crow that night. The war faction wanted to kill or drive out all the settlers, but others opposed that. Little Crow spoke last. He said he knew the numbers and power of the settlers, and that defeat lay at the end of the war trail. But then he said that if the tribe wanted war, he would lead them. It was agreed that a massive attack would take place.

One of the first killed was trader Andrew J. Myrick. A tuft of grass was stuffed in Myrick's mouth after he was killed.[22] An estimated 400 settlers died the first day of the uprising.[23] Alan Axelrod concluded that "the opening phase of the uprising would stand as the worst Indian massacre of whites in the nation's history."[24] Ralph K. Andrist added, "The word 'massacre' has been loosely used and misused, but what occurred in Minnesota was a massacre in the true sense of the word."[25] Duane Schultz reported on some of the details:

> Families [were] burned alive in their cabins, children nailed to doors, girls raped by a dozen braves and then hacked to pieces, babies dismembered and their limbs flung in the mother's face.[26]

Women who were not killed were held as captives and subjected to mass rape. The Indians left children alone according to the impulse of the moment. A few men who had been their friends were spared, but in general they killed friend and foe alike.[27] Several hundred whites were captured.[28]

The Indians even tried to trick the settlers in order to kill more. At Fort Ridgely, Little Crow appeared on horseback waving a blanket in an apparent request for a parley, then about 200 yelling warriors broke out of a ravine and headed toward the fort.[29] At the Lake Shetek settlement, the Indians made a surrender agreement with the settlers, then shot several as they left the settlement, clubbed 2 or 3 children, and took the remaining women and children.[30]

The courage of settler women was shown at Lake Shetek, where the Eastlick family suffered grievous losses. Wife Lavina was born in New York and married at 17. She and husband John had 5 sons and had already made several moves, each farther west, before settling in Minnesota.[31] When the uprising occurred, John was killed instantly. Lavina received 4 gunshot wounds and was clubbed over the head with a rifle until it broke. Two of the children were beaten and died. Then Lavina asked her 11-year-old son, Merton, to take care of her 18-month-old son, Johnny. Merton carried and led Johnny for 50 miles the next few days, finding enough berries to keep them alive. Lavina was finally able to come to their aid. She had been picked up by the mail carrier. (The boys' uncle Tom had come out of a slough to try to talk peace, but was shot with buckshot. He said good-bye to Merton, but he too got up and made it to safety.[32])

Sixteen-year-old Mary Boyeau was captured. She saw the Sioux go into a house where a woman was baking bread in an oven with her infant in a cradle nearby. They put the baby in the oven, the mother was cut and stabbed, then the baby was taken from the oven and its brains dashed out against the side of the house.[33]

The militia finally mounted a successful counteroffensive. Colonel Henry Sibley was in charge. He had been the first governor of Minnesota. After the decisive Battle of Wood Lake, the Indians were driven back so quickly that they left 14 dead behind, contrary to custom. Sibley discovered that all the dead Indians had been scalped. He gave his troops a lecture about acting like civilized gentlemen. It was claimed that the Indians were scalped by the Renville Rangers, many of whom had Sioux blood. Three days after the battle, 2,000 Indians surrendered and released about 370 captives.

Two similar estimates of the total number of settler dead came from reliable sources—one was President Lincoln, who thought at least 800 settlers lost their lives;[34] the other was historian William Brandon, who believed the Sioux "murdered some 700 settlers and killed 100 soldiers before they were driven out of Minnesota."[35] The Santee Sioux Uprising was the greatest Indian atrocity of the war.

Only a week after the Battle of Wood Lake, a military tribunal sentenced 303 Sioux to be hanged for participating in the uprising. The condemned men passed through the town of New Ulm, where the greatest settler losses occurred, on the very day the bodies of town defenders were being taken from temporary graves in the street to permanent graves in the cemetery. The townspeople, especially the women, attacked the Sioux with everything from hot water to pitchforks. The militia had to use bayonets to drive them back. Soldiers as well as prisoners were injured.

President Lincoln personally reviewed all the death sentences and reduced them substantially. One was given a reprieve, 2 Indians not on Lincoln's death list were hanged by mistake,[36] and 38 were hanged simultaneously at Mankato, Minnesota. It was the largest simultaneous hanging in United States history.[37] The hangman was William Duley, who had escaped at Lake Shetek. Three of his children were still lying dead on the frozen prairie, and his wife and 2 other children were still Sioux captives.[38]

The bodies were buried, but not for long. After dark a number of doctors dug up the bodies so they could use the skeletons.[39] One of the doctors was William W. Mayo. Later he and his 2 physician sons, William and Charles, founded the Mayo Clinic in Rochester, Minnesota.

Little Crow fled to Canada. He returned to Minnesota in 1863 to steal a few horses, according to his son, and was shot and killed stealing berries from farmer Chauncey Lamson.[40]

In December 1863, a party of soldiers found 15 Poncas people camped at night about 12 miles from their reservation. They were returning from a visit to Omaha. The soldiers offered the women money for sex, with revolvers in hand. The Poncas fled, and the soldiers destroyed their camp. The soldiers came upon them again the next morning, and wounded 3 as they were crossing the frozen river. Three women and a little girl hid, but their barking dog revealed their presence, and the soldiers killed all of them. Some of the Indians escaped, but the soldiers were never identified. The army called it "a very unfortunate occurrence."[41]

The Santee Sioux remained active after the uprising. Captive Fanny Kelly was forced to retreat with them after they were attacked by General Alfred Sully's army in 1864. An Indian came to her to read a letter he had taken from a soldier whom he had killed. The soldier had written that after an army topographical engineer had been killed, the soldiers had caught the Indians responsible, had cut their heads off, and stuck them on poles.[42] The Sioux later captured a settler who had been hunting on the prairie. They took off all his clothing, tied him hand and foot, and left him there to starve.[43]

One of the Sioux drew a picture of a white soldier for Fanny Kelly, representing him as a coward and an inferior being. Kelly grabbed it from him, tore it apart, and said the soldiers were her friends and she loved them. The Sioux became enraged and burned her severely with firebrands and the heated points of arrows.[44]

Shortly before Kelly finally escaped from the Sioux, they attacked a flatboat carrying about 20 people on the Yellowstone River. The bodies of those who were killed were at once thrown into the river. The women and children who survived were tortured to death that same day. The scalp of a woman whose red hair was 4 feet long struck Kelly. "Her glorious locks were needed to hang on the chief's belt."[45]

In 1864, Arizona rancher and Indian fighter King S. Wolsey had a peace council with the Apache. He (apparently by himself) massacred 24 of them. The territorial legislature congratulated him, gave him the rank of colonel, and tried to raise a militia to wipe out the rest of the hostile Indians.[46]

In January of that same year, Colonel Kit Carson won a decisive victory over the Navajo at their stronghold of Canyon de Chelly. By the middle of March, nearly 6,000 had surrendered to army bases and another 2,000 surrendered by the end of 1864. Soldiers took 2,400 prisoners across New Mexico. Dysentery caused 126 deaths even before the march started at Fort Canby. About 74 died on the way. There were reports that an unknown number not able to walk were shot by the soldiers.[47]

Not all Indians supported the wanton murder and torture of women and children. Shawnee chiefs Tecumseh and Black Hoof took the position, quoted by Bil Gilbert, that

> the occasional, slow, painful execution of an enemy warrior was one thing, an act of public policy, but burning women and children, torturing purely for pleasure, dishonored ancient traditions and was a sport for degenerates.[48]

The historian Thomas Goodrich has gathered together diaries, letters, and memoirs concerning soldiers and the Plains Indians during the years 1865–79. His book is called *Scalp Dance*. Some of these reports can be fixed in time; those that cannot are discussed first.

Lieutenant Charles Springer's diary told of a skirmish with the Sioux:

> 5 of our men were killed by arrow shots from the Indians, and one of them scalped, two were wounded, and one of them very severe. . . . Some of our men ran upon them killed two, and in the heat and excitement (also thirst for revenge) scalped the Indians.[49]

Goodrich said that Captain Henry Palmer

> found the bodies of three little children who had been taken by the heels by the Indians and swung around against the log cabin, beating their heads to a jelly. Found the hired girl some fifteen rods from the ranch staked out on the prairie, tied by her hands and feet, naked, body full of arrows and horribly mangled.[50]

Indians often dug up the bodies of soldiers to scalp them, but soldiers sometimes desecrated Indian graves as well. Lieutenant Edward Godfrey reported that soldiers robbed an above-ground Indian burial site in Montana.[51] Soldiers Jack Peate and Sigmund Shlesinger admitted they also had done the same thing.[52]

Captain Albert Barnitz wrote that during an Indian charge "Sergeant

[Frederick] Wyllyams . . . was killed. The Indians stripped, scalped, and horribly mutilated his body."[53]

After the Civil War, a Cheyenne* named Porcupine and his friends "tied a big stick" across the Union Pacific railroad tracks, hoping to salvage something valuable after the wreck. A handcar with 5 maintenance workers on it struck the big stick. The Indians scalped all 5, but one lived and escaped.[55]

ALTHOUGH THE Santee Sioux Uprising was the most murderous against settlers, only 2 years later the Sand Creek Massacre of the Cheyenne and Arapaho by Colorado militia became the greatest atrocity against the Indians in American history. The Cheyenne love of warfare was described by Duane Schultz, who has written the best and most recent detailed account of the massacre, *Month of the Freezing Moon:*

> Cheyenne boys were taught to fight and die gloriously, and their goal was to become the bravest of warriors. . . . To enjoy life fully, to feel satisfied, they needed someone to fight, and in their wanderings across the plains, it was seldom difficult to find strangers to attack. To the Cheyenne, anyone who was not of their own tribe was an enemy. . . . Scalping might be just a way of keeping score, but mutilation was also practiced out of tradition and habit. It was not uncommon for a Cheyenne warrior to cut off the arms of an enemy and preserve the severed limbs as trophies. Strangers captured by the Cheyenne faced a gruesome fate. Captives were stripped and spread-eagled over anthills, their hands and feet lashed to pegs driven deep into the ground. There they were abandoned, to go blind from staring at the sun, insane from hunger and thirst, and eaten by ants and wild animals. Sometimes the Indians heaped twigs and branches atop their victims and burned them alive.
>
> One Cheyenne brave recalled the killing of an old Shoshone man. "We cut off his hands, his feet, and his head. We ripped open his breast and his belly. I stood there and looked at his heart and his liver. We tore down the lodge, built a bonfire on it and its contents and piled the remnants of the dead body upon this bonfire. We stayed there until nothing was left but ashes and coals."

*The Cheyenne tribe first lived in Minnesota, then the Dakotas, and then moved westward to the banks of the Missouri River, probably pushed there by hostile bands of Sioux and Chippewa. They went into the Black Hills, but the Sioux pushed them farther south, and they settled in Wyoming and Nebraska. The Cheyenne made war against the Kiowa and Comanche, but then formed an alliance with these 2 tribes against the Crows, Pawnee, Shoshoni, Ute, and Apache.[54]

A captured woman became the common property of the war party, to be raped by all until they returned to camp, where she would belong exclusively to the man who first seized her. Treated as a slave, she would often be beaten and mutilated, eventually to be killed or traded into slavery with another tribe.[56]

The prelude to the massacre began in 1856, when an army officer tried to arrest some Cheyenne who were arguing with a trader about the ownership of a horse. Soldiers opened fire and a warrior was killed. The Cheyenne panicked and fled. A trapper was killed at that time. Two months later, Cheyenne looking for their ancient enemies, the Pawnee, killed a settler. The Cheyenne then tried to flag down a stagecoach, claiming they wanted tobacco. The situation escalated, as described in Chapter 3, and at least 33 died.[57]

The Santee Sioux Uprising of 1862 in Minnesota had alarmed the people of Colorado, where the Cheyenne lived. The Sioux had been docile much longer than the Cheyenne and Arapaho,* yet the Sioux had gone wild. Even worse, Denver was unprotected. All the soldiers had gone east to fight in the Civil War.

A new Colorado territorial governor, John Evans,† arrived in the summer of 1862.[60] Evans received 3 reports indicating that the Cheyenne and other tribes were going to attack.[61]

John M. Chivington‡ was appointed commander of the Colorado military district by Evans in 1863, and it was he who led Colorado volunteers against the Cheyenne. Chivington got a report that some drunk Indians had terrorized a rancher. He sent Major Jacob Downing to investigate. Downing reported he had found a half-Cheyenne, half-Sioux Indian and had questioned him by "roasting his shins." He finally guided Downing to the Cheyenne camp in Cedar Canyon, which Downing found to be peaceful and almost defenseless. The warriors were away hunting. He attacked anyway on the theory that the settlers were already at war with the Cheyenne. He reported that the attack lasted 3 hours. Twenty-six Indians were killed, 30 wounded, and everything burned.[63]

---

*At various times, the Arapaho fought the Shoshoni, Ute, Pawnee, Crows, Sioux, Comanche, and Kiowa.[58]

†Evans was a physician, a wealthy real-estate developer, and a good administrator, but cold-blooded and mercenary, and possessed with an overwhelming ambition to be Colorado's first United States senator.[59]

‡John M. Chivington was a Methodist minister from Ohio who preached to settlers, Indians, and miners in the West. Evans commissioned him a major in the Colorado militia, and he had fought well in the Civil War.[62]

Lieutenant George S. Eayre and his men were also looking for Cheyenne under orders from Chivington to burn lodges and kill Indians wherever they found them. They found Lean Bear's band of 400 Cheyenne. The militia version and the Cheyenne version of what happened differ greatly. Eayre said he was attacked by the Indians and defeated them in a 7-hour battle, killing 28. The Indian version is that Lean Bear went to the militia with the medal President Lincoln had given him to show he was friendly. When he got within 20 feet of Eayre, the lieutenant ordered his men to open fire. They killed Lean Bear at once, then riddled his body with bullets. Eayre fired his howitzers on the camp. Black Kettle,* the Cheyenne peace chief, came out and insisted that the fighting stop. After Lean Bear was killed, the angry Cheyenne raided up and down the stagecoach line, but they found no victims because all the settlers had fled.[65] Captain Parmeter was commander of Fort Larned. Arapaho peace chief Left Hand had warned Parmeter that some Kiowa Indians were going to steal his horses. Parmeter paid no attention to this. When the Kiowa arrived, he was drunk, and the dancing of the Kiowa women distracted the soldiers. No less than 240 horses and mules belonging to Eayre's men were stolen. Left Hand, bearing a white flag, arrived at the fort to offer his help in recovering the horses. Parmeter ordered his soldiers to fire on Left Hand and his men. The Arapaho weren't hurt, but they were mad. They terrified the settlers in their area to such an extent that they left their homes. Major General Samuel R. Curtis, the commander at Fort Leavenworth, Kansas, sent Major T. I. McKenny to investigate. He was seriously worried about the situation and made this accurate prediction:

> If great caution is not exercised on our part, there will be a bloody war. It should be our policy to try and conciliate them, guard our mails and trains well to prevent theft, and stop these scouting parties [of Chivington's men] that are roaming over the country, who do not know one tribe from another and who will kill anything in the shape of an Indian. It will require only a few more murders on the part of our troops to unite all these warlike tribes.[66]

Even as McKenny was writing his report, Cheyenne and Arapaho war parties were rumored to be searching out settlers along the Platte and Arkansas trails.[67]

---

*Black Kettle fought the Ute, Delaware, and other enemies of the Cheyenne in his youth. By the time of the Civil War, he wanted peace with the settlers.[64]

Evans asked Curtis to send soldiers "in strong force," but got no reply. He sent a second, more urgent message, which concluded, "I would respectfully ask that our troops may be allowed to defend us and whip those redskin rebels into submission at once."[68]

On June 11, 1864, 4 Arapaho killed the Ward Hungate family 25 miles from Denver. The father's body was found with more than 80 bullets in it. The bodies of the wife and 2 young daughters, ages 6 and 3, were mutilated, and the throats of the girls cut so deeply that their heads were almost severed. All 3 had been tied together and thrown into a well. Martial law was imposed in Denver.[69]

On July 17, there were Indian raids all along the Platte River. An unknown number of people were killed.[70] On July 19, Indians attacked a wagon train at Walnut Creek. Ten were killed, and 2 more were scalped but lived. In August more than 50 people were killed in raids, 10 of whom were tortured to death. The trail was closed for nearly 6 weeks, and supplies were short. Evans asked Curtis for more troops, but Curtis could not spare them. He did authorize formation of the Third Colorado Volunteer Cavalry Regiment, the troops Chivington would lead to the Sand Creek Massacre. They enlisted for 100 days.[71]

A little more than 2 weeks later, Evans issued a proclamation "calling on all friendly Indians to quit the company of those at war and report to designated military posts, 'places of safety' where they would be fed and protected." Few Indians responded.[72] He then issued a second proclamation on August 10, authorizing whites "to seek out and kill on sight all hostile Indians, defined as anyone who had not come in for protection." In addition, the public "could take or destroy all property of the hostiles."[73]

Black Kettle and other Cheyenne peace chiefs sent a letter to 2 Indian agents stating that the Cheyenne council had met and would make peace if the government would also make peace with the Kiowa, Comanche, Arapaho, Apache, and Sioux. He offered to exchange 7 Cheyenne prisoners for Indian prisoners held by the government in Denver. The letter was delivered to Major Edward Wynkoop, commander at Fort Lyon.

Wynkoop had strong feelings about Indians, and later admitted he "belonged to the exterminators." Wynkoop believed Indians were universally treacherous and had "nothing but instincts of a wild beast." He announced that as barriers to civilization, they "had no rights that we were bound to respect."[74]

Wynkoop took 127 troops and went to Black Kettle. He was met by

800 warriors with arrows at the ready. He noticed many of them had rifles and pistols as well. Black Kettle agreed to talk. Wynkoop proposed taking any delegation of chiefs they chose to talk peace with Evans and said he would do his best to procure peace for them. He suggested that the chiefs take their families to Fort Lyon, where they could wait "in safety" for the chiefs' return from the meeting with the governor in Denver. The next day the Cheyenne released 4 young female prisoners, stating the other 3 had been sold to the Sioux. They said they would go the 400 miles to Denver to see Evans to make peace.[75]

Just as soon as he arrived in Denver with the chiefs, Wynkoop immediately went to the Evans home. The governor couldn't see him. The next morning, Governor Evans came to Wynkoop's room and said he would not meet with the chiefs because they had declared war, and, more important, the Colorado Third had been formed to kill Indians, "and they must kill Indians." Wynkoop convinced the reluctant Evans to meet the chiefs. Colonel Chivington, as commander of the military district, wired the developments to General Curtis. Curtis replied, "I want no peace until the Indians suffer more."[76]

The meeting between Evans and the chiefs at Camp Weld on September 28, 1864, was tense. Black Kettle reminded the governor of the first proclamation he made, which promised that Cheyenne and Arapaho who went to Fort Lyon would receive protection. Black Kettle was not told it might no longer be applicable. Evans accused Black Kettle of being allied with the Sioux, who were at war with the settlers. Black Kettle and other chiefs denied that they had joined forces with the Sioux.[77]

At the end, Chivington, who had said nothing up to then, announced, "My rule of fighting white men or Indians is to fight them until they lay down their arms and submit to military authority. You [Indians] are nearer to Major Wynkoop [at Fort Lyon] than anyone else, and you can go with him when you get ready to do that."[78]

The Indians were pleased with the meeting. They thought they had ended the war and had made peace, but Evans and Chivington thought not. The next day Evans wrote to Sam Colley, the Indian agent for the Cheyenne and Arapaho, that he had not made peace with them, and that they must make peace with the military authorities. His annual report to the commissioner of Indian affairs characterized most of the Indians as hostile. They would have to be conquered by force. In a return message, the commissioner criticized Evans. He had the duty to encourage peace, he said, and a spirit of conciliation should have been shown.[79]

Wynkoop reported the situation to his commanding officer, Major General Samuel R. Curtis. Among other things, he suggested that "if peace terms were to be offered to the Indians, he could guarantee their fidelity by having all the Indian villages located near the fort where they would be subject to his control."[80] When Wynkoop's report was received, Curtis was away from Fort Riley, so his aide, Major B. S. Henning, read it and wired Chivington on the day of the meeting with Black Kettle that Wynkoop had somehow acted against policy. Henning relieved Wynkoop of command of Fort Lyon and put Major Scott J. Anthony in charge. No Indians were to be allowed in the vicinity of the fort for any reason. Anthony arrived and took command.[81] (Wynkoop learned after the battle that he had been relieved because he "left his district without orders to escort the chiefs to Governor Evans in Denver instead of to Curtis.")[82]

The Arapaho, 652 strong, made a camp near Fort Lyon. Anthony demanded to know why they were there. The Arapaho told him that although other tribes were at war, they came to the fort to show they wanted peace, to be where the public wouldn't be frightened of them and where they wouldn't be harmed by travelers or soldiers. Anthony was surprised because Henning had told him the Indians near the fort were hostile. Anthony told the Arapaho they could stay if they would surrender their weapons and stolen stock. They agreed. Anthony noticed they were hungry and gave them food, contrary to his orders. Ten days later, he changed his mind. He returned their weapons and recommended they kill game to live on.[83] He wrote to General Curtis, "I told them . . . that no war would be waged against them until your pleasure was heard."[84]

Shortly, Black Kettle and about 70 Cheyenne arrived. Anthony said he didn't have instructions to make peace with them, but he would let them know at once if and when he got such instructions. He said the Cheyenne should camp on Sand Creek, which was 40 miles away. Wynkoop had told them Anthony was now in charge and would treat the Cheyenne the same as he had done, and Anthony encouraged the Indians to believe this. But Anthony was acting with duplicity. Two weeks after arriving at the fort, he reported to Curtis that he intended to wait until he got reinforcements, then he would take to the field against all Indians. He specifically mentioned Black Kettle's Cheyenne village at Sand Creek. Chivington had decided to attack them also.[85]

Five days before the Sand Creek Massacre, on November 29, 1864, Chivington had supper with trader James Combs. Chivington inquired about the Indians. Were they well fed? Where were they located? Were they armed? Chivington then stated the purpose of his mission. He told Combs, "Scalps are what we are after."[86] As Combs was leaving, he heard Chivington say to his officers, "Well, I long to be wading in gore."[87]

Chivington wanted to take the Cheyenne at Sand Creek by surprise and made elaborate preparations. He did not tell General Curtis about the planned attack on Sand Creek.[88]

The night before the troops were to leave for Sand Creek, several officers and some civilians objected to what was about to happen because of the promises that had been made to the Cheyenne. They included Lieutenant James Cannon, Lieutenant W. P. Minton, Lieutenant C. M. Cossitt, Captain Silas S. Soule, and Lieutenant Joseph Cramer, who protested first to Anthony and then to Chivington that under the circumstances the attack would be murder. Chivington exploded. Cheyenne were evil and "damn any man who is in sympathy with them." As he left the room, he remarked loudly that Cramer should get out of the service. A last effort to call off the attack was made by Lieutenants Cossitt, Minton, and Maynard, Indian agent Sam Colley, and some other civilians. Chivington said again, "Damn any man who is in sympathy with an Indian."[89]

There were about 750 men in the attack, including Anthony with 125 from the Colorado First.[90] They were drunk, according to Carl Waldman and James Wilson.[91]

An elderly guide named Jim Beckwourth, a black trapper, became so stiff and cold he couldn't continue. Robert Bent, the half-Cheyenne son of William Bent, the founder of the first American settlement in Colorado, was ordered to take Beckwourth's place. Bent had 3 sisters and a brother in the camp at Sand Creek. Near daybreak, Bent suggested he might run off. Chivington tapped his revolver, looked at Bent, and said, "I haven't had an Indian to eat in a long time. If you fool with me, and don't lead us to that camp, I'll have you for breakfast."[92]

When they reached the village, Chivington first ordered 2 groups to run off the Indian horses. He addressed the troops, telling them to remove their coats so they could fight better, and in effect told them to take no prisoners. In the Indian camp, the 700 galloping horses awakened the Indians. Black Kettle hoisted an American flag that had been given to him by a commissioner of Indian affairs with the advice that it would protect the Cheyenne when approached by soldiers. He also raised a small white flag. He told his people not to be afraid because the camp was under the protection of the American flag.[93]

Then the troops opened fire, beginning the Sand Creek Massacre. The

Colorado Third Hundred Dazers, led by Chivington, dismounted and began firing right through Anthony's men. Chivington shouted, "Remember the murdered women and children on the Platte."[94] Anthony's troops fled to a creek to avoid the gunfire from the Third. All control was lost and never regained.[95]

Cheyenne chief White Antelope was a noted warrior who fought Comanche and Kiowa in the 1830s. He was one of the few Dog Soldiers (an Indian military society) to counsel peace with the settlers.[96] As the Sand Creek Massacre began, White Antelope ran toward the soldiers wearing his presidential medal and shouting in English for them to stop killing his people. Black Kettle called for him to run away. White Antelope halted in the creek, folded his arms, and chanted his death song:

> Nothing lives long
> Except the earth and the mountains

and waited to die. Bullets hit his chest, he fell, and the troops scalped him and cut off his ears and nose. Chief Left Hand said he would not fight his friends, the white men, and was killed. Others made no effort to fight or flee. Many walked toward the soldiers with raised hands, but all were killed. Every soldier was engaged except the troops of Captain Soule, who had pledged the Indians safety. He ordered his men not to fire. About 100 Indians fled for a mile along the creek bed to where the banks had gulleys and ravines. They dug in there with knives and bare hands. Soldiers fired at them from both banks. Soldiers then went into the banks and killed the wounded and the women and children who had not been hurt. The killing went on for almost 4 hours, then the troops left.[97]

There were many additional atrocities. A dismounted soldier standing near Chivington tried to scalp a dead woman. A naked 3-year-old was walking in the sand trying to reach the Indians ahead of him. A soldier shot at him and missed, another missed, but a third killed him. Five women crouched under a bank for shelter. When they were discovered, they showed the soldiers they were females, begged for mercy, but all were killed anyhow. An Indian woman with a broken leg was lying on the bank. A soldier came up with drawn saber, she raised her arm for protection, he broke it with his saber, she rolled over, raising her other arm, and he broke it as well. Some other women huddled in a hole for protection. They sent a girl about 6 out with a white flag. She was killed. A 5-year-old girl tried to hide in the sand. Two soldiers found her, killed her, and pulled her out by the arm. Several babies were killed along with their mothers in their mothers' arms.[98]

An old woman wandered around blinded because her entire scalp had been taken and the skin of her forehead had fallen over her eyes. Several soldiers quarreled over who should scalp a body. They all took part of the scalp. Soldiers took turns "profaning the body of a comely young squaw" who was dead. Fingers were cut off to get Indian rings. One soldier carried a heart impaled on a stick. Soldiers collected male genitals. The breasts of Indian women were sliced off; one was worn as a cap, another stretched over the bow of a saddle. A little boy was buried alive in a trench. A major blew off the top of the boy's head with a pistol. Three adult females and 5 children were being conducted down a road by soldiers when Lieutenant Harry Richmond of the Third appeared and killed and scalped all 8 while they were screaming for mercy. The soldiers shrank back, apparently disapproving.[99]

One soldier wrote, "They were scalped, their brains knocked out. The men used their knives, ripped open women, clubbed little children, knocked them in the head with their guns, beat their brains out, [and] mutilated their bodies in every sense of the word."[100]

More than 100 Indians were killed.[101] Robert Bent stayed at the site of the massacre for a time. He said that 163 were killed, of which 110 were women and children.[102] Wilson estimated the Indian dead at between 105 and 200,[103] and West believed there were around 150 dead.[104] Many estimates were higher, including Chivington's of 400 to 500.[105] Probably there were fewer than 70 armed warriors in the camp. They held off the 700 soldiers long enough to permit most of the Indians, about 500, to escape, including Black Kettle.[106] Afterward, Major Anthony wrote to his brother praising the bravery of the Indians, but adding that "we, of course, took no prisoners."[107] Nine soldiers were killed outright, and 4 more died later.[108]

What could have motivated Chivington and Evans? Both had run for Congress and lost. Schultz believed both thought they could get favorable publicity by fighting the Indians, thereby winning Chivington a seat in the House and Evans a seat in the Senate.[109] Although this belief may have been true, the only hard evidence as to either hoping an Indian fight would advance his career is congressional testimony about Chivington that "he thought he had done a brilliant thing which would make him a brigadier general. I think the expression was 'that he thought that would put a star on his shoulder.'"[110]

INDIAN RAIDS intensified greatly after Sand Creek. Axelrod observed that "far from disheartening the Indians, as Chivington had hoped, the

Battle of Sand Creek galvanized their resolve to fight, as Southern Sioux, Northern Arapaho, and Cheyenne united in a spasm of savage raids during late 1864 and early 1865 called the Cheyenne-Arapaho War."[111] In January 1865, more than 1,000 Cheyenne and Arapaho Indians raided Julesburg, about 190 miles northeast of Denver. War parties as large as 500 warriors burned coach stations and ranches as far as 80 miles west of Julesburg. Eight settlers were killed. For about 150 miles in the South Platte Valley, everything was burned and no settlers were safe. Denver was isolated and threatened with famine. Some 50 settlers died and others were captured. There was burning and violence from the Missouri River in Kansas to Salt Lake City. Chivington's successor declared martial law in Denver and closed down all businesses until 360 replacements could be found for the Hundred Dazers.[112] Debo and Wilson said this Cheyenne-Arapaho War killed more whites than the number of Indians killed at Sand Creek.[113]

THE INDIAN raids following Sand Creek could have been predicted. What was less predictable was the government reaction. On January 10, 1865, the U.S. House of Representatives directed the Joint Committee on the Conduct of the [Civil] War to investigate what eastern newspapers were calling a "massacre of friendly Indians." Curtis requested and received Chivington's immediate resignation, hoping to prevent an army inquiry. But the next day, Chief of Staff General George Halleck ordered Curtis to investigate charges that the conduct of Chivington toward the friendly Indians "had been a series of outrages calculated to make them all hostile." Curtis wrote to both Halleck and Evans condemning Chivington. He also ordered Wynkoop to take command of Fort Lyon again and investigate the massacre. Wynkoop collected affidavits and on January 15 sent Curtis a strong condemnation of Chivington. The report labeled him an "inhuman monster" and the attack an "unprecedented atrocity." It estimated there were from 60 to 70 killed at Sand Creek, two thirds of whom were women and children.[114]

A 3-day congressional hearing (the first) began on March 13, 1865. Evans himself testified evasively on the last day. Chivington gave an affidavit and answered questions put in writing by congressmen. He insisted he had attacked because he thought the Indians were hostile.

The committee's final report found the attack at Sand Creek to be "an atrocity of the highest order" and condemned it as "the scene of murder and barbarity." Men, women, and children were "indiscriminately slaughtered." "From the suckling babe to the old warrior, all who were overtaken were deliberately murdered." "The soldiers indulged in acts of barbarity of the most revolting character; such, it is to be hoped, as never before disgraced the acts of men claiming to be civilized." The report stated that the dead bodies revealed

> evidence of the fiendish malignity and cruelty of the officers who had so sedulously and carefully plotted the massacre, and of the soldiers who had so faithfully acted out the spirit of their officers. It is difficult to believe that beings in the form of men, and disgracing the uniform of the United States soldiers and officers, could commit or countenance the commission of such acts of cruelty and barbarity.[115]

Considerable blame was assigned to Evans. Anthony was chastised. The report dealt most harshly with Chivington. Schultz quoted from the report the assertion that Chivington had "deliberately planned and executed a foul and dastardly massacre." He took advantage of the Cheyenne "to gratify the worst passions that ever cursed the heart of man. [He] surprised and murdered, in cold blood, the unsuspecting men, women, and children on Sand Creek."[116]

Congress also made partial reparations to the widows and orphans of the Indians killed there. Each woman who lost a husband and each child who lost a parent was awarded 160 acres of land.[117] Another congressional report proclaimed, "To the honor of the government it may be said that a just atonement for this violation of its faith was sought to be made in the late treaty with these tribes."[118]

A second congressional investigation inquiring into plunder allegedly taken from the Indians by soldiers also concluded that Chivington's men had perpetrated a massacre of the Indians.[119] A third 3-man military commission met for 76 days but rendered no conclusions because the commission charter required that it simply find facts.[120]

About a month after the final committee report was released, Secretary of State William H. Seward advised Evans that President Andrew Johnson wanted his resignation without delay. Evans resigned.[121] Chivington was dismissed from the Methodist Church. Later he married his son's widow, prompting her parents to publish a letter condemning the marriage.[122]

ATROCITIES, OF course, continued elsewhere. Charles Bent, a Dog Soldier leader and another of William Bent's sons, was in Black Kettle's village at the time of the Sand Creek Massacre. He and some other

Cheyenne raided a station the following year, captured 2 men there, and in sight of their fellow workers staked one of the prisoners on the ground, cut out his tongue, built a fire on his stomach, and performed "other abominations."[123]

When settlers returned to Arizona after the Civil War, they confronted the Apache, who were a ferocious tribe. It was claimed that the Apache captured women, then literally tore their bodies apart. The settlers also reported that prisoners were hung head down over small fires, their uncontrolled jackknifing giving amusement to the Apache for hours while the prisoner's brain slowly roasted until death.[124]

In 1865, Lieutenant William Drew saw a soldier fall off a bluff during the Battle of Platte Bridge in Wyoming Territory:

> An Indian [Sioux] rode up to his body and commenced shooting arrows into it. After firing four or five arrows the Indian dismounted, took his tomahawk and commenced to hack him with it.[125]

Soldier Hank Lord fired his rifle, hitting the Indian when his hatchet was in midair. The next day, a supply train guarded by troops was attacked. After the Indians had withdrawn, troops went to the scene. Drew said,

> A horrible sight met our gaze. Twenty-one of our dead soldiers were lying on the ground, stripped naked and mangled in every conceivable way. I noticed one poor fellow with a wagon tire across his bowels, and from appearances, it had been heated red-hot and then laid upon him while still alive.[126]

A *Chicago Journal* reporter at the same scene wrote that "Lieutenant [Casper] Collins was horribly mutilated, his hands and feet cut off, heart taken out, scalped, and one hundred arrows in him."[127]

The Boxx, or Box, family was attacked by Kiowa Indians in Texas in 1865. Their home was destroyed, the father and the youngest daughter killed when she would not stop crying, the mother and 2 teenage daughters raped, and daughter Ida, age 7, tortured by being compelled to walk barefoot on live coals because she could not understand the commands of the Indian women. When rescued only 10 weeks later, Ida had almost forgotten the English language.[128]

FORT PHIL KEARNY, in Wyoming, was the site of Fetterman's Massacre in 1866. Colonel Henry Beebee Carrington was the commander of the fort, one of a series built to protect travelers on the Bozeman Trail. Captain William J. Fetterman, who was stationed there, had bragged that with only 80 soldiers he could defeat the entire Sioux nation. The Sioux had attacked a wagon train hauling wood. Colonel Carrington ordered Fetterman to relieve the besieged train, drive the Indians off, then return to the fort. He was not to pursue the Indians beyond Lodge Trail Ridge, which would be out of the range of the fort's howitzers.[129] Fetterman picked 49 experienced infantrymen. Lieutenant George W. Grummond followed with 27 cavalrymen, and 2 civilians and Captain Frederick H. Brown went along to observe. These 80 men left the fort in 2 groups, the infantrymen first, then the faster cavalrymen. The orders were repeated again to Fetterman and to Grummond at the gate. Disobeying orders, Fetterman led the group off the road, past Lodge Trail Ridge, and out of sight of the fort. Somewhere between 1,500 and 2,000 Sioux led by Crazy Horse were waiting in ambush for them.

Carrington heard heavy gunfire and sent 40 men to assist Fetterman. When they got to the ridge, they saw hundreds of warriors and 80 dead soldiers and civilians. Carrington was deemed partly responsible for the massacre and relieved of his command, but subsequent investigations exonerated him.[130]

He prepared his official report 2 weeks later. He stated that he had found his soldiers' bodies just at dark. They were naked and frozen with

> eyes torn out and laid on rocks; noses cut off; ears cut off; chins hewn off; teeth chopped out; joints of fingers, brains taken out and placed on rocks with other members of the body; entrails taken out and exposed; hands cut off; feet cut off; arms taken out from sockets; private parts severed and indecently placed on the person; eyes, ears, mouth, and arms penetrated with spear-heads, sticks, and arrows; ribs slashed to separation with knives; skulls severed in every form, from chin to crown; muscles of calves, thighs, stomach, breast, back, arms, and cheeks taken out. Punctures upon every sensitive part of the body, even to the soles of the feet and palms of the hand. All this only approximates the whole truth. . . . [One had] 105 arrows in his naked body.[131]

Once more, an entire military force had been wiped out by the Sioux. The army demanded vengeance, but there was a peace treaty instead. The Fetterman defeat, together with constant Sioux guerrilla warfare, had closed the Bozeman Trail and worn down the government.[132] The military capabilities of Red Cloud and his Sioux warriors resulted in the 1868 Second Fort Laramie Treaty, which provided that the Sioux would stop fighting and that a Sioux reservation would be established for the absolute and undisturbed use of the Sioux.[133] After gold was discovered in the Black Hills (part of the reservation), the government tried to keep prospectors out for a time, but with little success. Finally, President Grant reportedly met with the army, and it was agreed that the government would no longer interfere with the prospectors.[134]

MR. R. J. SMYTH was a teamster at Fort Phil Kearny. While making a trip to the hayfield outside the fort, he was accompanied by an artist from *Frank Leslie's Illustrated Weekly*. The artist insisted on getting off partway to make some sketches. Smyth advised him to stay with the outfit, but the artist insisted. On the way back he was found dead, a cross cut in his chest, indicating that the Indians thought him a coward, and his head completely skinned. Smyth speculated that the Cheyenne had killed the artist because they typically cut scalps into many pieces. Later, soldier Pate Smith got too far ahead of the outfit and the Crows claimed the Sioux caught him and skinned him alive.[135]

The Marysville, Kansas, *Enterprise* reported in 1866 that Indians surrounded a home, and while the husband looked on, his wife, who had fled,

> was led from her tent and every remnant of clothing torn from her body. A child that she was holding to her breast was wrenched from her arms and she was knocked to the ground. In this nude condition the demons gathered round her and while some held her down by standing on her wrists and their claws clutched in her hair, others outraged her person. No less than thirty repeated the horrible deed![136]

In Texas, attacks by the Indians had not abated either. In 1867, Texas governor Throckmorton reported that since the end of the Civil War, the Indians there (mostly Comanche and Kiowa) had killed 162 settlers and captured 43. Twenty-nine of the captives had been returned. Rupert Norval Richardson said,

> Ordinarily the Indians would not give up a captive without the payment of a reward. . . . Some of the more responsible chiefs tried to stop this stealing of white women and children. . . . But some of the most prominent Comanche chiefs either participated in or condoned this practice of taking captives.[137]

Cheyenne and Arapaho war parties also rode north into Kansas, killing 117 settlers and taking 7 women captive.[138]

The same year, after a fight with soldiers near Fort C. F. Smith, the Sioux retired, leaving a dead warrior behind. The soldiers "scalped the dead Indian in the latest and most artistic western style, then beheaded him, placing his head on a high pole, leaving his carcass to his friends or the wolves."[139]

Eight months after Fetterman's Massacre, there was another fight at the same place. The Sioux again attacked the woodcutters at Fort Phil Kearny. Earlier, Fetterman had had cumbersome muzzle-loaders, but at this second fight, called the Wagon Box Fight because the soldiers made a defensive formation behind a circle of wagons, the soldiers had more efficient breechloaders and survived. Surgeon Horton was appalled to learn that the soldiers had brought back the head of an Indian "for scientific study." Horton sent it to Washington.[140]

In the winter of 1867–68, the Cheyenne fought their old enemies, the Kaw and the Osage, and within a week after the Cheyenne got weapons from Wynkoop at Fort Lyon in August, they killed more than a dozen settlers, kidnapped some children, and forced hundreds of settlers to abandon their homes. In September there were more attacks. They continued into the fall.[141]

In the spring of 1868, the southern Plains tribes raided in Texas, Colorado, Nebraska, and Kansas. Goodrich noted that they burned, raped, and murdered. "In one month alone, seventy-five settlers were slaughtered."[142]

IN NOVEMBER, Black Kettle tried to surrender for the last time at Fort Cobb. He talked with Major General William B. Hazen. He told Hazen that his camp of 180 lodges located on the Washita River wanted to make peace. Hazen informed him that he was not authorized to make peace. Exactly one week after Black Kettle's talk with Hazen, Custer led the 700-man Seventh Cavalry to the peaceful Cheyenne camp and surrounded it. They charged at dawn. Major Joel Elliott led 15 soldiers along the riverbank, but was ambushed. He and all his men were killed, their naked bodies mutilated. But the soldiers killed 103 Indians. One of them was Black Kettle, who was buried in an unmarked grave so that soldiers would not find it, but his bones with his jewelry were recovered in 1934. The local newspaper put them on display in its window. The Battle of the Washita River was Custer's only victory over the Indians.[143] There were 4 white prisoners in Black Kettle's camp when the cavalry attack began. The Indians killed 2 of them, one a woman, the other a small child. Andrist said they were killed by the women.[144]

Custer, newspaper reporter DeBenneville Keim, and others went in search of Major Elliott and his men. Keim wrote,

> Within an area of not more than fifteen yards, lay sixteen human bodies . . . sixteen naked corpses frozen as solidly as stone. There was not a single body that did not exhibit evidences of fearful mutilation. They were all lying with their faces down, and in close proximity to each other. Bullet and arrow wounds covered the back of each; the throats of a number were cut, and several were beheaded.[145]

A scout for the army, Lem Wilson, was looking for water. He stumbled on an Indian, who attacked with a knife. Wilson killed the Indian instead and went wild. "I took his knife and scalped him. . . . It was th' happiest moment of my life. . . . I was like a wild man. I was wavin' th' bloody scalp in one hand and th' Indian's knife in th' other. All th' hatred I had for them cusses that had been tryin' to kill me for years was turned loose inside of me and outside."[146]

Some settlers sought vengeance for family members killed by Indians. In 1868, a newspaper reporter interviewed George Porter, who had witnessed the rape and murder of his entire family. He followed Indians wherever he could find them for the purpose of killing them. He carried with him a canebrake about 12 inches long and made a notch on it whenever he killed. The canebrake had 108 notches on it at the time of the interview. Other relatives seeking vengeance left pieces of poisoned meat where Indians were likely to pass. In one instance, more than 20 Indians were poisoned.[147]

Indians attacked a Montana trading post in 1869. Several warriors were killed. Their heads were cut off, their ears pickled in whiskey, and the flesh boiled from the skulls. Inscriptions such as "Let Harper's Tell of My Virtues" were put on them (*Harper's Weekly* was sympathetic to the Indians).[148]

Shoshoni chief Washakie was born around 1798, and by the 1850s he led 1,000 disciplined warriors.[149] In 1869, when Washakie was about 71 years old, he overheard some warriors complain that he was too old and should retire. He said nothing. The next day, he rode out of camp and wasn't seen or heard from for 2 months. When he returned, he brought 7 scalps (probably Indian), which he had taken by himself. That no doubt ended the talk about retirement, and he continued to take an active part in wars against the Sioux. After his son was killed in a barroom brawl, he converted to Christianity.[150] He died at age 101 or 102.[151]

Scout J. E. Welch wrote an account of the Battle of Summit Springs in

1869 to his comrade, Colonel Henry O. Clark. They found the trail of Cheyenne chief Tall Bull, who was a leader of the ferocious Dog Soldier Society, whose warriors earlier had raided the Pawnee, killing 15 men and raping 5 women.[152] The camp was charged.

Welch saw a white woman run from the Indians. One fired and hit her, but she was only wounded and survived. About the same time, Welch saw another white woman seized by an Indian, who hacked her with a tomahawk. Several men rode toward the Indian and killed him. Welch dismounted to see if he could help the woman, but she was dead. She had been far along in pregnancy.

Then Welch saw an Indian getting away by himself. Welch gave chase, the Indian turned, fired, and wounded Welch in the leg. Three arrows also were shot at him, the third splitting his left ear. Welch then shot the Indian through the head and scalped him. Welch later discovered that he was Chief Pretty Bear. The Pawnee scouts knew him and wanted his scalp, which Welch gave them. It was learned that the surviving white woman was German. She said both women had been "beaten and outraged in every conceivable manner."[153]

The Blackfeet had committed many crimes in Montana, so the army in 1870 under the command of Colonel E. M. Baker struck the Piegan camp of Heavy Runner and Red Horn. (The Piegans were a band of the Blackfeet.) The army was tracking several warriors who had killed a settler. There were 173 Blackfeet killed; 90 were women and 50 children. After the raid on the Piegans, General Sheridan estimated that at least 800 men, women, and children had been murdered by Indians since 1862. The *New York Times* countered that it was indefensible, needlessly barbaric and brutal, and a wholesale slaughter.[154]

KIOWA LEADER Satanta liked to live the good life. He lived in a carpeted tipi and called guests to dinner by blowing on a French horn.[155] Fanny Kelly heard the story that Satanta's people in Texas had captured Mrs. Clara Blynn, her 2-year-old son, Willie, and others in a raid on the Arkansas River. The Indians refused to give the Blynns any food after a couple of days except for the little bit Mrs. Blynn could get from the women, who were jealous of her. The women in Satanta's band believed that an Indian girl had become a spy because Satanta had murdered her best friend. The girl furnished food and carried a letter from Mrs. Blynn to the commanding general addressed to "Kind Friend," pleading for help. Whenever Satanta was gone, the women would burn the Indian girl with sharp sticks and resinous splinters. Her face, breasts, and limbs were scarred in this way and her baby was held by the hair and punished with a stick in her presence. The army arrived at the camp. Mrs. Blynn cried, "Willie, Willie, saved at last!" but Satanta buried his tomahawk in her brain, grabbed Willie, dashed his head against a tree, killing him, and threw his body on his dying mother.[156]

In north central Texas in 1871, 3 years after the Blynns were killed, Henry Warren, a government contractor, was at the head of his wagon train when the group was attacked by a raiding party of Indians, mostly Kiowa. The wagonmaster and 6 other men were killed. One of the men was tied to a wagon wheel and burned. At Fort Sill, Oklahoma, Satanta boasted that he had led the attack. He was convicted of murder and sentenced to death. Humanitarian groups (today they would be called Indian advocates) and the Bureau of Indian Affairs argued that the sentence was too harsh. The death sentence was revoked, he was imprisoned, and then paroled in 1873. The next year, General Sheridan ordered 74 militant Indians, including Satanta, to prison again. When Satanta was told he would never be released, he committed suicide by jumping from a prison hospital window.[157]

Even Custer wrote that except for Satanta's "restless barbarity" and "merciless forays" against the frontier, he was "a remarkable man—remarkable for his powers of oratory, his determined warfare against the advance of civilization, and his opposition to abandoning his accustomed way of life."[158]

THE ARMY had established several feeding stations where friendly Indians could find food and, they hoped, safety. One of these stations was at Camp Grant, north of Tucson. A band of Apache numbering 500 appeared there in 1871 and surrendered their weapons. Citizens of Tucson organized a vigilante group consisting of 7 white settlers, 48 Mexicans, and 92 Papago Indian mercenaries. The sleeping Apache were massacred.[159] Helen Hunt Jackson said that 21 women and children were killed.[160] This finally ended the war against the Apache begun by General James H. Carleton in 1862, a war that had cost many settler and soldier lives.[161]

In California, T. T. Waterman wrote that in 1871 some settlers with dogs chased a band of Indians into a cave because Indians had wounded a steer. On entering the cave, they found some small children. One of the men said he couldn't kill the babies with his heavy .56-caliber Spencer rifle because "it tore them up too bad," so he shot them with his .38-caliber revolver. About 30 were killed.[162]

Texas forces had attacked Mexican Kickapoos. Because the 2 were at war, the Kickapoos raided for horses and cattle in Texas and sold them in Mexico. Texas asked the federal government for troops. They were sent in 1873 under the leadership of Colonel Ranald S. Mackenzie. He learned when the men would be gone from the Kickapoo villages, raided them, burned them, and captured 40 women and children, who were held as hostages to try to get the group to go to the reservation in Oklahoma. About half of them did.[163]

A wagonload of 17 Modoc prisoners was being transported in Oregon to Boyle's camp in 1873. Some were women and children. They were unarmed and without an escort. A group of armed men thought to be Oregon volunteers attacked the wagon. Several of the Indians were killed before a squad of soldiers drove the volunteers away.[164]

The Modocs and Klamaths ceded most of their territory in 1864 and retired to a reservation in Oregon. The Modocs were unhappy there and asked for a reservation in California. Their request was denied. A group of Modocs under Captain Jack nevertheless went to California and established a village there. The government sent troops to evict them. There was a fight at the village, and a soldier and an Indian were killed. Captain Jack and his group escaped to a lava field. Another group of Modocs under Hooker Jim had been away from the village when the soldiers arrived. That group carried out raids on ranchers, killing 15, then fled to the lava beds.[165]

After Captain Jack had surrendered at the end of the Modoc War in 1873, 4 warriors decided to surrender too. They went to a friendly rancher, John Fairchild, to whom they had gone for counsel earlier to see if they could stay out of the war. Fairchild put them in his wagon to take them to surrender. Some settlers stopped the wagon, made Fairchild get out, and killed the 4 Indians. The settlers wounded a woman bystander in their enthusiasm.[166]

Captain Jack, Boston Charley, Black Jim, Schonchin John, and 2 others were tried by a military commission in 1873 for the murder of Peace Commissioner General Edward R. S. Canby* and Commissioner Reverend Eleasar Thomas, who were seeking to end the Modoc War. All were sentenced to death. Canby was the only general killed in the

---

*Edward Richard Sprigg Canby had an unusually varied military career commencing with actions against the Seminoles and the Mormons. After that, he commanded troops and Ute auxiliaries against the Navajo who had been raiding in New Mexico, where he was appointed brigadier general. With the aid of Chivington's volunteers, he drove invading Confederate forces into Texas. Finally he served to quell draft riots in New York City.[167]

American-Indian War. President Grant commuted the sentences of the other 2 to life imprisonment. The 4 named Indians were hanged. Their heads were removed and sent to the Army Medical Museum in Washington.[168]

THOMAS GOODRICH described a poignant atrocity occurring to the surviving members of the German family, which ended in 1874. Earlier, the family of 17-year-old Catherine German, consisting of her parents and her 6 siblings, were on the way west. Cheyenne Indians attacked, putting an arrow in her thigh and killing her parents, 2 sisters, and her brother. A sister with long hair was scalped. Catherine was compelled by the Indian who had captured her to become the tribe prostitute. When forced to get water or wood, she was often raped as many as 6 times a trip.

In 1874, the army attacked a Cheyenne village in Texas. The Indians fled, but one returned and fired his rifle at a pile of buffalo robes and blankets. He was killed by a soldier. The pile moved, so the soldiers investigated, thinking they might find a Cheyenne, but it was Catherine's sister, Julia German. Sister Addie, 5 years old when captured and now near starvation in a lodge, so moved Sergeant Mahoney that he wept and held her close. She asked the soldiers, "What kind of Indians are you?"

Catherine remained with some Cheyenne who decided they should return to the reservation. They got to the army camp, where the soldiers "stood at the side of the trail cheering."[169]

By 1874, the Cheyenne on their reservation in Oklahoma were starving to death. The army was directed to prevent them from leaving their reservation to search for food, but the next year they broke away and pillaged and even murdered. General Pope was sympathetic. "It is inhuman to compel Indians to remain at the agencies on their reservations slowly starving to death. . . . In other words, the military forces are required to compel these Indians to starve to death quietly or be killed if they are not willing to do it."[170] The same year, the Cheyenne under Tall Bull raided the Pawnee, killing 15 men and raping 5 women.[171]

Comanche and Cheyenne warriors, 700 in all, attacked Adobe Walls, Texas, in 1874. The trading post was defended by 27 buffalo hunters with long-range rifles. At the end of the unsuccessful all-day fight, the Indians turned on the Kansas travel routes, the Texas frontier, Colorado, and New Mexico. Robert M. Utley and Wilcomb E. Washburn stated that "men, women, and children were tortured, slain, or taken captive." About 80 settlers were killed. Patrick Hennessey and 3 other men were bringing a wagonload of supplies for the Indians, but the Cheyenne killed and scalped 3 of them. Hennessey was put on a pile of grain and burned to death by some Osages who just happened to be passing by.[172] Adobe Walls was abandoned after the attack. The defenders left behind them the heads of 12 warriors on posts.[173]

Troops destroyed the village of Cheyenne chief Dull Knife that same year. In the village a warrior was found with a necklace of human forefingers around his neck. There was also a bag containing the right hands of 12 Shoshoni babies and children (the Shoshoni were enemies of the Cheyenne).[174] Two scalps of 10-year-old girls were found, one white and one Shoshoni.[175]

That same year, a wounded Sioux warrior was discovered by a group of Crows. The Crows shot the wounded man 6 times and mutilated his body, said Coward, "until there was nothing recognizable as human."[176]

Colonel George Crook was engaged in a campaign in the Tonto Basin against the Apache in 1874. Some Tonto Apache on the San Carlos Reservation who had surrendered later killed an army officer, Lieutenant Jacob Almy, and left the reservation. There was a fresh outbreak of Tonto atrocities. Crook sent out troops. The San Carlos Apache tried to surrender again, but Crook demanded the heads of the 3 leaders of the outbreak and also offered the San Carlos Apache a bounty for the head of Western Apache chief Delshay. The Tonto Apache brought in 7 heads for the 3 San Carlos leaders and 2 for Delshay. Crook said about the Delshay heads that "being satisfied that both parties were earnest in their beliefs, and the bringing in of the extra head was not amiss, I paid both." He displayed one at Camp Verde and one on the San Carlos Reservation.[177]

In 1876, Lieutenant Colonel George A. Custer ordered Major Marcus A. Reno to pursue a party of around 40 Indians, but Reno's men suffered a disastrous defeat,[178] and Indian women and children mutilated the bodies of the dead. If a ring could not be taken off a dead soldier easily, the women would cut off the finger.[179]

The Battle of the Little Bighorn was the most significant of the entire war for many reasons. Because Custer had been popular with the people, his death galvanized many who had been opposed or indifferent to the war to support the generals,[180] something akin to the effect on the country of the attack on Pearl Harbor. Congress gave the army what it wanted to fight the Indians.[181] The military got the support of the civilian government and control of the Sioux agencies.[182] Many Cheyenne and Sioux surrendered.[183] Robinson concluded, "Custer was performing greater service [to the military] dead than he had ever done alive."[184] Custer's Last Stand was the beginning of the end for the Indian in the war.

The battle came about because the army had ordered the Sioux, Cheyenne, and Arapaho tribes to come to an agency within 2 months or be classified as hostile. They failed to report, so General Sheridan ordered forces commanded by General George Crook from the south, Colonel John Gibbon from the west, and General Alfred Terry from the east to make a winter strike on these tribes.

Army troops under General George Crook* fought the Sioux in the Battle of the Rosebud in 1876. Nine soldiers were killed. About midnight the bodies were wrapped in blankets and laid in a long trench on the bank of the Rosebud River. The grave was filled with stones and mud, the earth packed down, and a bonfire built on top. The entire column then was marched back and forth over the mass grave. Robinson reported, "It was hoped that the [Sioux] would not find it and desecrate the bodies." After the troops withdrew, the next morning about 20 warriors returned to the battlefield, found the mass grave, uncovered the bodies, took the burial blankets, took jewelry from the bodies, and scalped at least one dead soldier.[186] Crook retreated to Fort Fetterman, Wyoming.[187]

After the Battle of the Rosebud, the Sioux went to an encampment on the Little Bighorn River, where they met other Sioux, Cheyenne, and Arapaho. The Terry and Gibbon forces met, and when Major Reno reported the general location of the Indians, Terry ordered Custer to cut them off from the south while the remaining troops approached from the north.[188]

There were about 7,000 Indians (perhaps more), 1,800 of whom were warriors, at the Indian encampment on the Little Bighorn River. Custer

---

*George Crook fought in both the Yakima War and the Rouge River War. As a brigadier general in the Civil War, he fought in the Battles of Antietam and Chickamauga and in the Shenandoah campaign. After that war, he fought against the Northern Paiutes, the Apache (using Apache scouts), the Yavapais, and the Sioux and Cheyenne (using Pawnee scouts). He commanded 1 of the 3 prongs (using Crow and Shoshoni scouts) that were to converge on the Sioux and Cheyenne, but had to withdraw in the face of Crazy Horse's warriors and the Chiricahua Apache under Geronimo. Crook later campaigned for Indian rights groups and successfully campaigned for the release of Geronimo and other Apache who were in military prisons. He was never an advocate of total war because he believed limited strikes would succeed. He favored diplomacy over warfare. The Indians trusted him and called him Grey Fox.[185]

recklessly attacked immediately with only about 200 men instead of waiting another day for Terry and Gibbon, whom he knew were on the way. Not only was Custer vastly outnumbered, his carbines were older and inferior to those of the Indians.[189] He and all his soldiers were killed.[190]

Major Reno later wrote to General Sheridan that "Custer was whipped because he was rash."[191] President Grant told a reporter, "I regard Custer's massacre as a sacrifice of troops brought on by Custer himself that was wholly unnecessary—wholly unnecessary."[192]

Before the Battle of the Little Bighorn had begun, several Sioux boys announced that they would take a suicide vow to fight to the death in the next battle. A Dying Dance was put on to formalize the oath. The Sioux had borrowed the suicide vow from the Cheyenne. Not more than 20 took the vow, "and no one seemed to believe they would have to fulfill it."

The dance ended at dawn with a parade in honor of the suicide boys.[193] They fulfilled their vows at the battle. When it was nearly over, with fewer than 100 soldiers still alive, Sioux heralds arrived, shouting that the warriors should stand aside and watch the suicide boys, who were by the river preparing for their assault on Custer's position. As planned, the suicides plunged in among the troops, engaged them in hand-to-hand fighting, and distracted them while the rest of the warriors moved in and killed the soldiers. Robinson described what happened:

> The suicide boys charged. Some went among the army horses, stampeding the grays. The rest rode straight into the mass of soldiers. While the troops concentrated their fire on these youthful warriors, swarms of Indians swept in from all directions. . . . Every one of the young suicide warriors was either killed outright or mortally wounded.[194]

To this point, there had been no Indian atrocities in the battle. The atrocities occurred after the battle ended. The Indian women cut off fingers after Custer's defeat just as they had after the Battle of the Rosebud. Robinson said they were also "slashing and hacking away with sheath knives and hatchets. Hands and feet were cut off; limbs, torsos, and heads were repeatedly stabbed and slashed." A Cheyenne woman whose son had been killed in battle 8 days earlier wandered across the battlefield with an ax. "A wounded soldier tried to escape, but was grabbed and held by two warriors while the woman hacked him to death."[195]

After the battle, those who visited the field reported what they had found. Scout George Herendeen said, "Another man had strips of his skin cut out of his body. . . . Many bodies were gashed with knives, and some had their noses and other members cut off." Black interpreter Isaiah Dorman

> lay with his breast full of arrows and an iron picket pin thrusted through his testicles into the ground, pinning him down. . . . Dorman's penis was cut off and stuffed in his mouth. . . . [His] body had been ripped open, and a coffee pot and cup which he carried with him were filled with his blood.[196]

Major Reno also reported what he found:

> One ghastly find was near the center of the field where three tepee poles were standing upright in the ground to form a triangle. On top of each were inverted camp kettles, while below them on the grass were the heads of three men. The three heads had been placed within the triangle, facing each other in a horrible, sightless stare.
>
> Many of their skulls had been crushed in, eyes had been torn from their sockets, and hands . . . arms, legs and noses had been wrenched off. Many had their flesh cut off in strips the entire length of their bodies.[197]

Private Theodore Goldin said his party found "two human heads which were so charred and burned as to be beyond recognition."[198] Private Jacob Adams added that

> the men . . . were . . . scalped and horribly mutilated. Some were decapitated, while many bodies were lacking feet. . . . As I walked over the field I saw many unfortunate dead who had been propped into a sitting position and used as targets by bowmen who had proceeded to stick them full of steel-headed arrows. . . . Some bodies were set up on their knees and elbows and their hind parts had been shot full of arrows.[199]

Fred Girard saw his comrades "disembowled, with stakes driven through their chests." George Glenn found his bunkmate, Tom Tweed. "His crotch had been split up with an ax and one of his legs thrown over his shoulder."[200] Lieutenant Edward Godfrey discovered the body of Tom Custer, Lieutenant Colonel George A. Custer's brother. He had been scalped, his skull smashed in, arrows shot in his back, and "his belly had been cut open and his entrails protruded."[201] Thomas Goodrich added that nearby Jacob Adams saw the body of Colonel Custer which was stripped with the exception of his sox. He had a gunshot wound in his head and another in his side, and in his left thigh there was a gash about eleven inches long that exposed the bone. Custer was not scalped.

But Girard and Godfrey also reported they saw an arrow shaft rammed up Custer's penis.[202]

Two Cheyenne women claimed they punctured Custer's eardrums with awls to improve his hearing because he did not listen when their chiefs told him he would be killed if he ever made war on the Cheyenne again. The Sioux Good Fox was told this story by someone who saw it. Good Fox related, "I was there, but all I remember is one big cloud of dust."[203]

Many claimed they killed Custer. They included White Bull, Rain-in-the-Face, Flat Hip, and Brave Bear. Red Horse said it was an unidentified warrior. Low Dog said they didn't know who Custer was until the battle was over. Sioux war chief Rain-in-the-Face told his story of the battle to W. Kent Thomas in 1894 while he appeared at Coney Island, New York. He confirmed what Red Horse had to say about the soldiers asking to be taken prisoner. "Some of them got on their knees and begged; we spared none." Rain-in-the-Face claimed in Cyrus Townsend Brady's report that he shot Custer with his revolver, then

> I leaped from my pony and cut out his heart and bit a piece out of it and spit it in his face. I got back on my pony and rode off shaking it. I didn't go back on the field after that. The squaws came up afterward and killed the wounded, cut their boot legs off for moccasin soles, and took their money, watches, and rings. They cut their fingers off to get them quicker.[204]

Opinions differ concerning the extent of mutilation of the soldier dead. Axelrod indicated that all the soldiers were found naked and mutilated after the battle.[205] Robert M. Utley and Wilcomb E. Washburn stated, "The chief of scouts had counted 197 naked, mutilated bodies."[206] Marshall said a few of the dead were scalped or otherwise mutilated.[207] General Alfred H. Terry, who arrived 2 days after the battle, reported that his men found that the bodies of only some of the soldiers had been scalped or otherwise mutilated.[208]

Carl Waldman made this evaluation of Custer:

Custer is more important as a symbolic figure—a man whose ambitions, recklessness, and disregard for Indian peoples made him a victim of the last great Indian victory—than for his actual military contributions.[209]

Sioux chief American Horse was badly wounded in 1876 in the Battle of Slim Buttes in South Dakota. Soldiers had trapped him and others in a cave. He emerged from the cave holding his intestines from a wound, refused chloroform from an army surgeon, and endured his pain by biting on a piece of wood. After his death, the soldiers scalped him.[210] The American dead were buried in unmarked graves, and the troops walked over them to try to conceal them. Later, the Indians claimed they opened the graves and scalped the dead.[211]

Colonel Wesley Merritt was the leader of an expedition against the Cheyenne that same year. Buffalo Bill was his chief scout. They found some Cheyenne war parties in Nebraska and fought the Battle of War Bonnet Creek. Buffalo Bill shot Yellow Hair, the Cheyenne leader, in the leg and killed his horse. Yellow Hair killed Buffalo Bill's horse, according to Cody. They then exchanged shots at less than 20 paces. Yellow Hair missed, but Buffalo Bill hit Yellow Hair's breast, then drove his knife into Yellow Hair's heart. "Jerking the war bonnet off, I scientifically scalped him in about five seconds."[212] The Yellow Hair episode became the subject of a play called *The Red Right Hand, or Buffalo Bill's First Scalp for Custer.*[213]

In Oregon in 1877 General Oliver Otis Howard* had given the Nez Perce orders to leave their homes in the Wallowa Valley by June 14. The chiefs met to decide what to do. Three chiefs spoke for peace, but Shore Crossing, whose father had been murdered by a settler, demanded war, as did his cousin Red Moccasin Tops. When the meeting was over, a drunk Shore Crossing rode his horse across some camas bulbs a squaw had put out to dry. Her man, Yellow Grizzly Bear, yelled at him, asking why he didn't go after the man who killed his father.

Apparently as a result of this comment, the 2 Indians and another young Indian, Swan Necklace, went on a killing spree. Two settlers were killed, and a third was wounded. Nez Perce leader Toohoolhoolzote, along with 15 of his warriors and the 2 cousins, went on another raid, killing 2 more settlers and plundering houses. General Howard sent out 2 groups of soldiers to punish or bring in the guilty Indians. One group

---

*General Howard was a general in the Civil War. He fought in several battles, won the Congressional Medal of Honor, lost an arm, but continued to lead troops at Gettysburg and several other engagements. After the war, he was the first president of Howard University. He later returned to service and fought the Nez Perce, the Bannocks, and other tribes. He campaigned for the Indian Rights Association together with General Crook.[214]

with civilian guide Ad Chapman went to the White Bird camp. A small truce party carrying a white flag came out. Chapman fired on the flag, wounding an Indian. A return shot killed the bugler so that the force commander, Captain David Perry, could transmit no commands above the noise of battle. Even though less than half the Indians had rifles, 34 soldiers were killed.[215] Stung by these losses, the army under Howard mobilized 400 troops, and the Nez Perce began their long trek to try to reach Canada.[216]

During the exodus of the Nez Perce under Chief Joseph in 1877, the Bannock Indian scouts attached to the troops of General Howard disinterred and mutilated the bodies of recently killed Nez Perce.[217] General Sherman commented that after the Nez Perce were defeated by the army in Montana, it was extraordinary in that the Indians "abstained from scalping, let captive women go free, [and] did not commit indiscriminate murder of peaceful families, which is usual."[218] That was because of Chief Joseph's orders. One must wonder what the course of history would have been had all the chiefs and all commanders of soldiers given and enforced similar orders.

In the Bannock War in 1878, a group of Umatilla Indians approached the Bannocks and Paiutes on the pretense of joining them in the war. Instead, they persuaded Paiute chief Egan to leave his warriors and come with them. They then killed him and gave his scalp to General Nelson A. Miles. An army surgeon took Egan's head to make sure the scalp was his.[219]

In 1879, Nathan C. Meeker was the Indian agent for the Ute tribe in Colorado. He had been an agricultural reporter for the *New York Tribune* and had become overly zealous in trying to get the Indians to plow up their pony pastures in order to raise more crops. Medicine man Canalla, also known as Johnson, went to Meeker's house to protest. Meeker told him the Ute* had too many ponies and had better kill some of them. Johnson threw Meeker out of Meeker's own front door.

Meeker telegraphed for troops. By the time they came, the agency buildings were burned, Meeker and 9 other agency employees were found dead in the burned buildings, 3 women and 2 children were captured and taken into the mountains, and 13 soldiers were killed. Twelve Ute were charged with murdering Meeker and committing outrages on the captive women (2 were Meeker's wife and daughter). None was

---

*The Ute settled in Utah, Colorado, New Mexico, Nevada, and Wyoming. The name *Ute* means "high up" or "land of the sun." They fought other tribes as well as the Spanish, warred intermittently with the Arapaho, and captured slaves to trade with other tribes.[220]

tried because their personal situations were lost in the larger matter of whether or not the Ute should move from their homeland, where the miners hoped to discover silver. They moved.[221]

The *Times* summed it up:

No one doubts that Mr. Meeker meant well, but his conduct was nevertheless the immediate cause which precipitated the outbreak. He was a professional philanthropist. . . . It is a peculiarity of men of this type that they are prone to insist upon reforming other men by force. They are honestly anxious to do good, but they are determined to do good in their own way and in spite of the objections of those whom they propose to benefit.[222]

Events were beginning that would lead to the Wounded Knee Massacre. The Ghost Dance played an important role. The efforts of Wovoka, the Paiute medicine man, caused its spread among Indians. Wovoka was brought up as a youth on a ranch near Yerington, Nevada, with a devoutly Christian settler family named Wilson. When he was 32, he became ill with a fever. An eclipse of the sun happened during this time. Afterward, he said he had been taken to the spirit world, where he visited with the Supreme Being, and returned to spread the message that the world would soon end, then come alive again in a pure, aboriginal state with the Messiah present.[223]

When the Sun died [the day of the eclipse], I went up to heaven and saw God and all the people who had died a long time ago. God told me to come back and tell my people they must be good and love one another, and not fight, or steal, or lie. He gave me this dance to give my people.[224]

This new world would be inherited by all Indians, including the dead. Wovoka called for meditation, prayers, singing, and especially dancing, through which an Indian might briefly die and glimpse the paradise to come. This Ghost Dance spread rapidly. Some followers considered him the Messiah, and he was referred to as the Red Man's Christ. Kicking Bear and Short Bull, Sioux medicine men and brothers-in-law, visited him with others and thereafter they emphasized the possible elimination of whites and use of Ghost Dance shirts to stop white men's bullets.[225] Wovoka claimed he could produce fog, snow, a shower, a hard rain, or sunshine. As part of his claim to be the Messiah, Wovoka's message to the Indians was this:

All Indians must dance, everywhere, keep on dancing. Pretty soon in next spring Great Spirit come. He bring back all game of every kind. The game be thick everywhere. All dead Indians come back and live again. They all be strong just like young men, be young again. Old blind Indian see again and get young and have fine time. When Great Spirit comes this way, then all the Indians go to mountains, high up away from whites. Whites can't hurt Indians then. Then while Indians way up high, big flood comes like water and all white people die, get drowned. After that water go way and then nobody but Indians everywhere and game all kinds thick. Then medicine man tell Indians to send word to all Indians to keep up dancing and the good time will come. Indians who don't dance, who don't believe in this word, will grow little, just about a foot high, and stay that way. Some of them will be turned into wood and be burned in fire.[226]

Alan Axelrod described how the Ghost Dance

spread through the Sioux reservations with increasing fervor and excitement, reaching fever pitch in the summer of 1890. White authorities were alarmed, and it became apparent that the Sioux reservations were on the verge of a general uprising.[227]

Dee Brown reported that

by mid-November Ghost Dancing was so prevalent on the Sioux reservations that almost all other activities came to a halt. No pupils appeared at the schoolhouses, the trading stores were empty, no work was done on the little farms.[228]

The Ghost Dance was not well understood and, Robert G. Hays said, "terrified white society."[229] The towns around the reservations filled with hysterical people, and settlers appealed for protection. The new Indian agent at the Pine Ridge Reservation, Daniel F. Royer, telegraphed Washington, "Indians are dancing in the snow and are wild and crazy. We need protection and we need it now."[230] The settlers were alarmed because it was thought the Sioux reservations were near an uprising such as had occurred in Minnesota in 1862.

The government attempted to arrest Sioux chief and medicine man Sitting Bull on December 15, 1890, 14 days before Wounded Knee, because he had invited his nephew, Kicking Bear, to come demonstrate the Ghost Dance. Approximately 40 Indian police surrounded Sitting Bull's cabin. About 160 Ghost Dancers gathered outside to try to prevent the arrest. One of them, Catch-the-Bear, pulled a rifle and shot at Lieutenant Bull Head of the Indian police. Bull Head shot back and struck Sitting Bull. Indian police officer Red Tomahawk also fired, this time hitting Sitting Bull in the head. Several people were killed in the fight that followed, 7 Indian civilians and 5 Indian police officers. Women participated, armed with knives and clubs.[231]

Big Foot* was known as a peacemaker who settled disputes among the Sioux.[233] He received an invitation from Red Cloud to visit the Pine Ridge Reservation.[234] Red Cloud hoped that Big Foot could help solve Indian problems with the whites.[235] Big Foot set out from the Standing Rock Reservation in North Dakota with about 230 women and children and 120 men.[236] During the trip, he got pneumonia and had to ride in a wagon.[237]

Big Foot at one time had been a Ghost Dance believer. Unknown to the army, he had ceased to believe. When he moved his band south to Pine Ridge, General Nelson A. Miles in Rapid City, South Dakota, erroneously assumed he had been invited there by the Ghost Dancers. His name was on a list of "formentors of disturbances," so Miles ordered Big Foot taken prisoner.[238] The Seventh Cavalry found him 30 miles east of Pine Ridge,[239] and he was arrested.[240] Before his arrest, Big Foot had raised a white flag asking for a parley, but this was refused by Major S. M. Whiteside, who demanded unconditional surrender, which was at once given, and the Indians moved on with the troops to Wounded Knee Creek. Unconditional surrender meant that "all arms would be yielded peacefully upon request."[241] The Sioux were then surrounded by the army at Wounded Knee Creek, where they camped in the center of a ring of cavalrymen.[242]

Colonel James Forsyth commanded the Seventh Cavalry, Custer's old outfit. He saw that Big Foot was ill, so he provided a tent warmed with a camp stove for him, and he sent his own regimental surgeon to attend him.[243] Forsyth had instructions to disarm the Indians and take them to the railroad so that they could be removed from the "zone of military operation." A fight was not expected,[244] but Forsyth did have Hotchkiss guns or cannons, which fired 2-inch explosive shells at the rate of almost 50 a minute.[245] He ordered 4 of these guns placed in position around the Sioux camp.[246]

The Sioux warriors were wearing their Ghost Shirts. The soldiers began searching the Sioux for guns. They found about 40 weapons.[247]

---

*Sioux chief Big Foot was in Ghost Dance country. The dance was especially attractive to his people, most of whom were widows who danced in the hope it would bring their husbands back. Officials tried to stop these ceremonial gatherings, but Big Foot would not agree.[232]

Medicine man Yellow Bird took action, apparently expecting a fight. He began dancing the Ghost Dance, tweeted on his whistle, performed incantations, sang a holy song, and incited the warriors to fight, reminding them that the army bullets could not penetrate their Ghost Shirts. "You wear ghost shirts and no white man's bullet may hurt you."[248]

Indian Angie Debo observed in connection with this search by the soldiers that "in such a crisis the Sioux were always likely to give way to panic or blind rage, and in either case to begin shooting."[249] What did these Sioux do? They began shooting. Black Fox (some say Black Coyote) took out a rifle from beneath his blanket. He fired into the search party. Several other warriors did the same thing with the encouragement of Yellow Bird. Military historian S. L. A. Marshall stated that several Sioux simultaneously fired guns concealed under their blankets.[250] The fact that the Indians had not only rifles but also knives[251] and war clubs[252] is some evidence that the Sioux did not intend to surrender but were ready to fight.

When the Hotchkiss guns were fired into the Indian camp, they caused a stampede of the warriors, women, and children, who fled up a dry ravine and tried to hide. Marshall described what happened next:

> The frenzied cavalrymen and Indian scouts, once the heavy fire lifted, pursued to cut down many of these pitiful fugitives, showing them little or no mercy. Here is the sequence in Wounded Knee that is most generally condemned and really nothing sensible may be said in mitigation of it. . . . The grisly chase and killing went on for more than three hours and the trail of bodies extended outward from the camp for more than three miles.[253]

This was the atrocity.

James Mooney, who immediately investigated the battle under the auspices of the Bureau of American Ethnology and the Smithsonian Institution, concluded,

> There can be no question that the pursuit was simply a massacre, where fleeing women, with infants in their arms, were shot down after resistance had ceased and when almost every warrior was stretched out dead or dying on the ground.[254]

Dr. Charles Eastman, a Santee Sioux graduate of Dartmouth and the University of Boston medical school, had been serving as governmental physician to the Pine Ridge agency. He was one of the first on the scene after the battle. Brandon stated he described, "quite dispassionately, the way young girls had knelt, and covered their faces with their shawls so they would not see the troopers come up to shoot them."[255]

Oglala Sioux chief American Horse (possibly the nephew of the American Horse killed at the Battle of Slim Buttes) described firsthand some of the deaths:

> There was a woman with an infant in her arms who was killed as she almost touched the flag of truce. . . . A mother was shot down with her infant; the child not knowing that its mother was dead was still nursing. . . . The women as they were fleeing with their babies were killed together, shot right through . . . and after most all of them had been killed a cry was made that all those who were not killed or wounded should come forth and they would be safe. Little boys . . . came out of their places of refuge, and as soon as they came in sight a number of soldiers surrounded them and butchered them there.[256]

There were about 350 people with Big Foot. By the time the battle ended, the Indian dead, according to Angie Debo (who has made the only known breakdown among men, women, and children), included 84 men and boys of fighting age, 44 women, and 18 children.[257] Quite possibly most of the women and children were killed while fleeing, which means that the atrocity part of the battle took the lives of perhaps 62 Indian women and children.[258] The range of estimates of Indian dead is from 153 to "most likely" 300.[259] The range of soldier death estimates is 25 to 60.[260] Fair approximate figures would seem to be 170 Indian dead and 30 soldier dead. The fight was not completely one-sided. There were 39 wounded soldiers in addition to the 30 dead.[261]

There was a bad blizzard in the Dakotas after the battle, and Ralph K. Andrist stated that "the bodies were found partially covered with snow and frozen into the grotesque attitudes of violent death."[262] The blizzard prevented clearing the area for several days. A photograph of the body of Big Foot is said to be perhaps the most widespread photograph of the massacre. He was later buried with the rest of the dead in a common grave.[263]

The Wounded Knee Massacre ended the American-Indian War on December 29, 1890, 268 years after it began, even though there was a skirmish the following day. Wounded Knee caused Sioux factions to unite, and the day after the battle, they ambushed the Seventh Cavalry near the Pine Ridge agency. General Miles marshaled 3,500 troops and slowly and with patience contracted the ring of soldiers around the Sioux while urging them to surrender and promising them good treatment. They surrendered on January 15, 1891.[264]

After the battle was lost by the Indians, a shocked Wovoka started emphasizing peace with the settlers. His cult gradually died out, and he too finally died in 1932 at the Walker River Reservation in Nevada.[265] No organized Indian warfare followed Wounded Knee.

WHEN CONSIDERING Wounded Knee, it is easy to forget that the Sioux had had a fierce reputation for warfare in the period from 1850 to 1890. The year 1876 was the worst year for the army since the end of the Civil War. An extraordinary number of soldiers died at the hands of the Sioux and their allies that year.[266] The events that have been called the Sioux Wars included the Grattan Massacre in 1854–55 (the Mormon Cow War), the Santee Sioux Uprising in 1862–64, the War for the Bozeman Trail in 1866–68 (which included Fetterman's Massacre and the Wagon Box Fight), and the War for the Black Hills, which included 8 battles, one of which was Custer's Last Stand.[267] The Sioux were the predominant tribe in each of these wars, and they were not to be taken lightly anywhere, including at Wounded Knee, but they had suffered defeats in the last 5 battles in the War for the Black Hills, and, as Carl Waldman put it, the Sioux, "desperate in defeat for any glimmer of hope, took to the new religion"—that is, the Ghost Dance religion.[268]

Several conclusions were reached by officials who investigated Wounded Knee. The army investigation by General E. D. Scott found (perhaps predictably) the following: (1) There was nothing for the army to apologize for; (2) The firing was started by the Indians; (3) the killing of the women and children must have been mostly by Indian bullets; (4) the attack by the Indians was treacherous; and (5) their attack was explained in that they were under inexcusable religious hallucination.[269] Scott also concluded that "the wholesale slaughter of the women and children was unnecessary and inexcusable."[270] Marshall properly concluded that in the Scott report "there was some whitewash and some truth."[271] Although it was true that the Indians started the battle, it was also true that the killing of the Sioux, including women and children, in the dry ravine was unnecessary and inexcusable, an atrocity.

Mooney concluded that "the medicine man, Yellow Bird, at the critical moment urged the warriors to resist and gave the signal for the attack; that the first shot was fired by an Indian; and that the Indians were responsible for the engagement." "Suddenly Yellow Bird stooped down and threw a handful of dust in the air."[272]

S. L. A. Marshall in *Crimsoned Prairie: The Indian Wars* concurred:

There is no doubt who started that day's fight, though it is often called a massacre. . . . [D]eliberate Sioux action, so timed as to indicate that it had been well plotted, initiated the slaughter. *Bury My Heart at Wounded Knee* [the title of the Brown book] may be a lovely phrase. It is still a false and misleading sentiment, dignifying conspiracy and honoring treachery.[273]

Robert M. Utley and Wilcomb E. Washburn concluded in *Indian Wars* that Wounded Knee was "a tragic accident of war that neither side intended . . . for which neither side as a whole may be properly condemned."[274]

The frontier also ended in 1890. That year, the Census Bureau announced it could no longer designate a frontier on its map as it had done in previous decades.[275] Even more important, wrote Alan Axelrod, "it was becoming clear even to the most resolute that the [Indian] cause was hopeless . . . and [that] four centuries of war between white man and red had come to an end bitter and inglorious, suffused with exhaustion, sorrow, and shame."[276]

SOME CONCLUSIONS can be reached about the atrocities. There were many more atrocities committed in this war than in all other United States wars combined. As Gilbert noted, the war was one of "unique ferocity" in which "the savages—red and white—did things to each other which sensitive outsiders found unbelievable."[277] The reader may understandably find them unbelievable as well, but they are documented in the literature by credible historians, and it would appear that they are not disputed even by Indian advocates.

There is some irony in the fact that the war started with a hat— Trader Morgan's hat—which led to the Powhatan Wars and ended with some shirts—the Ghost Shirts that Yellow Bird at Wounded Knee claimed would protect the Sioux warriors from the soldiers' bullets. Two items of clothing played a part in starting a long, bitter war and bringing about its end as well. There isn't a moral here, but it is an interesting coincidence.

More than 16,000 atrocities connected with a death[278] are recorded in the atrocity chapters. This fact (an average of 60 atrocities each year during the 268-year war) is depressing. No attempt has been made here to calculate additional death figures not connected with atrocities.

Some historians and writers have attempted to estimate all deaths resulting from specific parts of the war. Indian casualties are especially hard to determine because of the Indian practice of carrying their dead from the field of battle whenever possible.

Carl Waldman's *Atlas of the North American Indian* estimated that "many tribal populations declined by more than 10 percent from Indian-white conflicts" (over a period of time not stated).[279] If we accept the estimate that there were 295,500 Indians in the United States in 1630, then more than 29,000 Indians (presumably mostly warriors) may have been killed when the Indians fought around that time. That was a big loss.

Here are some other estimates. Gallatin wrote that it was his opinion that more Indians were killed from 1600 to 1791 by the Iroquois alone than were killed by the Europeans.[280] Wilcomb E. Washburn estimated that in King Philip's War in 1675–76, the English (which included the Americans who fought with them) lost 600 men and the Indians 3,000.[281] Bil Gilbert in *God Gave Us This Country* calculated that 360 settlers were killed in the Wyoming Valley Massacre in 1778, 500 at Fort Mims in 1813, and 200 Cheyenne at Sand Creek in 1864.[282] Richard VanDerBeets concluded in his *Held Captive by Indians* that between 1782 and 1790, 1,500 settlers along the Ohio River were injured, killed, or captured.[283] Clark Wissler, author of *Indians of the United States,* figured that between 1707 and 1814 there were about 100 battles between Indians and whites. In addition, there were at least 1,000 raids on both sides. The losses from the raids alone were 8,000 whites and 4,000 Indians.[284] Washburn made an estimate that for the period from 1798 to 1898, not more than 4,000 Indians and some 7,000 soldiers and civilians were killed.[285] This is consistent with the figures reported from the atrocity information to the effect that more whites than Indians were killed.

Elliott West in *The Contested Plains* approached the question this way: The 1855 Census reported only 2 men for every 3 women among the Southern Cheyenne, Arapaho, and Comanche. The situation was even worse among some eastern tribes. West concluded the cause of this ratio was death from either hunting or fighting. A family among these tribes was 3 or 4 times as likely to lose a husband or son to fighting as a white family in the bloody Civil War at a later time. In short, the Civil War carnage did not approach that of these wars.[286]

In 1885, Helen Hunt Jackson in *A Century of Dishonor* held the opinion that "the Indian has no redress but war. In these [Indian] wars ten white men were killed to one Indian."[287]

To put the matter into perspective, the battle deaths in the other major wars in the history of the United States are: Revolutionary War,

6,824; War of 1812, 2,260; Mexican War, 1,733; Civil War, 140,414 (Union) and 74,524 (Confederacy), for a total of 214,938; Spanish-American War, 385; World War I, 53,513; World War II, 292,131; Korean War, 33,629; and Vietnam War, 47,393.

Pope John Paul II issued an encyclical entitled *Veritas Splendor* ("The Splendor of Truth") in late 1993, which asserted that there is a basic morality that transcends *all eras and cultures* and absolutely forbids certain actions.[288] History has given us some fundamental rules of conduct in hostile times, violation of which invokes the strong disapproval of contemporaneous and succeeding generations. Some of those rules are these: (1) Do not knowingly kill children; (2) Do not knowingly kill women unless they are showing hostility; (3) Do not torture your enemy; (4) Do not eat human flesh; (5) Do not kill your prisoner; and (6) Do not deliberately mutilate your enemy's body. Indians violated all these rules, and settlers and soldiers violated some of them, although the author has found no white cannibalizing of Indians and few instances of their torturing Indians.

The atrocities make it is easy to understand why this time and place in our history was called the wild frontier. The cataloging of these hard-to-believe atrocities is at an end.

Most of us are baffled by atrocious acts. Fortunately, we do have some clues that help us analyze the motives of those who committed them. Several of the causes have been mentioned above: hatred, revenge, unauthorized conduct, Indian love of warfare and desire to torture, desperation, cannibalism, and Indian conduct during the Revolution.

Two additional causes are the atrocities themselves and sadism. An atrocity was committed, word of it spread in the offended settler or Indian community, then a counteratrocity was committed in an escalating effect that sometimes led to full-blown war. Specific examples are the Raisin River Massacre of 1813, where 80 American prisoners were tortured and killed by Indians, which increased American resolve and "morally justified more or less anything they [the settlers] might be able to do to the savages";[289] the Santee Sioux Uprising in Minnesota in 1862, which caused white goodwill to "run out," according to S. L. A. Marshall, and which "would not be forgotten by the whites on the frontier";[290] and Sand Creek, which "the Plains Indians could neither forget nor forgive."[291]

Sadism is a little-understood mental illness characterized by the obtaining of pleasure from hurting someone else. Fanny Kelly reported that the Sioux were fond of recounting their exploits of torture. They would

> dwell with much satisfaction upon the number of scalps they have taken from their white foes. They would be greatly amused at the shuddering horror manifested, when, to annoy me, they would tauntingly portray the dying agonies of white men, women, and children, who had fallen into their hands; and especially would the effect of their description of the murder of [Kelly's daughter] little Mary afford them satisfaction.[292]

Regardless of whether or not it was proper, the settlers frequently attempted to justify their own atrocities on the grounds that the Indians were committing atrocities. Bil Gilbert said, "Whites frequently justified their own atrocious conduct on the grounds that it was necessary to fight fire with fire, that they had to be vicious because the savages were so vicious."[293] Denis Brogan also took this view: "The early settlers long needed to acquire a craft equaling the craft of the savages and a savagery not much inferior. It is hard to remember this today. . . . But it has to be remembered all the same."[294]

BELLIGERENTS IN any war have enemies. The enemies in this war were different. The principal enemy of the settlers, of course, was the Indians who fought them and committed many atrocities against them, but another enemy at times was the federal government, which spasmodically prevented settlers from encroaching on land occupied by Indians. One enemy of the Indians was the government that fought them and from time to time improperly assisted the settlers against them. A greater enemy was the settlers themselves, without right seizing land occupied by Indians and committing numerous atrocities against them. But paradoxically, the greatest enemy of the Indians was Indians themselves who warred ferociously with one another, weakening their ability to fight the settlers, and who refused to unite in defeating them.

CHAPTER 9

Some Other Aspects
of the War

The settlement of the United States was an invasion of European citizens on the East Coast commencing in 1607. After their War of Independence, they became one people. They then continued their invasion westward until it reached the Pacific Ocean. They were opposed by Indian tribes who did not unite to repel the invasion as urged by King Philip, Joseph Brant, Pontiac, and Tecumseh. The tribes were defeated by a united, much better armed invader.

The matter of treaties was an important subject for settlers and Indians from the beginning. Powhatan chief Opechancanough signed a peace treaty with the settlers in 1632, the first of hundreds of treaties that followed. Many problems arose because of them. The first report of the Board of Indian Commissioners established by Congress in 1869 found that "the history of the government connections with the Indians is a shameful record of broken treaties and unfulfilled promises."[1] President Rutherford B. Hayes was of the opinion that "many, if not most, of our Indian wars have had their origin in broken promises and acts of injustice on our part."[2]

Sitting Bull saw it that way too. "What treaty that the whites have kept has the red man broken? Not one. What treaty that the white man even made with us have they kept? Not one."[3] Peter Matthiessen charged that "the United States governments, one after another, had failed the Indian people in every moral and legal obligation."[4] Ralph K. Andrist, author of *The Long Death,* charged that every promise made by the government "had been cynically broken."[5]

But a more considered view is given by Alan Axelrod, who observed in *Chronicle of the Indian Wars* that the fault lay with the Indians as well as the whites:

> Treaties between whites and Indians were customarily violated almost as soon as they were signed.
>
> It is all too easy to ascribe these violations to white perfidy. Indeed, this was often the case, as white governments, colonial or federal, sometimes entered into treaties in bad faith. More often, however, white treaty commissioners had reasonably good intentions and fully expected their side would abide by the terms of the agreement. . . . There were grave problems on the Indians' side as well.[6]

Both sides were hindered by weak governments that could not keep their peoples acting in compliance with the treaties. The United States made 389 treaties with Indian tribes. Some treaties were made again and again with the same tribe as conditions changed. No less than 42 treaties were made with the Potawatomis and an additional 42 with the Chippewa.[7]

The last "treaty" with the Indians was made in 1871. Peter Matthiessen made the misleading statement that

> in 1871, the government repudiated the whole concept of treaties, most of which it had already broken; since the Indians who had not been exterminated were now mostly under control, the remnants could be administered by the Department of the Interior as a "national resource."[8]

The treaty concept was changed by an act of Congress because Indian advocates (called humanitarians then) did not like the treaty system and because the House of Representatives wanted to share with the Senate authority for dealing with the Indians. Under the Constitution, the House took no part in ratifying treaties.[9] The 1871 act did not repudiate "the whole concept of treaties." To the contrary, it expressly reaffirmed the validity of obligations incurred under earlier Indian treaties. The act provided "that nothing herein contained shall be construed to invalidate or impair the obligation of any treaty heretofore lawfully made and ratified with any such Indian nation or tribe."[10]

No evidence supports the conclusion that the United States broke most of its Indian treaties. Only Matthiessen, Sitting Bull, and a few others make that claim. Sitting Bull in the same statement quoted above also asserted that the Indians had broken "not one" treaty. There are many examples to the contrary, and indeed the violations are sometimes admitted by the Indians.

There is also a well-established rule of law that bears on the question of treaty-breaking by the United States. That rule is that Congress has the authority to break treaties when it wishes. Two Cherokee refused to pay taxes on tobacco required by an internal revenue act on the ground that they were exempt under a Cherokee treaty. In the *Cherokee Tobacco* case, the Supreme Court decided in 1870 that "a treaty may supersede a prior act of Congress, and an act of Congress may supersede a prior treaty. . . . In the case under consideration the act of Congress must prevail as if the treaty were not an element to be considered."[11]

ANGIE DEBO, in her *History of the Indians of the United States,* described several methods by which individual land-grabbers (and not the government) illegally obtained the land of individual Indians:

> Land-grabbers then flooded the country and obtained contracts of sale. Their methods are significant, for the identical techniques were repeated many times when Indians tried to hold land by individual title: misrepresentation, the Indian not knowing what he was signing; the use of intoxicants; the misuse of notary seals on blank instruments, to be filled in at the swindler's convenience; outright forgery and a specialized kind, the bribing of some subservient Indian to impersonate the owner and sign in his place; and rigged probate procedure in the state courts corrupted by the general dishonesty.[12]

Although Debo cited no specific cases to support her claim that individual land-grabbers illegally obtained land occupied by Indians, no one can doubt that this happened thousands of times. Laying aside what individuals illegally did to acquire land occupied by Indians, it is significant that no one explicitly claims the United States *government* illegally acquired such land. The word *explicitly* is used because of the nonspecific claims of some Indians or Indian advocates that someone, somehow, somewhere "stole" Indian land.

Land brought settlers to the New World, and land was the principal subject of the treaties. Despite the evidence that the federal government (sometimes state governments) had purchased very great quantities of land from the Indians under treaties, Edward H. Spicer found "the feeling was strong among Indians generally that the U.S. government owed them a great deal for taking nearly all their land and for failing to live up to the many treaties as settlers moved across the continent."[13]

Indian advocate Felix Cohen was asked if the more than $800,000,000 the United States paid for lands purchased from Indians after 1790 was an honest price. He said, "The only fair answer to that question is that except in a very few cases where military duress was present, the price paid was one that satisfied the Indians."[14]

Even those sympathetic to the Indians have acknowledged that the government legally obtained substantially all of the Indian land. Wilcomb E. Washburn pointed out in *The Indian in America* that "students of the subject as diverse as Thomas Jefferson and Felix Cohen have agreed that most of the lands acquired from the native inhabitants of the present area of the United States were acquired by purchase from their original possessors."[15] William T. Hagan, speaking of the government acquiring Indian land in *American Indians,* said, "Down to 1811 violence was not required and everything was done legally, if not ethically."[16] Carl Waldman's *Atlas of the North American Indian* showed clearly the areas ceded and the tribe or tribes making the cessation. These areas make up almost the entirety of the United States. Ralph K. Andrist, with reluctance and after making all the arguments the Indians made as to why they should not have been bound by the treaties ceding land, finally concluded,

> The government had always been completely correct in its relations with the Indian tribes, treating them as though they were independent nations.[17]

In 1946, the government set up an unprecedented judicial procedure for resolving Indian claims about land and other matters called the Indian Claims Commission Act. The act was broad and required the commission to hear almost any claim asserted by an Indian tribe or band, including

> . . . (3) claims which would result if the treaties, contracts, and agreements between the claimant and the United States were revised on the ground of fraud, duress, unconscionable consideration, mutual or unilateral mistake, whether of law or fact, or any other ground cognizable by a court of equity; (4) claims arising from the taking by the United States, whether as the result of a treaty of cessation or otherwise, of lands owned or occupied by the claimant without the payment for

such lands of compensation agreed to by the claimant; and (5) claims based upon fair and honorable dealings that are not recognized by any existing rule of law or equity. No claim accruing after the date of the approval of this Act shall be considered by the Commission.

All claims hereunder may be heard and determined by the Commission notwithstanding any statute of limitations or laches, but all other defenses shall be available to the United States.[18]

This act has been invaluable to the Indians. Under it the Sioux got a $105,000,000 judgment because land had been taken from them contrary to the Constitution. The Supreme Court held that under the Fort Laramie Treaty of 1868, the Sioux were to have exclusive occupation of the Black Hills, but then that land was effectively taken from them by an 1877 act of Congress, and the Fifth Amendment required the government to make just compensation to the Sioux.[19] A few of the other judgments are $31,000,000 for the Ute, $13,000,000 for the Delaware, $7,000,000 for the Pawnee, more than $5,000,000 for the California tribes, and almost $5,000,000 for the Miami. Other important claims are pending. So far as is known, although some Indians claimed that tribes possessed their land forever, the tribes such as the Sioux who dispossessed others to get the land on which their award was based never gave any part of the award to the dispossessed tribes.[20]

By 1951, 852 claims had been filed concerning more than twice the amount of land in the lower 48 states. (This resulted because of overlapping claims.) The government agreed to return 48,000 acres to the Pueblos and 21,000 acres to the Yakimas. Since 1970, the courts and Congress have returned more than 4,500,000 acres to Indians and have paid about $2,000,000,000 by way of compensation for land. The Indians did not win all their claims before the commission, but they did win 60 percent of them.

TRIBE AFTER tribe took by conquest land being occupied by others. A few examples: Iroquois by conquest displaced the Hurons. The Cree and Chippewa displaced the Sioux from their woodland homes in Minnesota and Wisconsin. The Sioux in turn displaced the Kiowa, Crows, Pawnee, Ioways, Omaha, Arikara, and Mandan in the West. The Navajo took the land of the Hopi.[21]

We know about the purchases of the Louisiana Territory in 1803, the Florida Purchase from Spain in 1819, the Gadsden Purchase from Mexico in 1854, and the Alaska Purchase from Russia in 1867. Under international law then and now, lands occupied by Indians in these territories purchased by treaty belonged to the government and not the Indians.

The same result obtained when the territory was conquered. In the *McIntosh* case, plaintiffs claimed title to land in Illinois by reason of purchases from the Indians. The defendant claimed title to the same land on the basis of purchase from the government. The Supreme Court, speaking through Chief Justice John Marshall in 1823, found for the defendant, holding in part that even without a treaty, title to the Indian land was acquired by the settlers by 2 additional means:

> Conquest gives a title which the Courts of the conqueror cannot deny. The title by conquest is acquired and maintained by force. The conqueror prescribes its limits. Second, title by conquest on the part of the settlers themselves. "If a country has been acquired and held under it [the rule of title by conquest]; if the property of the great mass of the community originates in it, it becomes the law of the land, and cannot be questioned.[22]

The law of complete conquest is described in this way in the *American Jurisprudence* legal encyclopedia:

> Complete conquest, by whatever mode it may be perfected, carries with it all the rights of the former government. In other words, the conqueror, by the completion of his conquest, becomes the absolute owner of the property conquered from the enemy nation or state. His rights are no longer limited to mere occupation of what he has taken in his actual possession, but they extend to all the property and rights of the conquered state, *including* even debts as well as personal and *real property* [emphasis added].[23]

Under international law then and now, lands occupied by Indians in those territories *conquered* by the government belonged to the government and not to the Indians.

Although the government was entitled to take all the Indian land without compensation under the law of conquest, the fact that it chose to try to purchase that land instead was to its credit. It was also perhaps unprecedented in world history.

It is still argued by some that most of the land was taken by force without compensation. One example did occur during the Revolutionary War. After the war, in 1783, the Americans, according to Edward H. Spicer, "took over the greater part of the land of the Cayugas, Mohawks, and Onondagas."[24] These 3 tribes fought against the Americans during the war.[25] They were not paid for their land because of their exceptionally atrocious conduct toward the settlers. The Americans held title to this land, however, under the law of conquest.

ONE OF the great tragedies of the war between the Indians and the settlers was that there was plenty of land for both. Black Hawk returned from a hunt in 1829 to find a settler family settled in his lodge. He got an interpreter and told the squatters not to occupy those lands and that "there was plenty of land in the country for them to settle upon." The family didn't leave, more settlers arrived, and the Black Hawk War started. S. L. A. Marshall observed in *Crimsoned Prairie* that at the time of the Plains wars, "the Far West was still a largely unpeopled land of magnificent distances. There remained plenty of room for the red man and for the white man."[26] As late as 1872 any newly arrived foreigner who declared his intention to become a citizen was given 160 acres of land and tools and stock.[27]

AS WE have seen, diseases were as destructive to the Indians as anything else. Carl Waldman in *Atlas of the North American Indian* put it succinctly:

> As devastating as warfare and forced removals were to Indian peoples, another result of contact with whites proved to be even more debilitating, demoralizing, and deadly—the spread of European diseases. It is estimated that, whereas many tribal populations declined by more than 10 percent from Indian-white conflicts, the average tribal loss of life from infectious diseases was 25–50 percent. For some tribes, these diseases meant near extinction. . . .
>
> The extent of the tragedy is staggering. The subject of infectious European diseases pervades every aspect of Indian studies. Disease was a principal disrupter of Indian culture, with shattering impact even on Indian faith and religion. The debilitating effects of these diseases also helped the whites win many of the Indian wars. . . . As for land cessions, disease through depopulation played a large part in the ultimate displacement of tribes.[28]

It may be that more Indians were killed by disease than by intertribal warfare and fighting the settlers combined,[29] and William T. Hagan concluded that had it not been for Indian diseases, the war "would have been bloodier and more protracted."[30] Wilcomb E. Washburn believed that "unwittingly, disease was the white man's strongest ally in the New World."[31]

Three years before the *Mayflower* arrived, an epidemic decimated the Indians from Rhode Island to Maine. Thus the Indians were not in as strong a position to oppose the Plymouth colony. "If they had been, it [Plymouth] could not have survived."[32] A smallpox epidemic struck the New England Indians in 1633 and 1634. Thousands died. Plymouth and the other colonies got a new life.[33]

In 1849, cholera swept through the western tribes. The Cheyenne were devastated, the Flexed Leg band vanished, the Sioux reported terrible losses, and a Pawnee agent reported that one fourth of the tribe, or 1,200, had died, with the epidemic still raging.

Disease almost wiped out the Omaha tribe. In the smallpox epidemic of 1800, the tribe's population dropped from about 3,000 to about 300. At that point, the tribe decided to commit collective suicide. Bordewich discussed how: "They formed a village-wide war party to attack their traditional enemies and fought through the Poncas, Cheyennes, Pawnees, and Otoes until those left realized some of them might survive after all. Then they returned home."[34]

Smallpox was the most harmful disease to the Indians. It was a serious disease among whites as well, but most survived it because they had built up some resistance by reason of centuries of exposure. This was not true, of course, of the Indians. The Mandan Indian tribe of 1,600 suffered a smallpox epidemic in 1837. Half committed suicide with knives, guns, or by leaping from a 30-foot ledge.[35] Only 31 survived. Those were enslaved by the Riccarees, a neighboring tribe, who later were attacked by the Sioux. The Mandan, not wishing to live, ran onto the prairie, calling out that they were Riccaree dogs and asking for the Sioux to kill them. The Sioux did.[36]

Edward Jenner developed his vaccine for smallpox in 1796. It was available for use not long thereafter. Various government officials made efforts to see to it that the Indians were vaccinated, but it is clear from the fact that epidemics continued that those efforts were not successful.[37]

There were smallpox epidemics in 1780–1800 in Texas, in 1830–33 in California, in 1837 in Wyoming, in 1837–70 in Kansas, and in 1869–70 in Montana.[38]

In 1805, Blackfoot Indians hired Alexander Culbertson to get a keelboat of goods for the Indians. Several passengers came down with smallpox. When he learned about their smallpox, Culbertson tried to stop the boat until cold weather, but the Indians refused, so the boat went on. Ten days later, the Blackfeet had an epidemic. No fewer than 4,000 out of the 6,000 members of the tribe died.[39]

The Blackfeet raided a Shoshoni camp in 1781. They found all the Shoshoni dead or dying of smallpox. More than half the Blackfeet then died of smallpox as well.[40] In 1801, a Pawnee war party returning from a raid in New Mexico (then Spanish territory) brought smallpox back with them. It spread from their territory on the lower Platte to Texas.[41] A war party of Pawnee took several Sioux prisoners in 1838. The prisoners had smallpox. About 2,000 Pawnee died of smallpox as a result. They in turn carried it south to the Osages, who also suffered many deaths and then passed the disease on to the Kiowa and the Comanche. The latter 2 tribes moved to north Texas to try to escape.[42]

George Catlin watched as Indians "in this [smallpox] as in most of their diseases, ignorantly and imprudently plunge into the coldest water, whilst in the highest state of fever, and often die before they have the power to get out."[43] But something devastating happened beyond the diseases themselves. James Wilson claimed European diseases "undermined the Native Americans' confidence in themselves and their view of the world. The failure of the shamans to contain and cure smallpox and bubonic plague was the failure of an entire system of belief."[44]

Diseases affected the soldiers as well and with similar consequences. Axelrod noted that "disease [in the army] was responsible for more casualties than Indian hostility."[45] In King William's War in 1690, the English army was overcome by both the French and by smallpox, which killed many soldiers, and the army withdrew.[46] During the French and Indian War, in 1757, the American army was in Halifax training for an assault on Louisbourg. The army was stricken with an epidemic, presumably smallpox. There were 200 deaths and an additional 500 hospitalizations. This army also withdrew.[47] In 1757, French general Montcalm promised the American commandant and his men safe passage out of their fort, Fort William Henry. His Indian allies ambushed the surrendered men and massacred the hospital patients, including the smallpox patients, and took their infected scalps back to their people, where many deaths occurred.[48] During the siege of Quebec in 1759, the British lost fewer than 250 soldiers. After the city was taken, however, an epidemic (no doubt smallpox) killed 1,000 more and 2,000 became unfit for service.[49]

Disease was not a one-way street. Columbus perhaps brought smallpox, but his crews took back syphilis and tobacco. The exchange was not a good one for the whites. Smallpox was made preventable in 1796 by Jenner's vaccine, but syphilis could not safely be cured until the late 1940s, when antibiotics were developed. This was more than 325 years after Plymouth was founded in 1620.[50] Syphilis was the most common medical problem for the Lewis and Clark Expedition.[51]

Indians over almost all of North America used tobacco before Columbus came. Catlin found in the 1830s that "the luxury of smoking is known to all the North American Indians. . . . In their native state they are excessive smokers."[52] Columbus took it back with him to Europe and from there its use spread all over the world.[53] More deaths have no doubt resulted from tobacco than from smallpox and syphilis combined. The World Health Organization estimates that about 2,500,000 people in the world die as a result of smoking each year, and about 400,000 of those deaths are in the United States.[54] Tobacco throughout the world kills more than 3 times as many people each year as there were Indians in the United States in 1492.

EXTERMINATION WAS a topic popular among both settlers and Indians. Indians and their advocates have argued that it was soon clear that settlers intended to exterminate the Indians either by deliberately spreading contagious diseases or by use of force. There is no evidence that settlers attempted to use diseases to exterminate Indians. The question remains whether the settlers tried to exterminate the Indians by use of force.

The Ottawa chief Pontiac said in 1763, "It is important to us, my brothers, that we exterminate from our lands this nation [Great Britain] which seeks only to destroy us." He then led an assault on Fort Detroit, the strongest British garrison in the area, which was unsuccessful.[55]

A great pan-Indian council was held near Detroit in 1786. Bil Gilbert said the Shawnee and the Miami urged all the tribes "to exterminate all the Americans who might be in those lands [the Ohio River line]." The Shawnee began acting on that policy immediately.[56]

Thomas Jefferson, quoted by Bernard W. Sheehan, wrote in 1813 about the Indians that "ferocious barbarities justified extermination."[57] Jefferson had left office 4 years earlier.

As we have seen, at the time of the California gold rush in 1848, much of the gold country was inhabited by Indians known as Diggers because they dug roots and picked berries for food. The governor of

California announced that "a war of extermination will continue to be waged until the Indian race becomes extinct. This must be expected."[58] In very little time, the prospectors had killed 10 percent of the Diggers.

Around 1855, Oregon territorial governor George Curry called for a military campaign to exterminate the Indians in that state. Instead, army regulars defended Indians from aggressive settlers.[59]

After the Rouge River War of 1855, a Modoc chief said, "I thought if we killed all the white men we saw, that no more would come. We killed all we could; but they came more and more like new grass in the spring."[60]

The fact that there were white people who did want extermination is exemplified by 3 editorials, the first from California in 1866, the next written in 1867 in Kansas, and the last dated 1870 in a Wyoming newspaper. The *Chico Courant* in California took the position that

> it is a mercy to the red devils to exterminate them, and a saving of many white lives. Treaties are played out—there is one kind of treaty that is effective—cold lead.[61]

The Kansas editorial described Indians as

> a set of miserable, dirty, lousy, blanketed, thieving, lying, sneaking, murdering, graceless, faithless, gut-eating skunks . . . whose immediate and final extermination all men, except Indian agents and traders, should pray for.[62]

The Wyoming editorial rationalized the elimination of the Indian in this way:

> The same inscrutable Arbiter that decreed the downfall of Rome, has pronounced the doom of extinction upon the red men of America. To attempt to defer this result by mawkish sentimentalism . . . is unworthy of the age.[63]

The Battle of the Little Bighorn of 1876 was a shock to the settlers— so much so that a bill was introduced in Congress by Senator Paddock calling for the extermination of Indians. But it did not pass.

After the Meeker raid in Colorado in 1879, Governor Frederick Pitkin even figured out the economic benefit of extermination:

> My idea is that, unless removed by the government, they [the Indians] must necessarily be exterminated. I could raise 25,000 men to protect

the settlers in twenty-four hours. The State would be willing to settle the Indian problem at its own expense. The advantages that would accrue from the throwing open of twelve million acres of land to miners and settlers would more than compensate all the expenses incurred.[64]

Was it ever the policy of either Indian or federal governments to exterminate the other? No. The holders of these extreme views never spoke for the government or for all the tribes. Fergus M. Bordewich put it best:

Although many modern polemicists call upon Americans to regard the nation's treatment of the Indians as a pattern of deliberate "genocide," the physical extermination of Native Americans was never an official policy of the United States government. With more realism than racism, the new republic initially worried less about ridding itself of Indians than about how to protect them from the depredations of its own citizens.[65]

Was this a race war? Alan Axelrod commenced his book, *Chronicle of the Indian Wars,* with the statement that the book is a "chronicle of protracted racial warfare."[66] Alvin M. Josephy, Jr., in *The Indian Heritage of America,* correctly referred to the war as a "total conflict of one race against the other."[67] And Carl Waldman in *Atlas of the North American Indian* cautioned that "the hostilities [of the war] cannot be viewed simply in terms of Indian versus white. The Indian wars are now generally interpreted as wars of native resistance."[68]

If the words *race war* simply mean a war between people of different races, the war was a race war because red people were at war with white people. If those words are taken in their normal sense, however, to mean a racially motivated war, it was not, because for the most part the white people were fighting for the land of the red people and would have done so regardless of the color of the defenders' skins, just as the defenders would have resisted regardless of the color of the attackers' skins. No one apparently contends that this was a racially motivated conflict in the sense of one where a belligerent tries to exterminate all the opponent's race. Waldman concluded that "the Indians' tribal identity was stronger than racial, just as for the whites national or religious identity took precedence over shared race."[69]

Most people of Jefferson's day did not consider that there were racial differences between whites and Indians. Sheehan observed that "divisions there were between white and Indian, but in the Jeffersonian age, they were not racial."[70] Jefferson himself wrote in 1785 that "I believe the Indian then to be in body and mind equal to the white man."[71] Clark Wissler argued in *Indians of the United States* that the war was economic and political, not racial:

> There was neither racial nor social incompatibility between Indian and white. On the frontier white men married Indian women, and we have seen that white captives married to Indian men were reluctant to leave them. In Europe the early tendency of scholars was to consider the Indians as belonging to the white race. The tragic struggle between the two was economic and political.[72]

Alan Axelrod put it like this:

> Contrary to the claims of some Indian as well as white activists in the twentieth century, it was never the federal government's official policy to practice genocide against the Native peoples of the West—though there was no shortage of individual racists and fanatics who advocated just that.[73]

The few who argue that this was a racially motivated war would no doubt be surprised to learn that 10 Indian army scouts were awarded the Congressional Medal of Honor by the United States government. Surely it is unlikely that a government in a racially motivated war would confer its highest medal on no fewer than 10 members of the other race in one war.

Unfortunately, as James Wilson noted, "the issue of race has become an ugly and painful running sore in some tribes" in that full-blooded Indians claim superiority over mixed bloods.[74]

THE INDIANS were conquered, but they continued to resist beyond heroism. A theory concerning why they resisted when all was lost can be based on a comparison between the many invasions of England and the settler invasion of America. People from Spain and France settled in England between 8000 and 3000 B.C. There were 8 more invasions.[75] The invaded English peoples repeatedly accepted the invaders to a large extent, and the invaders and the invaded even exchanged some of their culture.

In each of these invasions, the law of the invader governed when it conflicted with the law of the conquered. This is a fundamental principle of international law and should come as no surprise when given any thought at all. Some Indian advocates contend that Indian rights before the settler invasion should prevail after the invasion. They obviously did not, no more than our rights would have survived had we been invaded by the Germans or the Japanese in World War II or by the Russians or the Chinese in the Cold War.

CHAPTER 10

Government Indian Policy

Initially every English colony was responsible for dealing with the Indians as it saw fit.[1] The policy of the Jamestown colony could be and was different from that of the Plymouth colony. After the Powhatan attack of 1622, Governor Wyatt urged extermination,[2] but that was not true of Plymouth. Jamestown set up the first Indian reservations in 1653. A reservation was established for the Pamunkey Indians and the Chickahominy. Justices of the peace were required to remove whites who had settled in these reservations. The Massachusetts Bay Colony also created reservations for "praying Indians." These reservations were not available to hostile Indians who were not controlled by the colonists.[3] Finally, in 1754, in order to have a consistent Indian policy, the Albany Congress brought together Indian affairs under the royal government.[4]

The Continental Congress followed the British system of dealing with the Indians and in 1778 made its first treaty with the Delaware.[5] Esarey rather forthrightly concluded that after the Revolution, "by the laws of warfare they [the Indians] had forfeited all their rights to their land and almost to their lives; yet Congress had no idea of punishing them."[6] Indians in the territory allotted to the states by the Treaty of Paris, which ended the Revolution, were regarded, said Alan Axelrod, as "a conquered people without civil rights," yet the federal government did attempt "to regulate white settlement . . . and did offer to buy—albeit cheaply—territory rather than simply appropriate it."[7]

The government of the United States of America began in 1789. Once American Indian policy had been determined, the administration of that policy created many difficulties. One of the first arose out of the fact that territorial governors were also superintendents of Indian affairs for their territories. The governor reported to the secretary of state in his capacity as governor, but to the secretary of war in his capacity as superintendent of Indian affairs. Not only did this cause confusion, but in addition there were jurisdictional disputes between civilians and the military when it was necessary to bring in the army. This remained a frequent problem until almost the 1890s.[8]

The settlers themselves created a serious and continuing problem. The government was close to bankruptcy. Selling the western lands was the only way of raising revenue quickly. Bil Gilbert said,

> In this regard the Indians presented obvious difficulties, but the behavior of frontier whites was almost as vexing to federal officials. From their standpoint the thousands of unruly pioneers who took choice properties simply by squatting on them were stealing government property in such quantities as to threaten the solvency and therefore existence of the nation.[9]

The government's response was the Northwest Ordinance of 1787, which federalized most of the land in Ohio, Indiana, Michigan, Illinois, Wisconsin, and part of Minnesota, wiped out previous colonial and state claims to the land, and set up a form of government. Land was sold to the Ohio Company for 9 cents an acre and to other land companies for even less. For the next several years federal troops tried to keep squatting settlers off the unsold land, without much success.[10]

Despite its need for revenue, the government was not too anxious for the frontier to move west rapidly because the price of the land could be kept higher if there was not too much of it available. Peace commissioner Timothy Pickering instructed General Wayne that in treating with the Indians at the conclusion of Little Turtle's War, "peace and not increase of territory has been the object of this expensive War."[11]

The Louisiana Purchase was made in 1803. The land east of the Mississippi filled up, and by 1830 the frontier was west of the Mississippi to about 100 miles north of St. Louis. It then crossed northern Illinois, northern Indiana, and southern Michigan.[12] There was more room for the settlers, but there were new Indians to resist them.

Government policy from the Washington administration to the Jackson administration, said Bernard W. Sheehan, "persisted in trying to civilize the tribes," along with efforts to keep the settlers off Indian land. Secretary of War Knox instructed that the Indians should be treated with "entire justice and humanity." His successor, William H. Crawford, announced that the appearance of force or menace should be avoided and the government should "lean in favor of the Indians."[13]

Continued attempts to protect the Indians from the settlers failed. The Trade and Intercourse Act, which largely restated earlier laws, provided that anyone going onto Indian land without a passport was subject to fine and imprisonment, anyone committing a crime against the person or property of a friendly Indian should also be subject to fine and imprisonment, and anyone murdering a peaceful Indian should suffer death.[14] By the time Jefferson became president, however, it was evident that the frontier could not be controlled.[15]

In 1806, a new law created a superintendent of Indian trade, but as Logan Esarey commented, he was in the main powerless:

> The government factors were forbidden to sell whiskey to the natives, but unprincipled traders, most of them criminal outcasts from the east, swarmed into the Indian country, furnishing liquor to all who had anything to give in return, denouncing the government agents as robbers, and inciting the Indians to all kinds of deeds of violence on one another or to depredations on the settlers.[16]

Government Indian policy was not only inadequate but conflicting from the military point of view. Wilcomb E. Washburn reported that army generals "complained that the reservations were often regarded as sanctuaries from which Indians could issue forth to raid the settlements and to which they could return to avoid the risk of retaliation by settlers or soldiers."[17] For example, the Kiowa raided from the Kiowa-Comanche Reservation, then after the raid returned to the reservation (where they drew government rations), knowing the army could not follow them there.[18]

There was also disagreement between the War Department and the Interior Department. The *Times* said, "The Secretary of War and the Secretary of the Interior are constantly working at cross purposes, so far as the Indians are concerned."[19] This conflict was described by Edward Lazarus "as a heated and frequently vicious battle between the Departments of War and Interior for control of Indian policy. During the next decade, each would frustrate the other's policies and trade endless accusations and recriminations."[20]

When the eastern Indians were first taken west of the Mississippi under the Indian Removal Act in the 1830s and 1840s, they were allowed to go pretty much where they wanted to hunt or to farm. In the 1860s, however, the Indian Peace Commission negotiated separate treaties with each removed tribe. Those treaties required each to settle on a reservation, normally the land on which the tribe hunted or had already settled.[21]

The system made all those Indians wards of the government. They no longer had to provide for their own food, clothing, and shelter. The leaders of the tribes were bypassed and made ineffective. The tribes were not allowed to become economically independent, and there was a forced breakdown of tribal traditions and religious practices.[22] Reservations got the Indians off the lands the settlers wanted.[23] The more the Indians were insulated, the less likely they were to raid the settlers.

The reservations even had some advantages for the Indians. In addition to furnishing them food, clothing, and shelter, Wilcomb E. Washburn observed that

> whatever else the reservation system may represent it does mark an acceptance of the Indians' right to live and to retain land and resources for their support. While such a concession may not seem exceptional, on balance it ran against a persistent current of thought—not solely in America—that cared little whether aborigines disappeared from the face of the earth.[24]

Nevertheless, as Robert M. Utley and Washburn wrote in *Indian Wars,* "every big Indian conflict since 1870 had been essentially a war not of concentration but of rebellion—of Indians rebelling against reservations they had already accepted in theory if not in fact."[25]

A week before his inauguration in 1869, President-elect Grant said he planned a fresh and fair Indian policy. The general acclaim for that policy drowned out his statement that he would also have a sharp and severe war policy toward the Indians. The Indians were dissatisfied with reservation life, however, and by 1874 there were hostilities approaching a full-scale war on the southern Plains. The army had been stopping at the boundaries of the reservations, but that year Sheridan was authorized to make war on hostile Indians wherever they were found.[26] The Peace Policy collapsed. Inconsistency of policy characterized government-Indian relations for many years. And it was "at its worst," Alan Axelrod noted, "during the period of the Peace Policy as military and civilian authorities fitfully vied for control."[27]

THE GENERAL Allotment Act, or Dawes Act, of 1887 marked a major change in American policy. By that time most religious denominations had developed some experience dealing with Indians and had some ideas about policy. Their thoughts were the substance of the Dawes Act, which made the following provisions: (1) Each Indian head of family would be given 160 acres of reservation land as his own, 80 acres for each single person over 18, and 80 acres for each orphan under 18; (2) the land would be held in trust by the secretary of the interior for 25 years; (3) any land left over after these "allotments" were made could be sold (if the tribe and the government agreed on a price) to the government for resale to "actual and bona fide settlers"; and (4) every Indian who had been allotted land or who had resided apart from any allotted land was declared to be a citizen of the United States if the Indian "had adopted the habits of civilized life." Some of the land of 11 tribes was exempted.[28] The act had the effect of substantially decreasing the amount of land owned by the Indians. They owned over 136,000,000 acres in 1887 when the act became effective. By 1934, when the allotment policy was finally abandoned, the Indians owned less than 50,000,000 acres, a decrease of more than 63 percent.[29]

There is a telling footnote to the Dawes Act. The Cherokee and the Choctaw would not allow the government to make allotments. Indeed, they filed suit in federal court. Congress then passed the Curtis Act in 1898, which dissolved their tribal governments and all others in Oklahoma.[30]

The Meriam Report of 1928[31] was sharply critical of the Indian policies of the government. The report found that most Indians were poor and many destitute. Their diet, housing, sanitation, and health were appalling. Disease was a problem. Indians were discontented, unhappy, and lacking in hope and initiative.[32] After that report, Congress enacted the Wheeler-Howard Act, the so-called Indian Reorganization Act, in 1934. That act specifically rejected many of the provisions of the Dawes Act and the Curtis Act, which supplemented the Dawes Act. The Indian Reorganization Act did more than simply reverse provisions of the Dawes Act; it reversed Bureau of Indian Affairs regulations designed to force cultural assimilation. The act tried to relate reservation life to the economic life of the nation. It sought to develop Indian democracy and sought to use the tribal councils as training grounds for Indians to start managing their own communities.[33]

In most sessions of Congress after the act was passed, bills to terminate the reservations were introduced. Many thought that the reservations were overcrowded, a kind of concentration camp, and that the Indians should be set free. There were conflicts between the tribes and county governments, between the agency and the states.[34]

A joint resolution of Congress in 1953 declared that Indians should be granted all the privileges of citizenship and their status as wards of the government ended. Several tribes were specifically mentioned. This was called the process of termination. The Indians strongly opposed the resolution,[35] but the government proceeded to terminate its relationship with 2 of the named tribes, the Menominees in Wisconsin and the Klamaths in Oregon, both of whom voted in favor of termination, which meant loss of control of their timber lands. The Menominees reversed the termination in 1973, but the Klamaths never did.[36] Termination acts passed between 1954 and 1962 resulted in the termination of 61 Indian tribes and related organizations.[37] The policy of termination continued to be discredited both by Indians who wanted to remain separate political entities and others who thought the Indians were not yet ready for complete independence.

In a special message to Congress in 1970, President Nixon stated, "This policy of forced termination is wrong."[38] "Self-determination among the Indian people can and must be encouraged without the threat of eventual termination."[39] The 1984 Commission on Reservation Economics report stated flatly that the policy had failed.[40]

President Reagan addressed Indian affairs in 1983 and said, "The only effective way for Indian reservations to develop is through tribal governments which are responsive and accountable to their members." Reagan recognized the lack of constancy in American Indian policy, but he also added, "Throughout our history, despite periods of conflict and shifting national policies in Indian affairs, the government-to-government relationship between the United States and Indian tribes has endured."[41]

THE UNITED States' shifting governmental Indian policies were made even worse by incompetent administration of those policies. An indignant congressman complained, "No branch of the national government is so spotted with fraud, so tainted with corruption, so utterly unworthy of a free and enlightened government, as this Indian Bureau."[42] Under the 1786 act of the Continental Congress, the 2 superintendents of Indian affairs were to license all traders with the Indians and supervise them in their work. Esarey revealed the pitfalls of this system. "It was the hope of Congress to attract good men into this work, but the majority of the early traders were refugee criminals, seeking a field where their criminal propensities might have freer range."[43]

When the settlers flooded the Ohio Valley, they compounded problems of the administration of Indian policy. During the 5 years between 1785 and 1790, 20,000 people immigrated into the Ohio Valley. Most of them were dissidents, dissatisfied with life in the East and with no strong ties to the government. There was talk for a time that the western settlers might form their own nation or join the British or the Spanish. Secretary Knox told Congress that the "whole western territory is liable to be wrested out of the hands of the Union by lawless [white] adventurers or by the savages."[44]

In response to the flood of new settlers, the "wild nations"—the Shawnee, the Miami, and others—killed between 1,500 and 2,000 settlers in the 1780s. The settlers asked for military help from the government, preferably a general Indian war. The government responded that settlers should stay out of Indian country for now. The settlers were unhappy with this restriction.[45]

The Bureau of Indian Affairs, which was created in 1824, had deplorable administrators. According to Alan Axelrod,

> The Bureau of Indian Affairs [the administrator of the reservations] was regarded more as a cache of political favors than as a committed policy-making body. Between 1834 and 1907, no fewer than 21 men served as commissioner of Indian Affairs. Almost to a man, they were political hacks for whom the job was a patronage reward—an opportunity for profits both legal and illegal. Between 1834 and 1890, according to one authoritative estimate, 85 percent of all Congressional appropriations for Indian subsistence, education, and land payments were diverted by the Bureau of Indian Affairs to defray padded administrative costs, overpriced supplies, as well as unvarnished graft and fraud.[46]

One commissioner was ousted from office for giving a bribe. Another resigned after a House committee rebuked him for incompetence.[47] Indian fighter Kit Carson was appointed Indian agent for the Ute in 1853. He was said by Axelrod to have served "with honesty, intelligence, and compassion—qualities very rare in the generally corrupt and inept Indian agency system."[48]

Henry Benjamin Whipple, an Episcopal bishop, argued that corruption and mismanagement of federal Indian policy inevitably led to armed conflict.[49] After the Santee Sioux Uprising in Minnesota in 1862,

Whipple made a report about the causes of the uprising and reforms in the Indian Department necessary to correct them. He complained to President Lincoln that Indian agents were selected "without any reference to their fitness for the place" but largely as a reward for political party work. They appointed their subordinates on the same basis.

> They are often men without any fitness, sometimes a disgrace to a Christian nation; whiskey sellers, barroom loungers, debauchees, selected to guide a heathen people. Then follows all the evils of bad example, of inefficiency, and of dishonesty. The school a sham; the supplies wasted; the improvement fund squandered by negligence, or curtailed by fraudulent contracts. The Indian bewildered, conscious of wrong, but helpless, has no refuge but to sink into depths of brutishness never known to his fathers.[50]

Secretary of War Edwin M. Stanton was incensed by Whipple's blanket indictment and in 1864 asked General Henry Halleck,

> What does Bishop Whipple want? If he has come here to tell us of the corruption of our Indian system, and the dishonesty of Indian agents, tell him that we know it. But the Government never reforms an evil until the people demand it. Tell him that when he reaches the hearts of the American people, the Indians will be saved.[51]

Lincoln took a different view. He was shaken by Whipple's report. "If we get through this war," he said, "and I live, this Indian system shall be reformed."[52] Whipple proposed a complete reform of the Bureau of Indian Affairs, elimination of the appointment of agents through political patronage, and establishment of a cabinet post exclusively for the management of Indian policy. He was a respected voice on Indian issues through many administrations.[53]

In 1867, Grant's Peace Commission came down heavily on the bureau:

> The records are abundant to show that agents have pocketed the funds appropriated by the government and driven the Indians to starvation. It cannot be doubted that Indian wars have originated from this cause.[54]

Two years later, the *Times* charged that "the management of the Indian Bureau has brought about the present [Cheyenne] uprising, and that Bureau clearly is not fit to deal with them in the future."[55] Congressman Lawrence in 1869 joined the chorus of criticism, complaining, "The whole Indian Bureau is rotten and a mere den of thieves."[56] Helen Hunt Jackson wrote in 1885 that "the Indian Bureau represents a system which is a blunder and a crime."[57]

The government representatives who were to administer the Dawes Act, Edward Lazarus said,

> continued for the most part to be political appointees with little or no experience in Indian affairs. A state governor blithely admitted that for party workers fit for nothing else, he found jobs in the Indian service. One inspector found an "abandoned woman" in charge of one Indian school, a lunatic in charge of another.[58]

William T. Hagan added to the list of things gone wrong:

> Contracting to supply an Indian reservation was a lucrative business. Collusion between contractor and agent provided "steel chopping knives made of cast iron; best brogans with paper soles; blankets made of shoddy and glue, which fell to pieces when wet . . . forty dozen elastics . . . when there was not a stocking in the tribe." . . . Honest mistakes were as damaging. Sawmills were erected miles from any timber; bakeries were built which the Indians declined to patronize; agency farms were opened where drought was a chronic condition.[59]

The United States Senate itself made fundamental criticism of our Indian policy in Report No. 91-501, 91st Congress, 1st Session (1972):

> A careful review of the historical literature reveals that the dominant policy of the Federal government toward the American Indian has been one of forced assimilation which has vacillated between the two extremes of coercion and persuasion. At the root of the assimilation policy has been a desire to divest the Indian of his land and resources.

More recently, Fergus M. Bordewich said that President Reagan's Commission on Reservation Economics report in 1984 accused the Bureau of Indian Affairs of "excessive regulation and incompetent management, with the agency consuming more than two-thirds of its budget on itself, and recommends assigning the agency's programs to other federal agencies."[60]

The Bureau of Indian Affairs remains incompetent even today. In 1985, in what was called by Bordewich "one of the most stunningly shortsighted decisions for which it has become famous," the bureau announced that welfare recipients would no longer be permitted to attend school.[61]

Bureau financial affairs are equally bad. In a 1991 report, the Department of the Interior found Bureau of Indian Affairs accounting systems were "totally unreliable." Two specific examples: The Bureau of Indian Affairs Muskogee Area office inventoried 3 chainsaws at a total of $297 million, a television set at $96 million, and 2 typewriters at $114 million. The Albuquerque Area office valued a computer disk drive at $3 million; its actual cost was $495. "The agency could not locate $23 million worth of property in 1991."[62]

In 1993, federal inspectors reported that the Bureau of Indian Affairs' financial system was in such disarray that they could not audit $3.2 billion of $4.4 billion in bureau assets. Until recently, the Bureau of Indian Affairs was 8 years behind in paying its local telephone bills. The $2.1 billion Indian trust fund was never audited until 5 years ago. That fund has not been able to reconcile its accounts for more than 100 years, a fact that Congress has characterized as a national disgrace. Although the Bureau of Indian Affairs budget for 1994 was about $1.8 billion, some bureau officials estimate that less than 20 percent of money received trickled down to the reservations. Accountants at Arthur Andersen & Company have been hired to try to sort out the books, but estimate it could cost $390 million just to reconcile accounts in the $2.1 billion Indian trust fund.[63]

There is current litigation involving bureau financial affairs. The bureau manages 300,000 individual Indian land accounts worth an estimated $500 million.[64] It admits it cannot document $2 billion worth of transactions in tribal accounts over a 20-year period.[65] In February 1999, the judge in a class-action suit filed against the government held 3 government officials in contempt of court for failing to turn over bureau records, holding they "must take blame for years of delays and 'outright false statements.'"[66] He also said, "Justice has not been done to these Indian beneficiaries."[67] The same day, a joint statement from the Treasury and Interior Departments said, "We deeply regret the mistakes that we made in this case."[68]

In May 1999, Secretary of the Interior Bruce Babbitt charged that the bureau's critics were "racially motivated." He added that it was "a deep condescension to the fact that any institution which is primarily managed by Indians is incompetent of managing in the modern world." The bureau's workforce is 90 percent Indian. A Cherokee lawyer replied that "if criticizing the BIA is anti-Indian, then most Indians are anti-Indian."[69]

Minutes before the trial concerning the bureau's alleged failures concerning the land accounts started in June 1999, the government admitted that it "does not adequately control the receipts and disbursements of account holders."[70] Also in June, a court-appointed investigator found inappropriate storage of bureau records, which were kept in 108 different offices. Records were kept in wooden sheds; files were spilled loosely around and were stuffed in unmarked boxes strewn among truck tires. Many had been lost or ruined over the years.[71] Babbitt announced that the government was installing a new $60 million computer system to try to help the situation, but he added that because of the poor condition of some records, "the new computer system will not be totally accurate."[72]

When this current litigation is concluded, we should know more about the bureau and its impact on the Indians.

CHAPTER 11

Where We Are
and Where We May Go

The relations between the settlers and the Indians during the war were understandably hostile in view of the fact that each side was often trying to kill the other. After wars have been over for a period of time, however, there is usually a tendency to let bygones be bygones. One need only recall that after World War II our two major opponents, Germany and Japan, became our friends, and our old Cold War enemy, the former USSR, now has fairly cordial relations with us. This has not been true of settler-Indian relations, even though the war was ended more than a century ago. Some Indians today are frustrated, unhappy, and even bitter toward the descendants of the settlers. What accounts for this?

We know that most of the Indian tribes loved war. They were defeated in this war, and that defeat no doubt led to frustration that less warlike peoples might have more easily tolerated. We also know that after the war was ended, the Indians were victims of settlers who grabbed Indian-occupied lands, of the government's inconsistent Indian policies, and of misconduct on the part of the Bureau of Indian Affairs that continues to the present time. The low state of Indian health and economic status also continues. Unhappiness and bitterness resulted from all these things.

Bitterness and unrealistic expectations also came about from the doctrine of historical revisionism, or false history. Products of the doctrine mislead instead of inform, thereby impairing resolution of disputes. Arthur M. Schlesinger repeated this concept. He said, "Honest history is the weapon of freedom," then added that we can't allow our history to be dictated by pressure groups such as Indian advocates:

> Our schools and colleges have a responsibility to teach history for its own sake—as part of the intellectual equipment of civilized persons—and not to degrade history by allowing its contents to be dictated by pressure groups, whether political, economic, religious, or ethnic. The past may sometimes give offense to one or another minority; that is no reason for rewriting history.[1]

Lincoln said it first and said it better: "History is not history unless it is the truth."[2]

Apparently in an attempt to romanticize Indians and make them and their advocates feel better, in 1970 the Dee Brown book *Bury My Heart at Wounded Knee* was published. Admittedly, it was a history of the American West from the Indian point of view. The *New Statesman* said the book was "a deliberately revisionist history." *The New York Review of Books* noted that Brown's reason for writing the book was his belief that settlers "have for long had the exclusive use of history and that it is now time to present, with sympathy rather than critically, the red side of the story."[3] John M. Coward in *The Newspaper Indian* called *Bury My Heart at Wounded Knee* "polemical literature."[4]

Brown said, "The culture and civilization of the American Indian was destroyed" between 1860 and 1890.[5] Indian culture and civilization are not destroyed as one can see just by looking at the wealth of Indian cultural events available today. Brown also said that one of the most warlike tribes of all, the Iroquois, "strove in vain for peace."[6] Finally, *Bury My Heart at Wounded Knee* praised Little Crow and Cochise as "perhaps the most heroic of all Americans."[7] But among the highlights of Cochise's career was his vow to exterminate all whites in Arizona and his brutal murder of 14 prisoners. Little Crow led the Santee Sioux Uprising, where some 700 settlers were murdered and 100 soldiers killed. These multiple murderers are surely not heroic to present-day Indians. *Bury My Heart at Wounded Knee* is history that often leads us away from the truth so that it is more difficult to solve Indian problems. Terrorists such as Cochise and Little Crow have never been heroes in mainstream American history.

The Earth Shall Weep by James Wilson also relied heavily on revisionist history. Reviewer C. B. Delaney on Amazon.com accurately said that Wilson was "attempting to view the Indian-European encounter through their [Indian] eyes." *Kirkus Reviews,* February 15, 1999, noted, "He [Wilson] relies heavily on the work of revisionist historians." Wilson, an Englishman, seems to have a distorted view of America. He said we are a "racist, immoral society" where (speaking of Indian casinos) the "ultimate accolade of success [is] Mafia involvement."[8] We do have some racist, some immoral, and some Mafia people here, but that does not make America a racist, immoral, or Mafia society.

It has not been demonstrated that rewriting history helps the groups for which it is rewritten. Arthur M. Schlesinger said,

> Even if history is sanitized in order to make people feel good, there is no evidence that feel-good history promotes ethnic self-esteem and equips students to grapple with their lives.[9]

Schlesinger also quoted the Czechoslovakian Vaclav Havel, who pointed out one of the effects of historical revisionism:

> He who fears facing his own past must necessarily fear what lies before him. . . . Lying can never save us from the lie. Falsifiers of history do not safeguard freedom but imperil it.[10]

Those who falsify Indian history with the best of intentions, hoping to improve the Indian condition, will of course harm the Indians, not help them. To paraphrase Schlesinger, historical revisionism clouds the Indians' view (and that of all others as well) of where they have been and where they are going, and this is to their detriment. The rich cultural history of the many tribes is well worth preserving and presenting, but falsification of certain aspects of Indian life is not.

PARADOXICALLY, THE invasion of the settlers benefited the Indians in some important ways. The impact of white culture was most notable among eastern tribes. With their metal tools and weapons, the Indians were able to support themselves more easily, leaving more time for religion, war, and recreation. Old crafts declined. Some crafts reached new levels of excellence.[11] The acquisition of rifles allowed some tribes to drive out traditional enemies, which has been described as a "prodigious shifting of tribes." William T. Hagan has observed that

> the Iroquois in the East, the Apaches in the Southwest, and the Crees in the Hudson's Bay area were among those Indians who acquired metal

weapons and used them with devastating effect on their neighbors, driving them from choice hunting grounds, seizing their property, enslaving and killing them.[12]

White culture influenced western tribes as well. "Degeneration did not automatically follow tribal associations with the whites," observed Hagan. "The acquisition of metal tools and utensils, firearms, horses, and sheep simplified life for the Indian."[13] The horse made the greatest impression. It "facilitated a genuine revolution" and "produced a new culture" for the Plains Indians. With the horse, the Indians became mobile and could follow the buffalo herds. As a result, "an entirely new pattern of life developed, complete with a new religious orientation, new dances, and new games."[14] The horse was so important to the Navajo that they claimed there was never a time the 2 did not exist together. "If there were no horses, there were no Navajos."[15]

The horse and the gun allowed the Sioux to achieve a "rich and satisfying life."[16] Indeed, "some Indian groups, such as the Plains warriors, achieved their greatest power and fame as a direct result of such trade [with the settlers]."[17] The Creeks grew prosperous in dealing with colonial traders.[18] In addition to horses and guns, some tribes (the southern tribes and the Iroquois) began acquiring domestic animals and planting European fruit trees.[19]

In the long run, the Indian was changed dramatically by the settlers. Fergus M. Bordewich concluded that

> in the course of the past five centuries, Indian life has been utterly transformed by the impact of European horses and firearms, by imported diseases and modern medicine, by missionary zeal and Christian morality, by iron cookware, sheepherding, pickup trucks, rodeos and schools, by rum and welfare offices, and by elections, alphabets, and Jeffersonian ideals as well as by MTV, *Dallas,* and *The Simpsons* and by the rich mingling of native bloodlines with those of Europe, Africa, and the Hispanic Southwest.[20]

The invasion of the settlers greatly accelerated Indian material progress. The change was perhaps too rapid for the Indians, but it was arguably a change for the better. The Indian today is able to live more effectively in the modern world in many ways because of the impact of the settler invasion.

In addition to these benefits, starting nearly with the beginning of the United States, Bernard W. Sheehan noted, the Indians have "accepted incontinently a rich assortment of the products of civilized technology.

The list seems endless."[21] Federal money for Indian programs designed to alleviate their problems annually totalled $120 million by 1960 and was estimated to exceed $2 billion each year by the late 1970s.[22] That sum increased dramatically to about $3 billion each year by the 1990s.[23]

Whether or not these payments are well spent has been questioned by columnist Mona Charen:

> For years, but particularly since the 1960s and '70s when the Indian cause became chic, the U.S. government has lavished freebies on Indian reservations. Hendrik Mills, writing in the November/December *American Enterprise* magazine, described the cornucopia available to reservation Indians: free health care with no co-payments, extra education funds, tribal colleges complete with full scholarships and living expenses, exemptions from many local and state taxes, Head Start, loads of free food, and—of course—welfare.
>
> Mills, who was drawn to the reservation initially by leftist idealism, was appalled to see the unopened packages of food—most with Department of Agriculture stamps—rotting in local dumps.
>
> He was shocked that many Indian parents effectively have made their children orphans by failing to provide the most basic care. And he was disillusioned to discover that many Indians wait for the government check to come each month and then blow it all at the casino.[24]

Seminole chairman Buffalo Tiger has said that his people live in dependence on the United States government and are in effect living in a welfare state. He hopes, however, in the future to be able to refuse government grants so that his people can "return once again to independence," according to Peter Matthiessen.[25] The chairman clearly recognized that accepting federal money prevents independence.

The Indians have more than adequate room for economic activity. Their reservations in the lower 48 states total about 52,000,000 acres, an area about the size of Minnesota. The Indians in Alaska own an additional 44,000,000 acres there. Although they constitute less than 1 percent of the U.S. population, Indians own nearly 5 percent of the United States.[26]

ARE THE Indians dying out? The answer to this question is yes and no. There are fewer full-blooded Indians all the time, and in that sense the answer is yes. There are more people with some Indian blood all the time, and, to that extent, the answer is no. In 1970, more than 33 percent of all Indians were married to non-Indians, compared to just 1 percent of all Americans who married outside their race. By 1980, the number had grown to 50 percent, and it continues to climb. A 1986 congressional study estimated the percentage of Indians with one half or more Indian blood would decline from about 87 percent in 1980 to only 8 percent by 2080.[27] This mingling of Indian bloodlines obviously has important consequences for Indians and Indian culture.

"It is estimated that one-third to one-half of the Indians now live in cities."[28] James Wilson has said that figure is now 60 percent.[29] Indians moving to the cities have reduced the Indian population on reservations. The 1990 Census indicates 437,358, or only 22.32 percent, of the Indians live on the reservations.[30] More recent government statistics, however, according to a July 1999 AP press release, indicate that "there are 1.43 million Indians living on or near reservations."[31] If this is true, the figure for Indians living in cities is much smaller than the estimates stated above.

The Bureau of the Census has published statistics showing Indian education, employment, family income, and poverty figures for 1979 compared with those of the total population. Four years of high school were completed by 56 percent[32] of the Indians and by 67 percent of the total population (which, of course, includes Indians). Four years of college or more were completed by 8 percent of the Indians and by 16 percent of the total population. Participation in the labor force was 59 percent[33] by Indians and 62 percent by the total population. Median family income was $13,680 for Indians and $19,920 for the total population. Families in poverty (a family of 4 making less than $7,412) were 28 percent for Indians and 12 percent for the total population.[34]

The Department of Health and Human Services, Indian Health Service, has published figures comparing Indian health with that of the entire population. They are dismal. Indian mortality from several causes is compared with mortality figures for all races for 1987. Indian deaths are 780 percent greater for tuberculosis, 667 percent greater for alcoholism, 295 percent greater for accidents, 268 percent greater for diabetes mellitus, 134 percent greater for homicide, 95 percent greater for suicide, 77 percent greater for gastrointestinal diseases, 9 percent greater for cerebrovascular diseases, 1 percent greater for diseases of the heart, and 12 percent less for malignant neoplasms.

WE KNOW where the Indians have been. Where are they going? There is disagreement. Wilcomb E. Washburn said that "it is conceivable that the Indian will be able to retain his special status within the American nation and convert its former deficiencies into future advantages."[35] Indian arts and crafts are enjoying a renaissance. Tribes are being restored. Indians have new pride.[36] It is said that since 1917, the Indians "have shown gradual improvement in education, health, and economic well-being."[37] Indian leadership is coming of age. The Indian problem is not as complex as it was 200 years ago.[38] Some others say that the future of the Indian is not bright because most Indians are wholly dependent wards of the government.

Three tribes illustrate different directions the Indian could take. The first is the path of the Oglala Sioux on the Pine Ridge Reservation in South Dakota. The reservation has a population of 20,000. It is in Shannon County, the poorest county in the United States. Unemployment is at least 50 percent; some say it is even higher.[39] Jobs tend to be held with the tribal or federal government. Housing is scarce and poor. Many houses have no indoor toilets. There is no bank, no pharmacy, and a small taco stand is the closest thing to a restaurant. Tourist development is hampered by tribal infighting. The traditionalists oppose a gaming house on the ground that a casino with a liquor license is the last thing the town needs, but one was recently established there. Tribal council chairman John Yellow Bird Steele no longer thinks economic development can be handed to the tribes by the federal government or by firms bribed into the reservation by grants and loans. He insists that "Indians have to do things for themselves." A growing number of Indians and economists agree. Former Cherokee chief Wilma Mankiller spoke to tribal leaders in 1992, saying, "We have gotten too used to the BIA doing everything for us. . . . Getting away from the BIA is a major step for Indians. Self-government is an act of faith in ourselves."[40] *The Economist* has said that "traditionally, the Oglala Sioux have been thought of as a 'difficult' tribe."[41] Surely few Indians would take their path by choice.

Contrast the Oglala Sioux with the Choctaw tribe of Mississippi. Over the last few decades, the tribe has transformed itself from a welfare culture into one of the largest employers in the state. Its factories assemble wire harnesses, telephones, and audio speakers for blue-chip corporations. A greeting-card plant hand-finishes 83 million cards every year. Only 15 years ago, unemployment was 80 percent, but now the tribe is fully employed and half of the tribe's employees are white and black, not Indian. The tribe has its own television station, casino, golf course, conference center, and a 314-room hotel. By 1995, tribal sales were more than $100 million annually. The average income for a family of 4 is now about $22,000. The new Choctaw Health Center is among the state's best hospitals. Teachers' salaries in elementary schools are 25 percent higher than neighboring non-Indian schools.

These achievements were brought about primarily by the managerial skills of Phillip Martin, a high school graduate, Air Force veteran, and chief of the tribe. Almost everything once carried out by the Bureau of Indian Affairs for the Choctaw is now done by the tribal government, including law enforcement, schooling, health care, social services, forestry, credit, and finance.[42]

Further contrast the Oglala Sioux with the Wascos, the Warm Springs, and the Paiute tribes of Oregon, whose 2,300 members constitute the Confederated Tribes of Warm Springs Indians. Their reservation consists of 355,000 acres of Douglas fir and ponderosa pine. They were removed from the Columbia River in 1855. A settlement for loss of their fishing rights was made with the government in 1958 for $4,000,000. Instead of dividing it up, they paid Oregon State University $100,000 to make an economic feasibility study of their reservation. They purchased a sawmill and a plywood plant and built a luxury lodge with golf course, tennis courts, sauna baths, trout fishing, horseback riding, and an Olympic-size swimming pool fed by hot springs. There is a new trout and salmon hatchery. Wild horses are raised; the most unruly are rented to rodeos. The building of a $30,000,000 hydroelectric plant is being considered. The gross income of the confederation is nearly $50,000,000 annually. Profits provide a monthly dividend of $75 for every Indian (including children) and a Christmas bonus of $1,200 each. The confederation employs more than 1,000 people, with a combined payroll of $12,000,000 each year. Tribal pensions begin at age 60. Tribal funds are available for medical and psychiatric care, alcohol and drug therapy, and educational and vocational training. Low-interest loans help pay for modern houses and mobile homes. Members of the confederation are financially better off than many of the whites around them. Reservation college graduates fill important positions. Nevertheless, there is a great need for doctors, psychiatrists, and especially teachers.

There are problems at Warm Springs. Alcoholism is prevalent. The young generation is turned off, and some of them turned on to drugs. The school dropout rate is high—fewer than half graduate from high school. There is a foster-care program for children with severe family problems and a center for troubled teenagers. Both are staffed by Indians.

James Cornett, the Bureau of Indian Affairs superintendent on the reservation, comments that "this is the most viable Indian society in the country." What is the key to the confederation's success? General manager Kenneth L. Smith says his grandparents inspired him to get an education because "we're in the white man's world . . . and you're gonna have to learn to play the ball game."[43] Substantially all the confederation's customers for the sale of its forest products, hotel services, and fish hatchery products are white.

General manager Smith and the confederation did assimilate to some extent to the great benefit of the tribes without destroying their Indian way of life and without impairing their culture.[44] The confederation has followed the advice of tribal council chairman John Yellow Bird Steele of the impoverished Oglala Sioux, who realizes now that "Indians have to do things for themselves."

WILL INDIANS follow the path of the Oglala Sioux, the path of the Warm Springs and the Choctaw Indians, or some other path? The answer to that question does not lie in the hands of the federal government and its Bureau of Indian Affairs, in the hands of whites, or in the hands of Indian advocates. The answer lies almost exclusively in the hands of the Indians themselves. Some of those who decide to do things for themselves and who accept the fact that they can accommodate to the white man's world without losing their culture as many other cultures have done may be able to achieve the Warm Springs and Choctaw results and live a dignified and productive life.

There are elements of classic Greek tragedy at work in the relationship between whites and Indians. The federal government over the years alternately has tried to harm and to help, but on balance has treated the once proud tribes in such a way that many of them are now characterized by their own leaders as welfare-state wards.

No doubt the best of times in this country are yet to come. The descendants of the settlers, the descendants of the Indians, and all other Americans would be wise to join in that future just as Thomas Jefferson invited Indians in 1808 to join with the settlers and "spread with us over this great island."[45] Jefferson's invitation is appropriate today. No atrocities have been committed by present-day whites against present-day Indians or vice versa. No one at the Santee Sioux Uprising, the Sand Creek Massacre, or the Wounded Knee Massacre is alive today. The time has come to go forward together, unhindered by the mutual atrocities growing out of the war.

Intertribal Indian Wars

Events indicated by an * are those where members of one tribe fought another as scouts for an army.

Intertribal Wars Before the 1600s

1400s: Some Indian villages in America were found to be palisaded or fenced, a sign of "intensifying conflict."[1]

Before 1492: There were "fierce intertribal conflicts" for several reasons, including fights over women, material possessions, hunting rights, plunder, adventure, revenge, and sometimes territory.[2]

1519: When Spanish explorer Hernán Cortés marched on the Aztec capital near Mexico City, he found "ever-warring" city-states in the empire.[3]

1531: Conquistador Francisco Pizarro invaded Peru and found a civil war among the Incas.[4]

1534: Jacques Cartier sailed up the St. Lawrence River. The Algonquin tribes told him their Iroquois enemies had been driven from that region several generations earlier.[5]

The Iroquois invaded Algonquin territory before the settlers came. Many Algonquin lives were lost. That fighting continued after the settlers arrived.[6]

Around 1560–70: The first explorers of the American coast and settlers as well found many Algonquin fighting one another and the Iroquois.[7]

1584–90: The Powhatans fought the Chesapeakes.[8]

1500s: The Sioux were driven out of Minnesota and Wisconsin by the Chippewa.[9]
  The Sioux went west and took land from the Kiowa, Crows, Pawnee, and other tribes.[10]

Intertribal Wars in the 1600s

Early 1600s: The Pequots attacked and conquered the Montauks.[11]

Early 1600s: The Apache fought the Pimas.[12]

1607: The Shawnee and the Iroquois fought before the settlers arrived. John Smith reported that they were engaged in a "fierce war" at that time.[13]

1608–09: French explorer Samuel de Champlain found the Hurons and some Algonquin-speaking tribes fighting the Iroquois.[14]

Before 1621: There were about 40 tribes in the Chesapeake Bay area. Powhatan, the predecessor of Opechancanough, was chief of several dozen of these tribes. Years before the settlers arrived, he had been "consolidating his hold on the lesser tribes of the area while warding off the inland tribes of the Piedmont."[15]

1621: The Wampanoags and the Narragansets fought. They made a treaty with the Pilgrims for trade and mutual assistance. Miles Standish and other Pilgrims aided the Wampanoags against the Narragansets.[16]
  Fighting among Indians continued after the settlers arrived up to the outbreak of the Revolutionary War. It first occurred in the war between the Powhatans and the settlers, which began with the incident involving Morgan's hat in 1622.[17]

1624: The Mohawk fought the Mahican and Ottawas.[18]

1626: Four Dutch traders joined the Mahican in a raid on the Mohawk. All 4 were killed.[19]
  The Mohawk raided the Mohegans, Pequots, Narragansets, Wampanoags, Massachusetts, and Pennacooks to such an extent that, out of fear, some of them paid yearly tribute.[20]

1629: The Massachusetts and Pawtucket Indians agreed to exchange land with the Pilgrims for protection against their enemies, the Micmac.[21]
  The Navajo had raided and harassed the Hopi "from earliest times."[22] There was a land dispute between the 2 as late as 1960.[23]

Shortly after 1630: The Five Nations commenced fierce attacks against the Hurons. The attacks went on for 45 years.[24]
  At the same time, the Iroquois defeated the Algonquin allies of the Hurons to such an extent that they too paid yearly tribute.[25]

1636: Massachusetts Bay militia with Mohegan allies killed some Pequot Indians.[26]

1637: Mohegan and Narraganset Indians destroyed a Pequot town.[27]

1638: The Five Nations fought the so-called Iroquoian Beaver Wars against the Hurons, Tobaccos, Neutrals, Eries, Ottawas, Mahicans, Illinois, Miamis, Susquehannocks, Nipissings, Potawatomis, Delaware, and Sokokis.[28]

1639: The Hurons captured and burned 113 Iroquois.[29]

1643: The Mohegans fought the Narragansets.[30]

1647: Non-Christian Indians fought the Christian Apalachee.[31]

1649: A party of 1,000 Mohawk and Seneca attacked a large Huron village.[32]

1649–79: The Iroquois fought the Hurons and their allies in wars of annihilation.[33]

Before 1650: The Sioux fought the Chippewa for more than 200 years. That war ended about 1850.[34]

Around 1650: The Sioux fought the Hurons. Thousands were killed in that war. The Hurons were eliminated as an independent tribe.[35]

    The Shawnee became involved in a series of fights with the Iroquois.[36]

1660: The Five Nations made attacks in the west against the Tobaccos, the Neutrals, and the Eries. All 3 tribes were practically wiped out. The Five Nations then fought the Ottawas.[37]

1660: The Oneidas and the Piscataways fought.[38]

Around 1661: The Susquehannocks had an intense war with the Seneca, Onondaga, and Cayuga.[39]

1662: The Mahicans and Ottawas fought the Mohawk.[40]

Around 1670: The Iroquois of New York invaded the western country, what is now Indiana and Illinois.[41]

1671: In an attempt to curry favor, when the Englishman Nathaniel Bacon said he was going to fight the Susquehannocks, the Occaneechis offered to do the fighting for him. They captured some Susquehannock prisoners and furs; they gave the prisoners to Bacon, but kept the furs. Bacon's men attacked the Occaneechis, then retreated.[42]

1671: The Illinois fought the Winnebagos. The Winnebagos were badly beaten. The tribe was reduced from 4,000 to a single village.[43]

Before 1674: The Westos raided Guale, Cusabo, Cherokee, and Creek communities, taking slaves.[44]

*1675: Wampanoag chief Metacom was called King Philip by the settlers. Three of his tribe were hanged for murdering a Christian Indian. Settlers were killed in raids. The Nipmuc and Narraganset tribes and other warriors joined King Philip. The settlers used Mohegans, Pequots, Niantics, Sakonnets, and Massachusett Indians to assist them as warriors, spies, and scouts. The settlers employed friendly Indians in this war to fight hostile tribes.[45] Benjamin Church, commander of the settler troops, even recruited into his army some Indians he had captured.[46]

    Connecticut offered a bounty to the Narragansets for Wampanoag scalps or prisoners, and when the Narragansets attacked a Wampanoag village, 207 militia, perhaps 500 Indian warriors, and as many women and children were burned to death.[47]

1675–80: Susquehannocks and Iroquois raided against the Piscataways and Mattawoman.[48]

    By the close of the seventeenth century all of the tribes of the north-central woodlands were facing destruction, mainly because they could not forget their petty feuds and present a united front to oppose the intrusion of Europeans into their lands.[49]

1670s: The Cree and their allies forced the Sioux from the Mississippi headwaters into southern Minnesota.[50]

    The Iroquois destroyed the last of the Erie Indians.[51]

    The Iroquois fought the Susquehannocks.[52]

1676: The Piscataway and the Mattawoman fought the Susquehannocks.[53]

1680: The Sioux fought the Cheyenne and the Kiowa.[54]

1680: The Carolina planters contracted with a wandering group of Shawnee to fight the Westos. At the end of 3 years, there were fewer than 50 Westos left. The rest had been killed by the Shawnee or sold into slavery.[55]

1680s: The Winnebagos were crushed by disease and by a war they started with the Illinois.[56] The Iroquois attacked the Illinois, the Potawatomis, and the Miami.[57] They also fought the Algonquin, Ottawas, Delaware, Mahicans, and Wappingers.[58]

1680–84: The Five Nations fought the Illinois and the Miami.[59]

1680s: The Iroquois attacked the Miami and the Illinois.[60] They were defeated, ending the westward expansion of the Iroquois.[61]

The Ottawas and Hurons fought the Iroquois.[62]

At the height of their power, the Five Nations compelled Algonquin in Indiana and Michigan to pay tribute.[63]

Late 1600s: The Kickapoos suffered several massacres at the hands of their neighbors the Sioux and the Iroquois. In response they fled to the area around Green Bay, Wisconsin, and formed a confederacy with the Fox and the Mascouten.[64]

The Powhatans fought the Iroquois.[65]

1683: The Five Nations lost several hundred warriors in a battle with the Ojibway and Fox.[66]

Before 1690: The Iroquois drove the Shawnee from the Ohio River Valley.[67]

Around 1690: The Chickasaw allied themselves with Charleston, South Carolina, slave traders. The Chickasaw raided the Choctaw, killing more than 1,800 and taking about 500 slaves. The Chickasaw lost about 800 warriors in these raids. The 2 were still fighting as late as 1702.[68]

Late 1600s–early 1700s: The Creeks fought Indians who had been missionized by the Spanish, especially the Apalachee and the Timucuas.[69]

Before 1700: The Sioux fought their hereditary enemies, the Chippewa, beginning perhaps as early as this date. Time and time again over the course of many years, the Sioux were defeated.[70]

Intertribal Wars in the 1700s

Around 1700: The Comanche moved from territory between the Yellowstone and Platte rivers to the South Plains. They fought with the Apache and drove them away. The Comanche made raids along their borders against both Indians and settlers for the next 150 years.[71]

Around 1700: The Comanche supported by the French made "unrelenting war" on the Apache and Navajo.[72]

The Pawnee killed hundreds of Navajo.[73]

The Arapaho fought the Ute.[74]

The Sioux were driving the Crows to the west.[75]

1700: The French got help from the Choctaw, who overpowered the Natchez Indians, almost wiping them out.[76]

The Choctaw, at the request of the French, attacked the Chickasaw.[77] When that fight was ended, the Choctaw vowed they would continue to make war on the Chickasaw. They said they would "never cease to strike at that perfidious race as long as there should be any portion of it remaining."[78]

Early 1700s: Neighboring tribes repeatedly raided the Tuscarora in North Carolina. Their children were stolen and sold as slaves.[79]

The Tuscarora attacked English and German settlers, killing about 130 of them. South Carolina Indian trader John Barnwell led an army of 50 English and Indians from several tribes, especially Yamasees. His army entered Tuscarora territory, destroying houses and taking slaves.[80]

1701–04: The Creeks fought the Cherokee, Choctaw, Chickasaw, Guale, Apalachee, Westos, and Savannah.[81]

1702: The Creeks fought with the Timucuas.[82]

1704–10: Carolina Indian trader Thomas Moore led about 1,000 Creeks and 50 English against the Timucuas, Guale, and Apalachee. Somewhere between 10,000 and 12,000 Indians were captured and sold into slavery.[83] The Apalachee were practically destroyed.[84]

1710–75: The Comanche were at war almost all the time with the Apache, the Mescalero, and the Faraon.[85]

1711: The Cherokee fought the Tuscarora.[86]

1711: The Fox fought the Hurons, Ottawas, and Potawatomis. After the Fox surrendered, about 1,000 of them were killed.[87]

1711: After the Tuscarora killed 137 Carolinians, the settlers got the Catawbas and the Cherokee to help them fight the Tuscarora.[88]

1716: Cherokee fought Yamasees and Lower Creeks. Casualties were heavy on both sides.[89]

1720: The Fox fought the Miami and the Illinois.[90]

1723: The Fox fought the Ojibway.[91]

1724: The Seneca and the Cherokee fought. The Creeks offered to mediate. The Seneca said they could not afford to make peace because "we have no people to war against nor yet no meal to eat but the Cherokees."[92]

Around 1725: The Cree and Blackfeet were at war with the Shoshoni.[93]

1729: Tunica helped the French suppress the Natchez.[94]

Around 1729: The Kickapoos assisted the French against their former ally, the Fox, and fought them and the Chickasaw.[95]

Late 1720s: The French enlisted the Winnebagos, the Ottawas, the Chippewa, and the Menominees to try to exterminate the Fox. They almost succeeded in 1730.[96]

Before 1730: The Cherokee fought the Chickasaw and the Shawnee.[97]

1731: The French with Choctaw allies stormed Natchez strongholds. One thousand were killed, 400 sold as slaves, and many burned at the stake. By the end of the year, the Natchez tribe, which once had more than 5,000 people, had ceased to exist. The survivors obtained refuge with other tribes.[98]

1732: The Iroquois pressured a band of Delaware to give up their land near Philadelphia and move to where they lived under a minor Iroquois chief.[99]

Around 1734: The Chippewa fought the Fox and Sioux.[100]

Around 1740: The Comanche invaded Apache territory.[101]

1742: The Cherokee fought the Six Nations.[102]

1749: The Ottawas fought the Mississaugas.[103]

1750: The Shawnee fought the Chickasaw.[104]

Around 1750: The Apache invaded the Pimas, the Zuñi, and the Laguna.[105]

The Chippewa fought the Sioux. The Chippewa took over Sioux territory as far as the prairie.[106]

Last half of the 1700s: The Sioux and the Cheyenne expelled the Kiowa from the Black Hills.[107]

The Sioux and the Cheyenne drove the Pawnee south of the Platte River in Nebraska and the Crows from eastern Montana westward.[108]

1755: The Iroquois simply ordered the Delaware to leave eastern Pennsylvania. This forced the Shawnee to move to Ohio.[109]

1760s: The settlers obtained Indian help in suppressing the Cherokee. This war lasted 2 years.[110]

After 1763: Kickapoo territory was invaded by the Sioux from the west and by the Iroquois from the east. They then turned to warfare as a major pursuit and supported Ottawa leader Pontiac.[111]

1765: Pontiac helped the British (England, Scotland, and Wales had joined to form Great Britain in 1707) subdue Illinois tribes who were being incited by Frenchmen.[112] Warriors in one of the Peoria villages decided to kill Pontiac. One of their braves did so in 1769.[113]

Around 1770: The Sioux and Cheyenne drove the Kiowa out of the Black Hills.[114]

1770s: The Arikara, or Rees, who had been weakened by 3 successive smallpox epidemics, were driven from their territory by the Sioux.[115]

1775: Some Kickapoos had been forced out of Wisconsin into Illinois and even farther west by tribes moving into the Great Lakes area. This occurred as early as around 1775. The Kickapoos were defeated in 1811 and 1812 by these tribes.[116]

*After the Kickapoos were displaced by other tribes, they, the Delaware, the Shawnee, and other displaced tribes became mercenary soldiers for the Spanish and protected their settlements from the Chickasaw and later the Osages.[117]

Around 1776: There was an Iroquois civil war. Mohawk attacked Oneida, and Oneida attacked Mohawk. Iroquois fought Iroquois at the Battle of Bennington and the Battle of Saratoga, both of which were won by the American army. Mohawk leader Joseph Brant's warriors attacked one another.[118]

1777: The Comanche and Apache fought. The Spanish governor of New Mexico, Juan Bautista de Anza, who had encouraged the war, gave the Comanche cards to help them keep score.[119]

During the Revolutionary War, at the Battle of Oriskany, the army of American general Nicholas Herkimer with 60 Indians, mostly Oneida, was ambushed and mauled by the army of British leader Sir John Johnson with Mohawk chief Joseph Brant and a group of Seneca warriors. Five Seneca chiefs were killed.[120]

1778–79: The Iroquois continued their 70-year war against the Hurons.[121] Washington wrote to the commissioners of Indian affairs in 1778. He commented on a congressional resolution giving him authority to hire 400 Indians if they could be "procured upon proper terms." He stated that "divesting them of the Savage customs exercised in their Wars against each other, I think they may be made of excellent use."[122]

1779: General John Sullivan enlisted the aid of the Oneida against the Mohawk, Seneca, and Cayuga. The latter with British regulars and Tories destroyed Oneida settlements.[123]

1780: The Fox and Sioux were defeated by the Chippewa.[124]

Before 1790: The Kiowa and the Comanche had fought for many years, but then made peace and fought the Cheyenne and the Osages for 50 more years.[125]

1793: During Little Turtle's War between the Shawnee and other tribes and the new American army, a group of Ottawas and other Indians robbed and raped Shawnee women farmers in several villages.[126]

*1794: At the Battle of Fallen Timbers, the army of American general Anthony Wayne included a few Chickasaw and Choctaw scouts. It attacked the army of Miami chief Little Turtle, which had numbered 2,000 Shawnee, Miami, Creeks, Cherokee, and others before Indian defections occurred. At the time of the battle, no more than 1,300 were left. Little Turtle was defeated.[127]

1795: The Creeks invaded Chickasaw territory.[128]

1798: The Missouri tribe fought the Sac and the Fox. The Missouri were almost destroyed.[129]

End of the 1700s: The Kickapoos nearly exterminated the Illinois and other tribes in their area and then established villages in the conquered territory.[130]

Intertribal Wars in the 1800s

Early 1800s: The Missouri fought with the Osages. This time the Missouri were destroyed. Survivors went to live with the Otoe and the Iowa tribes.[131]

Early 1800s: The Puncahs were at war with the Sioux, the Pawnee, the Osages, and the Konzas.[132]

The Cheyenne fought the Mandan.[133]

Kiowa, Crows, and Pawnee were attacked by the Sioux.[134]

1800: The Sioux held the west bank of the Mississippi against Iroquois aggression as late as this date.[135]

1800: The Hidatsa attacked the Shoshoni.[136]

Around 1800: The Sioux became more warlike and made war on the Crows, the Pawnee, "and every other western tribe they met."[137]

The Winnebagos fought the Chippewa, Fox, Sac, and others.[138]

The Comanche were fighting the Apache.[139]

The Cheyenne carried on "almost unceasing war" with the Pawnee and Blackfeet.[140]

Most of the 1800s: The Comanche fought the Pawnee and the Osages.[141]

1803 or before: The Kaskaskia Indians in Illinois were mentioned in Jefferson's message to Congress. He said they were friendly and had never had a difference with the government, but they had been "reduced by the wars" to a few individuals and were "unable to defend themselves against the neighboring tribes."[142]

1804: The Hidatsa fought the Blackfeet.[143]

The Tetons fought the Omaha.[144]

The Sioux and Arikara attacked the Mandan.[145]

Early 1800s: The Winnebagos fought the Chippewa.[146]

Before 1806: The Flatheads fought the Blackfeet.[147]

*1811: General William Henry Harrison with an army of 1,000 men and some Delaware and Miami scouts was in battle with the Shawnee near the Tippecanoe River in Indiana. About 50 were killed on each side.[148]

1812: William Wells, an Indian agent in Indiana, left Chicago (Fort Dearborn) with 30 Miami. The Potawatomis attacked the party, killing Wells and many others.[149]

*1813: The Creeks had a civil war. The Lower Creeks, or White Sticks, wanted to cooperate with the settlers, but the Upper Creeks, or Red Sticks, wanted to drive them out.[150] After Red Stick attacks upon settlers, an army was authorized by the Tennessee legislature. Led by General Jackson and strengthened by White Sticks, Choctaw, and Cherokee, it made 3 attacks on the Red Stick towns. The Red Stick people were nearly wiped out.[151] Jackson learned that some friendly Indians were besieged by the main force of Creeks. He went to their relief. The Creeks lost 290 dead.[152]

*1813–14: The Chickasaw and the Americans fought the Creek Red Sticks.[153]

1814: The Sioux drove the Kiowa out of the Black Hills and drove the Crow from the Powder River country a few years later. The Pawnee also were attacked by the Sioux.[154]

*1814: General Jackson and his army defeated the Creeks. He required them to sign a treaty ceding nearly all their land in Alabama and some in Georgia. He then recruited about 1,000 Creek and Choctaw warriors for his campaign against the Florida tribes. William T. Hagan said that "the Indian capacity for self-destruction seemed limitless."[155]

Around 1820: The Delaware fought the Osages.[156]

The Sioux conquered the Arikara, the Mandan, and other tribes.[157]

1821: Crows stole horses from the Cheyenne, Arapaho, Comanche, and Kiowa and used them to fight.[158]

Around 1825–50: The Cheyenne fought the Ute, the Delaware, and other tribes.[159]

1829: The Sac and the Fox under Chief Black Hawk had been defeated by an army under General Winfield Scott. The Indians unsuccessfully tried to retreat by several routes. Finally they decided to try to cross the Mississippi into Sioux country. Soldiers and a gunboat killed many of them. Two hundred warriors who reached the west bank were killed or captured by the Sioux.[160]

1820s–30s: The Kiowa launched raids on the Caddos, Navajo, Ute, Apache (except the Kiowa-Apache band), Arapaho, Cheyenne, and Osages. Peace accords were reached in the 1830s.[161]

1830s: The Shoshoni with the Bannocks fought the Blackfeet and the Crows.[162]

1831: The Nez Perce and the Blackfeet fought.[163]

Ironically, the arrival of traders into an area sometimes brought about fighting among tribes. They would move to be nearer the traders, thus bringing them into conflict with the tribes already there.[164]

1832: Sioux fought the Sac and the Fox at the end of the Black Hawk War.[165]

1833: Several removed tribes were attacked by other tribes. The Pawnee removed and were attacked by Sioux, Cheyenne, and Arapaho.[166] The Sioux attacked the removed Otoes, Missouri, and Omaha.[167] The removed Potawatomis, Ottawas, Chippewa, Winnebagos, Delaware, and Sac and Fox were attacked by other Indians.[168]

1837: The army hired Shawnee, Delaware, Kickapoos, Sac and Fox, and Choctaw to fight against the Seminoles.[169]

1838: The Kiowa, Comanche, and Apache fought the Cheyenne and Arapaho at the Battle of Wolf Creek.[170]

1839: The Apache attacked a large Comanche village at Spring Creek in Texas. They killed a number of people in the village, including 5 settlers who had been captured by the Comanche.[171]

Before 1840: The Arapaho made war with the Shoshoni, Crows, and Sioux.[172]

Around 1840: The Kickapoos accepted the invitation of the Creeks to settle with them to provide protection from "the wild tribes."[173]

1840s: The Kiowa, Comanche, Cheyenne, and Wichitas made war on the Cherokee, Chickasaw, Choctaw, Creeks, and Seminoles. The latter were known as the Five Civilized Nations.[174]

1847: The Pawnee were attacked by the Sioux, who killed 23. Other Sioux warriors raided the same year. As a result, the Pawnee moved.[175]

1848: Because the buffalo were being exterminated, tribes encroached on one another for food. Catholic priest P. J. De Smet wrote that the Plains Indians' subsistence needs forced them into small bands who, "like hungry wolves," poached on their neighbors:

> The Sioux must necessarily encroach on the lands of the Arickaras, Crows, Assiniboins, Cheyennes and Pawnees—the Crows and Assiniboins on the Blackfeet and vice versa, and thus endless struggles, and murderous and cruel wars daily perpetrated and multiplied.[176]

1848: The Cheyenne and Arapaho fought their old enemies the Ute.[177]

Before 1850: The Shoshoni fought the Blackfeet and Crows, sometimes in alliance with the Bannocks.[178]

1800s: The Cheyenne were driven from their eastern homes by the Cree and the Sioux.[179]

1850s: The Shoshoni fought the Blackfeet, the Cheyenne, and the Sioux.[180]

1850s: A Fox war party attacked a Menominee camp because the Menominees had killed several Fox chiefs.[181]

    *In the First Seminole War, Jackson's army, joined by a large number of Creeks, attacked the Seminoles.[182]

By 1850: The Sioux themselves had been driven westward by the Cree.[183]

1851: During the meetings at Fort Laramie, Sioux chief Black Hawk acknowledged the fights between the Sioux on the one hand and the Kiowa and the Crows on the other. He said, "These lands once belonged to the Kiowas and the Crows, but we whipped these nations out of them, and in this we did what the white men do when they want the lands of the Indians."[184]

    The Cheyenne and Arapaho again fought the Ute.[185]

1855: Comanche fought a group of their old enemies, the Apache.[186]

1857: The Sioux fought the Pawnee.[187]

1857: The Assiniboine and Cree fought the Blackfeet and Sioux.[188]

1857: Mdewakanton Sioux chief Little Crow led his warriors in battle against another division of Sioux, the Wahpekute.[189]

1857: The Pimas had fought the Apache for generations.[190]

1850s: The Maricopas and the Yumas fought the Mojaves and the Yumas.[191] The Pimas and the Maricopas fought the Apache and the Yumas.[192]

1860–64: During the Civil War, the Choctaw and the Chickasaw sided with the Confederacy. Their buildings were burned and their livestock taken by Kansas settlers "and their willing Indian helpers."[193]

1862: The Shawnee, Delaware, and Kickapoos, at the request of Union officers, invaded the Wichita agency, which was being protected by the Tonkawa Indians. The Tonkawas were almost annihilated.[194]

*1864: Osage scouts helped the militia during the Sand Creek Massacre. After it was over, some of the scouts dangled Cheyenne scalps from their lances.[195]

1865: The Kickapoos fought the Cherokee, the Creeks, and others.[196]

1867: The Blackfeet defeated the Gros Ventres and the Crows.[197]

1867–68: The Cheyenne did battle with their old enemies, the Kaw and the Osages.[198]

1868: The Osages fought the Kiowa, Comanche, and other tribes.[199]

*1868: The Osages scouted for the army, especially in leading Custer's troops to Black Kettle's Cheyenne village at Washita.[200]

*1869: General Eugene A. Carr led about 450 cavalry and 150 Pawnee scouts under Buffalo Bill against the Sioux and the Cheyenne. At the Battle of Summit Springs, 52 defending Cheyenne were killed.[201]
   The Pawnee were scouts not only at the Battle of Summit Springs, but also for other campaigns against the Sioux, Cheyenne, and Arapaho.[202]

*1869: The Shoshoni scouted for the army in campaigns against the Sioux, Cheyenne, Arapaho, and Ute. They helped the army pursue Sioux chief Crazy Horse when he and his people were fleeing.[203]

1860s: The Shawnee, the Delaware, and the Kickapoos fought the Tonkawas.[204]

*1870s: The Crows served as scouts for the army against the Sioux and the Nez Perce.[205]

1871: Papago together with Mexicans and citizens of Tucson massacred Apaches.[206]

*1872: General Crook organized a number of mobile units to fight the Apache. Included were White Mountain Apache scouts, the only people who could track their fellow Apache.[207]

1873: A Sioux war party intercepted a Pawnee hunting party. Pawnee chief Sky Chief and 149 other members of the tribe were killed.[208]

1873: The Cheyenne under Tall Bull fought the Kaw.[209]

1874: The Comanche fought the Tonkawas.[210]

*1876: A delegation of Cheyenne, Miniconjou, and Sans Arc chiefs came to talk peace with General Miles. The general's Crow scouts attacked the peace party, killing 5 of them. Miles sent them the Crows' ponies as an apology.[211]

*1876: At the Battle of the Rosebud, Crazy Horse and his Sioux and Cheyenne met the army of General George Crook. Crook had about 1,050 soldiers and approximately 266 Crow and Shoshoni scouts.[212] The Crow and Shoshoni scouts attacked the flanks of the Sioux.[213] The Crows helped track the Nez Perce, who were trying to flee to Canada.[214]

*1876: General Crook had 225 Shoshoni and 25 Ute scouts with him at the Battle of Slim Buttes when he attacked and destroyed the village of Sioux chief American Horse and killed the chief.[215]

*1877: When the Nez Perce were at war with the army, some of the warriors of Crazy Horse's Sioux were recruited as army scouts and wore army uniforms.[216]
   The Sioux and Assiniboine fought for perhaps 100 or 200 years. The Sioux claimed they had taken more scalps from the Assiniboine than from any other tribe. It is not certain when their war began.[217]

*1877: General Howard had some Bannock scouts with him while fighting the Nez Perce. The Bannocks dug up Nez Perce dead to scalp and mutilate.[218]

*1877: At the Battle of Big Bear Paw, Colonel Nelson E. Miles had a number of Cheyenne warriors with him.[219] After that battle was over and while the defeated Nez Perce were trying to flee, some of them were killed by Assiniboine and by Hidatsa.[220]

Before 1882: The Apache fought the Pueblos.[221]

The literature refers to other intertribal wars, but the author has not found specific dates. Those fights include the following:

Chickasaw, Chocktaw, and Cherokee against the White Sticks.[222]

Shoshoni against the Blackfeet, Cheyenne, and Sioux.[223]

Seneca against the Catawbas.[224]

Chickasaw against the Muskohge, and the Shawano against the Muskohge.[225]

Chickasaw against the Shawnee.[226]

Blackfeet fought the Crows, Sioux, Shoshoni, Flatheads, and Kootenais.[227]

Chippewa fought the Kickapoos.[228]

Chippewa, Ottawas, Potawatomis, Sac, Fox, and Kickapoos defeated the Illinois.[229]

Crows fought the Sioux and Blackfeet for horses, hunting grounds, and fame.[230]

Navajo fought the Hopi.[231]

Klamaths fought other northern California tribes.[232]

Mojaves fought the Pimas and the Papagos.[233]

Pequots and Narragansets attacked the Montauks.[234]

Navajo and Apache fought the Pueblos for food, property, women, and slaves.[235]

Pawnee fought Kiowa and Comanche.[236]

Pequots fought Narragansets and Niantics for land.[237]

Tonwankas fought Apache.[238]

Caddo, Delaware, and Shawnee fought Tonwankas.[239]

Pawnee and Blackfeet fought each other "time out of mind."[240]

Deaths Caused by Specific Indian Atrocities

Date	Number of deaths*	Brief description of the atrocity
1511–12	3+	Dutch reported Indian eating wife and children
unknown	1	Tonkawas killed Comanche and made stew of him
unknown	1	Lipans cooked a Comanche
unknown	2+	New England Indians gnawed flesh from settlers
c.1625	1	Mohegan sachem ate Narraganset sachem
c.1630	1	Thumb of Father Jogues cut off
unknown	1	Indians made a hole in victim's breast and sucked blood from it
1632	32	Delaware Indians massacred Dutch settlers
c.1637	6+	Indians in Massachusetts flayed settlers alive, cut off members and joints and broiled them, and ate flesh of others in their sight
1637	1	Indians roasted settler in Massachusetts to death
1637	2+	Indian tribes gave English the heads of Pequots
1638–84	4	During the Beaver Wars, Iroquois captured by Hurons and killed by torture. Iroquois chief Ononkwaya roasted, scalped, thrown into the fire, hands and feet amputated, and finally decapitated

*Atrocities by Indians against other Indians are included

Date	Number of deaths	Brief description of the atrocity
1639	113	Hurons burned Iroquois to death
1643	80	Mohawk severed the heads of Wappinger Indians
1643	30	Mohawk tortured additional Wappingers to death for public amusement
1643	8+	Mohawk hacked babies to death, threw others in the water to drown, amputated hands and legs
1644	2	Susquehannock Indians tortured Maryland soldiers
1648	1	Iroquois hacked Father Daniel's body apart and threw it in the fire
1655	2+	Armed Indians killed settlers in retaliation for killing of Indian pulling peaches off tree
1659	8	Esopus Indians burned Dutch soldiers alive
unknown	5	Cheyenne scalped workers; one survived
1675	8	Heads of settlers put on poles at King Philip's village
unknown	1	Nipmucs captured a settler on a peace mission, beheaded him, and stuck his head on a pole in front of his home
1675	4+	Massachusetts towns attacked by Indians; men and women settlers scalped, their skins flayed
1675	37	Captain Beers and his men were beheaded by Indians, who put their heads on poles
1675	12	Narraganset Indians murdered settlers at Lancaster, Massachusetts
1675	36	Indians killed settlers in dispute over an account
1676	1	Indians burned an Iroquois to death
1689	1	Indians in Maine cut off fingers and slashed chest of fur trader Major Richard Waldron
1690	60	French-Canadians and Indians attacked Schenectady, hacking men, women, and children to death
1692	100+	Abnakis and French massacred soldiers in Maine who had surrendered on condition of safe conduct
1697	1+	Abnakis smashed the baby of Hannah Duston against a tree
1703	49	Abnakis and Mohawk killed settlers in Connecticut
1721	4	Cherokee presented king of England with scalps
1729	1	Shawnee tortured by cutting off his thumbs, pulling out his nails, burning prisoner's feet, legs, genitals, with red-hot gun barrels, stuck pine splinters into him and set them on fire, scalped him, and ran hot gun barrels up his rectum
c.1750	6+	Apache killed older women, took prisoners home where women could shoot them with arrows and rifles, cut off arms and legs, scalped
1752	1	Indians ate Miami chief Memeskia
1754	3	Indians ate Captain Donahew and others

Date	Number of deaths	Brief description of the atrocity
1754	17	Indians scalped Snider family, tomahawked and scalped Snider's servant, scalped Adams family, raped Mrs. Adams, scalped a trader and ate him, scalped and disemboweled prisoners who had escaped, then burned them to death and buried another in a hole, scalped him, burned him to death, and cut off his head
1754	20+	Indians took 20 scalps
1755	75+	Mohawk brought scalps from Braddock's defeat
1755	12	Prisoners burned to death by Mohawk
1755	1	Indian scalped Englishman
1755–59	95	Indians killed settlers, according to John M'Cullough memo
1756	1	An Indian woman who had fled to the settlers was stripped, tied to a post, and hot irons applied
1756	2	The Delaware tortured and killed Simon Girty's stepfather and killed his mother
1757	3+	Indians put prisoner into kettle and forced others to eat him and compelled mothers to eat the flesh of their children
1757	2+	Indians scalped the dead and ate some of them
1757	3	Indians scalped Captain Spikeman, who was beheaded and his head put on a pole; another prisoner was stuck with pine needles, which were set afire; and a third had his intestines cut open and was forced to walk around a sapling until he died
1758	1+	Montcalm took Fort William Henry and promised soldiers safe conduct, but Indians killed or took prisoner as many as 1,500
1758	3	Delaware Indians killed Thomas Potter, then a small child who was scalped, then Samuel Hunter, who was also scalped, and Daniel M'Manimy, who was burned, then his scalp was put on a pole before his face and finally red-hot gun barrels and a bayonet were passed over his body
1758	c.267	Scottish soldiers beheaded and heads put on stakes
1758	2+	Shawnee burned settlers and put their burned heads, arms, and legs along shore of Ohio River
1763	2,000	Pontiac's Rebellion resulted in many settler deaths
1763	8	Settlers murdered by Indians at Detroit
1763	12+	At Fort Michilimackinac, which was captured by Chippewa and Sac, a lieutenant was beheaded, the dead scalped and mangled, the dying tomahawked, some bodies ripped open and Indians drank their blood, 5 knifed to death by a Chippewa chief, and the fattest cooked and eaten

Date	Number of deaths	Brief description of the atrocity
1763	1	Commander of the garrison at Venango tortured for 3 days by Iroquois, then roasted to death by the Seneca
1763	1	Chippewa chief Wasson scalped Captain Campbell
1763	1	Captain Dalyell was killed; Pontiac's men cut out his heart, wiped it on prisoners' faces, cut off his head, and mounted it on a pole
1763	1	Pontiac served French settlers body of a British soldier, then showed them his severed head
unknown	2+	Sioux scalped Mandans
c.1770	1	The Boggs baby was not permitted to nurse, was thrown into the road intermittently, was sometimes kicked, then murdered and scalped
c.1775	1	Indians seared prisoner's body with heated gun barrels, scalped, hot coals applied to his skull, one end of his intestines tied around a tree around which he walked until they were all drawn out, his genitals cut off, and a hot gun barrel thrust into his heart
1777	2	A Wyandot and another Indian friendly to the British escorted American Jane MacCrea to a British post to meet her British fiancé. The Indians tomahawked and scalped her. Her scalp and that taken from an American officer were taken to the Indian camp
1778	360	The Wyoming Valley Massacre took 360 settler lives at the hands of the Iroquois, and the British commander Butler claimed 227 scalps were taken
1778	110	British colonel Hamilton claimed he bought 110 scalps that year alone
1778	30+	Indians attacked Cherry Valley, New York, and some engaged in cannibalism
1778	5+	Major Moses Van Campen's father and brother were scalped; he found an Indian village that had scalped 3 families
1779	2	Manheim twin sisters stuck with splinters dipped in turpentine and burned
1779	unknown	Mohawk struck town of Minisink, burning 12 houses
1779	2	Iroquois captured Oneida chief Hanyerry, hewed his body to pieces, and impaled his scalped head on a branch; at same time, Lieutenant Boyd was captured, his fingernails pulled out, nose and tongue cut off, eye gouged out, genitals cut off, and he was skinned alive and beheaded
1779	4+	Colonel Lochy and some of his men tortured by Mohawk
1779	18	Indians attacked town of Goshen and scalped all 17 hospital patients and their physician

Date	*Number of deaths*	*Brief description of the atrocity*
c.1780	1	Sutler Potts was scalped, hung upside down on a sapling, then cut open so that his intestines hung down over his head
1781	9	Settlers burned at the stake by Wyandots
unknown	3	Kwakiutl Cannibal Society bit flesh from arms of those watching them dance, then ate a slave
1782	3	Indians scalped Mrs. Wallace, her infant, and John Carpenter near Raccoon Creek
1782	5	Delaware women and boys tomahawked prisoners
1782	1	Delaware tortured Colonel Crawford: Powder was shot into his body from feet to neck, his ears cut off, his body burned with sticks, burning coals thrown on him, he was scalped, a squaw put more coals on his back and head, and his body burned almost to ashes
1782	5	The Reverend Corly's family was scalped by Indians
1782	7	Shawnee and Mingos killed captives by burning, the bodies of 3 given to the dogs
1783–90	c.1,500	Settlers killed in Little Turtle's War in the Old Northwest
1785	4	Scott family killed by Indians in Virginia
c.1785	1	This prisoner of the Indians was burned from all sides by women with torches; when he fell unconscious, he was scalped, dismembered, and all his extremities, including his genitals, cut off
1786	1	Grandfather of Abraham Lincoln killed by Indian in Kentucky
1788	3	Tecumseh and his men scalped at Drake Creek
1788	110	British colonel Hamilton bought these white scalps
1789	1	Medicine man Aiskawbawis ate his wife
1789	1	Indian showed Ironside the heart of a settler whom he had killed
1789	1	Charles Builderback, who had murdered Indians at Gnadenhutten, and his wife were captured; he was slowly emasculated and dismembered
1790	8	Johnston was captured, and others also captured scalped by Indians, then 6 more killed, 2 of whom were scalped by Indians
1790	3	Miamis killed prisoners
1790	1	William Flinn was burned at the stake and eaten by Miamis
1790	1	Abner Hunt was tied to a log, stretched out, a fire built around him, knife slits made in his body, and hot coals put in the slits
1791	24	Mingos captured boats on the Ohio River and killed passengers

Date	Number of deaths	Brief description of the atrocity
1791	2	Daniel Greathouse, who allegedly murdered part of the family of Mingo chief Logan, and his wife were captured by Mingos, pieces of their intestines lashed to a sapling, and they were made to walk around it until they died
1791	1	Officer Richard Butler was captured by Shawnee, who killed and scalped him, then cut out his heart and divided it into 14 pieces so that each tribe in the battle could eat it
1791	1	Soldier George Aikins was scalped by Kickapoos, then stabbed in every sensitive part of his body
1791	4	Soldiers were severely beaten, fainted, and were scalped and tortured
1791	6	Settlers scalped, perhaps by Wabash Indians
1792	12+	After St. Clair's defeat, captives were roasted, soldiers' intestines pulled out; they were flayed alive, their limbs hacked and pulled off, brains of children were dashed out, women run through with stakes, and some women's breasts hacked away before they were cut in 2
1792	2	The Herbeson boys, 5 and 3, were scalped
c. 1795	1	The Shawano captured Anantooeah, who tried to use strategy to escape. He sat on burning torches there to torture him. A Shawano warrior said he would not have died except that he was spoiled by fire, and tomahawked him
c.1800	12	Warrior captured by Catawba escaped and was pursued by Seneca; he killed them, chopped them to pieces, scalped them, went to the place he had buried other Seneca earlier, dug them up, scalped them too, and burned their bodies
c.1805	3	Chickasaw warrior went into enemy Muskohge country, killed a young man and 2 women, then scalped them
1806	4	Delaware medicine man Tenskwatawa had a witch hunt where an accused witch was roasted 4 days, then confessed, and 3 more burned
1807	7	Jordan and his children were put in holes dug in the ground up to their necks; dried branches were placed around them and burned
1812	1	The body of Captain Wells was beheaded by Indians and stuck on a pole, while other Indians took out his heart and divided it among chiefs
1812	10+	The garrison at Fort Dearborn surrendered, and troops, settlers, wives, and children evacuated and Potawatomis killed many by torture

Date	Number of deaths	Brief description of the atrocity
unknown	4	Moore family captured; infant and retarded son killed; mother and daughter roasted by Cherokee
1812	20	Tecumseh's Indians scalped prisoners at Fort Meigs
1813	400	Creeks attacked Fort Mims and massacred settlers
1813	850	American army failed in its attack on Frenchtown on the Raisin River in Michigan, and soldiers massacred by Indians
1813	40	At the Battle of Fort Meigs, Indians massacred prisoners
1816	4+	Creek and Seminole mothers killed their small children before going into battle
1820	1+	Every year the Pawnee kidnapped a young girl, and then cut out her heart
1832	15	Black Hawk murdered and mutilated after the Black Hawk War
1832	11	Militia turned 11 Indian bodies over to enemy Indians, who hacked them to bits
1832	c.120	Black Hawk Sac and Fox warriors retreated to west bank of Mississippi; Sioux there scalped them
1837	2+	During the Second Seminole War, Generals Thompson and Rogers were shot 15 times; both were scalped, and their skulls beaten in
1841	11	Comanche tortured prisoners
1847	13	Cayuse Indians killed Whitmans and other settlers
1849	5	Maidu Indians in California attacked miners who had raped their women
1849	2	Indians killed harsh ranchers
1850	11	California Indians attacked men who burned their ferry-boat, mangled their bodies, and burned them
1851	11	Yavapais (or perhaps Apache) killed Oatman family and tattooed daughter Olive Oatman
1851	72	Indians in California murdered settlers near Rattlesnake Creek
1851	7	Ferrymen killed by California Indians at Colorado River
1851	1	Settler murdered by Indians near Merced River
1851	13	California Indians massacred settlers at Four Creeks and tore out their entrails
1851	5	Cahuilla chief in California killed servant, then white invalids
1851	4	California Indians killed sheepherders near Gila
1851	3	California storekeeper Savage found his men murdered
1851	7	California Indians killed on Merced River
1852	130+	Legislators in California advised governor about murders by Indians in their counties
1853	1	Miner murdered by Indians in California

Date	Number of deaths	Brief description of the atrocity
1853	1	California chief learned an Indian had stolen, started to take him in, Indian tried to escape, and chief ordered him killed
1853	1	Mule train attacked by Indians in California and Dick Owen killed
1854	30	Sioux hacked soldiers to death at Grattan's Massacre
1855	3	Sioux killed settlers to avenge Grattan's Massacre
1855	1	Sioux caught trapper Levasseuer in the Black Hills and cut off his hands and cut out his tongue
1855	31	Oregon Indians raided settlement
1855	17	Comanche chopped off arms and hands, cut out some tongues, and scalped all
1855	2	Comanche scalped, cut, and finally crashed hatchets into skulls of captives, and dogs lapped up the blood
1855	1	Comanche hanged a soldier by his heels, cut off his ears
1855	27	Indians killed settlers in Oregon
1856	4	Cheyenne war party killed after misunderstanding about mail wagon
1857	70+	Indians and Utah citizens attacked troops, murdering many
1858	8	California Indians killed their medicine men because they were not effective
c.1860	1	A captured woman was brought on horseback into the Indian camp. When an Indian attempted to lift her from the horse, she shot him; the Indians cut her body in gashes, filled them with powder, then set fire to her
1861	8	Apache Cochise tied Mexicans to wagon wheels and set fire to them
1861	6	Cochise's hostages were perforated with lance holes to the extent that one could be identified only by his dental work
1861	1	Indians in California robbed a house and killed the cook
c.1862	6	A joint Apache-Comanche expedition in Texas resulted in a family being tortured and killed
1862	800	The Santee Sioux Massacre in Minnesota resulted in torture, rape, and murders
1862	2	Yahi Indians of California murdered children; one had a slit throat and was scalped
unknown	3	After an Indian raid in Colorado, a mother and her 2 children were discovered. The mother was stabbed, scalped, and perhaps raped, and the children had their throats cut and their heads nearly severed
unknown	1	Lieutenant Springer found a scalped soldier

Date	Number of deaths	Brief description of the atrocity
unknown	4	Captain Palmer found children whose heads had been beaten to jelly and a servant girl who had been staked out, her body full of arrows and horribly mangled
unknown	1	Sergeant Wyllyams was killed by Indians, scalped, and mutilated
1864	20	Sioux attacked a flatboat on the Yellowstone River, killed some and threw them in the river, and tortured women and children the next day
1865	1	Cheyenne raided a station, staked a prisoner out on the ground, cut out his tongue, and built a fire on his stomach
1865	21	After the Battle of Platte Bridge in Wyoming, soldiers were found mangled, one with a wagon tire across his bowels that had been heated red hot; Lieutenant Collins had his hands and feet cut off, his heart taken out, was scalped, and had 100 arrows in him
1865	6	The Boxx (or Box) family was attacked by Kiowa in Texas, the father and youngest child killed, the mother and 2 teenage daughters raped, and a 7-year-old compelled to walk barefoot on live coals
1865–67	162	Texas governor reported that during these years, Indians killed settlers
1866	80	Sioux, Cheyenne, and Arapaho killed and badly mutilated at Fetterman's Massacre in Wyoming, where eyes were torn out, noses, ears, and chins chopped off, hands, arms, feet, and genitals cut off, punctures all over bodies, even soles of feet and palms of hands; one body with 105 arrows in it
1866	1	Artist out of Fort Phil Kearny was separated from his party and was found with a cross cut in his chest and his head completely skinned
1866	1	Indians raided a tent home in Kansas, and 30 raped the wife
c.1866	1	Sioux completely skinned soldier Pate Smith
1867	117	Cheyenne and Arapaho war parties in Kansas killed settlers
1867	12+	Cheyenne killed settlers
1868	75	Settlers killed by Plains Indians
1868	2	Cheyenne camp killed a woman and a child prisoner when army attacked at Battle of the Washita River
1868	17	Cheyenne mutilated soldiers at same battle, some with cut throats, some beheaded
1868	2	When the army seemed about to rescue captive Blynn and her 2-year-old son from Kiowa leader Satanta,

Date	Number of deaths	Brief description of the atrocity
		Satanta tomahawked the mother, dashed the child's head against a tree, killing him, and threw his body on his dying mother
1869	1	Cheyenne killed a pregnant prisoner when attacked
1871	7	In Texas, a wagonmaster and others were killed; one was tied to a wagon wheel and burned
1872	12	Modoc Indians raided a ranch
1874	c.84	Comanche and Cheyenne tortured and killed settlers; 4 bringing supplies to Indians scalped and one burned
1874	6	The German family was captured by the Cheyenne; 5 were killed; Catherine was compelled to be the tribe prostitute and was frequently raped
1876	1+	Army buried its dead after a fight; Sioux dug up bodies and scalped at least one
1876	c.15	Found in a Cheyenne village were human forefingers, 12 severed right hands of babies and children, and 2 scalps
1876	1	Crows mutilated the body of a wounded Sioux so that he was no longer recognized as human
1876	2+	Before the Battle of the Little Bighorn, Reno's men were defeated, and Indian women and children mutilated bodies of soldiers, including cutting off fingers to get rings
1876	c.200	At the Battle of the Little Bighorn, the bodies of the Custer soldiers killed were mutilated in many ways: scalping, slashing and hacking of bodies, hands and feet cut off, stabbings, pieces of skin cut out, noses and other members cut off, an iron pin thrust through the testicles, penises cut off, disembowelment, heads cut off, eyes torn out, heads burned beyond recognition, bodies propped into sitting positions and used for target practice, buttocks shot full of arrows, and stakes driven through chests. Although Custer was not scalped, an arrow had been rammed up his penis. Rain-in-the-Face claimed he killed Custer, then cut out his heart and bit off a piece of it
1877	2+	Bannocks dug up bodies of Nez Perce and mutilated them
1877	4	Nez Perce Indian Swan Necklace and his men killed settlers
1878	1	Umatilla Indians killed and scalped Paiute chief Egan
unknown	4+	Apache reported to literally tear bodies of women prisoners apart and to hang prisoners head down over a small fire while they roasted to death
1879	10	Ute killed Indian agent Meeker and others

Total 9,156, or 56 percent of all atrocity deaths

Deaths Caused by
Specific Settler Atrocities

Date	Number of deaths	Brief description of the atrocity
c.1623	c.150	Governor Wyatt poisoned Indians
1634	1	Dutch soldiers tortured a Hackensack Indian, fed him his own flesh, castrated him, flayed him, dragged him through the streets alive, and finally beat his head off
1637	600	Settlers and Indians burned Pequot town
1643	80	Dutch soldiers murdered Wappingers
1655	2	Dutch killed Indian man and woman
1659	2+	Dutch killed peace emissaries
1675	32	Nanticokes killed over account dispute
1676	1	Connecticut militia severed Weetamoo's head
1676	1	Soldiers killed, drew, and quartered King Philip
c.1677	1	Soldiers beheaded Annawan, Philip's successor
1697	10	Hannah Duston scalped her Indian captors
1711	1	Swiss colonists roasted a chief alive
1713	366+	Slave trader Moore with settlers and Indians burned hundreds and murdered 166 Indians
1756	2	Settler M'Swine scalped his Indian captor and another Indian
1763	20	The Paxton Boys murdered 20 Indians
1764	5	Indian captive David Owens escaped, then scalped some of the Indians

Date	Number of deaths	Brief description of the atrocity
1778	5+	Major Moses Van Campen took several scalps
c.1778	5	Pennsylvanians took Indian scalps
1779	6	George Rogers Clark scalped 2 and murdered 4 Indians
1779	2	Soldiers skinned captured Indians
1781	15	Soldiers killed, then scalped, Indian prisoners
1781	1	Civilian murdered Indian chief during truce
1782	90+	Militia murdered Indians at Gnadenhutten
1786	1	Captain McGary murdered and scalped Indian chief
1791	6	Soldiers scalped 5 Indians and beheaded another
1794	1	Soldiers scalped Indian after the Battle of Fallen Timbers
1795	4+	Alexander Outlaw murdered women and children
1795	17	Benjamin Harrison murdered Creeks and beheaded some
1813	46	Davy Crockett burned Creeks alive in a house
1813	12	Militia scalped Indians at Frenchtown, Michigan
1824	9	Settlers murdered Indians on Fall Creek in Indiana
1832	27+	Trappers in Wyoming murdered 27 Indians
1832	2	Trappers in Wyoming burned Indians to death
1838	1	Catlin robbed the grave of Chief Black Bird
1848	25	Texas Rangers killed Wichita Indians
1848	20+	Oregon militia murdered Cayuse Indians
1849	20+	After miners in California raped Indian women and Indians killed miners, miners killed Indians
1849	1	Miner and Indian in California disputed ownership of horse, and Indian was killed
1849	1	Ruins of smoking house found, settlers followed tracks leading from it to California Indian, and he was killed
unknown	2	Army captain Naglee in California murdered 2 Indian chiefs
1849	27	White gang murdered Indians in California
1849	24+	After Indians in California killed 2 ranchers, soldiers surrounded 300 Indians, killed many; captain described it as "a perfect slaughter house"
unknown	1	Prospector in California accused Indian of stealing his pick; chief came to inquire about it and was killed
c.1850	1	Settlers dragged the father of Scarface Charley to death
1850	1	Ferryboat owner in California killed employee of competitor
1851	27	Savage, owner of store that had been raided in California, found Indian camp and killed occupants
unknown	1	California Indian stole horse, and owner killed him
1851	10	Store owner Savage surprised Indian camp in California
1851	1	Indian in California was called outside his home and knifed

Date	Number of deaths	Brief description of the atrocity
1852	153	Indians in California killed some cows, and ranchers retaliated
1853	200+	During their harvest dance, California Indians murdered
1853	2	Ranchers in California who had been raided hired men to kill Indians. One of these men killed an Indian and captured another, who was hanged
1853	13	Stock was stolen from a California ranch, a posse formed, Indians found in a cave and killed
1853	1	An Indian chief in California threatened vengeance on the whites, and he was hanged
1853	4	A store was robbed in California; an owner went to the ranch of the Indians he thought were the robbers, found some of his goods, and firing broke out
1853	18	There was a dispute in California between miners and Indians over some thefts, and killings occurred
1853	3	In Sonora, California, Indians stole some stock, and they were pursued and killed
1853	10	Cattle were stolen in California, ranchers attacked the Indians, and all were killed for this and other stealing offenses
1853	6	An army major learned that a white woman might have been kidnapped by Indians in California; his men went to the Indian camp; some Indians tried to escape and were killed
1854	3	Lieutenant Grattan killed Sioux
unknown	1	Army captain Wessels reported that an inoffensive Indian had been murdered by a white man near the post
1855	1	Militia cut off ears and scalp of Walla Walla chief
1855	23	Settlers murdered old men, women, and children in Rouge River War in Oregon
1855	86	Colonel Harney killed innocent Sioux in revenge for Grattan's Massacre
1856	9	Because the sugar of a California miner had been stolen by Indians, he put strychnine in it
1857	350	In the vicinity of Round Hill in California, it is claimed this great massacre took place. For reasons stated in the text, this report must be viewed with caution
1859	1	An Indian boy in California set fire to a house; a mob took him from the courthouse and hanged him
1859	87	California citizens complained Indians were putting their lives and property in danger, and the governor sent out a party to "chastise" them
1859	16	The governor sent out another party
1859	80	Yet another expedition was sent

Date	Number of deaths	Brief description of the atrocity
unknown	283	Captain Jarboe in California bragged about these killings (which may duplicate some of the above numbers)
1860	65	White men in California rowed to an island where Indians were dancing
1860	240	The *San Francisco Bulletin* reported this slaughter
1860	32	Stock had been stolen in Mendocino County, California, and settlers had formed a standing army
1860	60	Captain Jarboe's men in California killed Indians on South Eel River and near Round Valley
unknown	200+	This massacre occurred at the mouth of Eel River in California
1860	26	Settlers in Humboldt County, California, attacked Indians in retaliation for thefts by them
1861	46	In the same California county, settlers who had thefts found the Indians they believed responsible and killed them
1861	2	After a robbery by Indians in California causing a death, settlers killed these Indians
1861	3	Lieutenant Bascom hanged relatives of Cochise and left their bodies hanging for months as a warning
1861	35	Soldiers killed Navajo after a horse race
1862	2	Captain Graydon murdered Apache chiefs
unknown	2	Soldiers robbed Indian grave sites in Montana
1864	24	Rancher Wolsey in Arizona alone massacred these Indians at a peace council
1864	2+	Soldiers caught Indians who had killed another soldier and cut their heads off and stuck them on poles
1864	c.163	Indians murdered, scalped, dismembered, raped, etc., at Sand Creek Massacre in Colorado
1865	1	Whites in California tried to get possession of a 10-year-old Indian girl; a crippled Indian boy resisted and was killed
1867	1	Soldiers scalped and beheaded Sioux
c.1868	108	George Porter, whose family was killed by Indians, claimed he murdered Indians in retaliation
1868	1	Army scout Lem Wilson killed Indian in a fight, then scalped him
1869	2+	Indians in Montana killed in a fight; soldiers beheaded them, pickled their ears, and boiled flesh from their skulls
1869	1	Army scout Welch killed Cheyenne chief Pretty Bear in the Battle of Summit Springs, then scalped him
1870	173	The army attacked a Blackfoot camp, killing 90 women and 50 children

Date	Number of deaths	Brief description of the atrocity
1871	30	Settlers in California chased Indians into a cave and shot them
1871	21	Settlers, Mexicans, and Indians attacked sleeping Apache, killing women and children
1873	17	Modoc prisoners, including women and children, attacked by Oregon volunteers and killed
1873	4	The heads of the hanged killers of General Canby were sent to the army museum in Washington
1873	4	A settler was taking warriors in his wagon to surrender, but other settlers killed them
1874	12	After the Battle of Adobe Walls in Texas, soldiers beheaded Comanche and Cheyenne Indians and put their heads on posts
1874	2	General Crook demanded the head of Apache chief Delshay; 2 were brought in by another group of Apache, and Crook displayed both
1876	1	Buffalo Bill killed Cheyenne chief Yellow Hair in battle, then scalped him
1876	1	Sioux chief American Horse was badly wounded in South Dakota. After he died, soldiers scalped him
1878	1	Indians scalped Paiute chief Egan and gave the scalp to Colonel Miles; his surgeon brought back the head
1890	63	Sioux women and children gunned down by soldiers at the Battle of Wounded Knee

Total 7,193, or 44 percent of all atrocity deaths

Notes

Introduction

1. Coward, John M., *The Newspaper Indian: Native American Identity in the Press, 1820–90* (1999), 233, notes that the cultural gap between white Americans and Indians was fundamental and wide.

2. Hughes, Robert, *Culture of Complaint: The Fraying of America* (1993), 121.

3. Commager, Henry Steele (ed.), *The West: An Illustrated History* (1976), 267.

4. Schlesinger, Arthur M., Jr., *The Disuniting of America: Reflections on a Multicultural Society* (1992), 46.

5. Nash, Gary B., *Red, White, and Black: The Peoples of Early North America* (1992), introductory page.

6. Marshall, S. L. A., *Crimsoned Prairie: The Indian Wars* (1972), xiii.

7. Waldman, Carl, *Who Was Who in Native American History* (1990), v–vi.

8. Quoted in Josephy, Alvin M., Jr., *The Indian Heritage of America* (1991), 7.

9. Bordewich, Fergus M., *Killing the White Man's Indian: Reinventing Native Americans at the End of the Twentieth Century* (1996), 18.

10. Josephy, *Indian Heritage*, 280.

11. Waldman, Carl, *Atlas of the North American Indian* (1985), 109.

12. "Who Were the First Americans?" *Newsweek*, April 26, 1999, 57.

13. Ibid., 52.

14. *New York Times*, October 26, 1999.

15. *World Book Encyclopedia*, vol. 10 (1973), 108.

16. Josephy, *Indian Heritage*, 144.

17. Wissler, Clark, *Indians of the United States* (1940), 85.

18. Axelrod, Alan, *Chronicle of the Indian Wars from Colonial Times to Wounded Knee* (1993), 169.

19. Quoted in Brown, Dee, *Bury My Heart at Wounded Knee: An Indian History of the American West* (1991), 78.

20. Axelrod, *Chronicle of the Indian Wars*, vii.

21. Marshall, *Crimsoned Prairie*, 2.

22. Tebbel, John, and Keith Jennison, *The American Indian Wars* (1961), 261.

Chapter 1: Settler and Other American Attitudes About the Indians

1. Coward, *The Newspaper Indian*, 160.
2. Hays, Robert G. (ed.), *A Race at Bay: New York Times Editorials on "The Indian Problem," 1860–1890* (1997), 3.
3. The military shared the wrath of the *Times*. General Sherman wired General Sheridan in 1876 stating that he hoped that General Miles would "crown his success by capturing or killing Sitting Bull and his remnant of outlaws." Robinson, Charles M., III, *A Good Year to Die* (1995), 280.
4. Dippie, Brian W., *The Vanishing American: White Attitudes and U.S. Indian Policy* (1991), 133.
5. Quoted in Hays, *A Race at Bay*, 5–6.
6. Josephy, *Indian Heritage*, 281.
7. Nash, *Red, White, and Black*, 37.
8. Kraus, Michael, *The United States to 1865* (1959), 35.
9. Smith, Page, *A New Age Now Begins: A People's History of the American Revolution* (1976), 108.
10. Quoted in Bordewich, *Killing the White Man's Indian*, 35.
11. Josephy, Alvin M., Jr., *500 Nations* (1994), 204.
12. Pearce, Roy Harvey, *The Savages of America: A Study of the Indian and the Idea of Civilization* (1965), 12.
13. Sheehan, Bernard W., *Seeds of Extinction: Jeffersonian Philanthropy and the American Indian* (1973), 205.
14. Quoted in Axelrod, *Chronicle of the Indian Wars*, 11–12.
15. Gilbert, Bil, *God Gave Us This Country: Tekamthi and the First American Civil War* (1989), 2.
16. Waldman, *Who Was Who*, 40.
17. Quoted in Nash, *Red, White, and Black*, 76.
18. Waldman, *Who Was Who*, 223.
19. Quoted in Nash, *Red, White, and Black*, 84.
20. Smith, *A New Age Now Begins*, 1155.
21. Ibid., 1155.
22. Quoted in Prucha, Francis Paul, *Documents of United States Indian Policy* (1990), 2.
23. Waldman, *Who Was Who*, 187.
24. Quoted in Dippie, *The Vanishing American*, 122.
25. Prucha, *Documents of United States Indian Policy*, 13.
26. Waldman, *Atlas*, 114–15.
27. Dippie, *The Vanishing American*, 5.
28. Waldman, *Who Was Who*, 373.
29. Ibid., 167.
30. Quoted in Sheehan, *Seeds of Extinction*, 224.
31. Quoted in Dippie, *The Vanishing American*, 6.
32. Dippie, 6.
33. Quoted in Dippie, 5–6.
34. Dippie, 6.
35. Ibid., 9.
36. Quoted in Dippie, 7.
37. Quoted in Washburn, Wilcomb E., *The Indian in America* (1975), 19.
38. Jackson, Helen Hunt, *A Century of Dishonor* (1885), 254–55.
39. Dippie, *The Vanishing American*, 123.
40. Quoted in Dippie, 8.
41. Waldman, *Who Was Who*, 52–53.
42. Dippie, *The Vanishing American*, 30.
43. Ibid., 62–63.
44. Quoted in Dippie, 52.
45. Ibid., 58.
46. Washburn, *The Indian in America*, 209.
47. Quoted in Sheehan, *Seeds of Extinction*, 206.
48. Brinkley, Douglas, *American Heritage History of the United States* (1998), 154.
49. Dippie, *The Vanishing American*, 142.
50. Hays, *A Race at Bay*, 3.
51. Quoted in Coward, *The Newspaper Indian*, 2.
52. Quoted in Bordewich, *Killing the White Man's Indian*, 51.
53. Marshall, *Crimsoned Prairie*, 28.
54. Quoted in Coward, *The Newspaper Indian*, 118.
55. Ibid., 107.
56. Quoted in Hays, *A Race at Bay*, 52.
57. Hays, 132.
58. Quoted in Hays, 1.
59. Hays, 51.
60. Ibid., 234–35.
61. Coward, *The Newspaper Indian*, 201.
62. Debo, Angie, *A History of the Indians of the United States* (1989), 234.

63. Hays, *A Race at Bay,* 215.
64. Quoted in Hays, 178.
65. Ibid., 298.
66. Ibid., 26.
67. Hays, 27.
68. Quoted in Hays, 28.
69. Waldman, *Who Was Who,* 136.
70. Berkhofer, Robert F., Jr., *The White Man's Indian* (1978), 168.
71. Quoted in Coward, *The Newspaper Indian,* 198.
72. Hays, *A Race at Bay,* 327.
73. Quoted in Hays, 93.
74. Ibid., 33.
75. Lazarus, Edward, *Black Hills/White Justice* (1991), 89.
76. Hays, *A Race at Bay,* 141.
77. Coward, *The Newspaper Indian,* 170.
78. Dippie, *The Vanishing American,* 127.
79. Jackson, *A Century of Dishonor,* 198.
80. Dippie, *The Vanishing American,* 156; Hays, *A Race at Bay,* 21.
81. Hays, 37.
82. Brandon, William, *Indians* (1987), 348.
83. Hays, *A Race at Bay,* 283–84.
84. Ibid., 251.
85. Quoted in Dippie, *The Vanishing American,* 120.
86. Quoted in Hays, *A Race at Bay,* 227–28.
87. Quoted in Wilson, James, *The Earth Shall Weep: A History of Native Americans* (1998), 235.
88. Quoted in Hays, *A Race at Bay,* 322.
89. Quoted in Dippie, *The Vanishing American,* 183.
90. Ibid., 183.
91. Ibid., 184.
92. Ibid., 184
93. Ibid., 250.
94. Waldman, *Atlas,* 204.
95. Matthiessen, Peter, *In the Spirit of Crazy Horse* (1991), 34–35.
96. Wilson, *The Earth Shall Weep,* 396, 405.
97. Wilson, p. 400, criticized the government in connection with this occupation because it "failed either to provide decent accommodations for them [the occupiers] or . . . [to] arrange meetings with the President and other high-ranking leaders."

98. Lazarus, *Black Hills/White Justice,* 300–1.
99. Waldman, *Atlas,* 205.
100. Hagan, William T., *American Indians* (1979), 171–72.
101. Lazarus, *Black Hills/White Justice,* 301.
102. Quoted in Wilson, *The Earth Shall Weep,* 401.
103. Washburn, *The Indian in America,* 273–74.
104. Hays, *A Race at Bay,* xx.
105. Wilson, *The Earth Shall Weep,* xvii–xviii.
106. Leo, John, *Sarasota Herald-Tribune,* January 31, 1995.

Chapter 2: Some Indian Cultural Characteristics

1. Bordewich, in *Killing the White Man's Indian,* commented that "in the film *Dances with Wolves* [described as a New Age Western on p. 29], which is a virtual compendium of currently popular attitudes about Indians, Euro-Americans are portrayed almost without exception as sadists, thugs, or lost souls" (p. 211). Gary L. Ebersole, in *Captured by Texts: Puritan to Postmodern Images of Indian Captivity* (1995), 255–56, similarly said, "Few whites come off well in the film—most are portrayed as ignorant, prejudiced, and brutal, while the Sioux are wise, open-minded, and humane. Whites are largely written off as incorrigibly corrupt." Two realistic fictional motion pictures about Indians and settlers on the frontier are *The Unconquered* and *The Last of the Mohicans.*
2. Spicer, Edward H., *The American Indians* (1980), 19.
3. Debo, *A History of the Indians,* 3.
4. Wissler, *Indians of the United States,* 298.
5. Catlin, George, *Letters and Notes on the Manners, Customs and Conditions of the North American Indians Written During Eight Years' Travel (1832–1839) Amongst the Wildest Tribes of Indians of North America* (1841), 463.

6. Ibid., 6.
7. Tebbel and Jennison, *The American Indian Wars,* 1.
8. Marshall, *Crimsoned Prairie,* 2.
9. Sheehan, *Seeds of Extinction,* 193, paraphrasing James Adair.
10. Carey, Larry Lee, "A Study of the Indian Captivity Narratives as a Popular Literary Genre, ca. 1675–1875" (1978), Ph.D. diss., Michigan State University, 30.
11. Collier, John, *The Indians of the Americas* (1947), 174.
12. Wilson, *The Earth Shall Weep,* 27.
13. Ibid., 55.
14. Ibid., 260.
15. Smith, *A New Age Now Begins,* 107–8.
16. Quoted in Berkhofer, *The White Man's Indian,* 8.
17. Josephy, *Indian Heritage,* 93. To about the same effect Wissler said, "The Algonkin were not merely at war with the Iroquois but often with each other. There were about a hundred Algonkin tribes, all independent like tiny nations, all sooner or later quarreling and starting feuds—little vicious circles impossible to break. In revenge for past injuries a few members of one tribe would stealthily approach the camp of a hostile tribe, take a scalp or two and escape if they could." Wissler, *Indians of the United States,* 70.

The relationship between "Algonquian" and "Iroquois" is complex. Algonquian was a major Indian language spoken by several tribes with different dialects, and Indians speaking one dialect might not be able to understand those speaking another. Iroquoian is also an Indian dialect. The Iroquois are also the most widespread Indian tribe in upper New York and the Lake Ontario region of Canada. The Iroquois Confederacy (later the Iroquois League) eventually consisted of several tribes. Complexity is compounded by the fact that Algonquian is often spelled Algonkin, sometimes refers to a small Canadian tribe, and sometimes the names are misspelled. Waldman, *Encyclopedia of Native American Tribes* (1988), 6, 103.

18. Waldman, *Atlas,* 93.
19. Nash, *Red, White, and Black,* 25.
20. Waldman, *Encyclopedia,* 105–6.
21. Axelrod, *Chronicle of the Indian Wars,* 41.
22. Josephy, *Indian Heritage,* 96.
23. Wissler, *Indians of the United States,* 131–32.
24. Ibid., 145.
25. Sheehan, *Seeds of Extinction,* 196.
26. Esarey, Logan, *A History of Indiana* (1970), 10–11.
27. Quoted in Tebbel and Jennison, *The American Indian Wars,* 53.
28. Waldman, *Atlas,* 110.
29. Waldman, *Who Was Who,* 128–29.
30. Quoted in Sheehan, *Seeds of Extinction,* 194.
31. Catlin, *Letters and Notes,* 50.
32. Ibid., 94.
33. Ibid., 98.
34. Waldman, *Encyclopedia,* 78–79.
35. Catlin, *Letters and Notes,* 369.
36. Quoted in Jackson, *A Century of Dishonor,* 68.
37. Drimmer, Frederick, *Captured by the Indians* (1961), 277–79, 299–300.
38. Josephy, *Indian Heritage,* 280.
39. Axelrod, *Chronicle of the Indian Wars,* vii.
40. Driver, Harold E., *Indians of North America* (1969), 320.
41. *World Book,* vol. 10, 144.
42. Spicer, *The American Indians,* 104. The author spoke of the northern Plains Indians, but this language applies to all tribes.
43. Gilbert, *God Gave Us This Country,* 6–7.
44. Waldman, *Atlas,* 87.
45. Schultz, Duane, *Month of the Freezing Moon: The Sand Creek Massacre, November, 1864* (1990), 13.
46. Waldman, *Encyclopedia,* 223.
47. Quoted in Matthiessen, *In the Spirit of Crazy Horse,* 440.
48. Quoted in Utley, Robert M., and Wilcomb E. Washburn, *Indian Wars* (1977), 144.
49. Driver, *Indians of North America,* 309.
50. Quoted in Loudon, Archibald, *A Selection of Some of the Most Interesting Narratives, of Outrages, Committed by*

the Indians, in Their Wars, with the White People, vol. 2 (1908), 220.

51. Dippie, The Vanishing American, 54.

52. Ibid., 234.

53. Wissler, Indians of the United States, xiv.

54. Waldman, Encyclopedia, 211.

55. Waldman, Atlas, 167.

56. Utley and Washburn, Indian Wars, 144.

57. Quoted in Robinson, A Good Year to Die, 134.

58. Robinson, 313.

59. Schultz, Month of the Freezing Moon, 16.

60. The Appendix counts as several wars those between more than 2 tribes. For example, when the Iroquois fought the Beaver Wars against 13 other tribes, those wars are considered 13 intertribal wars, not just one.

61. Utley and Washburn, Indian Wars, 15.

62. Marshall, Crimsoned Prairie, 212.

63. Brady, Cyrus Townsend, Indian Fights and Fighters (1971), 313.

64. Waldman, Atlas, 87–88.

65. Brandon, Indians, 176.

66. Pearce, The Savages of America, 93.

67. Driver, Indians of North America, 309.

68. Smith, A New Age Now Begins, 1174–75.

69. Kelly, Fanny, Narrative of My Captivity Among the Sioux Indians (1871), 78.

70. Quoted in Commager, The West, 237.

71. Quoted in Journal of the Indian Wars, 1 (1): 1999, 9.

72. Axelrod, Chronicle of the Indian Wars, 180.

73. Brady, Indian Fights and Fighters, 185.

74. Ibid., 90.

75. Andrist, Ralph K., The Long Death: The Last Days of the Plains Indian (1964), 136.

76. Ibid., 131.

77. Robinson, A Good Year to Die, xxix.

78. Waldman, Who Was Who, 293–94.

79. Marshall, Crimsoned Prairie, 84.

80. Quoted in Sheehan, Seeds of Extinction, 195.

81. Catlin, Letters and Notes, 469.

82. Quoted in Pearce, The Savages of America, 116.

83. Catlin, Letters and Notes, 146.

84. Waldman, Who Was Who, 167–68.

85. Quoted in Sheehan, Seeds of Extinction, 200.

86. Quoted in Kelly, My Captivity Among the Sioux, 188.

87. Kelly, 143.

88. Josephy, Indian Heritage, 96.

89. Drimmer, Captured by the Indians, 18.

90. Axelrod, Chronicle of the Indian Wars, 56. Indians were not alone in imposing the punishment of running the gauntlet. As noted in Stephen E. Ambrose, Undaunted Courage (1996), 159, Private Moses B. Reed in the Lewis and Clark Expedition did so after he was convicted of desertion and theft.

91. Driver, Indians of North America, 324.

92. Quoted in Sheehan, Seeds of Extinction, 197.

93. Brandon, Indians, 181–82.

94. Ebersole, Captured by Texts, 196.

95. Quoted in Goodrich, Thomas, Scalp Dance: Indian Warfare on the High Plains, 1865–1879 (1997), 43.

96. Catlin, Letters and Notes, 444.

97. Driver, Indians of North America, 324–25.

98. Catlin, Letters and Notes, 167–74.

99. Waldman, Who Was Who, 328–30.

100. Ibid., 291–92.

101. Lazarus, Black Hills/White Justice, 87. To basically the same effect, it is said that "Sitting Bull, after permitting fifty pieces of flesh to be cut from his arms and chest and undergoing other tests of fortitude, had had a vision of soldiers falling into the Indian camp." Andrist, Long Death, 262.

102. Brady, Indian Fights and Fighters, 281–83. Catlin witnessed and described another Sioux Sun Dance (Catlin, Letters and Notes, 226–27).

103. Waldman, Atlas, 219.

104. Drimmer, Captured by the Indians, 237.

105. Richardson, Rupert N., The Comanche Barrier to South Plains Settlement (1933), 37–38.

106. Kelly, My Captivity Among the Sioux, 106.

107. Waldman, Encyclopedia, 100.

108. Sheehan, Seeds of Extinction, 196–97.

109. Brandon, *Indians*, 136.
110. Axelrod, *Chronicle of the Indian Wars*, 174.
111. Of course, settlers scalped as well. Wilson, in *The Earth Shall Weep*, p. 237, stated that "on good authority I can report the case of an old prospector-pioneer-miner-trapper of this region who had on his bed even in recent years a blanket lined with Indian scalps. . . . The Indians he had killed purely on his own account." This was a California prospector. Such a blanket would contain perhaps 150 scalps, which is 146 more than Wilson reported the Indians took.
112. Gilbert, *God Gave Us This Country*, 88.
113. Bordewich, *Killing the White Man's Indian*, 37.
114. Josephy, *Indian Heritage*, 283.
115. Utley and Washburn, *Indian Wars*, 15.
116. Quoted in Sheehan, *Seeds of Extinction*, 267–68.
117. Quoted in Gilbert, *God Gave Us This Country*, 207.
118. Brady, *Indian Fights and Fighters*, 323.
119. Tebbel and Jennison, *The American Indian Wars*, 99.
120. Smith, *A New Age Now Begins*, 1234.
121. Ibid., 1234.
122. Ibid., 1234–35.
123. Ibid., 1234.
124. Quoted in Sheehan, *Seeds of Extinction*, 192–93.
125. Quoted in Washburn, *The Indian in America*, 220.
126. Matthiessen, Peter, *Indian Country* (1984), 329.
127. Utley and Washburn, *Indian Wars*, 27.
128. Drimmer, *Captured by the Indians*, 236.
129. Ibid., 18.
130. Sheehan, *Seeds of Extinction*, 194.
131. *The American Heritage Book of the Revolution* (1958), 242.
132. Quoted in Coward, *The Newspaper Indian*, 4.
133. Wilson, *The Earth Shall Weep*, 292.
134. Quoted in Sheehan, *Seeds of Extinction*, 153.
135. Esarey, Logan. *A History of Indiana* (1970), 70–71.
136. Sheehan, *Seeds of Extinction*, 213.
137. Kelly, *My Captivity Among the Sioux*, 145.
138. Ambrose, Stephen E., *Undaunted Courage* (1996), 84, 88, 135.
139. Lazarus, *Black Hills/White Justice*, 151.
140. Quoted in Wilson, *The Earth Shall Weep*, 17.
141. Ambrose, *Undaunted Courage*, 190.
142. Andrist, *Long Death*, 178.
143. Catlin, *Letters and Notes*, 259–60.
144. Washburn, *The Indian in America*, 66. Other reports about unnecessary slaughter of buffalo by Indians are found in Waldman, *Atlas*, 4, and Brady, *Indian Fights and Fighters*, 5.
145. Waldman, *Atlas*, 25.
146. Ibid., 214.
147. Driver, *Indians of North America*, 218.
148. Quoted in Drimmer, *Captured by the Indians*, 158.
149. Kelly, *My Captivity Among the Sioux*, 76.
150. Bordewich, *Killing the White Man's Indian*, 212.
151. Utley and Washburn, *Indian Wars*, 254.
152. War chiefs were the principals in times of war, peace chiefs in times of peace.
153. Lazarus, *Black Hills/White Justice*, 99.
154. Nash, *Red, White, and Black*, 19.
155. Axelrod, *Chronicle of the Indian Wars*, 160.
156. Waldman, *Atlas*, 128.
157. Nash, *Red, White, and Black*, 243.
158. Waldman, *Who Was Who*, 264–65.
159. Quoted in Berkhofer, *The White Man's Indian*, 170.
160. Josephy, *Indian Heritage*, 120.
161. Waldman, *Atlas*, 63.
162. Ibid., 87.
163. Washburn, *The Indian in America*, 43.
164. Ambrose, *Undaunted Courage*, 188.
165. Waldman, *Encyclopedia*, 234.
166. Nash, *Red, White, and Black*, 126.
167. Ibid., 127.
168. Drimmer, *Captured by the Indians*, 191.
169. Debo, *A History of the Indians*, 192.
170. Schultz, *Month of the Freezing Moon*, 103.
171. Debo, *A History of the Indians*, 265.

172. Axelrod, *Chronicle of the Indian Wars,* 161.
173. Waldman, *Atlas,* 88.
174. Utley and Washburn, *Indian Wars,* 289–90.
175. Josephy, *Indian Heritage,* 280.
176. Washburn, *The Indian in America,* 88–89.
177. Quoted in Brodie, Fawn M., *Thomas Jefferson: An Intimate History* (1988), 434.
178. Prucha, *Documents of United States Indian Policy,* 36.
179. Quoted in Marshall, *Crimsoned Prairie,* 84.
180. Quoted in Lazarus, *Black Hills/White Justice,* 57.
181. Quoted in Brown, *Bury My Heart at Wounded Knee,* 38.
182. *Abraham Lincoln: Speeches and Writings, 1859–1865: Speeches, Letters, and Miscellaneous Writings, Presidential Messages and Proclamations* (1989), 441–42.
183. Quoted in Schultz, *Month of the Freezing Moon,* 198.
184. Quoted in Prucha, *Documents of United States Indian Policy,* 107.
185. Quoted in Hays, *A Race at Bay,* 191.
186. Quoted in Lazarus, *Black Hills/White Justice,* 116.
187. Jackson, *A Century of Dishonor,* 271.
188. Bordewich, *Killing the White Man's Indian,* 40.
189. Quoted in Jackson, *A Century of Dishonor,* 226.
190. Ibid., 162.
191. Jackson, 244.
192. Quoted in Bordewich, *Killing the White Man's Indian,* 329.
193. Quoted in Wilson, *The Earth Shall Weep,* 380.
194. Some slaveholding tribes follow: Mohegan, Narragansets, Niantics (Waldman, *Atlas,* 91); Osages (Debo, *A History of the Indians,* 73); Miami, Delaware, Shawnee (Drimmer, *Captured by the Indians,* 133); Ute (Debo, 159); Nootkas (Drimmer, 233); Apache and Navajo (Utley and Washburn, *Indian Wars,* 153); Wichitas, Comanche, and Creeks (Abel, Annie Heloise, *The American Indian as Slaveholder and Se-* cessionist, 166–67); Cherokee, Chickasaw, Choctaw, and Seminole (Debo, 128); Papagos, Northwest Pacific Indians, and Iroquois (Debo, 269; Josephy, *Indian Heritage,* 77; and *World Book,* vol. 1, 119); Makahs and Wascos (Spicer, *The American Indians,* 155, 153).
195. Axelrod, *Chronicle of the Indian Wars,* 35. The Yurok tribe of northern California held land individually and sold it to one another. Waldman, *Encyclopedia,* 261.
196. Kelly, *My Captivity Among the Sioux,* 195, 202–3.
197. Prucha, *Documents of United States Indian Policy,* 54.
198. Title was obtained by 2 methods other than treaties: title by conquest through the English government, and title by conquest on the part of the settlers themselves (both will be described later). When imperialistic Indians took the hunting grounds of other tribes by force, as they frequently did, it was done under title by conquest and was no more theft than was the taking of Indian-occupied land by the settlers.
199. Waldman, *Encyclopedia,* 106.
200. Bordewich, *Killing the White Man's Indian,* 104.
201. Ibid., 104–5.
202. Gilbert, *God Gave Us This Country,* 130.
203. Drimmer, *Captured by the Indians,* 287–88.
204. Pearce, *The Savages of America,* 43.
205. Quoted in Ambrose, *Undaunted Courage,* 173. Both Lewis and Clark were marvelously brave and resourceful leaders. They were not good spellers. Their original spellings are used here in order that their words are not mistranslated. An example is Clark's entry referring to the work entitled *A New and Complete Dictionary of the Arts and Sciences.* Captain Clark said he had been thumbing through the "Deckinsery of arts an ciences." Ambrose, 226.
206. Ambrose, 180.
207. Ibid., 340.
208. Quoted in Coward, *The Newspaper Indian,* 36.

209. Catlin, *Letters and Notes*, 121.
210. Ibid., 126.
211. Josephy, *Indian Heritage*, 95.
212. Ibid., 96.
213. Gilbert, *God Gave Us This Country*, 50.
214. Josephy, *Indian Heritage*, 173.
215. Quoted in Brown, *Bury My Heart at Wounded Knee*, 111.
216. Brown, 226–27.
217. Brady, *Indian Fights and Fighters*, 310; Waldman, *Who Was Who*, 4.
218. Quoted in Brown, *Bury My Heart at Wounded Knee*, 327.
219. Quoted in Schultz, *Month of the Freezing Moon*, 15–16.
220. Pearce, *The Savages of America*, 93.
221. Drimmer, *Captured by the Indians*, 13.
222. Quoted in Prucha, *Documents of United States Indian Policy*, 91.
223. Coward, *The Newspaper Indian*, 59.
224. Ibid., 59. Colonel Ethan Allen Hitchcock escorted the band of Seminole chief Pascofa out of Florida. His journal said this: "A story exists that in the early part of the [Seminole] war, the children of this band were put to death by their parents to prevent being discovered by their noise and to make themselves light for hasty retreats; and it is a fact that the children among them [on the boat] extend up from infancy to 4 years of age—mostly to but 3 and then jump to 15 or 16. It would really seem from this that some 4 years ago they did put some of their children to death." Quoted in Foreman, Grant, *Indian Removal* (1932), 383.
225. Foreman, 179.
226. Quoted in Ambrose, *Undaunted Courage*, 341.
227. Catlin, *Letters and Notes*, 214.
228. Ibid., 214.
229. Ebersole, *Captured by Texts*, 3.
230. Drimmer, *Captured by the Indians*, 12.
231. Quoted in Ebersole, *Captured by Texts*, 191.
232. Heard, J. Norman, *White into Red: A Study of the Assimilation of White Persons Captured by Indians* (1973), 21, quoting Coleman, Emma Lewis, *New England Captives Carried to Canada* (1925), 44–58.
233. Quoted in Heard, *White into Red*, 17.
234. Waldman, *Atlas*, 152; Waldman, *Who Was Who*, 265.
235. Debo, *A History of the Indians*, 288.
236. Heard, *White into Red*, 131.
237. Ebersole, *Captured by Texts*, 5.
238. Ibid., 4.
239. Ibid., 215.
240. Ibid., 206.
241. Ibid., 206–7.
242. Heard, *White into Red*, 138.
243. Brandon, *Indians*, 369.
244. Waldman, *Who Was Who*, 146.
245. Debo, *A History of the Indians*, 107.
246. Quoted in Hagan, *American Indians*, 121.
247. Richardson, Rupert. *The Comanche Barrier to South Plains Settlement* (1933), 53.
248. Matthiessen, *Indian Country*, 26.
249. Quoted in Hays, *A Race at Bay*, 102.
250. Wissler, *Indians of the United States*, 298.
251. Matthiessen, *Indian Country*, 156.
252. Quoted in Wissler, *Indians of the United States*, 138–39.
253. Ibid., 139.
254. Quoted in Coward, *The Newspaper Indian*, 49.
255. Waldman, *Encyclopedia*, 160.
256. Quoted in Brandon, *Indians*, 318–19.
257. Quoted in Andrist, *Long Death*, 317.
258. Quoted in Berkhofer, *The White Man's Indian*, 19.
259. Catlin, *Letters and Notes*, 47.
260. Wissler, *Indians of the United States*, 180.
261. Richardson, *The Comanche Barrier*, 27–28.
262. Quoted in Ambrose, *Undaunted Courage*, 163.
263. Ambrose, 193.
264. Quoted in Ambrose, 335.
265. Ambrose, 353.
266. Quoted in Ambrose, 355–57.
267. Ambrose, 384–85.
268. Ibid., 387–91.
269. Marshall, *Crimsoned Prairie*, 12–13.
270. Driver, *Indians of North America*, 323.
271. Jackson, *A Century of Dishonor*, 191.
272. Drimmer, *Captured by the Indians*, 278.
273. Quoted in Drimmer, 282–83.

274. Waldman, *Who Was Who,* 85–87.
275. Brown, *Bury My Heart at Wounded Knee,* 406–7.
276. Ibid., 211.
277. Waldman, *Atlas,* 61.
278. Quoted in Bordewich, *Killing the White Man's Indian,* 257.
279. Ibid., 257.
280. Quoted in Wissler, *Indians of the United States,* 293.
281. Schultz, *The Month of the Freezing Moon,* 19.
282. Washburn, *The Indian in America,* 107.
283. Sheehan, *Seeds of Extinction,* 239.
284. Quoted in Sheehan, 237.
285. Axelrod, *Chronicle of the Indian Wars,* 130.
286. Lazarus, *Black Hills/White Justice,* 12.
287. Drimmer, *Captured by the Indians,* 305.
288. Andrist, *Long Death,* 14.
289. Catlin, *Letters and Notes,* 480.
290. U.S. Department of Health and Human Services, Indian Health Service, *Regional Differences in Indian Health* (1992), 5.
291. Dippie, *The Vanishing American,* 34–35.
292. Ibid., 34–35.
293. Bordewich, *Killing the White Man's Indian,* 254.
294. Dippie, *The Vanishing American,* 35.
295. Driver, *Indians of North America,* 396–98.
296. Ibid., 391.
297. Catlin, *Letters and Notes,* 34–35.
298. Driver, *Indians of North America,* 447.
299. Ibid., 447.
300. Crèvecoeur, J. Hector St. John de, *Letters from an American Farmer and Sketches of Eighteenth-Century America* (1986), 215.
301. Prucha, *Documents of United States Indian Policy,* 161.
302. Brown, *Bury My Heart at Wounded Knee,* 265; Andrist, *The Long Death,* 184–85.
303. Andrist, *The Long Death,* 188.
304. Brown, *Bury My Heart at Wounded Knee,* 265–66. Isatai fared better than 6 or 8 Fresno medicine men in California who could not cure the sick. It was determined they would be killed, and they were. Trafzer, Clifford E., and Joel R. Hyer, *Exterminate Them!* (1999), 49.
305. Waldman, *Atlas,* 107.
306. Waldman, *Who Was Who,* 354.
307. Ibid.
308. Quoted in Andrist, *Long Death,* 177.
309. Waldman, *Atlas,* 132; Waldman, *Who Was Who,* 89.
310. Andrist, *Long Death,* 237.
311. Catlin, *Letters and Notes,* 143.
312. Kelly, *My Captivity Among the Sioux,* 252.
313. Andrist, *Long Death,* 340.
314. Ibid., 340–41.
315. Jackson, *A Century of Dishonor,* 374–80.
316. Quoted in Coward, *The Newspaper Indian,* 35.
317. Coward, 8.
318. Berkhofer, *The White Man's Indian,* 6.
319. Ibid., 28.

Chapter 3: Some Settler Cultural Characteristics

1. Crèvecoeur, *Letters from an American Farmer,* 9–13.
2. Ibid., 69–70.
3. Ibid., 80.
4. Ibid., 70.
5. Smith, *A New Age Now Begins,* 29–30.
6. Nash, *Red, White, and Black,* 69.
7. Smith, *A New Age Now Begins,* 31.
8. Ibid., 30.
9. Ibid., 31.
10. Ibid., 31.
11. Ibid., 32.
12. Ibid., 37–38.
13. Ibid., 38.
14. Sheehan, *Seeds of Extinction,* 266.
15. Quoted in Sheehan, *Seeds of Extinction,* 266.
16. Wallbank, T. Walter, and Alastair M. Taylor, *Civilization—Past and Present,* vol. 2 (1942), 228.
17. West, Elliott, *The Contested Plains* (1998), 88.
18. Peckham quoted in Tebbel and Jennison, *The American Indian Wars,* 99.
19. Quoted in Ebersole, *Captured by Texts,* 204.

20. Coward, *The Newspaper Indian,* 70.
21. Crèvecoeur, *Letters from an American Farmer,* 79.
22. Smith, *A New Age Now Begins,* 119.
23. Axelrod, *Chronicle of the Indian Wars,* 10.
24. Waldman, *Atlas,* 170.
25. Brogan, Denis William, *The American Character* (1944), 5–6.
26. Crèvecoeur, *Letters from an American Farmer,* 81.
27. Nash, *Red, White, and Black,* 49.
28. Ibid., 129–30.
29. Axelrod, *Chronicle of the Indian Wars,* 114.
30. Quoted in Sheehan, *Seeds of Extinction,* 268.
31. Quoted in Prucha, *Documents of United States Indian Policy,* 10.
32. West, *The Contested Plains,* 335.
33. Sheehan, *Seeds of Extinction,* 167.
34. Ibid., 268.
35. Quoted in Axelrod, *Chronicle of the Indian Wars,* 196.
36. Hays, *A Race at Bay,* 178.
37. Ibid., 27.
38. Erlich, J. W., *Erlich's Blackstone* (1959), 791.
39. Debo, *A History of the Indians,* 311. This statement refers to the Cherokee, but it could refer to all Indians.
40. Quoted in Commager, *The West,* 235.
41. Quoted in Bordewich, *Killing the White Man's Indian,* 35.
42. Crèvecoeur, *Letters from an American Farmer,* 121.
43. Quoted in Sheehan, *Seeds of Extinction,* 206.
44. Found at 8 Wheaton 543, 572 (1823).
45. Hagan, *American Indians,* 70.
46. Debo, *A History of the Indians,* 287.
47. Ibid., 287.
48. Sheehan, *Seeds of Extinction,* 12.
49. Washburn, *The Indian in America,* 43.
50. Josephy, *Indian Heritage,* 280.
51. Utley and Washburn, *Indian Wars,* 16.
52. Axelrod, *Chronicle of the Indian Wars,* 13.
53. Ibid., 13.
54. Ibid., 13.
55. Nash, *Red, White, and Black,* 124.
56. Quoted in Smith, *A New Age Now Begins,* 167.
57. Nash, *Red, White, and Black,* 263.
58. Axelrod, *Chronicle of the Indian Wars,* 34.
59. Nash, *Red, White, and Black,* 268.
60. Axelrod, *Chronicle of the Indian Wars,* 102.
61. Quoted in Prucha, *Documents of United States Indian Policy,* 1.
62. Debo, *A History of the Indians,* 88.
63. Ibid., 90.
64. Hagan, *American Indians,* 39–40.
65. Axelrod, *Chronicle of the Indian Wars,* 124.
66. Ibid., 124.
67. Quoted in Sheehan, *Seeds of Extinction,* 269.
68. Quoted in Debo, *A History of the Indians,* 121–22.
69. Quoted in Prucha, *Documents of United States Indian Policy,* 103.
70. Crèvecoeur, *Letters from an American Farmer,* 49.
71. Smith, *A New Age Now Begins,* 49.
72. Andrist, *Long Death,* 202.
73. Washburn, *The Indian in America,* 111.
74. Ibid., 112.
75. Hagan, *American Indians,* 89, 127–28.
76. Jackson, *A Century of Dishonor,* 124.
77. Crèvecoeur, *Letters from an American Farmer,* 78.
78. Quoted in Waldman, *Encyclopedia,* 215.
79. Quoted in Smith, *A New Age Now Begins,* 108.
80. Ibid., 108.
81. Quoted in Pearce, *The Savages of America,* 21.
82. Ibid.
83. Pearce, 23.
84. Quoted in Hays, *A Race at Bay,* 181.
85. Debo, *A History of the Indians,* 349.
86. Quoted in Kraus, *The United States to 1865,* 430.
87. Kraus, 431.
88. Waldman, *Atlas,* 88.
89. Hays, *A Race at Bay,* 78.
90. Quoted in Wilson, *The Earth Shall Weep,* 271.
91. Driver, *Indians of North America,* 63.
92. Utley and Washburn, *Indian Wars,* 289.

93. Axelrod, *Chronicle of the Indian Wars,* 113–15.
94. Waldman, *Atlas,* 119.
95. Ibid., 120.
96. Ibid., 138–39.
97. Utley and Washburn, *Indian Wars,* 198.
98. Brown, *Bury My Heart at Wounded Knee,* 114–15.
99. Debo, *A History of the Indians,* 223.
100. Ibid., 223. Axelrod, in *Chronicle of the Indian Wars,* p. 210, said Custer seized 2 and sent the third back with the surrender terms.
101. Waldman, *Atlas,* 103.
102. Caesar, *The Gallic War,* l.xxi.
103. Sallerst, *Jugurtha,* L-VIII 102; Caesar, *The Gallic War,* l.xxi.
104. Schultz, *Month of the Freezing Moon,* 24; Jackson, *A Century of Dishonor,* 79–80.
105. West, *The Contested Plains,* 173–74.
106. Ibid., 258.
107. Ibid., 210.
108. Ambrose, *Undaunted Courage,* 43–44.
109. Ibid., 148.
110. Ibid., 149–50.
111. Ibid., 181.
112. Ibid., 192.
113. Marshall, *Crimsoned Prairie,* 43.
114. Schultz, *Month of the Freezing Moon,* 90.
115. Brogan, *The American Character,* 10.
116. Utley and Washburn, *Indian Wars,* 50.
117. Driver, *Indians of North America,* 310.
118. Ibid., 310.
119. Josephy, *Indian Heritage,* 118.
120. Axelrod, *Chronicle of the Indian Wars,* 27.
121. Wissler, *Indians of the United States,* 188.
122. Ibid., 286.
123. Axelrod, *Chronicle of the Indian Wars,* 181.
124. Andrist, *Long Death,* 188–89.
125. Axelrod, *Chronicle of the Indian Wars,* 181.

Chapter 4: Pre-Colonial Atrocities

1. *World Book,* vol. 7, 3.
2. Wallbank, T. Walter, and Alastair M. Taylor, *Civilization—Past and Present,* vol. 1 (1942), 345.
3. Ibid., 208–9; Bernard Grun, *The Timetables of History* (1979), 84.
4. *World Book,* vol. 10, 215.
5. Wallbank and Taylor, *Civilization— Past and Present,* vol. 1, 345.
6. Ibid., 421.
7. *World Book,* vol. 10, 215.
8. Ibid., vol. 11, 107.
9. Waldman, *Atlas,* 13.
10. *Newsweek,* Fall/Winter 1991, 26.
11. Wissler, *Indians of the United States,* 236.
12. Brandon, *Indians,* 71.
13. Waldman, *Atlas,* 13.
14. *World Book,* vol. 1, 311.
15. Kraus, *The United States to 1865,* 165.
16. *World Book,* vol. 21, 311.
17. Ibid., vol. 5, 3.
18. Wallbank and Taylor, *Civilization— Past and Present,* vol. 1, 511.
19. *Newsweek,* December 21, 1992, 75.
20. Quoted in Axelrod, *Chronicle of the Indian Wars,* 1–2.
21. Utley and Washburn, *Indian Wars,* 11–12.
22. Ibid., 12.
23. Debo, *A History of the Indians,* 21.
24. Ibid., 21.
25. Wilson, *The Earth Shall Weep,* 192.
26. Brandon, *Indians,* 98. The engraving is also found in Washburn, *The Indian in America,* on p. 106, fig. 3.
27. Waldman, *Atlas,* 98.
28. Debo, *A History of the Indians,* 37.
29. Waldman, *Atlas,* 98.
30. Debo, *A History of the Indians,* 43.
31. Bordewich, *Killing the White Man's Indian,* 35.
32. Heard, *White into Red,* 1.
33. Ebersole, *Captured by Texts,* 2.
34. Ibid., 5.
35. Ibid., 89.
36. Ibid., 89.
37. VanDerBeets, Richard, *Held Captive by Indians: Selected Narratives, 1642– 1836* (1972), xi.
38. Ebersole, *Captured by Texts,* 275. The words *white Indians* were widely used to refer to whites who had abandoned white civilization.

39. Quoted in Heard, *White into Red,* 6.
40. Heard, 7.
41. Quoted in Carey, "A Study of the Indian Captivity Narratives," 11.
42. VanDerBeets, *Held Captive by Indians,* xii.
43. Drimmer, *Captured by the Indians,* 11.
44. Carey, "A Study of the Indian Captivity Narratives," 151, 178.
45. Kelly, *My Captivity Among the Sioux,* vi–vii.
46. Ibid., 251.
47. VanDerBeets, *Held Captive by Indians,* xvi.
48. Ebersole, *Captured by Texts,* 150.
49. Ibid., 159.
50. Ibid., 185.
51. Ibid., 169.
52. Ibid., 160.
53. Ibid., 184.
54. Ibid., 74.
55. Ibid., 165.
56. Ibid., 121.
57. Ibid., 169.
58. Ibid., 189.
59. Kelly, *My Captivity Among the Sioux,* v.
60. VanDerBeets, *Held Captive by Indians,* xxiv.
61. Ibid., xxiii.
62. Ibid., i.
63. Carey, "A Study of the Indian Captivity Narratives," 4.
64. Berkhofer, *The White Man's Indian,* 7.
65. Josephy, *Indian Heritage,* 264.
66. Ibid., 28.
67. Ibid., 28.
68. Quoted in Berkhofer, *The White Man's Indian,* 8–9.
69. Berkhofer, 10.
70. Axelrod, *Chronicle of the Indian Wars,* 75.
71. Driver, *Indians of North America,* 329.
72. Ibid.
73. "Cannibals of the Canyon," *The New Yorker,* November 30, 1998, 77.
74. Waldman, *Encyclopedia,* 106.
75. Heard, *White into Red,* 111–12.
76. Axelrod, *Chronicle of the Indian Wars,* 75.
77. Brinkley, *American Heritage History of the United States,* 30.
78. Ebersole, *Captured by Texts,* 77.
79. Heard, *White into Red,* 67.
80. Ebersole, *Captured by Texts,* 223.
81. Axelrod, *Chronicle of the Indian Wars,* 75.
82. Wilson, *The Earth Shall Weep,* 97.
83. Quoted in Axelrod, *Chronicle of the Indian Wars,* 75.
84. Washburn, *The Indian in America,* 59.
85. Debo, *A History of the Indians,* 6.
86. Waldman, *Encyclopedia,* 197–98.
87. Axelrod, *Chronicle of the Indian Wars,* 71.
88. Coward, *The Newspaper Indian,* 33.
89. Axelrod, *Chronicle of the Indian Wars,* 84.
90. Sheehan, *Seeds of Extinction,* 192–93.
91. Quoted in Axelrod, *Chronicle of the Indian Wars,* 75.
92. Drimmer, *Captured by the Indians,* 165–66.
93. Josephy, *Indian Heritage,* 77.
94. Debo, *A History of the Indians,* 177.
95. Andrist, *Long Death,* 184.
96. Quoted in Robinson, Charles M., III, *The Men Who Wear the Star: The Story of the Texas Rangers* (2000), 49.
97. Ibid., 49.
98. Sheehan, *Seeds of Extinction,* 200–201.
99. Quoted in Wilson, *The Earth Shall Weep,* 119.
100. Robinson, *The Men Who Wear the Star,* 46.
101. Gilbert, *God Gave Us This Country,* 88.
102. Ibid., 88.
103. Ibid., 89–90.
104. Ibid., 90.
105. Drimmer, *Captured by the Indians,* 14.
106. Wissler, *Indians of the United States,* 278.

Chapter 5: Colonial Atrocities

1. Brinkley, *American Heritage History of the United States,* 28.
2. Ibid., 29–30.
3. Waldman, *Who Was Who,* 332.
4. Brinkley, *American Heritage History of the United States,* 30–31.
5. Ibid., 34.
6. Waldman, *Who Was Who,* 256.
7. Utley and Washburn, *Indian Wars,* 15.

8. Nash, *Red, White, and Black,* 60.
9. Utley and Washburn, *Indian Wars,* 16.
10. Steele, Ian K., *Warpaths: Invasions of North America* (1994), 46.
11. Utley and Washburn, *Indian Wars,* 16.
12. Quoted in Utley and Washburn, 17.
13. Axelrod, *Chronicle of the Indian Wars,* 11.
14. Ibid., 11.
15. Utley and Washburn, *Indian Wars,* 17.
16. Waldman, *Who Was Who,* 256. Wilson, in *The Earth Shall Weep,* p. 67, argued that "the Powhatans were not really savage." The 847 settlers killed in these 2 attacks might have disagreed.
17. Waldman, 257.
18. Axelrod, *Chronicle of the Indian Wars,* 57. Jogues later tried to establish a mission to the Mohawk, but was killed while trying to do so. Waldman, *Who Was Who,* 169.
19. Axelrod, 38.
20. Utley and Washburn, *Indian Wars,* 36.
21. Quoted in Utley and Washburn, 39; Axelrod, *Chronicle of the Indian Wars,* 18.
22. Axelrod, 19.
23. Brandon, *Indians,* 173; Waldman, *Atlas,* 90–91.
24. Axelrod, *Chronicle of the Indian Wars,* 22.
25. Waldman, *Encyclopedia,* 99–101.
26. Axelrod, *Chronicle of the Indian Wars,* 41–42.
27. Waldman, *Atlas,* 214.
28. Axelrod, *Chronicle of the Indian Wars,* 39.
29. Quoted in Axelrod, 39–40.
30. Waldman, *Who Was Who,* 184.
31. Brandon, *Indians,* 168.
32. Axelrod, *Chronicle of the Indian Wars,* 46.
33. Ibid., 43.
34. Ibid., 43–44; Waldman, *Who Was Who,* 42.
35. Axelrod, 40; Waldman, *Atlas,* 96.
36. Axelrod, 40; Waldman, 96.
37. Waldman, *Encyclopedia,* 246.
38. Debo, *A History of the Indians,* 49.
39. Quoted in Debo, 49.
40. Quoted in Axelrod, *Chronicle of the Indian Wars,* 35–36.
41. Brandon, *Indians,* 176.
42. Waldman, *Atlas,* 93; Waldman, *Who Was Who,* 270–72.
43. Waldman, *Who Was Who,* 272.
44. Quoted in Sheehan, *Seeds of Extinction,* 197. However, "captive women were seldom in danger of rape. Among most Indian groups, forcible rape was seen as deviant and unacceptable behavior, and in any case, Indian men often professed a disdain for white women, whom they claimed to find unattractive." Axelrod, *Chronicle of the Indian Wars,* 57.
45. Tebbel and Jennison, *The American Indian Wars,* 39.
46. Ibid., 43.
47. Quoted in Axelrod, *Chronicle of the Indian Wars,* 27.
48. Wilson, *The Earth Shall Weep,* 144.
49. Ibid., 186.
50. Drimmer, *Captured by the Indians,* 15–16, 375.
51. Bordewich, *Killing the White Man's Indian,* 37.
52. Ibid., 37.
53. Brady, *Indian Fights and Fighters,* 91fn.
54. Axelrod, *Chronicle of the Indian Wars,* 174.
55. Quoted in Coward, *The Newspaper Indian,* 82.
56. Axelrod, *Chronicle of the Indian Wars,* 174.
57. Josephy, *Indian Heritage,* 179.
58. Drimmer, *Captured by the Indians,* 27.
59. Wilson, *The Earth Shall Weep,* 186.
60. Kelly, *My Captivity Among the Sioux,* 95–96.
61. Drimmer, *Captured by the Indians,* 17.
62. Axelrod, *Chronicle of the Indian Wars,* 54.
63. Debo, *A History of the Indians,* 67.
64. Ibid., 48.
65. Ibid., 73; Axelrod, *Chronicle of the Indian Wars,* 67.
66. Brandon, *Indians,* 201.
67. Axelrod, *Chronicle of the Indian Wars,* 76.
68. Brandon, *Indians,* 201–2.
69. Drimmer, *Captured by the Indians,* 373. Sergeant Moses Van Campen claimed bounties for scalps he took before the bounty was in effect. He

scalped the Indians who captured him and retrieved the scalps of his father and brother that they had taken. He and 2 fellow prisoners, Pike and Pence, killed 9 of the 10 Indians who had captured them. When the action was at its most desperate and it appeared he would be killed by the Indians, Van Campen looked and saw that Pike was trying to pray and doing nothing else and that Pence was swearing at Pike for not helping. It is not known whether Van Campen got any money for his scalps.

70. Smith, *A New Age Now Begins*, 1151.
71. Wissler, *Indians of the United States*, 71. Brandon, in *Indians*, p. 201, said they were adopted by most of the colonies.
72. Esarey, *A History of Indiana*, 47–48.
73. Axelrod, *Chronicle of the Indian Wars*, 162.
74. This happened in 1847 when Mexico offered bounties for Apache scalps. Mexicans, Americans, runaway slaves, and Indians brought in scalps from other Indians, then even Mexican scalps. Special examination committees were set up to authenticate Apache scalps, to no avail. Axelrod, *Chronicle of the Indian Wars*, 161–62.
75. Wilson, *The Earth Shall Weep*, 232.
76. Ibid., 232.
77. Trafzer and Hyer, *Exterminate Them!* 28–29.
78. Schultz, *Month of the Freezing Moon*, 160.
79. Quoted in Schultz, 160.
80. Axelrod, *Chronicle of the Indian Wars*, 28.
81. Quoted in Coward, *The Newspaper Indian*, 32.
82. Ibid., 32.
83. Axelrod, *Chronicle of the Indian Wars*, 31.
84. Ebersole, *Captured by Texts*, 6.
85. "The first American 'best seller' was published in Boston in 1682 [and was] *The Sovereignty & Goodness of God . . . A Narrative of the Captivity and Restauration of Mrs. Mary Rowlandson*." Axelrod, *Chronicle of the Indian Wars*, 30.

86. Waldman, *Who Was Who*, 307.
87. Ibid., 307.
88. Ebersole, *Captured by Texts*, 65.
89. Axelrod, *Chronicle of the Indian Wars*, 46–50.
90. Ibid., 35.
91. Utley and Washburn, *Indian Wars*, 63; Axelrod, *Chronicle of the Indian Wars*, 53.
92. Sheehan, *Seeds of Extinction*, 205.
93. Waldman, *Who Was Who*, 125.
94. Utley and Washburn, *Indian Wars*, 63–64.
95. Brandon, *Indians*, 257.
96. Waldman, *Who Was Who*, 125–26.
97. Waldman, *Encyclopedia*, 3.
98. Axelrod, *Chronicle of the Indian Wars*, 54.
99. Ibid., 54.
100. Waldman, *Who Was Who*, 108.
101. Ibid., 161.
102. Waldman, *Encyclopedia*, 152–53.
103. Debo, *A History of the Indians*, 74.
104. Waldman, *Encyclopedia*, 152–54.
105. Utley and Washburn, *Indian Wars*, 69; Waldman, *Who Was Who*, 108.
106. Utley and Washburn, 71–72.
107. Brandon, *Indians*, 217; Waldman, *Atlas*, 104; Utley and Washburn, *Indian Wars*, 72; Axelrod, *Chronicle of the Indian Wars*, 59; Nash, *Red, White, and Black*, 136.
108. Nash, 137; Waldman, *Atlas*, 104.
109. Waldman, *Encyclopedia*, 216–19.
110. Nash, *Red, White, and Black*, 111.
111. Quoted in Coward, *The Newspaper Indian*, 33.
112. Goodwin, Grenville, *Western Apache Raiding and Warfare* (1971), 284–86.
113. Loudon, Archibald, *A Selection of Some of the Most Interesting Narratives*, vol. 1 (1808), 81–82.
114. Drimmer, *Captured by the Indians*, 29–30.
115. Brandon, *Indians*, 203.
116. Waldman, *Atlas*, 215.
117. Loudon, *Narratives*, vol. 2, 179.
118. Ibid., 17–46.
119. Ibid., 181–84.
120. Waldman, *Who Was Who*, 133; Boyd, Thomas Alexander, *Simon Girty: The White Savage* (1928), 33–34.
121. Waldman, *Who Was Who*, 133.

122. Axelrod, *Chronicle of the Indian Wars*, 83–84.
123. Tebbel and Jennison, *The American Indian Wars*, 79.
124. Utley and Washburn, *Indian Wars*, 83–84.
125. Quoted in Drimmer, *Captured by the Indians*, 62–72.
126. Loudon, *Narratives*, vol. 1, 113.
127. Ibid., 111–18.
128. Ibid., vol. 2, 47–64.
129. Ibid., 195–98.
130. Utley and Washburn, *Indian Wars*, 85–86.
131. Sheehan, *Seeds of Extinction*, 199.
132. Axelrod, *Chronicle of the Indian Wars*, 93.
133. Waldman, *Who Was Who*, 279–80.
134. Ibid., 279–80.
135. Waldman, *Atlas*, 106–8; Axelrod, *Chronicle of the Indian Wars*, 99.
136. Waldman, *Who Was Who*, 279–80.
137. Tebbel and Jennison, *The American Indian Wars*, 89.
138. Waldman, *Encyclopedia*, 57–60.
139. Ibid., 210–12.
140. Tebbel and Jennison, *The American Indian Wars*, 90–91.
141. Drimmer, *Captured by the Indians*, 85–86.
142. Ibid., 84.
143. Ibid., 74.
144. Tebbel and Jennison, *The American Indian Wars*, 92; Axelrod, *Chronicle of the Indian Wars*, 97.
145. Tebbel and Jennison, 92.
146. Waldman, *Atlas*, 108; Tebbel and Jennison, 92.
147. Hagan, *American Indians*, 25.
148. Axelrod, *Chronicle of the Indian Wars*, 98; Utley and Washburn, *Indian Wars*, 99.
149. Tebbel and Jennison, *The American Indian Wars*, 96.
150. Waldman, *Atlas*, 108–9; Utley and Washburn, *Indian Wars*, 99–100.
151. Loudon, *Narratives*, vol. 2, 172–77.
152. Quoted in Tebbel and Jennison, *The American Indian Wars*, 96.
153. Quoted in Sheehan, *Seeds of Extinction*, 203.
154. Waldman, *Who Was Who*, 280.
155. Waldman, *Encyclopedia*, 102.

Chapter 6: Atrocities During the Eras of the British Wars

1. Brinkley, *American Heritage History of the United States*, 53.
2. Ibid., 51.
3. Ibid., 53.
4. Ibid., 53.
5. Ibid., 54–56.
6. Ibid., 61–63.
7. Ibid., 63.
8. Ibid., 66–67.
9. Ibid., 67.
10. Waldman, *Who Was Who*, 213.
11. Smith, *A New Age Now Begins*, 906.
12. Hagan, *American Indians*, 36.
13. Smith, *A New Age Now Begins*, 906.
14. Ibid., 906; Hagan, *American Indians*, 36; Utley and Washburn, *Indian Wars*, 107; Waldman, *Who Was Who*, 213.
15. Tebbel and Jennison, *The American Indian Wars*, 58–59.
16. Quoted in Smith, *A New Age Now Begins*, 1155.
17. Smith, 719–21.
18. Quoted in Smith, 1155.
19. Wissler, *Indians of the United States*, 278.
20. Quoted in Sheehan, *Seeds of Extinction*, 267–68.
21. Smith, *A New Age Now Begins*, 1235.
22. Quoted in Smith, 912–13.
23. Ibid., 913–14.
24. Ibid., 1156.
25. *The American Heritage Book of the Revolution*, 319.
26. Loudon, *Narratives*, vol. 1, 106.
27. Axelrod, *Chronicle of the Indian Wars*, 108.
28. *The American Heritage Book of the Revolution*, 318.
29. Loudon, *Narratives*, vol. 1, 104.
30. Waldman, *Who Was Who*, 42.
31. Gilbert, *God Gave Us This Country*, 107.
32. Smith, *A New Age Now Begins*, 1157–58.
33. Loudon, *Narratives*, vol. 1, 65–66.
34. Waldman, *Who Was Who*, 142; Esarey, *A History of Indiana*, 48.
35. Loudon, *Narratives*, vol. 1, 229–30.
36. Tebbel and Jennison, *The American Indian Wars*, 123.

37. Smith, *A New Age Now Begins*, 1159–60; Waldman, *Who Was Who*, 43.
38. Axelrod, *Chronicle of the Indian Wars*, 109.
39. Drimmer, *Captured by the Indians*, 105–18.
40. Smith, *A New Age Now Begins*, 1160.
41. Ibid., 1161–62.
42. Loudon, *Narratives*, vol. 1, 58–59.
43. Ibid., vol. 2, 193.
44. Loudon, vol. 1, 62–64; quoted in Sheehan, *Seeds of Extinction*, 204.
45. Smith, *A New Age Now Begins*, 1199–1210; Waldman, *Who Was Who*, 68–69.
46. Waldman, *Who Was Who*, 341–42.
47. Waldman, *Atlas*, 111.
48. Quoted in Smith, *A New Age Now Begins*, 1163.
49. Waldman, *Who Was Who*, 342.
50. Hagan, *American Indians*, 38; Tebbel and Jennison, *The American Indian Wars*, 70; Waldman, *Who Was Who*, 341–42.
51. Wilson, *The Earth Shall Weep*, 129.
52. Quoted in Axelrod, *Chronicle of the Indian Wars*, 112; Smith, *A New Age Now Begins*, 1170.
53. Smith, 1181.
54. Wilson, *The Earth Shall Weep*, 242.
55. Wilson chose to rely on oral Indian traditions when they conflicted with written reports. He said such written reports were by 17th- and 18th-century people who sometimes "straightforwardly lied" about the Indians. He added that even those writers sympathetic to the Indians "probably misinterpreted what they saw." Wilson, 44. This stance is disturbing in that it implies that almost no written report can be relied upon if it conflicts with an oral Indian tradition.
56. Waldman, *Who Was Who*, 95.
57. Smith, *A New Age Now Begins*, 1171.
58. Loudon, *Narratives*, vol. 2, 69–159.
59. Boyd, *Simon Girty*, 123–25.
60. Ibid., 117–19.
61. Ibid., 119–20.
62. Sheehan, *Seeds of Extinction*, 187.
63. Drimmer, *Captured by the Indians*, 105–18.
64. Axelrod, *Chronicle of the Indian Wars*, 121.
65. Waldman, *Atlas*, 113.
66. Boyd, *Simon Girty*, 137–38; Sheehan, *Seeds of Extinction*, 187–88.
67. Axelrod, *Chronicle of the Indian Wars*, 121; Gilbert, *God Gave Us This Country*, 106.
68. Axelrod, 121.
69. Drimmer, *Captured by the Indians*, 120.
70. Ibid., 125.
71. Ibid., 125.
72. Loudon, *Narratives*, vol. 1, 1–15; Drimmer, *Captured by the Indians*, 119–29; Sheehan, *Seeds of Extinction*, 185–87. Dr. Knight's description comes to us in 3 somewhat different forms, one from Loudon, one from Drimmer, and one from Sheehan. The material quoted in the text consists of direct quotes from all 3.
73. Loudon, vol. 1, 1–15; Drimmer, 119–29; Sheehan, 185–86.
74. Drimmer, 119.
75. Ibid., 120.
76. Loudon, *Narratives*, vol. 1, 60–62.
77. Drimmer, *Captured by the Indians*, 133.
78. Ibid., 134–35.
79. Ibid., 135.
80. Waldman, *Who Was Who*, 228.
81. Drimmer, *Captured by the Indians*, 137.
82. Ibid., 137.
83. Ibid., 138–41.
84. Waldman, *Atlas*, 114.
85. Tebbel and Jennison, *The American Indian Wars*, 79.
86. Quoted in part in Smith, *A New Age Now Begins*, 1762–72.
87. Loudon, *Narratives*, vol. 1, 33–34.
88. Gilbert, *God Gave Us This Country*, 109–10, 121.
89. Beveridge, Albert J., *Abraham Lincoln*, vol. 1 (1928), 11; Drimmer, *Captured by the Indians*, 14–15.
90. Gilbert, *God Gave Us This Country*, 126–27.
91. Waldman, *Who Was Who*, 350–51.
92. Gilbert, *God Gave Us This Country*, 126–27.
93. Ibid., 124.
94. Ibid., 109.
95. Drimmer, *Captured by the Indians*, 188–89.

96. Ibid., 189–92.
97. Ibid., 210.
98. Waldman, *Who Was Who,* 145.
99. Ibid., 206.
100. Axelrod, *Chronicle of the Indian Wars,* 124.
101. Esarey, *A History of Indiana,* 76–78.
102. Waldman, *Encyclopedia,* 132–33.
103. Gilbert, *God Gave Us This Country,* 137–39.
104. Quoted in Axelrod, *Chronicle of the Indian Wars,* 105.
105. Boyd, *Simon Girty,* 195–96.
106. Gilbert, *God Gave Us This Country,* 141–42.
107. Ibid., 142.
108. Waldman, *Encyclopedia,* 109–10.
109. Loudon, *Narratives,* vol. 1, 88–90.
110. Quoted in Loudon, vol. 1, 88–100.
111. Andrist, *Long Death,* 190.
112. Waldman, *Who Was Who,* 310–11.
113. Esarey, *A History of Indiana,* 116.
114. Quoted in Gilbert, *God Gave Us This Country,* 145.
115. Gilbert, 145–46.
116. Utley and Washburn, *Indian Wars,* 113.
117. Ibid., 113.
118. Axelrod, *Chronicle of the Indian Wars,* 125.
119. Utley and Washburn, *Indian Wars,* 114.
120. Gilbert, *God Gave Us This Country,* 150.
121. Tebbel and Jennison, *The American Indian Wars,* 84.
122. Quoted in Axelrod, *Chronicle of the Indian Wars,* 125–26.
123. Loudon, *Narratives,* vol. 1, 69–73.
124. Gilbert, *God Gave Us This Country,* 183.
125. Quoted in Sheehan, *Seeds of Extinction,* 204.
126. Sheehan, 204.
127. Ibid., 6.
128. Quoted in Sheehan, *Seeds of Extinction,* 197–98.
129. Drimmer, *Captured by the Indians,* 235.
130. Ibid., 224.
131. Quoted in Gilbert, *God Gave Us This Country,* 222–23. Tecumseh himself was an excellent orator. William Henry Harrison heard him reviewing atrocities against the Indians in 1803, including Gnadenhutten and the death of Moluntha described above. Harrison reported to the War Department, "Every instance of injustice and injury which have been committed by our citizens upon the Indians from the commencement of the revolutionary war (There are unfortunately too many of them) was brought forward and exaggerated." Quoted in Gilbert, 206.
132. Loudon, *Narratives,* vol. 1, 107–10.
133. Ibid., vol. 2, 186.
134. Ibid., 187.
135. Ibid., 187–89.
136. Ibid., 309–11.
137. Ibid., 310–12.
138. Ibid., 313.
139. Ibid., 313–15.
140. Ibid., 316–17.
141. Kelly, *My Captivity Among the Sioux,* 238–40.
142. Brinkley, *American Heritage History of the United States,* 131.
143. Ibid., 131–32.
144. Wilson, *The Earth Shall Weep,* 156.
145. Brinkley, *American Heritage History of the United States,* 132–33.
146. Waldman, *Who Was Who,* 164–65.
147. Goodrich, *Scalp Dance,* 190.
148. Axelrod, *Chronicle of the Indian Wars,* 134.
149. Tebbel and Jennison, *The American Indian Wars,* 156.
150. Wilson, *The Earth Shall Weep,* 242.
151. Waldman, *Atlas,* 120–21.
152. Quoted in Carey, "A Study of the Indian Captivity Narratives," 164.
153. Gilbert, *God Gave Us This Country,* 286–87.
154. Drimmer, *Captured by the Indians,* 256–57.
155. Ibid., 258–63.
156. Ibid., 263–64.
157. Quoted in Drimmer, 264–67.
158. Gilbert, *God Gave Us This Country,* 294.
159. Ibid., 297.
160. Waldman, *Encyclopedia,* 81.
161. Ibid., 179–81.
162. Ibid., 181.
163. Ibid., 179–81.

164. Washburn, *The Indian in America,* 19–20.
165. Josephy, *Indian Heritage,* 331.
166. Coward, *The Newspaper Indian,* 18.

Chapter 7: Atrocities from the Trails of Tears to the Civil War

1. Quoted in Sheehan, *Seeds of Extinction,* 244.
2. Sheehan, 245.
3. Spicer, *The American Indians,* 181.
4. The phrase "Trail of Tears" was given to their last removal by the Cherokee, but now the name means the removal of all 5 tribes. Waldman, *Atlas,* 185.
5. Prucha, *Documents of United States Indian Policy,* 52–53.
6. Remini, Robert V., *The Legacy of Andrew Jackson: Essays on Democracy, Indian Removal, and Slavery* (1988), 67.
7. Quoted in Prucha, *Documents of United States Indian Policy,* 55.
8. Ibid., 54.
9. Waldman, *Encyclopedia,* 63.
10. Ibid., 213–15.
11. Ibid., 74–75.
12. Ibid., 53–54.
13. Ibid., 43–48.
14. Waldman, *Atlas,* 183–85.
15. Foreman, *Indian Removal,* 399.
16. Ibid., 3.
17. Ibid., preface 2. In similar fashion, Helen Hunt Jackson stated, "The army are not responsible for Indian wars; they are 'men under authority, who go where they are sent.'" Jackson, *A Century of Dishonor,* xx.
18. Quoted in Utley and Washburn, *Indian Wars,* 140.
19. Axelrod, *Chronicle of the Indian Wars,* 143.
20. Exploring-party members David and Robert Folsom quoted in Foreman, *Indian Removal,* 31–32.
21. Foreman, 35.
22. Ibid., 42.
23. Ibid., 42.
24. Ibid., 47.
25. Quoted in Foreman, 98.
26. Ibid., 76–77.
27. Foreman, 88–89. Disease, especially dysentery and cholera, were tremendous problems at this time and even at later times. Both can be caused by infected water or food, and either can be found in cramped quarters such as a detainment camp. General Jackson himself got dysentery in the field a few years before he became president. Tebbel and Jennison, *The American Indian Wars,* 170.
28. Ambrose, *Undaunted Courage,* 225, 235.
29. Letter to *Cherokee Phoenix* quoted in Foreman, *Indian Removal,* 97.
30. Document quoted in Foreman, 79. U.S. Senate Document No. 512 is a compilation of the correspondence in the War Department concerning Indian removal from 1831 to 1833 and is cited hereafter as "Document."
31. Foreman, 53.
32. Ibid., 53.
33. Ibid., 64–65.
34. Ibid., 69–70.
35. Quoted in Foreman, 63.
36. Document quoted in Foreman, 63–64.
37. Ibid., 63.
38. Foreman, 64.
39. Quoted in Foreman, 68–69.
40. Ibid., 72.
41. Foreman, 72.
42. Ibid., 66–67. A Choctaw council act of 1829 recognized that it was an old Choctaw custom to punish persons "said to be wizzards [*sic*] or witches with death, without giving them a fair trial" and sought to regulate the practice. Quoted in Foreman, 67.
43. Quoted in Foreman, 74.
44. Ibid., 83–84, 89.
45. Spicer, *The American Indians,* 84.
46. Waldman, *Atlas,* 122.
47. Quoted in Foreman, *Indian Removal,* 332.
48. Ibid., 333.
49. Foreman, 334.
50. Ibid., 339–40.
51. *Army and Navy Chronicle* quoted in Foreman, 343.
52. Foreman, 367–68.
53. Ibid., 370.
54. Ibid., 378.

55. Ibid., 385.
56. Document quoted in Foreman, 108.
57. Foreman, 126–28.
58. Ibid., 128.
59. Ibid., 152–57.
60. Ibid., 158.
61. Quoted in Foreman, 159.
62. Foreman, 160.
63. Ibid., 162–63.
64. Quoted in Foreman, 163–64.
65. Ibid., 160–62.
66. Ibid., 166.
67. Ibid., 170.
68. Ibid., 119.
69. Ibid., 173.
70. Ibid., 173–74.
71. Ibid., 176.
72. Ibid., 182–83.
73. Foreman, 185.
74. Ibid., 187.
75. Ibid.
76. Catlin, *Letters and Notes,* 396.
77. Foreman, *Indian Removal,* 197.
78. Quoted in Foreman, 206.
79. Foreman, 219.
80. Quoted in Foreman, 220.
81. Foreman, 209–12.
82. Quoted in Foreman, 222–23.
83. Foreman, 229.
84. Ibid., 231–32.
85. Wilson, *The Earth Shall Weep,* 170.
86. Remini, *The Legacy of Andrew Jackson,* 78.
87. Waldman, *Atlas,* 185.
88. Foreman, *Indian Removal,* 253.
89. Quoted in Foreman, 254.
90. Ibid., 257.
91. Foreman, 257.
92. Ibid., 260–61.
93. Quoted in Foreman, 262–63.
94. Foreman, 263.
95. Ibid., 273–74.
96. Quoted in Foreman, 287.
97. Foreman, 290–91.
98. Quoted in Foreman, 291–93.
99. Foreman, 294–96.
100. Ibid., 301.
101. Ibid., 299.
102. Ibid., 300.
103. Ibid., 300.
104. Ibid., 302–3.
105. Ibid., 310.
106. Ibid., 303.

107. Ibid., 305.
108. Ibid., 309, 311.
109. Ibid., 311.
110. Catlin, *Letters and Notes,* 392.
111. Spicer, *The American Indians,* 81.
112. The report and recommendations are summarized in a pamphlet entitled *An Overview of the Labor Market Problems of Indians and Native Americans,* published in 1989 by the National Commission for Employment Policy. The report and recommendations are hereafter referred to simply as "Report from Overview." This reference is from p. 3.
113. Wilson, in *The Earth Shall Weep,* p. 227, said that it was "the U.S. practice of forcibly removing Indians." The only Indians forcibly removed (principally Cherokee) were those who agreed to leave for Oklahoma by a date stated in their treaty and then stayed beyond that time.
114. Spicer, *The American Indians,* 84.
115. Waldman, *Atlas,* 184.
116. Spicer, *The American Indians,* 88.
117. Ibid., 81.
118. Debo, *A History of the Indians,* 124.
119. Foreman, *Indian Removal,* 310.
120. The same method of making computations is used in Appendices B and C relating to the number of atrocity deaths.
121. Remini, *The Legacy of Andrew Jackson,* 47.
122. Ibid., 45.
123. Ibid., 81–82.
124. Foreman, *Indian Removal,* 386.
125. Jackson, *A Century of Dishonor,* 381–82.
126. Waldman, *Encyclopedia,* 86–87.
127. Quoted in Axelrod, *Chronicle of the Indian Wars,* 152.
128. Axelrod, 152.
129. Tebbel and Jennison, *The American Indian Wars,* 194.
130. Utley and Washburn, *Indian Wars,* 138.
131. Quoted in Waldman, *Encyclopedia,* 212.
132. Catlin, *Letters and Notes,* 271–72.
133. Tebbel and Jennison, *The American Indian Wars,* 216.
134. Waldman, *Who Was Who,* 259; Utley and Washburn in *Indian Wars* said that

Dr. Weedon cut off Osceola's head and kept it as a souvenir for years.

135. Matthiessen, *Indian Country*, 24–25.
136. Tebbel and Jennison, *The American Indian Wars*, 218.
137. Brandon, *Indians*, 239.
138. Waldman, *Encyclopedia*, 68–70.
139. Washburn, *The Indian in America*, 173.
140. Richardson, *The Comanche Barrier*, 111.
141. Quoted in Washburn, *The Indian in America*, 178.
142. Waldman, *Encyclopedia*, 110–12.
143. Richardson, *The Comanche Barrier*, 348.
144. Debo, in *A History of the Indians*, p. 154, suggested the Indian children may have died because the Indians dealt with measles by giving a "treatment of a steam bath followed by a plunge in cold water."
145. Brandon, *Indians*, 306–7.
146. Axelrod, *Chronicle of the Indian Wars*, 170.
147. Trafzer and Hyer, *Exterminate Them!*, 104; Andrist, *Long Death*, 204.
148. Spicer, *The American Indians*, 142.
149. Andrist, *Long Death*, 204–5; Trafzer and Hyer, *Exterminate Them!*, 104.
150. Driver, *Indians of North America*, 490.
151. Quoted in Trafzer and Hyer, *Exterminate Them!*, 65.
152. Quoted in Axelrod, *Chronicle of the Indian Wars*, 165.
153. Andrist, *Long Death*, 205.
154. Quoted in Debo, *A History of the Indians*, 159.
155. Trafzer and Hyer, *Exterminate Them!*, 12.
156. Spicer, *The American Indians*, 140.
157. Josephy, *Indian Heritage*, 332.
158. Trafzer and Hyer, *Exterminate Them!*, 43.
159. Axelrod, *Chronicle of the Indian Wars*, 165.
160. Trafzer and Hyer, *Exterminate Them!*, 30.
161. Quoted in Trafzer and Hyer, 128–29.
162. Trafzer and Hyer, 28.
163. Josephy, *Indian Heritage*, 332.
164. Trafzer and Hyer, *Exterminate Them!*, 18.
165. Jackson, *A Century of Dishonor*, 483.
166. Trafzer and Hyer, *Exterminate Them!*, 118.
167. Quoted in Trafzer and Hyer, 116–17.
168. Ibid., 120.
169. Ibid., 121.
170. Ibid., 121–22.
171. Ibid., 122.
172. Ibid., 51.
173. Ibid., 13, 65.
174. Ibid., 71.
175. Andrist, *Long Death*, 204–5.
176. Spicer, *The American Indians*, 142.
177. Trafzer and Hyer, *Exterminate Them!*, 17.
178. Ibid., 36.
179. Ibid., 37.
180. Ibid., 14.
181. Ibid., 114–15.
182. Ibid., 18.
183. Ibid., 56–58.
184. Ibid., 73.
185. Ibid., 39.
186. Ibid., 64.
187. Ibid., 74, 116.
188. Ibid., 112.
189. Ibid., 98–111.
190. Ibid., 98.
191. Ibid., 119.
192. Ibid., 43.
193. Ibid., 118.
194. Ibid., 107.
195. Ibid., 138.
196. Quoted in Bordewich, *Killing the White Man's Indian*, 50.
197. Trafzer and Hyer, *Exterminate Them!*, 154. Trafzer and Hyer said on p. 136 that letters like this were "questionable at best," yet they erroneously said the total of murdered whites in the letter was only 110 instead of 130.
198. Bordewich, *Killing the White Man's Indian*, 50.
199. Trafzer and Hyer, *Exterminate Them!*, 44.
200. Ibid., 45.
201. Ibid., 66–67.
202. Quoted in Trafzer and Hyer, 68.
203. Trafzer and Hyer, 119–20.
204. Ibid., 123.

205. Quoted in Trafzer and Hyer, 69.
206. Ibid., 124.
207. Quoted in Debo, *A History of the Indians*, 165.
208. Jackson, *A Century of Dishonor*, 382–83.
209. Quoted in Trafzer and Hyer, *Exterminate Them!*, 47–48.
210. Trafzer and Hyer, 130.
211. Ibid., 49.
212. Quoted in Trafzer and Hyer, 76–77.
213. Ibid., 125.
214. Trafzer and Hyer, 126.
215. Quoted in Trafzer and Hyer, 127.
216. Trafzer and Hyer, 28.
217. Wilson, *The Earth Shall Weep*, 233.
218. Trafzer and Hyer, *Exterminate Them!*, 129.
219. Ibid., 70.
220. Quoted in Trafzer and Hyer, 77.
221. Bordewich, *Killing the White Man's Indian*, 32.
222. Quoted in Trafzer and Hyer, *Exterminate Them!*, 29.
223. Trafzer and Hyer, 78.
224. Ibid., 78.
225. Ibid., 79.
226. Ibid., 29.
227. Ibid., 133.
228. Ibid., 132.
229. Ibid., 79.
230. Spicer, *The American Indians*, 142–43.
231. Waldman, *Who Was Who*, 313.
232. Brandon, *Indians*, 373.
233. Kelly, *My Captivity Among the Sioux*, 208.
234. Ebersole, *Captured by Texts*, 229.
235. Waldman, *Who Was Who*, 136–37.
236. Axelrod, *Chronicle of the Indian Wars*, 179.
237. Robinson, *A Good Year to Die*, 12.
238. Marshall, *Crimsoned Prairie*, 19–20.
239. Quoted in Lazarus, *Black Hills/White Justice*, 73.
240. Axelrod, *Chronicle of the Indian Wars*, 173.
241. Ibid., 173.
242. Quoted in Utley and Washburn, *Indian Wars*, 179–80.
243. Drimmer, *Captured by the Indians*, 278.
244. Quoted in Drimmer, 301.
245. Robinson, *The Men Who Wear the Star*, 46–47.
246. Quoted in Drimmer, *Captured by the Indians*, 303.
247. Drimmer, 282–313.
248. *World Book*, vol. 20, 194fn.

Chapter 8: Atrocities in the Civil War and Post–Civil War Eras

1. Waldman, *Atlas*, 128.
2. Reported in Brinkley, *American Heritage History of the United States*, 213.
3. Schultz, *Month of the Freezing Moon*, 50–51.
4. Brady, *Indian Fights and Fighters*, ix.
5. Axelrod, *Chronicle of the Indian Wars*, 184.
6. Utley and Washburn, *Indian Wars*, 175–77.
7. Tebbel and Jennison, *The American Indian Wars*, 238.
8. Waldman, *Atlas*, 140.
9. Axelrod, *Chronicle of the Indian Wars*, 184.
10. Ibid., 184–85.
11. Quoted in Goodrich, *Scalp Dance*, 3.
12. Waldman, *Who Was Who*, 58–59.
13. Axelrod, *Chronicle of the Indian Wars*, 187.
14. Quoted in Robinson, *The Men Who Wear the Star*, 47.
15. Axelrod, *Chronicle of the Indian Wars*, 185.
16. Ibid., 190.
17. Ibid., 190.
18. Waldman, *Who Was Who*, 204.
19. Quoted in Axelrod, *Chronicle of the Indian Wars*, 190.
20. Ibid., 190.
21. Axelrod, 190–91.
22. Ibid., 190–91.
23. Utley and Washburn, *Indian Wars*, 203.
24. Axelrod, *Chronicle of the Indian Wars*, 193.
25. Andrist, *Long Death*, 39.
26. Quoted in Schultz, *Month of the Freezing Moon*, 60.
27. Debo, *A History of the Indians*, 186.
28. Schultz, *Month of the Freezing Moon*, 60.

29. Andrist, *Long Death,* 46.
30. Ibid., 51.
31. Drimmer, *Captured by the Indians,* 315.
32. Andrist, *Long Death,* 51–52.
33. Kelly, *My Captivity Among the Sioux,* 117; Mary Boueau had been captured in the Santee Sioux Massacre and told her story to Fanny Kelly.
34. Drimmer, *Captured by the Indians,* 314.
35. Brandon, *Indians,* 341. Debo, in *A History of the Indians,* p. 187, stated that 500 dead was a conservative estimate. Schultz, in *Month of the Freezing Moon,* p. 60, estimated close to 600. Utley and Washburn, in *Indian Wars,* p. 203, said, "Fully 800."
36. Axelrod, *Chronicle of the Indian Wars,* 194.
37. Waldman, *Who Was Who,* 203.
38. Andrist, *Long Death,* 64.
39. It should be added that this was an accepted practice in the medical community at the time.
40. Marshall, *Crimsoned Prairie,* 27.
41. Jackson, *A Century of Dishonor,* 193–94.
42. Kelly, *My Captivity Among the Sioux,* 104–5.
43. Ibid., 134–35.
44. Ibid., 144.
45. Ibid., 165.
46. Bret Harte in Commager, *The West,* 235.
47. Waldman, *Atlas,* 145; Axelrod, *Chronicle of the Indian Wars,* 189.
48. Quoted in Gilbert, *God Gave Us This Country,* 90.
49. Quoted in Goodrich, *Scalp Dance,* 18.
50. Ibid., 44.
51. Goodrich, 44–45.
52. Ibid., 113–14.
53. Quoted in Goodrich, 66.
54. Waldman, *Encyclopedia,* 48–53.
55. Debo, *A History of the Indians,* 217–18.
56. Schultz, *Month of the Freezing Moon,* 13–15.
57. Ibid., 13–16; Jackson, *A Century of Dishonor,* 79–80. The series of incidents leading to 33 deaths is described in Chapter 3 as a classic example of escalation.
58. Waldman, *Encyclopedia,* 17–19.
59. Waldman, *Who Was Who,* 115.
60. Schultz, *Month of the Freezing Moon,* 61–63.
61. Ibid., 65–66.
62. Waldman, *Who Was Who,* 66–67.
63. Schultz, *Month of the Freezing Moon,* 74–75.
64. Waldman, *Who Was Who,* 29.
65. Schultz, *Month of the Freezing Moon,* 75–76.
66. Quoted in Schultz, 77.
67. Schultz, 77.
68. Quoted in Schultz, 79–80.
69. Schultz, 80–82.
70. Ibid., 85.
71. Ibid., 85–90.
72. West, *The Contested Plains,* 291.
73. Quoted in West, 291.
74. Ibid., 294.
75. Schultz, *Month of the Freezing Moon,* 98–104.
76. Quoted in Schultz, 104–7.
77. Schultz, 109–10.
78. Quoted in Schultz, 113.
79. Schultz, 113–14.
80. Quoted in Schultz, 115.
81. Schultz, 115–16.
82. Ibid., 149.
83. Ibid., 116–17.
84. Quoted in West, *The Contested Plains,* 299.
85. Schultz, *Month of the Freezing Moon,* 117–19.
86. Quoted in Schultz, 126.
87. Ibid., 126.
88. Schultz, 127–30.
89. Quoted in Schultz, 130–32.
90. Schultz, 132.
91. Waldman, *Who Was Who,* 29; Wilson, *The Earth Shall Weep,* 275.
92. Quoted in Schultz, *Month of the Freezing Moon,* 133.
93. Schultz, 134.
94. Quoted in West, *The Contested Plains,* 304.
95. Schultz, *Month of the Freezing Moon,* 134–35.
96. Waldman, *Who Was Who,* 380.
97. Schultz, *Month of the Freezing Moon,* 135–37.
98. Ibid., 133–38.
99. Ibid., 137–39.
100. Quoted in Goodrich, *Scalp Dance,* 4.

101. Schultz, *Month of the Freezing Moon,* 139; Josephy, in *Indian Heritage,* p. 337, said that almost 300 Indians were massacred. Other estimates go down to 60 or 70 in the first congressional report.
102. Quoted in Marshall, *Crimsoned Prairie,* 39.
103. Wilson, *The Earth Shall Weep,* 274.
104. West, *The Contested Plains,* 305.
105. Coward, *The Newspaper Indian,* 109.
106. Schultz, *Month of the Freezing Moon,* 139. Chivington claimed his troops killed Black Kettle there, but he survived for 4 more years. Coward, *The Newspaper Indian,* 109.
107. Coward, *The Newspaper Indian,* 110.
108. West, *The Contested Plains,* 305.
109. Schultz, *Month of the Freezing Moon,* 73–74 for Chivington and 62–63 for Evans.
110. Quoted in Schultz, 5.
111. Axelrod, *Chronicle of the Indian Wars,* 197.
112. Schultz, *Month of the Freezing Moon,* 155.
113. Debo, *A History of the Indians,* 196; Wilson, *The Earth Shall Weep,* 275. West, in *The Contested Plains,* disagreed. West thought the dead totaled fewer than 50. West, 307.
114. Quoted in Schultz, *Month of the Freezing Moon,* 148–50.
115. Ibid., 165.
116. Ibid., 157–66.
117. Schultz, 184.
118. Quoted in Prucha, *Documents of United States Indian Policy,* 103; Andrist, *Long Death,* 94; Commager, *The West,* 236; Debo, *A History of the Indians,* 198.
119. Schultz, *Month of the Freezing Moon,* 166.
120. Ibid., 174.
121. Ibid., 165.
122. Coward, *The Newspaper Indian,* 121.
123. Quoted in Andrist, *Long Death,* 96.
124. Brandon, *Indians,* 377.
125. Quoted in Goodrich, *Scalp Dance,* 12.
126. Ibid., 13.
127. Ibid., 14.
128. Heard, *White into Red,* 100, 107.
129. Robinson, *A Good Year to Die,* 20.
130. Waldman, *Who Was Who,* 58.
131. Quoted in Goodrich, *Scalp Dance,* 29–30.
132. Robinson, *A Good Year to Die,* 20.
133. Ibid., 21; Prucha, *Documents of United States Indian Policy,* 110.
134. Robinson, 41.
135. Brady, *Indian Fights and Fighters,* 62–64.
136. Goodrich, *Scalp Dance,* 119.
137. Richardson, *The Comanche Barrier,* 293–94.
138. Andrist, *Long Death,* 148.
139. Quoted in Goodrich, *Scalp Dance,* 44.
140. Axelrod, *Chronicle of the Indian Wars,* 202; Brady, *Indian Fights and Fighters,* 69fn.
141. Schultz, *Month of the Freezing Moon,* 199–201.
142. Goodrich, *Scalp Dance,* 93.
143. Schultz, *Month of the Freezing Moon,* 203–4.
144. Andrist, *Long Death,* 160.
145. Quoted in Goodrich, *Scalp Dance,* 147–48.
146. Ibid., 190.
147. Goodrich, 128.
148. Andrist, *Long Death,* 170.
149. Waldman, *Who Was Who,* 372.
150. Ibid., 372.
151. Wissler, *Indians of the United States,* 249–52.
152. Utley and Washburn, *Indian Wars,* 221.
153. Brady, *Indian Fights and Fighters,* 173–78.
154. Waldman, *Encyclopedia,* 33; Hays, *A Race at Bay,* 216.
155. West, *The Contested Plains,* 48.
156. Kelly, *My Captivity Among the Sioux,* 248. Although Kelly had not witnessed these things, Generals Sheridan and Custer gave substantially the same report. However, in *Satanta: The Life and Death of a War Chief* (1997), Charles M. Robinson III expressed doubts that these events occurred.
157. Richardson, *The Comanche Barrier,* 347.
158. Quoted in West, *The Contested Plains,* 373–74.

159. Utley and Washburn, *Indian Wars*, 217.
160. Jackson, *A Century of Dishonor*, 333.
161. Waldman, *Atlas*, 139–43.
162. Brandon, *Indians*, 299.
163. Debo, *A History of the Indians*, 208; Spicer, *The American Indians*, 69.
164. Hays, *A Race at Bay*, 217–18.
165. Waldman, *Encyclopedia*, 138–39.
166. Andrist, *Long Death*, 212–13, 235–36.
167. Waldman, *Who Was Who*, 54.
168. Utley and Washburn, *Indian Wars*, 253–54.
169. Goodrich, *Scalp Dance*, 117, 122, 124, 186, 191.
170. Quoted in Hays, *A Race at Bay*, 160.
171. Utley and Washburn, *Indian Wars*, 221.
172. Andrist, *Long Death*, 189.
173. Utley and Washburn, *Indian Wars*, 231; Andrist, 189; Debo, *A History of the Indians*, 230.
174. Brady, *Indian Fights and Fighters*, 318.
175. Robinson, *A Good Year to Die*, 300.
176. Coward, *The Newspaper Indian*, 172.
177. Quoted in Debo, *A History of the Indians*, 272–73.
178. Waldman, *Atlas*, 157.
179. Robinson, *A Good Year to Die*, 197.
180. Ibid., 216.
181. Ibid., 216.
182. Axelrod, *Chronicle of the Indian Wars*, 227.
183. Ibid., 229.
184. Robinson, *A Good Year to Die*, 216.
185. Waldman, *Who Was Who*, 85–87.
186. Robinson, *A Good Year to Die*, 149, 152.
187. Waldman, *Atlas*, 157.
188. Ibid., 157.
189. Brady, *Indian Fights and Fighters*, 260.
190. Waldman, *Who Was Who*, 91–92.
191. Quoted in *Journal of the Indian Wars*, (1999) (1), 7.
192. Ibid., 7.
193. Robinson, *A Good Year to Die*, 172.
194. Ibid., 195.
195. Ibid., 197.
196. Quoted in Goodrich, *Scalp Dance*, 260.
197. Ibid., 260–61.
198. Ibid., 260.
199. Ibid., 261.
200. Ibid., 261.
201. Goodrich, 262.
202. Ibid., 262.
203. Quoted in Matthiessen, *In the Spirit of Crazy Horse*, 170.
204. Quoted in Brady, *Indian Fights and Fighters*, 289.
205. Axelrod, *Chronicle of the Indian Wars*, 227.
206. Utley and Washburn, *Indian Wars*, 246.
207. Marshall, *Crimsoned Prairie*, 155.
208. Ibid., 155.
209. Waldman, *Who Was Who*, 92.
210. Waldman, *Who Was Who*, 4.
211. Robinson, *A Good Year to Die*, 253.
212. Quoted in Brady, *Indian Fights and Fighters*, 296.
213. Waldman, *Who Was Who*, 73–74.
214. Ibid., 157–58.
215. Marshall, *Crimsoned Prairie*, 188.
216. Debo, *A History of the Indians*, 263.
217. Andrist, *Long Death*, 311. Their trek and Chief Joseph's speech are described in the chapter on Indian characteristics.
218. Quoted in Brandon, *Indians*, 317.
219. Waldman, *Who Was Who*, 111.
220. Waldman, *Encyclopedia*, 244–45.
221. Utley and Washburn, *Indian Wars*, 270–74.
222. Quoted in Hays, *A Race at Bay*, 276–77.
223. Waldman, *Who Was Who*, 392.
224. Quoted in Josephy, *500 Nations*, 437.
225. Waldman, *Who Was Who*, 392–93.
226. Quoted in Brown, *Bury My Heart at Wounded Knee*, 416.
227. Axelrod, *Chronicle of the Indian Wars*, 250.
228. Brown, *Bury My Heart at Wounded Knee*, 435–36.
229. Hays, *A Race at Bay*, 323.
230. Quoted in Utley and Washburn, *Indian Wars*, 295.
231. Utley and Washburn, 297–98. There is irony in the fact that both Crazy Horse and Sitting Bull were killed after an arrest and with the participation of Indians.
232. Waldman, *Who Was Who*, 24.
233. Utley and Washburn, *Indian Wars*, 298.
234. Waldman, *Atlas*, 158

235. Ibid., 158; Utley and Washburn, *Indian Wars*, 299.
236. Waldman, *Who Was Who*, 24.
237. Axelrod, *Chronicles of the Indian Wars*, 253.
238. Waldman, *Atlas*, 158.
239. Waldman, *Who Was Who*, 24.
240. Mooney, James, *The Ghost Dance Religion and Wounded Knee* (republished 1973), 867. Mooney was a well-known anthropologist who immediately after the battle investigated Wounded Knee. Similarly, Andrist, in *Long Death*, p. 348, quoted Whiteside as insisting "on nothing other than unconditional surrender, and the Sioux chief . . . was in no position to resist even if he had been of a mind to."
241. Marshall, *Crimsoned Prairie*, 239–44.
242. Brandon, *Indians*, 349.
243. Andrist, *Long Death*, 348.
244. Axelrod, *Chronicle of the Indian Wars*, 254.
245. Andrist, *Long Death*, 351.
246. Waldman, *Atlas*, 158. Colonel Forsyth was later charged with the killing of innocents, but he was exonerated. Waldman, *Atlas*, 159. Wilson, in *The Earth Shall Weep*, pp. 284–85, asserted that the night before Wounded Knee, "the soldiers cracked open barrels of whisky and some of the Indians heard them drunkenly boasting that they would avenge the Little Big Horn." No confirmation of these statements can be found, and of course Wilson gives no source.
247. Andrist, *Long Death*, 350.
248. Quoted in Marshall, *Crimsoned Prairie*, 242–43.
249. Debo, *A History of the Indians*, 292.
250. Marshall, *Crimsoned Prairie*, 243.
251. Andrist, *Long Death*, 350.
252. Debo, *A History of the Indians*, 293.
253. Marshall, *Crimsoned Prairie*, 246.
254. Quoted in Robinson, *A Good Year to Die*, 346.
255. Brandon, *Indians*, 386.
256. Josephy, *500 Nations*, 441.
257. Debo, *A History of the Indians*, 293.
258. Ibid., 292.
259. Estimates of Indian dead (in alphabetical order) are 200 (Andrist, *Long Death*, 351); 153 and "most likely 300" (Axelrod, *Chronicle of the Indian Wars*, 255); 153 (Brown, *Bury My Heart at Wounded Knee*, 444); 146 (Debo, *A History of the Indians*, 293); 170 plus (Marshall, *Crimsoned Prairie*, 246); 150 plus (Utley and Washburn, *Indian Wars*, 300); and 170 plus (Waldman, *Atlas*, 159).
260. Estimates of soldier deaths are from Axelrod, *Chronicle of the Indian Wars*, 255 (25); Brown, *Bury My Heart at Wounded Knee*, 444 (25); Marshall, *Crimsoned Prairie*, 246 (60); Utley and Washburn, *Indian Wars*, 300 (25); and Waldman, *Atlas*, 159 (25).
261. Waldman, *Atlas*, 159.
262. Andrist, *Long Death*, 352.
263. Marshall, *Crimsoned Prairie*, 247.
264. Axelrod, *Chronicle of the Indian Wars*, 255.
265. Waldman, *Who Was Who*, 392–93.
266. Robinson, *A Good Year to Die*, xxiii.
267. Waldman, *Encyclopedia*, 224–27.
268. Waldman, *Atlas*, 158.
269. Tebbel and Jennison, *The American Indian Wars*, 303–4.
270. Quoted in Robinson, *A Good Year to Die*, 346.
271. Marshall, *Crimsoned Prairie*, 247.
272. Mooney, *The Ghost Dance Religion*, 869–70.
273. Marshall, *Crimsoned Prairie*, 243–44.
274. Utley, Robert M., *The Last Days of the Sioux Nation* (1973), 200–230, quoted in Washburn, *The Indian in America*, 222.
275. Waldman, *Atlas*, 159.
276. Axelrod, *Chronicle of the Indian Wars*, 255. The 400-year period is the time from the landing of Columbus in 1492 to Wounded Knee in 1890, but the war did not begin until 1622, although there were skirmishes before then.
277. Gilbert, *God Gave Us This Country*, 2.
278. The phrase "atrocities connected with a death" needs to be explained. The death of a soldier or warrior killed in battle is not an atrocity without more. If his body is mutilated in some way, for example, his head cut off and stuck on a pole, that is an atrocity, although his death was not.

279. Waldman, *Atlas*, 166.
280. Sheehan, *Seeds of Extinction*, 194.
281. Washburn, *The Indian in America*, 132.
282. Gilbert, *God Gave Us This Country*, 107.
283. Carey, "A Study of the Indian Captivity Narratives," 125.
284. Wissler, *Indians of the United States*, 187.
285. Washburn, *The Indian in America*, 207.
286. West, *The Contested Plains*, 256.
287. Jackson, *A Century of Dishonor*, xx–xxi.
288. *The Indianapolis Star*, October 3, 1993, C10.
289. Gilbert, *God Gave Us This Country*, 294.
290. Marshall, *Crimsoned Prairie*, 28.
291. Ibid., 40.
292. Kelly, *My Captivity Among the Sioux*, 143–44.
293. Gilbert, *God Gave Us This Country*, 339–40.
294. Brogan, Denis William, *The American Character* (1944), 10.

Chapter 9: Some Other Aspects of the War

1. Quoted in Prucha, *Documents of United States Indian Policy*, 131.
2. Quoted in Dulles, Foster Rhea, *The United States Since 1865* (1959), 40–41.
3. Quoted in Matthiessen, *In the Spirit of Crazy Horse*, 33.
4. Matthiessen, 441.
5. Andrist, *Long Death*, 154–55.
6. Axelrod, *Chronicle of the Indian Wars*, 34.
7. Driver, *Indians of North America*, 484.
8. Matthiessen, *Indian Country*, 247.
9. Quoted in Prucha, *Documents of United States Indian Policy*, 136.
10. Quoted in Prucha, 136.
11. Ibid., 136.
12. Debo, *A History of the Indians*, 118.
13. Spicer, *The American Indians*, 199.
14. Quoted in Bordewich, *Killing the White Man's Indian*, 312.
15. Washburn, *The Indian in America*, 82.

Felix Cohen is described as "the nation's foremost expert on Indian law"; his book, *Handbook of Federal Indian Law*, is "the deepest reservoir of knowledge in its field and the bible of Indian rights advocates." Lazarus, *Black Hills/White Justice*, 185.
16. Hagan, *American Indians*, 56. It is not clear whether he was speaking of just Governor Harrison's tenure or of the entire period from 1783.
17. Andrist, *Long Death*, 8.
18. Quoted in Prucha, *Documents of United States Indian Policy*, 231.
19. Lazarus, *Black Hills/White Justice*, 392–94.
20. Matthiessen, in *Indian Country*, p. 5, asserted without authority and contrary to law that the right of the tribes to stand upon the land was "inalienable."
21. Bordewich, *Killing the White Man's Indian*, 36, 104; Lazarus, *Black Hills/White Justice*, 117, 413, 417.
22. Quoted in Prucha, *Documents of United States Indian Policy*, 35–37.
23. 30 *American Jurisprudence*, 465, citing *Downes vs. Bidwell*, 182 US 244, and *United States vs. Huckabee*, 16 Wall 414.
24. Spicer, *The American Indians*, 47.
25. Waldman, *Atlas*, 110.
26. Marshall, *Crimsoned Prairie*, 14.
27. Prucha, *Documents of United States Indian Policy*, 140.
28. Waldman, *Atlas*, 166–67.
29. Nash, *Red, White, and Black*, 300.
30. Hagan, *American Indians*, 94.
31. Washburn, *The Indian in America*, 106–7.
32. Bordewich, *Killing the White Man's Indian*, 180.
33. Catlin, *Letters and Notes*, 488.
34. Ibid., 487.
35. Ibid., 491.
36. Waldman, *Atlas*, 166 (map).
37. Washburn, *The Indian in America*, 105–6.
38. Tebbel and Jennison, *The American Indian Wars*, 20.
39. Nash, *Red, White, and Black*, 78.
40. Washburn, *The Indian in America*, 105.
41. Andrist, *Long Death*, 14.

42. Ibid., 15.
43. Catlin, *Letters and Notes,* 489. Debo, in *A History of the Indians,* p. 154, added that measles would be treated by a steam bath followed by plunging into cold water.
44. Wilson, *The Earth Shall Weep,* 76. Apparently no other author mentions bubonic plague among the Indians. The disease almost vanished in the late 1800s, but entered New York City in 1899 and San Francisco the next year. It also appeared in New Orleans and Seattle. Fortunately, it has been stamped out wherever it has appeared in the United States. *World Book,* vol. 2, 545.
45. Axelrod, *Chronicle of the Indian Wars,* 160.
46. Ibid., 54.
47. Ibid., 83.
48. Ibid., 84.
49. Ibid., 89.
50. Hobhouse, Henry, *Seeds of Change* (1985), 39.
51. Ambrose, *Undaunted Courage,* 196.
52. Catlin, *Letters and Notes,* 228.
53. Waldman, *Atlas,* 60.
54. American Cancer Society, *Cancer Facts and Figures—1993,* 21.
55. Nash, *Red, White, and Black,* 267.
56. Gilbert, *God Gave Us This Country,* 122.
57. Quoted in Sheehan, *Seeds of Extinction,* 244.
58. Quoted in Axelrod, *Chronicle of the Indian Wars,* 165.
59. Waldman, *Atlas,* 139.
60. Quoted in Debo, *A History of the Indians,* 159.
61. Quoted in Trafzer and Hyer, *Exterminate Them!,* 1.
62. Quoted in Hagan, *American Indians,* 104.
63. Ibid., 117.
64. Quoted in Andrist, *Long Death,* 331.
65. Bordewich, *Killing the White Man's Indian,* 37.
66. Axelrod, *Chronicle of the Indian Wars,* vii.
67. Josephy, *Indian Heritage,* 279.
68. Waldman, *Atlas,* 87.
69. Ibid., 87.
70. Sheehan, *Seeds of Extinction,* 43fn.
71. Quoted in Ambrose, *Undaunted Courage,* 53.
72. Wissler, *Indians of the United States,* 280.
73. Axelrod, *Chronicle of the Indian Wars,* 157.
74. Wilson, *The Earth Shall Weep,* 423–24.
75. Lunt, W. E., *History of England* (1945).

Chapter 10: Government Indian Policy

1. Waldman, *Atlas,* 190.
2. "It is infinitely better to have no heathen among us, who were but as thornes in our sides, than to be at peace and league with them," wrote Wyatt. Utley and Washburn, *Indian Wars,* 17.
3. Washburn, *The Indian in America,* 211–12.
4. Waldman, *Atlas,* 190.
5. Ibid.
6. Esarey, *A History of Indiana,* 89.
7. Axelrod, *Chronicle of the Indian Wars,* 123.
8. Hagan, *American Indians,* 46.
9. Gilbert, *God Gave Us This Country,* 134.
10. Ibid., 134–35.
11. Quoted in Gilbert, 186.
12. Wallbank and Taylor, *Civilization—Past and Present,* vol. 2, 229.
13. Knox and Crawford quoted in Sheehan, *Seeds of Extinction,* 121–23.
14. Prucha, *Documents of United States Indian Policy,* 18.
15. Sheehan, *Seeds of Extinction,* 268.
16. Esarey, *A History of Indiana,* 230.
17. Washburn, *The Indian in America,* 205.
18. Axelrod, *Chronicle of the Indian Wars,* 211.
19. Quoted in Hays, *A Race at Bay,* 55.
20. Lazarus, *Black Hills/White Justice,* 32.
21. Spicer, *The American Indians,* 181.
22. Report from Overview, 4.
23. Utley and Washburn, *Indian Wars,* 193.
24. Washburn, *The Indian in America,* 209.
25. Utley and Washburn, *Indian Wars,* 289.
26. Ibid., 226–31.

27. Axelrod, *Chronicle of the Indian Wars,* 212.
28. Prucha, *Documents of United States Indian Policy,* 171–74.
29. Report from Overview, 4; Driver said these figures are about the same, 138,000,000 in 1887 and 48,000,000 in 1934. Driver, *Indians of North America,* 491.
30. Spicer, *The American Indians,* 184; Prucha, *Documents of United States Indian Policy,* 197–98.
31. Prucha, 219; Debo, in *A History of the Indians,* p. 336, summarized the report by saying it indicated that the condition of the Indians was deplorable for several reasons.
32. Wilson, *The Earth Shall Weep,* 342.
33. Spicer, *The American Indians,* 190–91.
34. Waldman, *Atlas,* 194; Spicer, *The American Indians,* 194.
35. Prucha, *Documents of United States Indian Policy,* 233.
36. Spicer, *The American Indians,* 194.
37. Waldman, *Atlas,* 194.
38. Quoted in Prucha, *Documents of United States Indian Policy,* 257.
39. Ibid., 257.
40. Report from Overview, 6.
41. Quoted in Prucha, *Documents of United States Indian Policy,* 301.
42. Quoted in Utley and Washburn, *Indian Wars,* 291.
43. Esarey, *A History of Indiana,* 90.
44. Quoted in Gilbert, *God Gave Us This Country,* 133.
45. Gilbert, 133.
46. Axelrod, *Chronicle of the Indian Wars,* 158.
47. Hagan, *American Indians,* 111–12.
48. Waldman, *Who Was Who,* 379–80.
49. Ibid., 379–80.
50. Quoted in Washburn, *The Indian in America,* 216.
51. Ibid., 216.
52. Ibid., 216.
53. Waldman, *Who Was Who,* 380.
54. Quoted in Wilson, *The Earth Shall Weep,* 291.
55. Hays, *The Newspaper Indian,* 212–13.
56. Quoted in Hays, 24.
57. Jackson, *A Century of Dishonor,* xx.

58. Lazarus, *Black Hills/White Justice,* 105.
59. Hagan, *American Indians,* 126–27.
60. Bordewich, *Killing the White Man's Indian,* 293.
61. Ibid., 293.
62. *U. S. News & World Report,* February 22, 1993, 26.
63. *U. S. News & World Report,* November 28, 1994, 61–64.
64. AP, December 24, 1998, release.
65. AP, January 7, 1999, release.
66. Quoted in AP, February 23, 1999, release.
67. Quoted in *Sarasota Herald-Tribune,* February 23, 1999, 14A.
68. Ibid., 14A.
69. AP, May 14, 1999, release.
70. AP, June 10, 1999, release.
71. AP, June 7, 1999, release.
72. AP, June 25, 1999, release.

Chapter 11: Where We Are and Where We May Go

1. Schlesinger, *The Disuniting of America,* 136–37.
2. Beveridge, Albert J., *Abraham Lincoln,* vol. 1 (1928), 1.
3. *Contemporary Authors,* New Revision Series, vol. 11, 94.
4. Coward, *The Newspaper Indian,* 121.
5. Brown, *Bury My Heart at Wounded Knee,* xvii.
6. Ibid., 4.
7. Ibid., introduction.
8. Wilson, *The Earth Shall Weep,* 393, 418.
9. Schlesinger, *The Disuniting of America,* 93.
10. Ibid., 52.
11. Hagan, *American Indians,* 5.
12. Ibid., 6.
13. Ibid., 4.
14. Ibid., 4–5.
15. Ibid., 5.
16. Utley and Washburn, *Indian Wars,* 146.
17. Washburn, *The Indian in America,* 80.
18. Josephy, *Indian Heritage,* 320.
19. Debo, *A History of the Indians,* 70.
20. Bordewich, *Killing the White Man's Indian,* 332.

21. Sheehan, *Seeds of Extinction,* 219.
22. Josephy, *Indian Heritage,* 364.
23. Bordewich, *Killing the White Man's Indian,* 13.
24. Mona Charen, *Indianapolis Star,* July 12, 1999, A6.
25. Matthiessen, *Indian Country,* 46.
26. Josephy, *Indian Heritage,* 378.
27. Bordewich, *Killing the White Man's Indian,* 78.
28. Waldman, *Atlas,* 200.
29. Wilson, *The Earth Shall Weep,* xxiv.
30. United States Department of Commerce, Bureau of the Census, document number CP-1-1A.
31. AP, July 7, 1999, release.
32. That figure has risen to 63 percent according to an AP, July 7, 1999, release.
33. Estimated by the government to be only 50 percent in 1999. AP, July 7, 1999, release.
34. Bureau of the Census, *We, the First Americans,* 5–7. The government reported in 1999 that Indian per capita income was $21,619. AP, July 7, 1999, release.
35. Washburn, *The Indian in America,* 274.
36. Waldman, *Atlas,* 210–11.
37. Washburn, *The Indian in America,* 272.
38. Hagan, *American Indians,* 172–73.
39. *The Economist,* December 19, 1992, 29 (at least 50 percent).
40. Bordewich, *Killing the White Man's Indian,* 57.
41. *The Economist,* December 19, 1992, 29.
42. Bordewich, *Killing the White Man's Indian,* 302–9.
43. Quoted in *National Geographic,* April 1979, 494–505.
44. The Kickapoos demonstrate that Indian culture can be maintained despite upheavals. "Kickapoo history is in many respects the most remarkable of all the Indian histories in the United States. Some of them have maintained the major elements of their aboriginal way of life through 350 years of the most varied social and physical conditions experienced by an Indian group....

Yet even without a long-sustained and stable land base, many kept their traditional ways.... [In Oklahoma] each time BIA employees attempted to force cultural assimilation programs on them ... [they refused]." Spicer, *The American Indians,* 65, 69–70.
45. Quoted in Brodie, *Thomas Jefferson,* 434.

Appendix A: Intertribal Indian Wars

1. Nash, *Red, White, and Black,* 18.
2. Washburn, *The Indian in America,* 63–64.
3. Axelrod, *Chronicle of the Indian Wars,* 2.
4. Ibid., 4.
5. Nash, *Red, White, and Black,* 18.
6. Wissler, *Indians of the United States,* 69.
7. Josephy, *Indian Heritage,* 93; Wissler, in *Indians of the United States,* p. 70, said, "The Algonkin were not merely at war with the Iroquois but often with each other. There were about a hundred Algonkin tribes, all independent like tiny nations, all sooner or later quarreling and starting feuds—little vicious circles impossible to break. In revenge for past injuries a few members of one tribe would stealthily approach the camp of a hostile tribe, take a scalp or two and escape if they could."
8. Steele, *Warpaths,* 39.
9. Lazarus, *Black Hills/White Justice,* 117.
10. Ibid., 413, 417.
11. Waldman, *Encyclopedia,* 146.
12. Debo, *A History of the Indians,* 67.
13. Gilbert, *God Gave Us This Country,* 42–43.
14. Wissler, *Indians of the United States,* 69.
15. Nash, *Red, White, and Black,* 53.
16. Ibid., 76.
17. Josephy, *Indian Heritage,* 301.
18. Steele, *Warpaths,* 73.
19. Waldman, *Atlas,* 95. The Mohawk were members of the Iroquois Confederacy.

20. Tebbel and Jennison, *The American Indian Wars*, 35.
21. Nash, *Red, White, and Black*, 79.
22. Matthiessen, *Indian Country*, 89.
23. Ibid., 90.
24. Tebbel and Jennison, *The American Indian Wars*, 55.
25. Ibid., 55.
26. Waldman, *Atlas*, 90–91.
27. Ibid., 91.
28. Ibid., 93–94.
29. Brandon, *Indians*, 187.
30. Utley and Washburn, *Indian Wars*, 45.
31. Steele, *Warpaths*, 32.
32. Driver, *Indians of North America*, 217. Between 6,000 and 8,000 Hurons retreated to an island, where all but 500 starved to death.
33. Josephy, *500 Nations*, 233.
34. Wissler, *Indians of the United States*, 183.
35. Ibid., 183.
36. Gilbert, *God Gave Us This Country*, 39.
37. Waldman, *Atlas*, 94.
38. Axelrod, *Chronicle of the Indian Wars*, 46.
39. Steele, *Warpaths*, 73.
40. Ibid., 118.
41. Esarey, *A History of Indiana*, 10–11.
42. Utley and Washburn, *Indian Wars*, 28–29.
43. Spicer, *The American Indians*, 57.
44. Steele, *Warpaths*, 51.
45. Waldman, *Atlas*, 92–93.
46. Axelrod, *Chronicle of the Indian Wars*, 34.
47. Debo, *A History of the Indians*, 48.
48. Axelrod, *Chronicle of the Indian Wars*, 50.
49. Hyde, George E., *Indians of the Woodlands from Prehistoric Times to 1725* (1962), 269.
50. Robinson, *A Good Year to Die*, 5.
51. Wissler, *Indians of the United States*, 134.
52. Ibid., 134.
53. Axelrod, *Chronicle of the Indian Wars*, 49.
54. Spicer, *The American Indians*, 107–8.
55. Nash, *Red, White, and Black*, 133.
56. Brandon, *Indians*, 196.
57. Ibid., 196.
58. Waldman, *Encyclopedia*, 106.
59. Waldman, *Atlas*, 94.
60. Esarey, *A History of Indiana*, 11.
61. Waldman, *Encyclopedia*, 102.
62. Nash, *Red, White, and Black*, 231.
63. Wissler, *Indians of the United States*, 135.
64. Washburn, *The Indians in America*, 94.
65. Spicer, *The American Indians*, 31.
66. Steele, *Warpaths*, 125.
67. Spicer, *The American Indians*, 99.
68. Nash, *Red, White, and Black*, 140.
69. Waldman, *Encyclopedia*, 75.
70. Lazarus, *Black Hills/White Justice*, 4.
71. Richardson, *The Comanche Barrier*, 15.
72. Marshall, *Crimsoned Prairie*, 7.
73. Ibid., 7.
74. Ibid., 7.
75. Ibid., 7.
76. Debo, *A History of the Indians*, 74.
77. Ibid., 74–75. The Choctaw took about 400 Chickasaw scalps when they captured 3 Chickasaw villages.
78. Ibid., 75.
79. Nash, *Red, White, and Black*, 135.
80. Ibid., 136.
81. Steele, *Warpaths*, 152–53.
82. Ibid., 153.
83. Nash, *Red, White, and Black*, 133.
84. Waldman, *Atlas*, 215.
85. Richardson, *The Comanche Barrier*, 52.
86. Spicer, *The American Indians*, 80.
87. Steele, *Warpaths*, 163.
88. Debo, *A History of the Indians*, 78.
89. Axelrod, *Chronicle of the Indian Wars*, 62.
90. Steele, *Warpaths*, 163.
91. Ibid., 163. "Fox warriors were raiding virtually all their neighboring tribes."
92. Debo, *A History of the Indians*, 6.
93. Driver, *Indians of North America*, 320.
94. Waldman, *Encyclopedia*, 242.
95. Washburn, *The Indian in America*, 94.
96. Spicer, *The American Indians*, 64.
97. Ibid., 99.
98. Nash, *Red, White, and Black*, 111.
99. Ibid., 100.
100. Waldman, *Encyclopedia*, 87.
101. Ibid., 14.

102. Steele, *Warpaths*, 167.
103. Ibid., 173.
104. Gilbert, *God Gave Us This Country*, 49.
105. Brandon, *Indians*, 353.
106. Spicer, *The American Indians*, 51–52.
107. Robinson, *A Good Year to Die*, 6.
108. Ibid., 6.
109. Spicer, *The American Indians*, 99.
110. Waldman, *Atlas*, 105.
111. Spicer, *The American Indians*, 66–67.
112. Tebbel and Jennison, *The American Indian Wars*, 105.
113. Waldman, *Atlas*, 108.
114. Robinson, *A Good Year to Die*, 6.
115. Ibid., 6.
116. Spicer, *The American Indians*, 67.
117. Ibid., 67.
118. Waldman, *Atlas*, 110.
119. Debo, *A History of the Indians*, 98.
120. Washburn, *The Indian in America*, 149.
121. Esarey, *A History of Indiana*, 72.
122. Smith, *A New Age Now Begins*, 1125.
123. Ibid., 1125.
124. Waldman, *Encyclopedia*, 87.
125. Spicer, *The American Indians*, 94.
126. Gilbert, *God Gave Us This Country*, 176; Axelrod, *Chronicle of the Indian Wars*, 128.
127. Hagan, *American Indians*, 51–52.
128. Spicer, *The American Indians*, 91.
129. Brandon, *Indians*, 264.
130. Spicer, *The American Indians*, 67.
131. Brandon, *Indians*, 264.
132. Catlin, *Letters and Notes*, 209.
133. Ibid., 118.
134. Lazarus, *Black Hills/White Justice*, 7.
135. Wissler, *Indians of the United States*, 174.
136. Ambrose, *Undaunted Courage*, 260.
137. Wissler, *Indians of the United States*, 190.
138. Spicer, *The American Indians*, 57.
139. Richardson, *The Comanche Barrier*, 51, 53, 66.
140. Jackson, *A Century of Dishonor*, 66.
141. Richardson, *The Comanche Barrier*, 51, 53, 66.
142. Quoted in Gilbert, *God Gave Us This Country*, 200.
143. Ambrose, *Undaunted Courage*, 188.
144. Ibid., 172.
145. Ibid., 189.
146. Spicer, *The American Indians*, 57.
147. Waldman, *Encyclopedia*, 86.
148. Axelrod, *Chronicle of the Indian Wars*, 132–33.
149. Gilbert, *God Gave Us This Country*, 287.
150. Axelrod, *Chronicle of the Indian Wars*, 139.
151. Debo, *A History of the Indians*, 111–12.
152. Tebbel and Jennison, *The American Indian Wars*, 170.
153. Spicer, *The American Indians*, 91.
154. Lazarus, *Black Hills/White Justice*, 7.
155. Hagan, *American Indians*, 60–61.
156. Spicer, *The American Indians*, 77.
157. Utley and Washburn, *Indian Wars*, 146.
158. Waldman, *Encyclopedia*, 78.
159. Axelrod, *Chronicle of the Indian Wars*, 197.
160. Waldman, *Who Was Who*, 29.
161. Waldman, *Encyclopedia*, 111.
162. Waldman, *Who Was Who*, 372.
163. Debo, *A History of the Indians*, 15.
164. Josephy, *Indian Heritage*, 326.
165. Tebbel and Jennison, *The American Indian Wars*, 194; Utley and Washburn, *Indian Wars*, 135.
166. Washburn, *The Indian in America*, 185.
167. Ibid., 185.
168. Ibid., 185.
169. Foreman, *Indian Removal*, 348.
170. Richardson, *The Comanche Barrier*, 179.
171. Ibid., 179.
172. Waldman, *Encyclopedia*, 19.
173. Spicer, *The American Indians*, 69.
174. Marshall, *Crimsoned Prairie*, 11.
175. Washburn, *The Indian in America*, 188.
176. Quoted in Washburn, 171.
177. Schultz, *Month of the Freezing Moon*, 51.
178. Waldman, *Who Was Who*, 372.
179. Robinson, *A Good Year to Die*, 6.
180. Wissler, *Indians of the United States*, 249.
181. Waldman, *Atlas*, 119.

182. Axelrod, *Chronicle of the Indian Wars,* 140.
183. Utley and Washburn, *Indian Wars,* 145–46.
184. Quoted in Washburn, *The Indian in America,* 193.
185. Debo, *A History of the Indians,* 190.
186. Drimmer, *Captured by the Indians,* 299–300.
187. Lazarus, *Black Hills/White Justice,* 24–25.
188. Waldman, *Encyclopedia,* 25.
189. Waldman, *Who Was Who,* 204.
190. Brandon, *Indians,* 372.
191. Ibid., 373.
192. Ibid., 373.
193. Debo, *A History of the Indians,* 182.
194. Ibid., 177.
195. Schultz, *Month of the Freezing Moon,* 205.
196. Spicer, *The American Indians,* 69.
197. Waldman, *Encyclopedia,* 89.
198. Schultz, *Month of the Freezing Moon,* 199.
199. Waldman, *Atlas,* 154.
200. Ibid.
201. Brady, *Indian Fights and Fighters,* 173.
202. Waldman, *Atlas,* 154.
203. Waldman, *Who Was Who,* 372.
204. Debo, *A History of the Indians,* 172.
205. Waldman, *Encyclopedia,* 78.
206. Utley and Washburn, *Indian Wars,* 217.
207. Waldman, *Atlas,* 143.
208. Ibid., 154.
209. Utley and Washburn, *Indian Wars,* 221.
210. Andrist, *Long Death,* 184.
211. Axelrod, *Chronicle of the Indian Wars,* 228.
212. Andrist, *Long Death,* 261.
213. Brady, *Indian Fights and Fighters,* 196.
214. Waldman, *Atlas,* 153.
215. Andrist, *Long Death,* 294–95.
216. Brown, *Bury My Heart at Wounded Knee,* 310.
217. Wissler, *Indians of the United States,* 177.
218. Andrist, *Long Death,* 311.
219. Ibid., 313.
220. Ibid., 315.
221. Josephy, *Indian Heritage,* 171. The name *Pueblo* includes the Hopi, Jemez, Keres, Pecos, Piro, Tiwa, and Zuñi tribes.
222. Waldman, *Atlas,* 121.
223. Wissler, *Indians of the United States,* 249.
224. Loudon, *Narratives,* vol. 2, 313–15.
225. Ibid., 316–17.
226. Ibid., 311–12.
227. Waldman, *Encyclopedia,* 32.
228. Ibid., 59.
229. Ibid., 59.
230. Ibid., 77.
231. Ibid., 98.
232. Ibid., 113.
233. Ibid., 144.
234. Ibid., 146.
235. Ibid., 156.
236. Ibid., 180.
237. Ibid., 185.
238. Ibid., 240.
239. Ibid., 240.
240. Catlin, *Letters and Notes,* 240.

Bibliography

Most but not all of the books cited by the author are listed here.

Abel, Annie Heloise. *The American Indian as Slaveholder and Secessionist.* Cleveland: Scholarly Press, 1915.

Ambrose, Stephen E. *Undaunted Courage: Meriwether Lewis, Thomas Jefferson, and the Opening of the American West.* New York: Simon & Schuster, Inc., 1996.

American Heritage Book of the Revolution, The. New York: American Heritage, 1958.

Andrist, Ralph K. *Long Death: The Last Days of the Plains Indians.* New York: Macmillan Publishing Company, 1964.

Axelrod, Alan. *Chronicle of the Indian Wars from Colonial Times to Wounded Knee.* New York: Prentice Hall, 1993.

Berkhofer, Robert F., Jr. *The White Man's Indian.* New York: Vintage Books, 1978.

Beveridge, Albert J. *Abraham Lincoln.* Boston: The University Press, 1928.

Bolt, Christine. *American Indian Policy and American Reform.* Boston: Routledge, 1987.

Bordewich, Fergus M. *Killing the White Man's Indian: Reinventing Native Americans at the End of the Twentieth Century.* New York: Doubleday, 1996.

Boyd, Thomas Alexander. *Simon Girty: The White Savage.* Minton Balch & Company, 1928.

Brady, Cyrus Townsend. *Indian Fights and Fighters.* University of Nebraska Press, 1911.

Brandon, William. *Indians*. New York: American Heritage, 1987.

Brinkley, Douglas. *American Heritage History of the United States*. New York: American Heritage, 1998.

Brodie, Fawn M. *Thomas Jefferson: An Intimate History*. New York: W. W. Norton & Company, 1988.

Brogan, Denis William. *The American Character*. New York: Alfred A. Knopf, 1944.

Brown, Dee. *Bury My Heart at Wounded Knee: An Indian History of the American West*. New York: Henry Holt and Company, 1991.

Carey, Larry Lee. "A Study of the Indian Captivity Narratives as a Popular Literary Genre, ca. 1675–1875." Ph.D. diss., Michigan State University, 1978.

Catlin, George. *Letters and Notes on the Manners, Customs and Conditions of the North American Indians Written During Eight Years' Travel (1832–1839) Amongst the Wildest Tribes of Indians of North America*. New York: Viking Penguin, 1996.

Collier, John. *The Indians of the Americas*. New York: New American Library, 1947.

Commager, Henry Steele (ed.). *The West: An Illustrated History*. New York: Exeter Books, 1976.

Coward, John M. *The Newspaper Indian: Native American Identity in the Press, 1820–90*. Urbana: University of Illinois Press, 1999.

Crèvecoeur, J. Hector St. John de. *Letters from an American Farmer and Sketches of Eighteenth-Century America*. New York: Penguin Books, 1986.

Crosby, Alfred W., Jr. *The Columbian Exchange: Biological and Cultural Consequences of 1492*. Westport, Conn.: Greenwood Press, Inc., 1972.

Debo, Angie. *A History of the Indians of the United States*. Norman: University of Oklahoma Press, 1989.

Dippie, Brian W. *The Vanishing American: White Attitudes and U.S. Indian Policy*. Lawrence: University Press of Kansas, 1991.

Drimmer, Frederick. *Captured by the Indians*. New York: Dover Publications, Inc., 1961.

Driver, Harold E. *Indians of North America*. Chicago: The University of Chicago Press, 1969.

Dulles, Foster Rhea. *The United States Since 1865*. Ann Arbor: The University of Michigan Press, 1959.

Ebersole, Gary L. *Captured by Texts: Puritan to Postmodern Images of Indian Captivity*. Charlottesville: The University Press of Virginia, 1995.

Erlich, J. W. *Erlich's Blackstone*. San Carlos, Calif.: Nourse Publishing Company, 1950.

Esarey, Logan. *A History of Indiana*. Indianapolis: Hoosier Heritage Press, Inc., 1970.

Febrenback, T. R. *Greatness to Spare*. Princeton, N.J.: D. Van Nostrand Company, 1968.

Foreman, Grant. *Indian Removal*. Norman: University of Oklahoma Press, 1932.

Gilbert, Bil. *God Gave Us This Country: Tekamthi and the First American Civil War*. New York: Doubleday, 1989.

Goodrich, Thomas. *Scalp Dance: Indian Warfare on the High Plains, 1865–1879*. Mechanicsburg, Penn.: Stackpole Books, 1997.

Goodwin, Grenville. *Western Apache Raiding and Warfare.* Tucson: University of Arizona Press, 1971.

Grun, Bernard. *The Timetables of History.* New York: Simon & Schuster, Inc., 1979.

Hagan, William T. *American Indians.* Chicago: The University of Chicago Press, 1979.

Hays, Robert G. *A Race at Bay: New York Times Editorials on "The Indian Problem," 1860–1900.* Carbondale: Southern Illinois University Press, 1997.

Heard, J. Norman. *White into Red: A Study of the Assimilation of White Persons Captured by Indians.* Metachen, N.J.: Scarecrow Press, 1973.

Hobhouse, Henry. *Seeds of Change.* New York: Harper & Row, 1985.

Hughes, Robert. *Culture of Complaint: The Fraying of America.* New York: Oxford University Press, 1993.

Hyde, George E. *Indians of the Woodlands from Prehistoric Times to 1725.* Norman: The University of Oklahoma Press, 1962.

Jackson, Helen Hunt. *A Century of Dishonor: A Sketch of the United States Government's Dealings with Some of the Indian Tribes.* Norman: The University of Oklahoma Press, 1995.

Josephy, Alvin M., Jr. *The Indian Heritage of America.* Boston: Houghton Mifflin Company, 1991.

———. *500 Nations.* New York: Alfred A. Knopf, 1994.

Kelly, Fanny. *My Captivity Among the Sioux Indians.* New York: Carol Publishing Group, 1993.

Kraus, Michael. *The United States to 1865.* Ann Arbor: The University of Michigan Press, 1959.

Lazarus, Edward. *Black Hills/White Justice.* New York: HarperCollins Publishers, 1991.

Leupp, Francis E. *The Indian and His Problem.* New York: Charles Scribner's Sons, 1910.

Lincoln, Abraham. *Speeches and Writing, 1859–1865, Speeches, Letters, and Miscellaneous Writings, Presidential Messages and Proclamations.* New York: Literary Classics of the United States, 1989.

Loudon, Archibald. *A Selection of Some of the Most Interesting Narratives of Outrages Committed by the Indians in Their Wars with the White People.* Carlisle, Penn.: Ayer Company Publishers, 1808.

Lunt, W. E. *History of England.* New York: Harper & Brothers, 1945.

Marshall, S. L. A. *Crimsoned Prairie: The Indian Wars.* New York: Da Capo Press, 1972.

Matthiessen, Peter. *Indian Country.* New York: Viking Penguin, 1984.

———. *In the Spirit of Crazy Horse.* New York: Viking Penguin, 1991.

Mooney, James. *The Ghost Dance Religion and Wounded Knee.* Washington, D.C.: Smithsonian Institution, 1973.

Nash, Gary B. *Red, White, and Black: The Peoples of Early North America.* Englewood Cliffs, N.J.: Prentice Hall, 1992.

National Commission for Employment Policy, *An Overview of the Labor Market Problems of Indians and Native Americans.* 1989.

Norton, Jack. *Genocide in Northern California.* San Francisco: Indian Historian Press, 1979.

Pearce, Roy Harvey. *The Savages of America: A Study of the Indian and the Idea of Civilization.* Baltimore: Johns Hopkins Press, 1965.

Prucha, Francis Paul. *Documents of United States Indian Policy.* Lincoln: University of Nebraska Press, 1990.

Remini, Robert V. *The Legacy of Andrew Jackson: Essays on Democracy, Indian Removal, and Slavery.* Baton Rouge: Louisiana State University Press, 1988.

Richardson, Rupert Norval. *The Comanche Barrier to South Plains Settlement.* Austin, Tex.: Dover Publications, 1933.

Robinson, Charles M., III. *A Good Year to Die.* Norman: University of Oklahoma Press, 1995.

————. *Satanta: The Life and Death of a War Chief.* Austin: State House Press, 1997.

————. *The Men Who Wear the Star: The Story of the Texas Rangers.* New York: Random House, 2000.

Schlesinger, Arthur M., Jr. *The Disuniting of America: Reflections on a Multicultural Society.* New York: W. W. Norton & Company, Inc., 1992.

Schultz, Duane. *Month of the Freezing Moon: The Sand Creek Massacre, November, 1864.* New York: St. Martin's Press, 1990.

Sheehan, Bernard W. *Seeds of Extinction: Jeffersonian Philanthropy and the American Indian.* Chapel Hill: University of North Carolina Press, 1973.

Smith, Page. *A New Age Now Begins: A People's History of the American Revolution.* New York: McGraw-Hill Book Company, 1976.

Spicer, Edward H. *The American Indians.* Cambridge, Mass.: The President and Fellows of Harvard College, 1980.

Steele, Ian K. *Warpaths: Invasions of North America.* New York: Oxford University Press, 1994.

Tebbel, John, and Keith Jennison. *The American Indian Wars.* New York: Harper, 1961.

Thornton, Russell. *American Indian Holocaust and Survival.* Norman: University of Oklahoma Press, 1987.

Trafzer, Clifford E., and Joel R. Hyer. *Exterminate Them!* East Lansing: Michigan State University Press, 1999.

Utley, Robert M. *The Last Days of the Sioux Nation.* New Haven, Conn.: Yale University Press, 1973.

Utley, Robert M., and Wilcomb E. Washburn. *Indian Wars.* New York: American Heritage, 1977.

VanDerBeets, Richard. *Held Captive by Indians: Selected Narratives, 1624–1836.* Knoxville: The University of Tennessee Press, 1972.

Waldman, Carl. *Atlas of the North American Indian.* New York: Facts on File Publications, 1985.

————. *Encyclopedia of Native American Tribes.* New York: Facts on File Publications, 1988.

————. *Who Was Who in Native American History.* New York: Facts on File Publications, 1990.

Wallbank, T. Walter, and Alastair M. Taylor. *Civilization—Past and Present.* New York: Scott, Foresman and Company, 1942.

Washburn, Wilcomb E. *The Indian in America.* New York: Harper & Row Publishers, 1975.

West, Elliott. *The Contested Plains: Indians, Goldseekers, and the Rush to Colorado*. Lawrence: University Press of Kansas, 1998.

Wilson, James. *The Earth Shall Weep: A History of Native Americans*. New York: Atlantic Monthly Press, 1998.

Wissler, Clark. *Indians of the United States*. New York: Doubleday, 1940.

Index

ABOUT THE AUTHOR

WILLIAM M. OSBORN was born and educated in Indiana and Michigan. He practiced law in Indiana for many years. Upon his retirement several years ago, he began researching this book about settlers and Indians, in part because the Massachusetts home of one of his father's ancestors was burned by Indians in colonial days and, according to family tradition, one of his mother's ancestors, a settler on the frontier, married a Cherokee named Lydia. Osborn and his wife, Pat, spend half their time in Indiana and half in Florida.

ABOUT THE TYPE

This book was set in Sabon, a typeface designed by the well-known German typographer Jan Tschichold (1902–74). Sabon's design is based upon the original letter forms of Claude Garamond and was created specifically to be used for three sources: foundry type for hand composition, Linotype, and Monotype. Tschichold named his typeface for the famous Frankfurt typefounder Jacques Sabon, who died in 1580.